T0354935

PLAYING IT WELL

THE LIFE AND TIMES OF JACK O'LEARY
PART I

by John J. O'Leary

"THE GAME OF LIFE IS NOT SO MUCH IN HOLDING A GOOD HAND AS IN PLAYING A POOR ONE WELL."

H.T.LESLIE

Order this book online at www.trafford.com
or email orders@trafford.com

Most Trafford titles are also available at major online book retailers.

Printed in the United States of America.

ISBN: 978-1-4269-6156-4 (sc)
ISBN: 978-1-4269-6157-1 (hc)
ISBN: 978-1-4269-6158-8 (e)

Library of Congress Control Number: 2011904684

Trafford rev. 04/04/2011

 www.trafford.com

North America & international
toll-free: 1 888 232 4444 (USA & Canada)
phone: 250 383 6864 ♦ fax: 812 355 4082

FOR
My daughters
Patti and Eileen
and
My grandson
James Patrick McKenna

TABLE OF CONTENTS

PREFACE

Our 1998 trip to Italy took us to Castellamare del Golfo in Sicily, the hometown of Jean's maternal grandparents, Mariano Gennaro and Josephine Corallo; and in Molise (formerly Abruzzo until 1963), the town of Colle d'Astine, the birthplace of Nunzio DiPaolo, Jean's other grandfather; and grandmother Angelina Buttino's hometown at Campochiaro. As a result of these journeys we eventually uncovered a line of Jean's ancestry in Campochiaro, eventually leading back to a previously unknown great-great-great-grandfather, Angelino, and many cousins and other relatives in the Buttino line of descent.

These exciting discoveries roused my curiosity about my own ancestry; at that time I didn't even know the name of my father's father or most of the family origins. In uncovering some of the family genealogy, I began to realize that the only things I was discovering were dates of birth, marriage, and death, but nothing about who these ancestors were. What did they do in their lives? How did they spend their days; their holidays; their special occasions? What were they like as people?

I soon realized that my own life would follow a similar scenario; a life that would someday close and eventually be forgotten as years and living memories passed. I regretted not having documented our family's history while the elders were still around to relate their stories. My father, Dan, for instance, had an interesting history during his younger days in the bootlegging business during prohibition and no one ever recorded his reminiscences. These stories are now all lost to his descendants; never to be told.

I want my grandson, James (and any other grandchildren that may join him) to have knowledge of my humble life so that he can understand another time and another place, and so that his family is not just another list of dates of birth and death.

I have not attempted to impart any of my philosophical attitudes in this story of my life, although I don't doubt that much could be read between the lines in the events that have shaped my years.

I have attempted to be faithful to events as seen through my eyes (or at least as I think I remember them.) As I delved further into a study of my own life, I was astounded at how many clear memories have been stored away in the hard drive of my brain for these many years. In some instances my memory proved somewhat inadequate, particularly for events that occurred many decades in the past. My recollection proved most vague in remembering some of the names from long ago. In the interests of a more even flow of prose, and to add a bit of mischief, I have used some substitute names in the early pages. These names can be identified by the **bold type.**

I have attempted to present the times as I remember them, nothing more and nothing less. I apologize for any inaccuracies that may occur in these pages.

In the chapters dealing with my long career as an Engineer, I have avoided getting involved in technical details; most of which I have probably forgotten and, even if I remembered would not be understood by many... nor would they care. I will say that most of the projects I worked on were state-of-the-art for the day and always on the cutting edge of technology, but which today would be considered relics of the dark ages.

I have seen much, done much, and I have done some good and some bad (but I hope not too bad), and I have made my share of mistakes in this life. The one mistake I will not make at this juncture of my life is to leave my grandson without an appreciation of a least one part of his family heritage.

...and so it is to James Patrick McKenna (and all of his descendants) that I dedicate this book

.... John J. O'Leary

PROLOGUE

1932 was the bridge year. It spanned the Age of Innocence before the Great War and the attempt after the war to renew that time against the harsh realities then enfolding on the world. Economically, the world had slipped into a deep depression and, politically, the forces of evil were afoot in the world with Nazism raising its ugly head in Germany, Japan's militarists starting to move out into the world, and the Soviet Union reaching the heights of cruelty. These things would soon plummet the world into a terrible war that would forever crush any hopes of a return to the more irenic times before the conflict.

With 12 million jobless in the United States, 1932 was a year when the concern of most Americans was to feed and shelter their families. They were glad to be rid of the foreign entanglements that took so many American lives in a war that most American felt was not theirs. We had turned inward and were not yet ready to engage the nefarious forces that were, even then, starting to emerge on the other side of the world.

Herbert Hoover was in the last year of his presidency; soon to be replaced by Franklin D. Roosevelt who would usher in his "New Deal" and permanently change the political landscape of America.

The eighteenth amendment to the Constitution with its prohibition against alcohol was still in effect until 1933. The country was still on the gold standard; Bryan's "Cross of Gold."

The only foreign relations that concerned Americans was the return of the Heavyweight boxing crown to the United States when Jack Sharkey defeated Germany's Max Schmeling in 15 rounds in New York City.

1932 was the only year in which there was a tie for the Oscar for Best Actor when Frederick March (Dr. Jekyll and Mr. Hyde) shared the award with Wallace Beery (The Champ). Helen Hayes took the best actress prize for "Sin of Madelon Claudet" and the best picture Oscar went to "The Grand Hotel."

The Pulitzer Prize for Fiction that year went to Pearl Buck for "The Good Earth."

Elsewhere, in sports, the Yankees swept the World Series over Chicago in four straight games, while the Rangers were losing the Stanley Cup to Toronto.

Outside the United States, Hirohito was Emperor of Japan but the nativist militarists had seized control of the government and had started the Japanese quest for hegemony over Eastern Asia and the Pacific with the establishment of a puppet government in Manchuria that they named Manchukuo.

In the Soviet Union the tyrant dictator, Josef Stalin, was completing his brutal collectivization program that left millions dead in his country. Hitler was just days away from being named Chancellor of Germany by President Hindenburg (January 1933) to start the world on the first steps toward world war and one of the most wicked governmental regimes ever to stain the world.

Closer to home, the United States was still playing hemispheric policeman with American troops still occupying Haiti.

Into this world of rapidly evolving change, a child was born. There was no star rising in the east to announce his birth; if anything, there may have been a full moon to greet this newcomer. The narrative to follow is the story of that child.

1932-1936

1932-1936

IN THE BEGINNING

I was born at home at 30-55-49th Street in Astoria, Queens, New York City, having been delivered by a Mrs. Sarah Smith, a mid-wife from Long Island City, at 5:30 P.M. on July 8, 1932. It was a normal birth and I weighed in at a hefty eight pounds and fifteen ounces.

I was the third child born to Daniel J. O'Leary, Sr. and Florence Beiser, following Francis Xavier who was born eighteen months before and the oldest brother, Daniel Joseph, Jr. born in August of 1929. We also had a half sister, Helen; though we never thought of her as any but a full sister. Helen Florence Roepke was born in New York City to our mother, Florence, and Edward Roepke, her first husband.

By the time I arrived on the scene in 1932, depression had set in pretty badly across the United States and our family was greatly effected by it. This is the reason I was only given one name; the family could no longer afford two names.

In those days it was common practice not to put off the Baptism of newborn babies until a caterer could be hired and a party arranged. The important thing was to welcome the child into the church at the earliest time so that the baby would be prepared for any eventuality. My Baptism took place at St. Joseph's Church in Astoria, only nine days after I was born. My grandfather, John Schwab and my mother's sister, Aunt Ruth Beiser (later to be Ruth Schwartz) sponsored me as my godparents.

Mother (we always called our Mother by that name; not Mom, or Ma, or Mommy) kept a written record of each of the eight siblings, tracking their illnesses, medical records, places of residence, schools attended, and significant events in each of our lives. It was from this record that I informed myself of the earliest days.

Before I was four years old, I had been through some of the major childhood sicknesses such as Chicken Pox, Mumps, and Whooping Cough; never did get the Measles or Scarlet Fever.

At eighteen months, I fell on my forehead three times; out of the high chair, I believe; and spent eight days in Bellevue Hospital in New York City being treated with flaxseed poultices for Cellulitis of the forehead which had caused my eyes to be swollen shut.

It seems that my head accounted for a large part of this motherly ledger. In the first grade, at the age of 6, I fell on the concrete in St. Joseph's schoolyard and required stitches in the back of the head. Just before turning ten, my head was split open in a "rock war" in Woodside.

I can remember in one of the English classes during my attendance at St. Joseph's Elementary School, being required to write an autobiography which was to be read to the class. When I was about halfway through my recital, Sister interrupted me to say, "This is supposed to be the story of your life, not only an autobiography of your head." I have often wondered if all this attention to my head led to my current hat size, 7-3/4.

My earliest, though somewhat hazy, recollection is while I was in a baby carriage being pushed by Mother with a young Dan and Fran holding on to each side. I must have been about two years old; surely no older than three.

A wheel came off the carriage and Mother was quite perplexed, but her usual calm self. She sought assistance at a nearby store. I believe it was a saloon located on 30th Road where Public School 10 and a park would be built at a later date.

I believe it was the traumatic impact to my young mind that made some of these events stand out above all others and to be remembered over seventy years later.

One of the most traumatic of these happenings took place at our apartment on 44th Street, which was the third place we had lived in my three short years on earth. I believe those were the days when you received a free month's rent when you moved into a new apartment, and moving was a way to cut down the cost of rent.

One day, we three boys were playing in the apartment and Mother was sitting in the rocking chair knitting. She started to hemorrhage profusely over the rocker with the blood flowing onto the floor. Mother remained quite calm and told us to call the neighbor next door. We were quite frightened; first, by the blood, then by the droves, or what seemed to be droves, of agitated women, excitedly rushing in and out of the apartment, barking orders; and then by the arrival of police and an ambulance.

It seemed like an eternity before things quieted down after they took Mother out on a stretcher. The house emptied and we three boys were taken to another apartment by one of the neighbor women until Daddy came home. Earlier, one of the women told us not to worry that, "Your mother sat on a knitting needle and will be all right."

Several days later, Mother returned home with a little baby girl in her arms. I later realized that she had been taken to the hospital and she was bringing home a sister for us; my sister Marilyn (the spelling of which was "Marylin" on her birth certificate.)

I didn't react too pleased at this new addition that would supplant me as the baby of the house. My first words to her were, "Dinky one" (Stinky

5

One). It was not until years later that I learned that babies did not come from sitting on a knitting needle, but until that time, I was very vigilant to make sure that there were no knitting needles where Mother might sit and cause another baby.

This latest addition to our growing household was probably the impetus for us to move to different quarters around the corner on 46th Street, where we would spend the next seven years.

We moved into a four-room apartment on the ground floor of a clapboard house that was probably one of the oldest existing structures in Astoria. It was here that I started to grow up, to meet new friends, and to begin my exploration of the world of Astoria.

1936-1943

THE APARTMENT

Our new home on 46th Street was a modest "railroad" apartment in a building with four apartments; two upstairs and two downstairs(see page 340.) Our four rooms included a front room; no doubt called that because it was in the front of the house facing the street. We used it as a living room and family room. The furnishings that I recall were a sofa that was usually adorned with slipcovers and lace doilies on the arms; a small bookcase with glass doors and a number of books which we all avidly read over the next few years, the rocking chair of knitting needle infamy, and a kerosene burner. Hanging over the mantle was a two by three foot oil painting on black velvet depicting a scene in Venice, Italy with some Renaissance characters.

At the rear of the house was the kitchen, which was of sufficient size to accommodate a large kitchen table. When pulled from its normal place against the wall, the table provided seating for our family of seven (soon to be eight with the arrival of brother Bob in May of 1937). We didn't have enough chairs for all of us to sit at the table at the same time, so we made up

9

the deficit by putting the ironing board across two chairs to give us two to three extra places.

There was a toilet at the rear of the kitchen; no bath, no shower, no sink; just a small closet of a room with a toilet that had an overhead tank and a chain for flushing. In the wintertime when the temperature was below freezing, the water in the toilet would freeze up overnight. There was a race amongst the boys in the morning to be the first to get to use the toilet so that we could thaw out the ice in the bowl with that first pee of the day. I can still hear Mother yelling out, "Pull the chain!"

The other two rooms in the center of the apartment were used as bedrooms. The one closest to the kitchen had two single beds; one for Helen (who later shared this bed with Marylin after Bobby joined the household), and the other bed I shared with Danny and Franny. There was a doorway without a door on one side to the kitchen and one on the other side to the other bedroom. There was also a clouded glass double hung window between the kitchen and the bedroom. The only other furniture that I can recall in this bedroom was a small, narrow dresser about four feet high, which gave us an excellent platform to jump off onto the beds; which usually collapsed from the impact of the flying bodies. We did this, of course, when Mother and Daddy were not at home.

Helen, who was often left to baby sit us, tried to control us but we were incorrigible and she usually had to resort to force. She would grab us one at a time, hold us down, and give us a "mulligan", which was a blow delivered by a fist with a bent, protruding middle finger and applied with great force to the upper arm, the thigh, or most often, the top of the head.

One night as we were doing our "suicide dives" onto the bed, Mother and Daddy arrived unexpectedly and caught Franny in the air just before he hit the bed that collapsed as it often did. Daddy was so irate that he picked Franny up and banged his head into the plaster wall leaving a dent in the wall of about three inches in diameter. That dent was never fixed, and until we left the house a few years later, whenever we got out of line, Daddy would point to the dent in the wall and we were all well aware of the implications.

The second bedroom was for Mother and Daddy, who slept in a double bed. This room opened up through a wide archway into the front room. Above the archway was decorative beading that must have been fashionable during the "Gay Nineties." The baby's crib was also located in this room.

The only clothes closet in the house was built into this room; double vertically hung doors at the top and two tiers of drawers at the bottom.

A sister painting of another Venice scene on velvet completed the décor in this "master bedroom".

The floors in each room were covered in linoleum which was subject to much wear and was periodically changed by Daddy when it was affordable.

There was no central heating. A black coal stove in the kitchen provided the primary heat to the apartment and was supplemented by the kerosene burner in the front room. In the wintertime when the coal stove was in daily use, the stove was also used for cooking. Another use for the stove in the winter was to place our feet in the oven to warm up after playing in the snow and coming in wet and cold.

Coal for the stove was stored in the cellar in a bin; every apartment was assigned a bin that was used to store personal belongings and the coal. Coal was delivered by trucks to the neighborhood houses. Metal chutes were run into the cellar from the cellar window and the coal was put into large barrels to be rolled to the chute for transfer to the cellar bins.

Fuel for the "oil burner" was purchased from Brandt's Hardware Store around the corner and put directly into the oil can which was then placed in a reservoir tray on the back of the burner. A large pot of water was placed on top of the burner console to humidify the air and had to be refilled continuously.

In the kitchen, in addition to the coal stove, was a four-burner gas range and oven for cooking, a sink, an icebox and a double section soapstone washtub. Daddy took the separator out from between the two tubs so that we had a place to bathe, albeit in the kitchen.

Most of the time, we doubled up in the tub to save water. A gas-fired boiler that was located between the sink and the coal stove provided hot water.

Mother and Daddy took their baths when everyone was out of the house or late at night after we had all gone to sleep. Helen, being a young teenager at the time, wouldn't use this kitchen bathing facility. I can remember her packing up her towel and bathing supplies and a change of clothes into a brown paper bag and going to Aunt Lily's house on 43rd Street to use her bathtub.

The alternate use for the washtubs was, of cause, to scrub the laundry manually on a washboard. When the budget would permit the modest expenditure for "wet wash", Mother would send the clothes out and they would be delivered "wet" in a bag to be hung on the backyard clothes line to dry.

The icebox was a constant source of aggravation in the kitchen. A block of ice was placed in the upper compartment and as it thawed, the melted ice dripped into a pan placed underneath. If, as often happened, the pan were not emptied, the overflow would soak the kitchen floor.

The ice was usually purchased from the iceman who peddled the ice from a truck or a horse drawn wagon. He would carry it into the house directly into the icebox. A fifteen-cent piece of ice off the wagon measured about one cubic foot. We were often sent to the Knickerbocker Ice House about a half-mile from the house so that we could purchase a larger piece of ice for the same price. We hauled the ice back to the house in our homemade wagon. With all the detours and diversions that we encountered along the way, by the time we got home, the ice was melted down to about a half a cubic foot.

Lighting for the apartment was miniscule. The largest bulb, 100 watts, was in the kitchen in a ceiling fixture with a pull chain. This was the sole lighting in the kitchen. There was a single 25-watt bulb in a ceiling fixture in each of the other three rooms and a standing lamp in the front room that also had a 25-watt bulb. The front windows were fitted with shutters which when closed added to the dimness of the room.

Entry to the apartment was usually through a door leading to the kitchen, and less often through a door from the hallway into the front room. The doors were usually left unlocked in those days unless the whole family was leaving the house.

Besides the clothes closet in the "master bedroom", the only cabinetry in the house was a small cabinet in the kitchen where we stored the food and dishes which in the main were an odd assortment of broken and irregular pieces. Our "crystal ware" was old jelly jars that were often chipped.

Behind the house was a small yard that was variously used as a ball field, a battlefield, a mud pie factory, or anything that our young imaginations could conjure. Access to the yard was through the cellar (remember, "... slide down my cellar door"?) The more usual entry to the yard, however, was directly out the kitchen window in the back of the house using the adjacent fence as a ladder.

Daddy built us a grand shack in the backyard from old wood scraps. The upper half of the shack was constructed of a thin layer of tarpaper whose integrity was short lived. A small tear on in the side of the tarpaper soon expanded into a gaping hole which became an alternate ingress and egress for us; which only led to a larger hole.

Some of the most memorable times in that multi-purpose edifice were when we were permitted to stay up after dark. We would gather in the shack with a flickering candle and in the semi-darkness we would listen with wide-eyed awe to Danny or one of the older kids as they delightfully frightened us with tales of horror, gore, and mystery. And how we loved to be scared out of our wits!

One day Daddy constructed a chicken coop in the backyard and stocked it with young chicks. After a few weeks, the chickens had reached maturity and with Mother's prodding to be rid of them, Daddy prepared to dispatch them all in the cellar of the house.

I don't recall how many chickens there were, but Daddy quickly chopped off each of the heads and let the headless chickens run around the cellar until they expired. This was quite an exciting event for us kids, and for me it was my first experience in observing a typical session of a governmental legislative body. However, these "chickens running around with their heads cut off" were more delectable roasted and served at our dinner table than any of those politicians would have been.

The apartment was small, but it provided adequate living space for a host of occupants. Besides Mother and Daddy and we six kids, we had an abundance of cockroaches whose presence was usually most noticeable after dark.

We also had a colony of mice to keep us company. Hardly a week went by without having our "big game hunt" in which we chased the mice with brooms or any other weapon that was available. The captured mouse would be executed by drowning in the toilet where with a quick flush he joined his mates in the city sewers.

The evening was also time for the guests who joined us in bed and who we didn't notice until after we went to sleep and they started to feast on our flesh. There was many a night of bed bug banquet followed by Daddy pulling the mattresses off in the morning to be beaten and aired in the back yard, attempting to get rid of these night crawlers. He would then spray the springs on the bed with an insecticide, if it was available, or in the event it was not, he would scrape the inside of the springs to remove the bedbugs and kill them by hand. You could tell the ones that had gorged on us the night before because they were the bloodiest.

In the summer, the invaders were flies and mosquitoes; there being no air conditioning and windows and doors were usually wide open to cool the house. We would kill the flies on a sticky flypaper trap hanging from the light string or, more directly, with a swatter. The most entertaining way to kill them, though, was with a spring-loaded pistol that shot a dart with a small suction cup on the end. When the flies would land on a wall or on the ceiling we would take our target practice on them. It wasn't long before the wall and ceiling were covered with squashed fly bloodstains. The stains were usually washed off with the Saturday cleaning, but there was one particularly large spot on the kitchen ceiling that remained for years and was still there the day that we moved.

Mother was a very fastidious housekeeper in spite of the pests that swarmed around us. Every Saturday was house-cleaning day, and every room was cleaned from top to bottom. All of the furniture was moved into an adjacent room, every week, and the floors were scrubbed, usually with a heavy concentration of Pine-Sol, and then waxed. Walls and windows were cleaned and all furniture and moldings were dusted. Only then was all the furniture replaced in the room.

When we were younger, we were allowed to dust but it wasn't too long before we were into the heavy moving and cleaning. It seemed to me at the time, that because of the small age difference in the three older boys, me being the youngest of the three, that when it came to "privileges" of age, I was always told that I would have to wait until I was old enough or the same age as Danny and Franny were when they were given these privileges. However, when it came to chores and other onerous tasks, we would all reach the age of responsibility simultaneously; an early lesson in life's inequities.

My earliest recollection at our 46th Street residence took place when I was about four years old, shortly after we had moved in.

Around that time period there was a parade and picnic every June 1st, called a "June Walk". I don't know what the genesis of the event was or who sponsored it but I do recall them quite vividly.

On this particular June day, we joined in the usual parade, which also featured many decorated floats, and marched to the picnic grounds where we were treated to whatever goodies were provided for the day. Toward the end of the day, Daddy went off to do something, perhaps the men's room, and cautioned me to stay exactly where he left me and not to move anywhere. The curiosity of a four year old led me to wander off... and off... and off. Before long I had wandered not only out of the park but wound up several blocks away.

However, I was not particularly disturbed, because even in those days, at four years old, I knew my numbers, knew how to read street signs, and also knew that I lived on 46th Street and 30th Avenue. I walked to the corner, noted the present street location and then walked to the next corner and discovered that the numbers were going in the right direction and continued going in the right direction along the way. It wasn't too many blocks before I came to a solid concrete barrier and was completely at a loss as to how to proceed. (I deduced in later years that this barrier was the wall along the Grand Central Parkway)

I noticed some people coming out of a nearby house and approached them. I was too shy to say anything (in those days they called me "Bashful"). So, I used my most effective means of communications, I started to cry. After ascertaining my predicament, those kind people took me over to Steinway Street and turned me over to a policeman who had me taken home in a Police car, which in those days was a solid green, single seat coupe.

When I arrived home, which was several hours after the start of this journey, Mother and Daddy were ecstatic; they hugged me and kissed me. They thanked the policeman profusely and Daddy even tried to give the cop a tip; which he thankfully declined. (Daddy tipped everyone even when he couldn't afford a penny)

After the cops left, Daddy turned on me and laced into me something fierce. He whacked me across the ass until I cried and said, "And now look what you've gone and done. Disgracing the family by being dropped off by the cops. How will we ever explain to the neighbors about a police car in front of our house?" I felt like "Jackie O'Leary – FELON" and wondered if they were going to drag me off to jail.

It wasn't too long after that episode, my flirtation with crime, that Mother had some neighbor's in for tea and coffee in the evening after we had all been put to bed. During the night I awoke with pains in my stomach and felt very sick. I came out to the kitchen where the ladies were gathered at the table and in my usual fashion, cried that I was sick. Everyone started to offer advice. I don't know how many women were there but it seemed like, and sounded like, an army. All I can see today in my mind's eye is a bunch of yelling, distorted faces.

Someone offered the suggestion that I should be given an enema. Before I knew it I was on the kitchen table with my bare ass hanging over the oval shaped wash basin that Mother used for multiple purposes; and now she was about to find another use for it. I was frightened and couldn't stop crying, women were babbling all around me. "Lift up his behind". "Put some Vaseline on it". "Stick it up his behind." "Gently now." Oh, Yeah!

I could feel my stomach filling up with something warm. It was starting to hurt and then all of a sudden ("I couldn't help it. Please, don't beat me," I was thinking) I exploded. Most of the excrement went into the pan, but it was all over the table and all over the floor, but, most gratifyingly, it splattered on the gaggle of hens hovering around the pan. Women were scampering around yelling and in a panic. The last thing I recall hearing was someone saying, "BAD BOY!" My last thoughts were, "Shit on all of you!"

I don't recall all of the neighbors in our house for they were changing from time to time, but some of them do stand out. Next door for a period of time lived Katy Doran, Daddy's second cousin, her husband and children, Joanie, Jimmy (who we called "Zombie" because he was the skinniest kid on the block), Ray-Ray, and Marilyn.

Upstairs were the Cavanaughs; whose only claim to my memory was a daughter called "Tansy", which name had a lyrical sound to me.

Next door to them were the McKies. Mrs. McKie had a physical impediment, perhaps M.S., and did not leave her apartment too often. We used to go to the store for Mrs. McKie; always to get a can of Franco-American beef gravy. I think that this was the reason that, after the McKies moved in, the hallway had the constant stale smell of old brown gravy.

Mikey, was the older son. Gussie, the younger, would later marry Ann Pruziner, a cousin of Ann Mulraney. Ann was Jean's maid-of-honor at our wedding in 1959. Gussie and Marilyn Doran caused a short-lived scandal in the neighborhood when they were found outside the house, cavorting in the nude. They were both about three or four years old at the time.

I remember one especially shocking day with Mikey McKie. I was about seven years old at the time and Mikey and I and a couple of friends, Eddie Ryan from my class in school and Gussie, Mikey's brother, took our homemade wagons to the remains of the old Madison Square Garden Bowl on Northern Boulevard, which had been demolished except for a large bowl shaped concrete crater that was ideal for riding our wagons to the bottom, climb back to the top, and repeat. [Madison Square Garden Bowl was used as the site for several boxing championship matches, including the Heavyweight contest in 1932 when Jack Sharkey took the title from Max Schmeling of Germany and brought the title back to the United States. It was also used for the Soap Box Derby, which we often attended.]

After several runs down the slopes of the bowl, we were sitting on our wagons at the bottom of the hill when a man at the top of the south end of the bowl called to us. Mikey ran up the hill to find out what the man wanted. When he returned to us waiting at the bottom, he said, "The man up there said he'd give us fifty cents if we would suck his cock." We were so frightened that we ran straight up the north end of the bowl with our wagons and hotfooted it for home. When we arrived home, Mikey finally caught up with us and showing great disappointment said, "Why'd you guys run? We coulda made fifty cents."

LIFE IN THE NEIGHBORHOOD

For the first couple of years at our 46th Street home, the apartment and the street between 28th and 30th Avenues were all I knew. (There was no 29th Avenue at this location). The neighborhood was a typical working class area with primarily multi-family apartment houses and a few two or three family attached homes. The only single family house was a small wooden frame house that was occupied by two spinster sisters who lived a reclusive life. The house had shutters that were continuously closed.

One of the sisters never left the house and the only time we were aware of her presence was when she peered furtively out of the window behind the shutters while her sister tended to the garden. The garden was planted in a large rectangular hole alongside their house that I realized in later years, was the foundation for the cellar of a house that was never built. Access to the garden was by a ladder that the sister brought back into the house when she was not in the garden.

The sisters dressed in long house dresses and bonnets, and fit the description of what we conceived of as a "witch". Often when playing ball in the street, the ball would go over their fence and land in the garden. None of us had the courage to hop the fence to retrieve the ball unless we were "dared" to go in and face the wrath of the "witches". I particularly remember one day when we goaded Georgie Wunderlin into hopping the fence to get a ball that had gone into the "witches" yard. The sister that was the only one to leave the house came out and quietly climbed down into the pit without Georgie noticing. When he turned around and saw her approaching, it seemed that he ran up the side of the wall, over the fence, and out of harms way.

When he joined us on the other side of the street, safe from his frightening encounter, we all burst out with laughter; Georgie had peed his pants and he wasn't even aware of it. After that day, it was difficult to get any of us to retrieve lost balls in the "witches" garden. Usually we would wait until after dark when their lights went out and then we would send someone in to get any balls that were lost during the day.

[Georgie died of polio before we moved away from the block. This may have been my first experience with the death of someone I knew; other than the kittens that my brothers, Danny and Franny, allege that I killed before moving to 46th Street.]

Other than these cloistered sisters, most of the people on the block were working men and their families: that is, those who had jobs. With the depression still in full swing in 1936, there were probably as many people on the block on home relief as there were with low paying jobs.

The ethnic makeup of 46th Street and its environs was mixed; predominantly, Irish, German, Italian, and other Western European types. There were no Negroes (not yet called "African-Americans" nor even "black"). There were Greeks in Astoria, but they were primarily found around Ditmars Boulevard at the other end of town, and had not yet reached the density that would later make them the majority group in the community.

There was a small Jewish community centered around a Synagogue on 34th Street and in those days did not play a noticeable role in our end of the community other than as shopkeepers or as door to door salesmen. Mother had one of the vendors who regularly came to the house to sell a large selection of merchandise from slipcovers and rugs to pots and pans and dishes. She called him "My Jew", and that's the way we referred to him when he made his house call. "Mother, your Jew is here."

The only Asian people we were exposed to were, the Chinese Launderer and the waiters at the Chinese Restaurant. In our innocent youth we weren't aware of any differences between these various groups but the adults we lived around quickly filled our vocabularies with a whole catalogue of descriptive titles which we picked up and used but actually had no idea of the significance. (Nor the ignorance and hatred behind it)

There were: Micks and Guineas (also Wops and Dagoes), Kikes and Mockies, Niggers (not yet just the "n" word), Heinies and Krauts. These epithets shaped many an Astoria young mind; many of which are still tainted by this early exposure. However, this is not a place for apology or explanation - that's just the way it was.

A German delicatessen was on the corner of 30th Avenue across from our house that was at mid-block. Across the street from the deli was Will's Bar and Grill or as we called it, "Nickel Will's", because it was the last bastion of the five cent beer.

["Nickel Will's" was also the first place that had a television in the neighborhood.

Prior to the outbreak of World War II, New York City had the privilege of presenting the first television shows in the country for a short time. Daddy went every Friday night to see the boxing matches and often would take one of us to join him. While he drank beer, we would drink coca cola until we got sick. After the fights, which lasted until about 11 P.M., the television broadcast would end with the National Anthem and I would go home to puke; that is, if I were still awake.

It was here, at Will's that I had the opportunity to see the first Joe Louis and Billy Cahn Heavyweight Championship fight; and, after the War, the return match. It was probably also the place where the seeds were sown for my later brief foray into the world of pugilistics.]

The only other stores of any note on the block were directly across the street; Mike the Shoemaker's and Foley's Candy Store. Foley's was, understandably, one of our favorite places. There was nothing more pleasurable at my age than to have a penny to spend on a piece of candy; unless it was a nickel which could occupy me for at least a half hour, making a selection of whatever would give me the greatest quantity. (Quantity always took precedence over quality). Especially enjoyable was sidling up to the counter and saying, "A frozen Roly-Poly, Mr. Foley." (A Roly-Poly was a chocolate covered caramel bar similar to a Milky Way and sold for two cents frozen or one penny unfrozen.)

A pleasant memory of Foley's was a young man (older to us at the time) who would buy all the neighborhood kids a soda on Friday nights when he came home from work with his paycheck. We really looked forward to this special treat. "Dutch" Sokol just did this out of the goodness of his heart and we were all distraught when he was drafted into the Navy with the outbreak of World War II. The last time we saw him was when he was home on leave in his uniform. He came around to buy the old gang one last soda. We never heard from him again. I don't know if he ever returned from the war.

No one in the neighborhood had a telephone in the home and we all relied upon the public telephone in Foley's Candy Store to service us for both outgoing calls at five cents a call and incoming calls. In that rare instance when someone was called, usually a death or sickness of some relative, Mr. Foley would send one of the kids hanging around the street to summon the neighbor. Quite often it would just be yelling up into the window from the street that would serve to fetch the call recipient.

In the dog days of summer, the streets would be filled with men and women sitting in front of their houses to get away from the unbearable heat inside. Some of the apartment houses had stoops that were a popular gathering place. Our house had no stoop so Mother and Daddy had to provide their own chairs if they wanted to sit outside to escape the heat.

Most of the men wore hats both in the winter and in the summer. In the summer they would switch to their straw hats from the felt hats of winter. The men were always polite to the women and would tip their hat to the ladies when they would greet them on the street.

Summertime was also a time for swimming at Astoria Pool, a New York City Parks Department Public facility that was a good distance from 46th Street. We would walk there on many summer mornings to take advantage of the free swim time from nine to noon. In the afternoon the price of admission went to nine cents and it was a very rare occasion when we had the money to pay. We would climb the fence near the exit from the men's dressing room and sneak into the pool through that exit. The worst that ever happened to us, if we did get caught, was to be thrown out of the pool. Usually, though, we were pretty adept at getting in without being discovered.

When the polio epidemic was on, Mother insisted that the pool was a major spreader of the disease and vigorously opposed our swimming in those waters. And when Georgie Wunderlin died, she felt she was vindicated in her thinking.

One of the fixtures on the block was an old German shepherd that belonged to the Webster's about three houses down from ours. Betsy, as she was called, was a timid soul that just lay outside the house during the day and didn't bark and didn't bother anyone. Most of the neighborhood kids, however, would torment the poor dog by rubbing or pulling her tail. Betsy would run in circles for long periods of time trying to catch whatever she felt was biting on her tail. We were all sad when Betsy finally died.

Most of the youngsters in the neighborhood were mischievous at worst and there were few whom we considered really "bad kids." One of these, Eddie Koberski, stands out as exceptionally destined for a life of crime. One of the first indications we had took place at our house on 46th Street.

Our sister, Helen, a teenager attending high school in Long Island City, had some of her classmates over to the house one evening. There they listened to records on our old wind up Victrola console, drank soda, and just talked. Mother and Daddy were out for the evening. Danny, Franny, and I were supposed to be in bed sleeping, but we were "spying" on the activities in our front room. Helen chided us many times to get back in bed; which we did, but not for long.

When it was time for everyone to leave, they all said their goodbyes and departed while Ed Koberski lingered. After the last one had left and the door was closed, Koberski immediately started to force himself upon Helen while she pleaded with him to go. He just laughed and continued his attack. When he started pulling at her clothes, presumably to tear them off, Danny, Franny, and I ran into the room and jumped on Koberski's back after he had pushed Helen onto the sofa. We weren't much of a match for a boy of his size but we intimidated him enough to get him off Helen and out of the house. I don't recall if Helen ever told Mother and Daddy about this, but I know she was grateful to us for disobeying her orders to get to sleep that night.

I learned in later years that prior to this incident, while Koberski was a student at P.S. 151, he would get his kicks by tying girls to a tree or telephone pole, removing their clothes and in other ways humiliating them.

One day as we were playing outside the house, Koberski came flying out of Foley's Candy Store across the street and landed on his stomach outside the store. Mr. Foley came to the door and stood there with his hands on his hips and shouted for the whole neighborhood to hear, "You son-of-a-bitch, you come in here again trying to sell me stolen goods, I'll kick your ass clear to kingdom come." Koberski had some nasty retort but he didn't have the courage to hang around and feel Mr. Foley's reply.

We soon learned that Koberski stole many cases of cigarettes from a freight car at the railroad yards and was trying to peddle them to the local storekeepers. Koberski was destined for worse things. He would soon be on the front page of the Daily News for having killed a soldier after he and an accomplice raped the soldier's girlfriend in Central Park. It would subsequently come out that this was not the first rape or murder for this sick pair. They were also accused of several other successful and unsuccessful attempts, including a double murder and rape in Astoria Park. Both Koberski and his friend were convicted of murder and were executed in the electric chair shortly after their conviction. In those days, justice was meted out more swiftly than today.

SCHOOL DAYS

When I was five years old in 1937, I started school in Kindergarten at Public School 151 in Woodside. At that time Danny and Franny were both attending St. Joseph's Parochial School two blocks away from us on 44th Street. Helen was in her eighth and final year at P.S.151 before attending Long Island City High School and so it fell upon her to take me to school and home again. (Bryant High School was not yet built at that time, so most of the neighborhood kids attending high school had to travel the long distance to Long Island City)

Kindergarten was relatively forgettable and the only incident that stands out in my mind is what happened when a group of us students were asked to go to the blackboard and draw something. I was on one end of the blackboard and my selected subject was a train engine. Partway through this production, the teacher was so impressed with my efforts that she made the rest of the students sit down so that I could draw, not just the engine, but also the entire train. I did this with great pride and as I remember it, it was quite an impressive accomplishment for a young five year old. (Little did I know at the time that today my grandson, James, would be obsessed with trains; particularly, Thomas the Train.)

The following year, I joined Danny and Franny at St. Joseph's. My first grade teacher was Sister Mary Clement, O.P. (for Order of Preachers), a Dominican Nun. It was quite a shock for most of us to suddenly come under the rigid discipline of these dedicated ladies. We got right into the swing of things.

Every day would start off with our morning prayers and the Pledge of Allegiance to the flag, followed by our first lesson of the day, Catechism, which we learned to recite by heart by constant repetition day after day.

"Who made the World?"

"God made the World."

"Who is God?"

"God is the Creator of heaven and earth and of all things"

"What is man?"

"Man is a creature composed of body and soul and made in the image and likeness of God."

"Why did God make you?

"God made me to know Him, to love Him, and to serve Him in this world and to be happy with him forever in Heaven."

Sister Clement was relentless in her pursuit of perfection from everyone in the class. Any breaches of discipline or failure to be prepared were dealt with by a slap across the face, a blow from the pointer or yardstick, or in extreme case of misconduct, a trip to the principal's office for major behavior adjustments.

Sister Mary Honorata, O.P., the principal of the school at that time, was known to have a very effective tool for dealing with recalcitrant students, a cat-o-nine-tails, a nine corded whip with knots at the end of each cord. This is the kind of punishment device popular in the old sailing Navy days and hardly the kind of thing one should be using on six-year-old children. I was fortunate in never having to face the whip even though I was constantly on the carpet for something.

Perhaps more feared than the cat-o-nine tails, was the threat of being transferred out of St. Joseph's to the Public School. We were so indoctrinated into the verities of the Catholic religion that the thought of losing our privileged position as students in a Catholic School was the worst punishment we could bear.

One day, one of the girls in our class was feeling the sting of Sister's wrath for some transgression and was directed to, "Go down to the Principal's office and get a transfer slip." This was too much for the poor young thing. She got down on her knees and cried and begged Sister to forgive her and that she wouldn't do it again. "Please, please," she said, "I'm a Catholic, not a Public." Sister restrained her laughter but she did let the dear girl off the hook with a threat that the next time there will be no forgiveness.

On another occasion, Sister Clement was out of the class for a brief time, when one of the boys went to the pencil sharpener in the front of the class to sharpen his pencil. On the way back he must have seen a target of opportunity, my head, and spontaneously stuck the newly sharpened pencil into the middle of my forehead. Sister Clement was just returning to the classroom and caught the attacker in the act. She directed me to go to the front of the room and to sharpen my pencil. When I returned to the seat, she held the malefactor by the arms and directed me to stab him in the head with my pencil. Being always the obedient student, I did as directed; my first contact with Hammurabi, "an eye for an eye, and a head for a head."

Every day during our reading lesson, we were expected to be prepared with the day's assignment and be able to read it well. If not, you joined the line of students who were also delinquent in their lesson and, at the end of the lesson, Sister would go down the row of students and give each one two sharp slaps across each cheek. Most of the nuns had bony-fingered hands that seemed especially constructed to mete out the maximum amount of pain when used as a disciplinary weapon.

One day, I rose to give my recitation, which I usually was able to easily read. This day, however, I discovered too late that the page was missing from the book. As the third boy in the family, I got the hand me downs of the hand me downs and in the case of the schoolbooks, they were in pretty ragged shape by the time they got to me. I wasn't too kind to the books myself. I had continuous hunger pains in those days and I satisfied some of my food needs by eating the parts of the pages that were not printed on.

On top of this, the nuns made it a special point to single out the "poor kids" in the class and I often found this to be very humiliating. At Christmas time, for instance, toys would be donated to the school to give to these poor wretches and there would invariably be a nun poking her head into the classroom door asking that all of the "poor children" come down to the principal's office to get the Christmas dole.

So when it came to the reading of the book with no page, I was reluctant to again call attention to the fact that I was one of the "poor kids" and could not afford a new book. I lined up with the rest of the miscreants and took my bony-fingered punishment from Sister.

[One thing stands out about being poor. When it came to hand me downs, I got the hand me downs from Franny that he got from Danny, who in many cases got them as well from someone else. When I finally got the hand me down overalls (that's what we called them before they became Levi's or Jeans), they were bleached white with hardly a trace of their original blue color. Seeing me in these obviously old pants, Kieran Manning, one of my earliest classmates and buddies, sarcastically said, "What are you, a poor kid?" I ran into Kieran many years later when we were both in Navy Boot Camp in Great Lakes, Illinois. He was wearing a pair of jeans that he had bleached so that he would look like an "Old Salt" and not just a recruit. I was tempted to ask him if he were a poor kid but I don't think he would have remembered his uncharitable remarks so many years before. I last saw Kieran at the fiftieth anniversary gathering of the Astoria Ramblers in 1994 at the Granit in upstate New York. He was ailing then and died a couple of years later.]

In first grade at St. Joseph's I made my first friend that did not live on our block. Alan Balchi lived around the corner and we started a good relationship that gave me an opportunity to journey to distant climes (around the corner). This didn't last too long. One day while we were playing in front of his house on 45th Street, I decided to entertain the group of kids that had gathered with what I thought was a very amusing trick. I inserted my hand inside my short pants and pushed the index finger out through the button fly (there were no zipper flies in those days) and made it look like I was flashing my penis. They did not give me the reaction I thought they would. Instead, they were aghast and told me to leave and never come back. I was not only a felon now, but I was also a "filthy boy"; so ended my friendship with Alan Balchi.

It was while in the first grade that I had one of my major head trauma experiences. Every morning before class and after lunch before returning, we would gather in the schoolyard to play before being summoned to queue up to go to class. We lined up by class with the boys on one side and the girls on the other side in columns of two. The signal to stand in line was a bugle call made by one of the members of the school band. After lining up we would be marched by Sister, in very military style, to the classroom where we were expected to immediately and quietly take our seats; boys on one side of the room and girls on the other.

While running to my position, Mary Agnes Quinn, one of my classmates, was running after me shouting, "Wait for me, be my partner." This was my first experience, but not the last, of having a pretty young lady chase after me to get my attention. On hearing the siren's call, I turned around while still running and collided with one of the upperclassmen. I was knocked into the air and came down of the top of my head, which split open and bled profusely. I was taken to the emergency room at St. John's Hospital, which was then located in Long Island City, where I was stitched up. This was not to be my last visit to the ER at St. John's.

We had a special teacher, Mrs. Imhof, who came to class once a week to instruct us in the Palmer Method of handwriting. She was schooled in the disciplinary arts as well as manuscription and the usual penalty for an errant letter was a rap on the knuckles with a ruler. I was a regular recipient of Mrs. Imhof's reproaches. Though I was always first in the class in the academic subjects, my handwriting was atrocious. I credit a major part of this to Mrs. Imhof forcing me to adapt to a right handed writing style when I was naturally left handed. Perhaps this was because I was the only "southpaw" in the class of about fifty students and the nuns and lay teachers had a mania for uniformity.

I carried this lack of penmanship all through elementary school and, even today, carry the scars of that inauspicious start. To qualify for graduation from the eighth grade at St. Joseph's all students had to pass a test of their writing skills in the Palmer Method. The students were permitted, yes mandated, to keep retaking the test until a satisfactory script was produced. Other than me, the test repeaters went a maximum of three additional trials. I went on and on, perhaps as many as twenty repeats. With graduation rapidly approaching in June, I thought that I would be spending the greater part of the rest of the year repeating and repeating my futile attempts. I believe the only reason I finally got a "passing" grade was that the teacher was worn out and just wanted to be rid of me.

Before going to school in the morning, we would generally have a breakfast of coffee with canned evaporated milk that we got from the Home Relief, and day old rolls and buns. Danny was usually the one designated to go to the bakery in the morning to get about ten cents worth of "stale" rolls and buns, as we called them. On the weekends we would sometimes have Farina or oatmeal in the winter and on special occasions, pancakes smothered with Karo dark syrup, which was also provided by the Home Relief.

The stale buns and coffee would hold us until lunchtime when we would come home to eat, being only two blocks from the school. Lunch was also pretty routine; sandwiches of baloney, ham baloney, spiced ham, Taylor ham, liverwurst, or American cheese. (I thought for years that the only kind of cheese was American cheese.)

One of us would be sent to the grocery store for fifteen cents worth of whatever was the chosen sandwich fill of the day. One day, I made the terrible mistake of asking for "sliced ham" instead of "spiced ham". Sliced ham being infinitely more expensive than spiced ham, the result was a thorough beating when Mother opened the package and discovered that everyone was going to be treated to a spare lunch that day.

After lunch, we always pleaded for a "penny for candy" and more often than not were disappointed. Those occasions when the penny could be spared were rare but always greeted with such enthusiasm that one would think we had struck gold.

Some of the students at St. Joseph's who came from the farther reaches of the Parish did not have time to go home during lunch hour and would "eat out" at one of the local luncheonettes or ice cream parlors. I always thought of them as the "rich kids" and longed for the day when I could eat my lunch out.

The opportunity finally came one day when the landlord was repainting our house. I was eagerly anticipating the one day that we could not eat at home because the kitchen was being painted. When I woke in the morning after a restless night of anticipation, I waited for Mother to give us our lunch money for this long awaited luncheon adventure.

To my disappointment, Mother told us to meet her in the basement of the school at lunchtime and she would bring us our lunch. We all ate sulkily in that school basement. I believe we all would have rather been at the corner ice cream parlor where we could have spent our money for something more substantial and nutritious like an ice cream sundae or at least a Mello-roll.

By the time school was let out at three o'clock, when we would be again marched in military style from the classroom to the corner of the street where we would be released, we were ready to eat again. Most often we were told to wait for supper. On occasion when there were extra slices of bread, Mother would butter the bread, cover it with sugar and give each of us a slice, to hold our appetites at bay until suppertime.

Supper would be whatever the budget could provide. One of our favorites was Mother's baked spaghetti, made in a baking dish with canned, stewed tomatoes, covered with slices of the ubiquitous American cheese, and dotted with sparse pieces of breakfast sausage which Mother would squeeze across the cheese. We would all be very alert at suppertime to how many pieces of sausage each of us would get and any inequities would be loudly protested; "He's got more than me," was an often-heard complaint.

A regular supper entrée was soup made from a soup bone acquired gratis from the butcher. Mother would always send us to get the bone "for the dog". The soup bone would be added to fifteen to twenty cents worth of mixed soup greens, which the greengrocer would select from the abundance of fresh vegetables at what we called the vegetable store. Daddy, being the workingman of the house (when he had a job) would get to pick the few scraps of meat off the bone. If it were a particularly meaty bone, some of us would often get a small piece. The meat was particularly satisfying when Daddy decided to eat it with horseradish. The soup was always delicious and would be adequate for the entire family.

Later, when we became a bit more affluent, every Wednesday night was "liver day". How I hated the vile taste of the beef liver that was fried with bacon, but if we didn't eat what was on the table, we would get no substitutions.

Two of the things that we never saw in the house were steaks and chops, which were the costlier cuts of meat, particularly for an indigent family of eight. I never saw a real steak other than an occasional skirt steak, which is not steak at all, until I joined the Navy in 1950. We were fortunate to have occasional large roasts such as fresh and smoked ham, stuffed chicken and, something Mother was particularly adept at, a delicious pot roast or a sauerbraten. These cuts were evidently more cost effective for a large family.

Another stranger at our table was the marvelous cuisine of Italy. Other than the baked spaghetti, the closest we came to pasta was buttered noodles or the occasional can of Franco-American Spaghetti for lunch.

On Thanksgiving Day, we always had a turkey dinner even in our poorest days. It was a day we all cherished; not only for the dinner feast but because it was also "Ragamuffin Day", when we would dress in costumes or, more often, Mother's old clothes, make up our faces with greasepaint or Mother's face powder, lipstick and rouge to go from door to door in the neighborhood begging for coins and goodies by pleading, "Anything for Thanksgiving?"

After our morning round of petitioning the neighbors, we usually had acquired enough money to enable us to buy Christmas presents for the family; a luxury we could hardly afford without the Thanksgiving offerings. Mother used to get for Christmas such wondrous things as a pair of salt and pepper shakers, ten cents for the pair at the 5 and 10 cent store; or her favorite perfume, "Evening in Paris" (or at least she always said that it was her favorite perfume); also ten cents at the 5 and dime.

For dessert at suppertime, we would often have canned plums or stewed prunes if the Home Relief had provided these. At other times it was Mother's delicious bread pudding, which she made with the left over stale bread that she accumulated for this purpose. Or perhaps, it would be a rice pudding, which I could never get myself to eat, although everyone else raved about it. Occasionally, Mother would bake a cake. In those days the cake was made from all raw materials, as boxed cakes were not in vogue. Before using the flour, Mother invariably would have to sift the mealy bugs and maggots out of the flour before putting it into the mix. We would help sometimes by manually removing some of these unwanted pests. (Actually, had she left them in, it would have been a good protein supplement for our diet.)

At school, I found a unique way to cadge a meal from time to time. I was an excellent student academically, but I had a chronic behavior problem; I was disruptive in class, violated all the rules of good manners and gentlemanly conduct, and, worst of all, I never did my homework assignments; always with a lame excuse, such as, "I forgot", "I left it home", "I lost it." Or "I was attacked by some rowdies on the way to school and they stole it." At first, I was kept after school in the classroom to complete the assigned homework and to help in cleaning the room or cleaning the erasers for the blackboard.

After a while, when the weather permitted, I was obliged to stay after school on the open porch at the convent which was adjacent to the convent kitchen. The nun who did the cooking would bring me cookies and milk; fresh milk, not canned; or at other times would bring me a sandwich. This turned out to be an excellent way to ease those hunger pangs I always had at three o'clock when we normally finished school for the day, but did little to discourage me from continuing the bad habits that I would carry with me through most of my school years.

I never did like to recite in class even when I was prepared. However, I developed a bad habit from the early days of school that I carried with me throughout school. I was never hesitant to speak out when one of the teachers made an error in their presentation to the class. I always felt that I should not let the class be misinformed. This may have made me look like a bit of a wiseass kid, but it was an uncontrollable need on my part to keep the record straight. This also kept me in the bad graces of many teachers.

35

FUN AND GAMES

In the days prior to the Second World War, no home had a television; except for the short time that Nickel Will's had the neighborhood's first black and white TV set. In our house we didn't even have a radio until 1939. I can remember that first radio because Daddy let us stay up late one Monday night to listen to "Lux Presents Hollywood", with Cecil B. DeMille as the commentator. This first program that I heard at home was a weekly digest of a recent movie; this night it was "Snow White and the Seven Dwarfs."

The radio was a table model and was placed on a shelf in the kitchen. We all sat or stood around the radio while we listened and were fascinated by "Snow White" and the magic of the voices coming out of that small box.

We would listen to the adventure shows on the radio in the afternoon. These were especially exciting fifteen-minute stories that were usually continuous like a soap opera; some had a format that would present a completed episode in five days. Some of the evening shows, such as the Lone Ranger or Inner Sanctum, which lasted a full half hour, would complete the story in one episode. The daytime shows I especially remember are: Hop Harrigan,

Don Winslow of the Navy, Mandrake the Magician, Bulldog Drummond, Jack Armstrong the all American boy, and the Inner Circle. This last show encouraged us to mail in a dime for a ring with a secret compartment. The dime was taped to a card and placed in an envelope with a three-cent stamp on it. We never questioned sending cash through the mail and always received the treasures that we ordered. If you mailed the envelope unsealed with the flap just tucked in, the postage was 1-½ cents.

Later on, when we were a bit older, we listened to such popular favorites in the evening as; Fibber McGee and Molly, The Great Gildersleeve, The Shadow, Bob Hope, Fred Allen, Inner Sanctum (with the "Squeaking door"), Jack Benny, and Henry Aldrich. There were many more, but those are the first ones that come to mind.

Prior to the advent of the radio, most of indoor activities were either reading or playing games that required little or no costly equipment.

One of our favorite reading pastimes was the many comic books that were then being published for five or ten cents; comic books such as: Superman, Mandrake the Magician, Captain Marvel (SHAZAM!), Archie and Jughead, the Human Torch, Batman, and a host of others. [I can't believe that I still remember what SHAZAM! stood for; the incantation that would change a young boy, Billy Batson, into the comic book hero, Captain Marvel – S for Solomon, H Hercules, A Atlas, Z Zeus, A Achilles, M Mercury]

The comic books we purchased were usually from the used bookstore where we could pick up old books for a penny or less, depending on condition. We would further supplement our collection by trading with some of our friends. We would go to a friend's house and barter for the books we wanted.

Some of our more heavy reading came from our own bookcase at home. My favorite in those early days was "Hans Brinker and the Silver Skates" which I must have read from cover to cover at least a half dozen times. We also had a large collection of the "Bobsy Twins", Horatio Alger, and several of the other popular series of the time. When we were old enough to join the

Public Library on Steinway Street there was no limit to the kinds of books we could read. At that age, I was still reading the adventure stories and had not yet started to search the library for the "risqué" books that had such forbidden terms as: "pubic hair", "breast", "rectum", and a whole gamut of words that were not mentioned in "polite society" but would always titillate our young minds.

[Mother had a large medical book entitled "Eugenics" which, in addition to the obscure text, was filled with colored pictures and overlays. One of these overlays depicted the human body; skeleton, muscles, organs, etc. One night Daddy had me on his lap and was describing the various parts of a woman's body as we went through one of the overlays. At one point Daddy said, "That's a womb." I asked, "What's that?" He got rather flustered and said that I was too young to hear about that and that he would tell me when I was old enough. It piqued my curiosity enough to make me find out what it really was. Such was the innocence of the day – or backwardness.]

A peculiarity I had when I was young was that every time I read a biography or vocational book, I would immediately change my life's ambitions to be whatever it was that was in the book. For instance, I read an especially remarkable book entitled, "The Man That Got Even with God". It was the true story of a young man who went through life avenging any wrong that he may have felt was perpetrated against him. There came a time in his life when he realized what an important part of life God was to him and that he owed God for all of his good fortune. He vowed to get even with God.

He did this by joining the Trappist Order of Monks, one of the most austere of all the religious orders. I was so moved by the passion with which the young man approached his vocation to the church that it inspired me to want to join him in this wondrous experience.

This determination lasted until the finish of the very next book that I read. This time the book was about a professional burglar. When I finished that book, that was my new goal in life; to become a burglar. I don't know how long this lasted but at various times I had my hat set on being a pilot, a fireman, a cop, and, of course, President of the United States.

We played many games in the house, most of which required no equipment, such as guessing or word games like "Actors and Actresses" where one would try to guess the name after being given the initials; as TM = Tom Mix. Other games usually required no more than a pencil and some scrap paper; we used to make our own matrix to play "Battleships" or "Categories".

We also had some board games such as "Monopoly", "Parcheesi", "Checkers" and others. On rainy days and dark nights, we were never at a loss for things to do and games to play (even without the not yet ubiquitous television).

One of the games we loved to play that would probably be forbidden in today's protecting households is "Soldiers". This was a game in which we would amass an army of lead or paper, toy soldiers by alternately selecting a piece from our joint collections until we had evenly divided our entire stockpile of parts. The two players would then set the "armies" in battle formation on opposite sides of the room. The objective of the competition was to alternately roll a small rubber ball into the opposing army to knock the soldiers down; with the losing army to be the first one to have all soldiers knocked over. The only prize in any of these games was the victory itself.

The outdoors were a source of limitless activities from sports and street games to just plain mischief; the latter being my characteristic choice of entertainment.

Most popular, of course, was the great American pastime, Baseball and its many derivatives; Softball, Stickball, Punchball or Slapball, or Kick the Can or Kick the Stick which were variations of the traditional ball and bat games using a tin can or a piece of stick in place of the ball. Other than baseball and softball, these games were played in the street; in the thirties and early forties not too many people owned cars and the streets were always clear of parked vehicles.

There were Softball, Stickball, and Touch Football leagues organized by Mr. Nash at the 30th Road Park after it was built. More often than not we would play softball with an old ball that had the cover torn off from frequent use and was patched up with black electrical tape. (Adhesive tape was sometimes used, but was not as good as the black tape.) The prize for first, second or third place in any of these leagues was usually a certificate for each of the winning team members or a small maple leaf pin (symbol of the park) for wearing on the lapel.

Usually, though, we organized our own games. Stickball was played in the street with the sawed off handle of an old broom for a bat and a "spaldeen" ball (Spalding). Home plate was a manhole cover in the middle of the road and second base was the next manhole cover down the street. First and third bases were appropriately marked off with chalk along the curb; not always geometrically perfect.

The teams would be selected by two of the players (usually the oldest or biggest) who would "choose sides" by one of them throwing the bat (stick) to the other. The bat would be caught with one hand near the center and each of the choosers would alternately grasp the stick with a hand until one of the hands was at the end of the stick. This player would then rotate the stick over his head and behind his back three times without dropping it. If this were accomplished, this player would get to select the first player for his team, with each chooser making alternate picks. When I was younger, with Dan and Fran being such accomplished players, I was often the last one to be picked. If I were the odd man, I would have the dubious pleasure of being the "steady pitcher" or "steady catcher".

Quite often the ball would land on a garage roof and would have to be retrieved by climbing the roof or the ball would land on someone's property; like the "witches" garden. When the ball rolled into the sewer at the corner of the block, the manhole cover over the sewer would be lifted and the smallest player or spectator would be reluctantly volunteered to be dropped into the sewer while being held by the ankles to pick the ball out of the sewer water. Fortunately, no one was ever dropped in. Occasionally, a window would be broken and we would all run for cover.

[We were very resourceful in those days: the stickball bat served a dual function. When not being used to play ball, we would put a wad of chewing gum on the end of the bat to search for "treasures" down the grates along 30th Avenue and Steinway Street. On a good day we would return with some precious coins: to be used for candy, ice cream, or some other necessity.]

Other options for playing ball with the stickball bat were one on one games of either fast pitch against the wall in the school yard or pitching the ball against the wall with the batter hitting the ball on one bounce off the wall. Each game had its own complex set of rules for scoring that were completely understood by every kid in the neighborhood.

One summer afternoon, I was walking behind the batter in one of these "against the wall" ball games. I really should not have been there. The batter swung the bat and caught me square across the face and my right eye immediately swelled and reddened. I had to fight back the tears and I could not let this "insult" go unchallenged. I gave a left cross to the batter and he answered with a barrage of blows that had me on my backside in quick order. He outweighed me by a considerable margin and I was grossly outclassed. My brother Fran was playing in a ball game nearby and I yelled for him to come and take care of this upstart. (Franny was always coming to my defense when I overreached myself in a fight.)

This time Franny himself was out of his realm. He did come to avenge the family honor but in doing so, he was given a bit of a shellacking himself. He was embarrassed by it all and probably, even at this late date, would not want this episode revealed, but I was still proud that my brother Franny was there to protect the family reputation.

I went home with such a huge "shiner" (black eye), that Mother sent me to Sugar's Drug Store for a leech to suck the blood out of the eye lid. I was horrified at having a slimy leech on my eye. I was delightfully surprised when Mr. Sugar, the druggist, told me that they no longer use leeches for black eyes. We didn't have any steak to place on the eye, which was a popular remedy for black eyes in the comic books, so Mother just applied an ice pack and took me for another visit to St. John's Hospital.

Some of the street games that were popular were: Red light – Green Light; Giant Steps, and a game we called "Jew Boy". We never realized at the time what the connotation of this last game was and played it "just because we did". One boy was selected as the "Jew Boy" and another was selected as the "guard". Both of them would take a position in the middle of the street and all of the other players would stand on the sidewalk on one side of the street.

The "guard" would then put one hand on the "Jew Boy's" head and walk around him three times. At any time that he lost contact with the JB or when he completed three circles, he was obliged to run to the opposite side of the street from the other participants and to touch the wall or fence on that side. In the meantime, everyone would race to the "Jew Boy" to pummel him with their fists. The "guard" would race back to the group and attempt to tag someone who would then become the new "Jew Boy", if he was tagged before returning to the sidewalk. This is the kind of game that would continue until we just got tired of it because there were never any winners or losers.

[Had this been a game proposed in the not too distant future when the world became aware of the Nazi atrocities in Germany, all of us would have rejected any attempts to play this kind of insensitive game or at least have given it a different name.]

Some of the other street games were: tag, ring-o-levio (who the hell knows how to spell this strange name), hide-and-seek (which was particularly enjoyable in early teen years when we used to hide in the cellar with the young girls), and a pastime that was long a favorite but came to a sudden halt when someone got killed during the game, "Johnny-ride-the-Pony".

Johnny was a game where one team would stand one of the players against the wall as a "pillow" and the others would line up against the pillow, bent at the waist and in tandem. The opposing side would, one at a time, jump on the back of the "pony" formed by the bent players and attempt to get them to collapse by "bucking" while on the pony. The main strategy was to get as many players as possible on one back to hasten the collapse. Most of us, being "tough and obstinate", held on as long as we could.

One day, one of the fellows held on too bravely and had his back broken. The word of this spread through the neighborhood very quickly and I believe that this was the end of "Johnny-ride-the-Pony" in Astoria.

Marbles (we called them "mibs") were very popular in the warm weather and were played in one of the many vacant lots in the neighborhood. Each player put an agreed number of regulation-sized marbles into a circle scribed in the dirt with a stick, a nail, or any other handy scribing tool. The circle was of a random size in the range of 10 to 20 inches diameter.

The objective of the game was to take one marble, called the "shooter", and shoot it from outside the circle in an attempt to hit as many marbles out of the circle as possible. The rotational turn would be ended when no marbles were successfully knocked out of the circle. If the "shooter" was left stationary within the circle, the "shooter" would be dead and the participant eliminated from that round.

Special marbles were: the "peewee", a smaller than regulation sized marble which was excellent as a shooter for knocking out of the circle a small number of marbles but was less inclined to be left inside the circle; a "shooter", any marble usually roughed up on the surface for better control. Rolling a "mib" under the shoe or sneaker on a coarse concrete sidewalk roughed it up.

Another marble of note was the "Kabola", much greater than regulation size and "illegal" for play.

A variation of the marble game was to replace the marbles with caps from soda bottles. The "shooter" in this game was made by pressing an orange peel into the cap to give it more weight. The game was then played similar to marbles.

Autumn was the time to purchase a putty blower from the local candy store to be used to shoot out small green berries that we would get off the trees alongside the railroad tracks. These devices were similar to a pygmy's blowgun; a metal tube about ten inches long with a wooden mouthpiece; and cost one penny.

A secondary effect of picking the berries at the railroad line was poison ivy. After the first time I contracted poison ivy, I had a bad case of it for six more successive years. A belief at that time was that seven years of poison ivy gave one permanent immunity to it. I believe it; I haven't had poison ivy since then. In any case, I sure went through many bottles of calamine lotion in those seven years.

Another activity that we participated in was "guns". These were wooden guns made with the corner of an apple or orange crate and fitted with a rubber band to expel square shaped missiles at a target; an inanimate object or, more likely, a person. These projectiles were usually stiff cardboard of about one inch by one inch, or when we wanted a more lethal ammunition, a piece of linoleum or metal. Our parents regularly cautioned us about using these "dangerous" weapons, but we never heeded their admonitions. We were very fortunate that no one ever had his eye injured.

A variation of these single shot guns was what we called a "machine gun". Three single shot guns were fastened together. Single shot or multi-shot, we became quite proficient and accurate with these homemade "toys". [Later generations would be making Zip guns that would shoot real bullets; we never went that far.]

Most of us collected trading cards; baseball players, American Indians (as they were called at the time), war cards, and others. We could purchase them in a pack of bubble gum for a penny or "flip' for them. This was a game wherein one player "flipped" an agreed number of cards to the ground by allowing the cards to rotate randomly from the hand, and the opposing player would try to match each card, heads or tails. If all cards were matched, the "flipper" would win; if not, he would forfeit the agreed number of cards.

My brother Dan was the champion "flipper' and card collector in the neighborhood. If he had kept all of the cards that he had won or purchased in those days, today his collection would be priceless. I especially remember the trading cards that depicted the Sino-Japanese War of the early thirties. The depiction of body parts being torn to pieces and the general gore represented in these cards was very exciting for our young, impressionable minds.

Roller-skating in the streets was another diversion for us during fair weather. The skates we used were fastened to the shoes with metal clamps and strapped around the ankles. When the skates became too worn for comfortable skating, the skates were used to construct scooters. One skate was split into two parts that were mounted on each end of a two by four board about four or five feet in length. An old apple or orange crate was placed on the forward end of the board, and on top of the crate were placed two wooden handles. [These scooters were very popular in those days and quite common. Artie Anderson, a Plainview neighbor many years later, made one of these contraptions for his son, Tommy. Tommy was embarrassed to be seen by his friends with this relic of ancient technology so it gathered dust in the Anderson garage.]

Ice-skating in the winter was moderately popular but I never got into it because I never had a decent pair of ice skates. Our winter sports when it snowed were mainly building forts and having snowball fights. (So many of our activities were aggressive and war like. Today, anyone with these hostile tendencies would probably be given psychiatric help and be put on Ritalin; especially those of us who enjoyed making "ice balls" in place of snowballs when engaged in neighborhood combat.)

Saturdays and Sundays at any time during the year were days to go to one of the many local movie theatres. Saturday matinees were special times and Mother found it quite convenient to pack us off with a lunch in the morning to spend the day at the Hobart, Cameo, Steinway, or Broadway Theatres for a double feature and, usually, an extra-added attraction of a Tom Mix, Hopalong Cassidy or some other oater. These three feature length movies would be shown with about five cartoons and an extra added attraction such as: The Three Stooges, Edgar Kennedy, Leon Errol, an Our Gang Comedy or other "selected short subject".

The show would sometimes be topped off with a filmed comedy race with prizes awarded to the holders of the winning number that would be given to us at the door when checking in. Often the theatre would give out free ice cream or other premium; all included in the ticket price – ten cents. And to top all of this off, there was one chapter of a serial that would end each week in a cliffhanger, to bring you back to the movie the next week. These serials usually ran for fifteen weeks, with one chapter a week. The first one I can remember is, "The Clutching Hand". Others were, "Spy Smasher", "The Lone Ranger", "Buck Rogers".

On weekday nights, the theatres would often give away dishes, pots, or other premiums. The theatre was not only a place for entertainment but was a neighborhood social gathering place. The movies I mentioned before were our normal haunts because they were the least expensive. (Fortunately they weren't as disreputable and filthy as other neighborhood theatres such as the Meriden and the Crescent.)

There was a hierarchy of theatres in those days. The first run movies would always start in a Manhattan theatre, pass on to the Valencia in Jamaica and then go to our local "high class" theatres, the Triboro or the Astoria; I call them that because they were more expensive and more plush. The Triboro was especially noted for its starlit ceiling décor. After finishing a normal one-week stint at one of these theatres, the movies would filter down to the other local venues.

Movies were viewed differently in those days compared to today's viewing habits. We would enter the movies at any time during the film and leave at the point where we came in. Today, of course, everyone views the movie from the start and leaves at the end.

Other highlights at the movies in those early days were the occasional addition on certain nights of "five live acts of vaudeville", a raffle for prizes, or an "amateur show". It was at one of these amateur shows that my brother Franny won a banjo for his performance. But I was the one who took the banjo lessons from one of Daddy's fellow ushers at the Church. The banjo teacher gave us a real break and charged only twenty-five cents for a one-hour lesson every week. I plucked away at the banjo for about a year but never became too proficient in playing because I didn't have the fortitude to give it the practice time required.

In the summer, we went to what we called "summer school" at Public School 6. This was not actually school, but a summer recreational activity. We engaged in sports, games, and were provided with lunch and snacks. There would be a weekly talent show and other programmed activities. My favorite participant was my brother Dan, when he did the "auctioneer" by rolling his index finger up and down across his lips while making "auctioneer" sounds. He won a prize for this masterful performance. This summer school kept us out of mischief for at least the time we were there.

A summer alternative activity when we didn't have the money to swim at Astoria Pool and did not have any success in "sneaking in," would be to go swimming "BA" (bare-ass) in the East River. We had no trepidation at all for sharing the water with rats, "white eels" (condoms), and the raw sewage that was expelled into the river from the city sewer system. The only caution we did take was not to open our mouths while in the water to prevent ingesting any of the solid waste that was floating in the river. We were quite fortunate that none of us contracted any disease from swimming in those highly polluted waters.

The girls had their own set of games to play, in which many of the boys would quite often join them. Jump rope was always a favorite, whether solo or with "enders" turning a single rope or two ropes in synch ('Doubly Dutch'.) I finally learned how to properly jump rope when I started to box as a teenager

"Potsy" was another preference of the girls, if a piece of chalk was available to mark off the eight boxes on the sidewalk. It always seemed that there were a limitless number of games to be played with a minimum or no equipment required.

It was acceptable for boys and girls to play together in many of these games as long as the girls didn't attempt to play in strictly masculine games like football, baseball, and others. However, it was not de rigueur for boys to spend too much time in the company of girls, particularly at strictly girl like activities such as dolls, and playing house. If there were such a "sissy" in the neighborhood, he would be the foil for the rest of the boys and constantly tormented.

[I can remember one of my classmates, John Lynam, a gentle young fellow who spent an inordinate amount of time in the company of his sister and her girl friends; that is, as judged by his male classmates.

For a time in school, we had a daily routine going where the first two or three boys to arrive at the schoolyard before class would "jump" the next arrival and pummel him with punches about the head and body. He would then join with the group to present the same greeting to the next boy to arrive.

By the time the bugle sounded the call to line up for class, there would be about thirty to forty boys to "jump" the latest arrivals.

John Lynam was always a latecomer and would attempt to hide out until the last minute before rushing to school to avoid the inevitable fate awaiting him at the hands of the mob. We sent scouts out to search for John who invariably would find him and alert us to his whereabouts. We would attack poor John en masse. You can well imagine his fear as forty wild-eyed boys came charging at him with no hope of escape. His tears and pleadings only led the crowd to greater torment.

Many years later, when I was an Engineer at Powertronic Systems in New Rochelle, I had the opportunity to lead a small group of our people to North American Aviation in California to make a presentation for a major project that we were bidding on. Upon arrival at North American, we were greeted by an impressive roomful of Administrators, Engineers, Accountants, and Managers. We were informed that we would have to wait for the Program Director before making our presentation.

When the Program Director finally arrived, I was shocked to see that it was an old classmate from St. Joe's (and a much abused punching bag), John Lynam. Little would I have expected that meek little John would end up as the headman on such a large and prestigious program and a manager of thousands of personnel.

I said to myself, "This is get even time, and this time it's me that should be hiding in that alley back on 43rd Street in Astoria.

I was very thankful that John either didn't remember or chose to ignore those events of the past. We went to dinner together that evening and talked a little business and a lot about the old days and the old class, but fortunately we avoided certain past incidents.

In the end, we did get that contract, on the merits, and satisfactorily completed the job for North American. I never saw John Lynam again.]

"ALLEY WHACKIN" AND OTHER MISCHIEF

I was always "Peck's Bad Boy" (as Mother always called me.) I was a ragtag kid and really looked and acted the part. My shirt tail was constantly hanging out, my socks were always sagging to the ankle, long blond locks of hair covered my eyes, and if it were my school uniform or Sunday clothes, my tie was awry and stained; a characteristic carried with me to my golden years. Completing this picture of sartorial dishabille were dirty hands and face and, quite often, a runny nose. My friends were also attired in similar fashion.

There was never an end to the mischief that we discovered. "Alley whackin" was a popular winter pastime. Many people in those days constructed shelves on the outside of their kitchen windows where they would store perishable food and beverages during the cold weather to relieve the burden on the icebox. The food would often include fresh baked pies or cakes, milk and soda. "Alley whackin" was the name we gave to our nighttime forays to pilfer whatever we could from these window storage shelves, which were often located adjacent to the alleyway between houses. I don't know how many babies were deprived of their fresh milk because of our petit larceny, but at that time those considerations never entered our minds; and we never did consider this activity of sufficient magnitude to confess to the priest on Saturdays.

It was my brother Danny that initiated me into the finer aspects of hitching rides on buses and trucks when I was less than six years old. My recollection is a bit hazy but he has often in later years told of the time that he boosted me onto a truck in Astoria that pulled away faster than he could get on the truck himself. He chased after the truck for a long distance, from Astoria to Long Island City, yelling at me to hold on and fearing that I would fall off the truck.

He knew that he couldn't go home without me nor could he tell Mother and Daddy that he last saw me clutching desperately to a truck speeding towards Long Island City or, worse, that I fell off the truck. After an uncertain number of miles and a lot of running, Danny finally caught up with the truck at a red light to safely retrieve me.

After that, it didn't take me long to get the knack of hitching rides alone, or with some of my pals. Usually, the trucks would be required to stop at a red light and we could alight and hop another truck back home or we would continue on as the mood suited us.

One day, Willie Dooley and I hopped aboard the rear of a truck near home that rapidly took off toward the Triborough Bridge. It didn't stop at any stoplights or stop signs and was moving too fast for us to jump off so we were obliged to hold our position on the back of the vehicle.

Before we knew it, we were on the bridge headed away from Queens. The truck stopped at the toll plaza but we couldn't jump off there. Eventually, the truck stopped at a light or a stop sign and we got off as the truck rapidly sped away. We were in the Bronx with no money in our pockets and I had absolutely no idea of where we were. I was probably only eight or nine years old at the time but had confidence that we would somehow get back home.

It was a different kind of neighborhood than Astoria with signs in a language I couldn't understand. I assumed, in retrospect, that it must have been Yiddish.

Willie said that this was near where he used to live when he lived in the Bronx and that we could go to his old neighborhood to see if we could locate some of his former neighbors. So, we walked in a direction of his choosing but it wasn't long before I realized that he didn't know where he was going, or how to get there.

The sun started to set and the air was starting to chill when we passed an entrance to the elevated subway. I could already feel Daddy's strap on my butt for staying out "playing" so late. I suggested that we try to sneak onto the subway and take a train back to Astoria. At that time, I had no idea of how or where the trains ran, but we were up to this new adventure.

We went up the stairs where, fortunately for us, there was a line of people at the change booth. (Tokens were not yet in use on the subways in New York at that time and the fare was only a nickel.) With the attendant distracted, we raced quickly under the turnstile and hotfooted it for the platform; still not knowing where we were going.

We got on the first train into the station, not knowing where it was headed but confident that no matter what predicament we got ourselves into, as long as we had a buddy to share it with, everything would resolve itself.

We asked one of the passengers how to get to Astoria and we found that we were on the right train to start our journey. We didn't realize that we would have to make several changes of trains and travel for nearly two hours to get to a station in Astoria near home.

We followed the instructions and finally returned home well after dark with great expectations for the reprimand facing us. The obligatory beating with the strap was given as expected. I was put to bed without supper; not the first nor the last time. At this point I was just thankful that I made it safely home and was now under a warm blanket in familiar surroundings, reliving that day's adventure in the far-off Bronx.

Like most youngsters we were fascinated by fire. We would gather scrap wood and build a large fire in a pit in one of the many vacant lots. We surrounded the pit with stones to contain the fire. This occasion was especially popular during the late fall when the air was starting to get cold and we could warm ourselves around the open fire.

We would bake "mickeys" (potatoes) by tossing them directly into the fire and burn them until they were cooked as determined by poking the potato with a stick or a twig from a tree. We ate the potato, including the charcoal burnt outer skin, without salt or butter. There was nothing that ever tasted as good in those days, unless it was the peaches we purloined from a local orchard or a watermelon filched from a watermelon truck when the driver wasn't looking. The potatoes we either got from home when no one was looking or helped ourselves to at one of the local vegetable stands.

We would arrive home with black rings around the eyes from the time around the open fire and clothes reeked of the smell of the burning wood. Mother, who forbade us to play around fires, was always livid with rage when I came home in this condition and would scream," You've been around fires again. Haven't you?" an accusation I would always deny. The end result was always the same, a thorough beating and threats of more punishment, "especially for lying."

Mother could always tell when we were lying by the white streak that would appear on the tongue when we lied; or so she said. She'd say, "Open your mouth and let me see your tongue." Of course, I would clamp my mouth shut so as not to reveal my duplicity. She would then grab me by the nape of the neck and attempt to extricate my tongue from my clenched jaws with her stiffened index finger or a spoon. Her most effective device to open my mouth was to grab my face in her hand and press severely on both cheeks until the mouth was forced open and the stool pigeon tongue was exposed. A quick look at my tongue always uncovered the truth.

I always ran into the bathroom afterward to look at my tongue in the mirror but never saw that white streak. I figured that only Mother's had the ability to read tongues; after all, they seemed to know everything and they even had eyes in the back of the head.

In the evenings when we weren't just hanging around on the block, we would engage in such diversions as climbing garage "rooves." One night as we were running across the tops of a line of garages, jumping over the short divider wall between each building, I took a jump over the last wall in the pitch-black darkness. Before I realized that there were no more garages, I found myself free falling to the concrete pavement. I landed flat on my back, knocking the wind out of me, and banged my head against the ground. For an instant I thought that I had sustained some serious damage but after getting my breath back, walked away, miraculously unharmed and with no noticeable bruises or contusions.

On other nights, when we felt bored, someone might have offered the suggestion, "Let's knock over some garbage cans." Never turning down an opportunity for additional mischief, we would proceed to walk the neighborhood doing just that.

An alternative activity to wile away the hours was to gather some small stones to throw at targets such as a street light lamp or a window (always on an empty or vacant building, of course.) One day we were throwing rocks behind the Astoria Theatre at a wall of small glass blocks on one of the buildings, when we noticed a police car coming in our direction. Guilt made us hightail it out of there. I ran down 30th Road behind "Jimmy's Corner" where we used to get a hot dog and a chocolate malted for ten cents.

As I turned the next corner at 41st Street, a police car was approaching in my direction. I knew they were after me for breaking the windows, so I reversed course back down 30th Road where I met another obstacle to my escape.

In the early days of World War II, there were many volunteers for air raid wardens and other emergency positions. Daddy was a volunteer fireman and would put his identifying armband on and leave the house for his post during the air raid and blackout drills that were held. (Fortunately, they were only drills and we never experienced the real thing.)

Now I found myself facing one of these volunteers; this man was a volunteer policeman in khaki shirt and trousers with the auxiliary police armband in plain view. He was walking hastily in my direction and as I turned to get away I noticed the police car now at the corner blocking my getaway in that direction. Caught between the cops and the Auxiliary policeman, I realized that the jig was up and threw myself at the auxiliary cop with my arms held out for the expected handcuffs and said to him, "I surrender."

He gave me a surprised look but glancing up and seeing the waiting cops at the corner, he took me by the arm and led me to the police car. There he turned me over to two policemen sitting in a solid green two-door coupe that was common in that era. I was trembling and frightened about what was going to happen to me at that point and decided that the best course of action was to deny everything.

I stood outside the car as the cop on my side started his interrogation.

"What's your name?" "Joseph", I lied.

"Where do you live?" "47th Street", I lied again.

He wrote this all down in an official looking book and I started to feel somewhat relieved that he believed my answers.

"What were you doing around here, kid?" "Nothing", I replied.

"Well, now we have you in the book and if we ever catch you doing what you did again, we'll have to take you down to the station and lock you up."

"Now get out of here and go right home and stay out of trouble."

With that, I quickly rushed away and told the officer as I left, "I'm going, officer, and I promise, I won't do it again." I don't know whether that was a scowl on the faces of the cops as I left or whether they were going to burst out laughing. I was too terrified to wait around to find out.

One of our favorite places to explore, and which often was the source of unexpected treasures, was the garbage dump down by St. Michael's Cemetery. As long as the rats didn't bother us, we spent countless hours rummaging through the garbage searching for things of value that could be either traded at the junkyard for cash or were things that could make our imaginations soar.

One day, after a big rainstorm, there was a large lake created by the downpour in one of the large craters at the dump. Eddie Ryan and I found an old door in a pile of rubbish and decided that it would make an excellent raft to explore the lake. We pushed the door into the water and, having found a suitable piece of wood for use as a rafting pole, we set out on our cruise.

Our first objective was a mound of debris in the center of the lake. We poled our way out across the water feeling like Huckleberry Finn and Tom Sawyer, and not knowing what adventures were before us.

When we reached the island of garbage in the center, we jumped off the raft and pulled it onto this "Treasure Isle." In doing so, we accidentally knocked our pole into the water and it floated out beyond our reach. The water was filthy and there were a couple of large rats in view so we wouldn't attempt to jump into the water to rescue our pole.

As we searched the garbage island for another pole, it started to rain again. We tried to push the door back into the water but it was snagged on something. We both pushed hard against the door until it suddenly snapped loose, into the water and moved beyond our reach. We were now stranded on this island of trash.

We tried desperately to come up with a plan for getting back across the water. Night was falling and the water level of our little isle was rising rapidly. We were soaking wet from the rain that continued to pelt us so the tears from our crying weren't evident. We were afraid that we would either drown or be attacked by the rats.

We yelled loudly for help into the dark night across the empty dump. We alternately cried and yelled.

Finally, after what seemed an eternity, a couple of older boys came along and heard our anguished cries for help. They found our makeshift raft on the other side of the water. They tied a piece of rope to the raft and managed to push it over to us. We jumped on the door and these good Samaritans pulled us across the water to safety.

That was the last time we went boating at the garbage dump, but there were many more adventures to be had.

[When I think back to how we stuck by our buddies and shared everything equally together, I sometimes long for a return to those more innocent days. There was a warm camaraderie as we walked alongside each other with our arms around the other's shoulder; eager to face the world together and to fight and die for your friend. If we found anything on the street, a coin or anything of value, it was always share and share alike. We may not have had any material possessions in those days but we had something more important, buddies that could be trusted to be at your side when you needed help.]

On the other hand, there were many of our contemporaries in the neighborhood that were intent on tormenting or fighting anyone who was not in their particular "clique", whether it be someone from a different class in school, one from another block, or a member of a different sports team.

I would fight at the slightest provocation and was always in a brawl; usually on the winning side. I would always avoid fighting someone smaller than myself because I felt that if I was going to be "whipped", I would rather it be from someone bigger than face the ignominy of a shellacking from some runt.

Everyone fought by the rules in those days – a fair fight; no hitting below the belt, no kicking, biting, eye gouging or crotch kicking. When the opponent said, "I give", the fight was ended. This was unlike in later years when fighting became a serious business and no holds were barred and it was a fight for survival.

One day my brother, Franny, was walking along minding his own business when Dr. Malerba's kid confronted him.

"What's your name, kid?" said the bully in an intimidating way.

"Francis", replied Franny.

"Oh! A sissy name, eh?" the provocateur shot back.

This was the kind of insult that couldn't go unanswered, even if the guy was a bit taller and had twenty pounds on you. So Franny did what any self respecting O'Leary had to do and landed a fast right cross into the center of the harasser's face and crushed his nose in fine fashion. Any attempt by this maggot to defend himself after Fran's initial volley of punches was futile. Franny walked away with the family honor still in place and a thoroughly chastened wise guy put in his place.

(About fifty years later, while talking to Franny one night, this incident came up. I suddenly realized that that poor "bully" who got his lumps that day may have only been saying "OH! Assisi", referring to the famous Saint and was just making an innocent pun.)

Actually these early skirmishes were merely training for the many tougher battles that were to come during our teen years.

It wasn't all misbehavior and mischief. In some of our quieter moments Mother taught us how to do such "manly" things as knitting, crocheting, and sewing samplers. I liked the samplers best because that didn't take too much talent and the results were quite nice. I was fairly accomplished in knitting but the only thing that I ever made was a scarf – a long one. I didn't take to crocheting too well; I got tired of doing those frilly, lace doilies and the fancy edging on handkerchiefs.

YOUTHFUL ENTREPRENEURS

One of my first attempts at 'making a buck" was something I alluded to earlier; gathering saleable treasures at the garbage dump and selling them at the junkyard. We would pull our homemade wooden wagon with the wheels from old baby carriages to the dump and forage for useful items that were thrown away. Although we were queasy about the many rats at the dump, they never bothered us.

Another early moneymaking scheme was to take the handle of a broom, which we cut off to play stickball, place a wad of chewing gum on the end and walk the streets of Astoria searching down the grates alongside the buildings for any coins or other valuables. The gummed end of the stick would be dropped down the grate to retrieve the items. We usually tied a rope to the stick in case we released it from our tenuous grip.

In the summer months we would buy (or purloin) a few lemons for lemonade, which we would peddle from a homemade stand on the street, or we would put the lemonade on a wagon to sell to the road workers who were often fixing the streets on some WPA project. We offered a variety of cup sizes with the prices set without regard to the capacity of the cup; five ounces may have sold for one penny and eight ounces for two pennies.

My first "regular" job was selling newspapers at a commission outside St. Joseph's Church on Sunday Mornings. The papers we sold were the Diocesan paper, the "Tablet" and "Social Justice", a tabloid newspaper published by Father Charles Coughlin, a controversial Catholic Priest and radio personality during the 1930's and the founder of the "National Union for Social Justice." At the time, I had no idea of who Father Coughlin was or what the content of the newspaper was. I was only seven or eight years old at the time. Father Coughlin was accused of printing anti-Semitic articles and was a virulent opponent of President Franklin Roosevelt. He was forced by his Bishop to return to his Parish work in 1942 after being indicted by the Federal government for some of his contentious remarks.

Danny and Franny also sold these newspapers and would take the prime selling spots in the front of the Church while I was relegated to the side doors where the paper sales were miniscule. However, at that age I was happy to make a few pennies for just standing by the Church chanting, "Tablet!" "Social Justice!"

Another source of income was to stand outside the A & P Supermarket on 30th Avenue with our wagon to offer assistance to the women doing their Saturday grocery shopping. When we were successful in our solicitation, which was offered without first negotiating a fee, we would load the bags of groceries on the wagon, follow the lady home, and carry the bags to the apartment, even if it was a five story walkup.

The payment was left to the discretion of the customer, which usually worked out quite well. Some of the customers were more parsimonious in their payment and would pay only a few pennies. Most of the customers, however, paid more than we probably would have charged as a fixed fee.

In the summer, a man would park his car on the corner and enlist the help of the neighborhood boys to sell the Saturday Evening Post Magazine door to door. He would provide us with a canvas bag with a shoulder strap for carrying about ten to twenty magazines. The bag was imprinted with the Saturday Evening Post logo and name.

Each of us would be assigned a territory to cover, which we would do during the week. He returned at a set time the following week to collect our sales receipts and to give us the next week's magazines. Payment was based on sales and the payment was not in cash but a selection of premiums. Points could be accrued over time to save up for some of the more expensive premiums.

All of these moneymaking labors took place before we moved from 46th Street in 1943 when I was ten years old.

A VACATION IN PORT JEFFERSON

Our summers were always spent at home; a vacation to anywhere was not an option in those days. Usually our summer entertainments were local with an occasional, at most twice a year, trip to Coney Island by subway for a day. The destination at Coney was always Steeplechase Park where for a modest entry fee (I believe it was in the order of twenty-five cents for kids) one would get a circular punch card on a string to be attached to the garment and which entitled the bearer to fifty-two attractions at the amusement park.

The attractions ranged from real rides like the Scenic Railway, as we called the roller coaster, Merry-go-round, and others, to more quiescent things such as the "Red Bats". This latter attraction entailed climbing up a high ladder to a screened in cage at the top of the ladder to observe the eponymous display. When one reached the top of the ladder, inside the cage were not two red mammals, but two baseball bats painted red. Of course, no one would tell the next suckers what was in the cage to make sure that they were also forced to climb the ladder if they wanted to see this rare species.

One year, there was a singular exception to the usual rule of no vacations away from home. **Dolores Malone**, a friend of Mother's and a sister member of the Rosary Society at St. Joseph's, owned a summer home in then rural Port Jefferson on the north shore of Long Island in Suffolk County. Mrs. **Malone** offered the use of the house to our entire family for a couple of weeks. Mother, feeling this would be a great opportunity for the family to get out of the hot city, enthusiastically accepted.

Although Daddy couldn't come to join us until later in the week, we were all excited at the prospect of spending time "in the country." It must have been a big strain on the family's meager budget to prepare for this new adventure but Mother and Daddy managed to put together an adequate sum to cover our expenses.

When the Monday morning for departure finally came we were all eager to get going. Mother had packed our one small suitcase with as much of our necessities as could fit. The suitcase was tied with two pieces of clothesline to secure the bag. The remainder of our supplies for the week; clothes, food, sheets and towels, games and toys, and other essentials were packed into cardboard boxes that we got from the grocery store. These boxes were also tied with pieces of the old clothesline.

Mother had allowed herself one major extravagance. When she saw the magnitude of the job of getting all of these bundles and six kids to the Long Island Railroad Station in Woodside, she sent one of us to Steinway Street to hail a taxicab and bring it to the house.

When the taxi arrived, Mother convinced the driver that it was possible to load up all of our entourage, all of our traveling luggage, and a baby carriage for my brother Bobby, into one vehicle. After we stuffed the trunk and tied the remaining pieces on the roof of the car, eight of us, including the driver, jammed ourselves into the car like clowns in the Barnum and Bailey Circus and started off on the first leg of our journey to Port Jefferson. We must have looked like an "Okie" family headed across country to California during the thirties.

We arrived at the Woodside Station where Mother purchased the tickets and, with the help of the taxi driver, the train conductor, and some helpful passengers, got all of our things loaded onto the train.

At the station we met our benefactor's son, **Roscoe,** who was about thirteen years old, and his sister, **Molly.** They would be staying with us for the week and Roscoe would orient us to the house and the surrounding neighborhood. His mother, who worked during the week, was expected to join us for the weekend.

Soon we were on our way.

At Jamaica Station we managed to transfer to the Port Jefferson train with the assistance of some helpful passengers who felt sorry for Mother, who was now leading a troop of eight youngsters. This second train must have been one of the last of the coal-fired engines on the Long Island Railroad.

The trip to Port Jefferson seemed to take all day. The train was hot on that summer day and the stifling heat was not relieved when Mother made us close the windows for fear of our falling out.

An eternity after leaving home, we arrived at Port Jefferson station. We were the only passengers to leave the train and the station was otherwise deserted. There was no transportation available to take us to the house after we alighted from the train. Roscoe said that the house was not too far from the station and he would show us the way. Mother, being delighted at the prospect of saving the cost of the taxi, readily agreed that we would all walk to the house.

We piled as many boxes as we could onto Bob's baby carriage and, carrying the remainder of our belongings by hand, we started out to find our summer palace.

The walk was much longer than we had anticipated but after a while, hot, sweaty, and all in a terrible mood, we arrived at the house. After our long trek by taxi, train, and finally, on foot, we were all anxious to start playing, swimming, or relaxing, but were shocked by what met our eyes at that moment.

The small house was completely surrounded by grass and weeds that had grown to about five feet in height and had not been cut since the previous year. It was so dense that we couldn't move our baggage into the house.

Roscoe, the only one familiar with this property, volunteered to open the house where there was a sickle inside and to cut a path between the dirt road and the house, so that we could get our cargo to the front door.

When the grass had been cut, we finally got our first look at the inside of the house. The first thing that we noticed was the terrible stench of mold, mildew, and something that smelled like rat shit. The visual impact was even more devastating.

It was a small house consisting of four rooms; a kitchen on the left side running from front to back, about eight feet wide by sixteen feet deep. In the center of the house as we entered the front door was a living room about ten feet wide by the same sixteen feet to the rear of the house, and to the right of the living room were two bedrooms, each about eight feet square with doors leading to the living room.

Every room in the house was filthy. The small amount of furniture that filled the house was threadbare and dilapidated. It was difficult to appreciate the full nature of the house because the dirt-impacted windows were filtering out most of the light from the sun.

I think Mother would have cried or, at least, have wanted to just pack up and go back to Astoria, but she didn't want to upset all of the youngsters and was quick to take command of the situation. "Open the windows and doors," was the first thing she said. We opened those windows that weren't stuck and left both doors wide open, including the one leading from the kitchen to the back yard.

It wasn't long before we had a realization of what we had to contend with. There was no electricity or running water in the house. There was a hand cranked pump on the right side of the house connected to a well that provided all of our needs for water. The water was filtered though a rag which was tied to the spout of the pump. This filtered out the large particulate matter and the small creatures found in the unfiltered water but I doubt if it was effective in removing the smaller microorganisms.

Kerosene lamps provided light for the house. Kerosene was also used to fuel the small stove used for cooking in the kitchen. We soon determined that there was an adequate supply of fuel for the lamps in a large rusted can underneath the kitchen sink. The sink had a drain that emptied directly out the side of the house and did not have any spigots.

About five feet from the rear of the house was a steep incline that led to our toilet facility, a single hole outhouse at the bottom of the hill. Before attacking any of the in house problems, Mother had us all pitch in to clear a path to the outhouse so that the girls could have some much needed relief. We boys had no problem; we just peed in the grass.

The small bedrooms had one bed in each of the rooms. Mother would be sharing one bedroom with baby Bob and little Molly, and the girls, Helen and Marilyn, would use the other. The four boys would spend the week sleeping on the living room floor.

In the remaining daylight hours, there was to be no playing for the children, as we were all assigned tasks to get the house into a livable condition. While Roscoe continued the job of cutting down the high grass to give us access to the pump and other outdoor locations, we all pitched in to clean the floors, wash down the kitchen, and especially to remove all the bedding to air outdoors and to beat out any crawling creatures that may have sought harbor in the mattresses. The windows were cleaned to bring more light into the rooms. Mother put all of our belongings that could fit into the one dresser in her bedroom. The remainder of the goods was left stored in the boxes we had carried from Astoria.

We worked as long as daylight permitted to get most of the tasks done so that tomorrow we could start enjoying the vacation we had come for. As the sun set, we lit the kerosene lamps and settled down to the modest meal

Mother had prepared for us. We were tired from all of the work and the long trip, but we were content with our accomplishments, especially after filling our empty and growling stomachs. We laughed at this first day's adventures and listened with rapt attention to Roscoe's promises for tomorrow.

We slept well. In the morning, I was the first to waken. I looked up from the floor to the rear window and screamed in fright. Peering into the window was the wizened face of the oldest and ugliest woman I ever saw. She had bulging eyes that were red as blood and a head of gray hair that hadn't been combed in a fortnight and flared out in all directions like the head of Medusa.

Everyone in the house awoke from the sounds of my loud shrieks. Danny and Franny looked at the apparition in the window and were as startled as I was. We huddled together as Mother ran into the living room in her nightgown. Roscoe roared with knowing laughter.

"That's our neighbor, **Mrs. Katy Mahoney.** She lives in that house down the road. She uses our pump to get her water," Roscoe said, "Don't be afraid."

Without a word, Mrs. Mahoney moved away from the window and disappeared into the brush.

Later we would find out a little more about Mrs. Mahoney, who one of us dubbed "Crazy Mary." She had been a native of Ireland and now lived alone in a small cottage just a few hundred feet from our summerhouse and was our closest neighbor. Roscoe said that she was a bit strange, but harmless.

In the evening, after dark, she would keep a lantern lit in her window to "keep the banshees away". Around her house, she kept several black snakes, which were claimed to be a defense against the poisonous rattlesnakes that inhabited the nearby woods.

These mystical tales fascinated us, but we avoided contact with "Crazy Mary" because of her presumed magical powers and wizardry. Her only forays onto our property were her early morning visits to get her days supply of water. If I heard her at the pump, I would feign sleeping for fear that she might give me the evil eye or some other occult thing.

We arose early after this intrusion and were prepared to make the most of this day. Mother made coffee on the kerosene cooking stove, gave each of us our cup of coffee and evaporated milk, and stale buns and rolls that we had brought from home.

With Roscoe's lead, we put on our bathing suits, a shirt, and sneakers and started on our exploration of the area. Roscoe explained everything as we went along; he seemed very knowledgeable about the ways of the country, including pointing out a snake that he said was a poisonous copperhead that ran across the path in front of us.

(We had been told before we left home that there were no poisonous snakes on Long Island and now we discovered not only the rattlesnakes which reportedly infested the woods, but now, a copperhead. Later, Roscoe would also point out a deadly Water Moccasin. Years after this day, Jim Ronacher's father killed a rattlesnake during a summer trip to Lake Ronkonkoma and brought it home for all of us to see on 45th Street, so much for "no poisonous snakes on Long Island.")

Everything was so interesting; the flora and the fauna, and even the insects. We were in a new world and delirious with anticipation of what would happen or what we would see next.

Eventually we came to a small rocky beach abutting Port Jefferson Harbor. We could see the other side of the bay and it looked like it was miles away. Roscoe had the foresight to bring two or three inner tubes from a car tire from which the filler valve was extracted. We blew the tubes up by mouth and capped the tubes. We now had our vessels to sail this vast body of water.

With one boy lying across each tube on his back, we entered the water. We used our hands as oars to propel us further into the water. I felt a freedom I never felt before. I was on the high seas, following in the wake of Columbus,

Magellan, and of course as a Catholic School student, St.Brendan, the Irish Monk and Navigator.

We went further and further, never once considering the fact that I couldn't swim. After a long time, we made it to the other side of the bay. I was so proud of my accomplishment that I ignored the reddening of the front of my body and thighs from the bright summer sunshine on this cloudless day. I looked forward to the return journey.

We made it back late in the day to the other side of the bay where we started from. By this time I realized that we hadn't eaten since breakfast and that I was also burned to a crisp and began to feel the painful sting of the sun.

We deflated our tubes and returned directly to the house. Mother was mad as hell for our being gone all day and was especially irate when we proudly told her of the trip across the bay. By this time, my sunburn hurt so much that I started to cry. Mother had no medicating salves so she rubbed me down with butter, which didn't seem to relieve the burning ache on the front of my body; the back was not burned at all, having been on my back in the tube all day. Her every touch was a special pain that I thought she inflicted on me as punishment for today's transgressions.

I was forbidden to go into the water on a tube for the rest of our time at the summer retreat and was ordered to go only in the low water by the shore and only when Helen or Danny was there to supervise.

The rest of the week was a daily dose of dips in the water and exploring the woods around us. I learned about ticks and leeches, many varieties of butterflies, birds and bugs and many of the wonders of nature that stimulated the imagination and curiosity of a boy from the city.

When the weekend came, we were anxious to tell Daddy of our week's fun when he arrived. The first arrival however was our hostess, Mrs. **Malone,** accompanied by three of her friends. (Mother would later refer to them as Mrs. **Malone's** "bar fly friends."

Mrs. **Malone** promptly took over as the "Lady of the Mansion." She took over Mother's bedroom and told her to move into the girl's bedroom. She complained about the state of the house that we had so diligently cleaned and that she had left in such disrepair and filth.

Mrs. **Malone** and her cronies started drinking heavily and grew boisterous and abusive to Mother and the children. Mother was appalled by their behavior but really got angry when **Malone** and her drunken friends tried to order her around like a bondservant.

This was more than Mother's patience could endure. Before this horrible night ended, we were directed to pack our things. "We're going home in the morning," Mother declared. We dared not protest losing our second week in the country.

When Daddy arrived in the morning, he was surprised to find us packed and ready to go home before he had a chance to spend even an hour at this place. So ended our Port Jefferson vacation.

CELEBRATING THE HOLIDAYS

The holiday that we enjoyed the most was what every child thought was the King of Holidays, Christmas. It was a very rare occasion when we were treated to a toy or a game that required an outlay of money during other times of the year, but Christmas was a special time when, no matter how poor we were, we would get a surprise from Santa Claus. Mother and Daddy always held over our head the threat of getting only coal in the stocking on Christmas from Santa if we misbehaved. We learned very quickly that behaving was only required a week before Christmas because none of us ever received the much deserved coal for our conduct during the rest of the year.

We were like any other kid in any generation. We went to bed early knowing that Santa would be coming and that we couldn't be awake when he arrived or he wouldn't leave us anything. It seemed impossible to sleep; we would toss for the longest time and be unable to sleep. Eventually we would fall asleep but would be wide awake at the crack of dawn to see what Santa had brought us the night before. (I think that our generation held on to our Santa belief for a longer time than later generations; probably the effect of not having the countervailing influence of television to destroy our happy delusion.)

Other than a wreath in the window, Christmas decorations would not be put up until Christmas Eve. We always waited until Christmas Eve to buy our Christmas tree when the price of the trees plummeted. Mother would make one of us follow her with the wagon while she went from one vacant lot to another, where the trees were usually brought in for sale from upstate New York or New England. She would bargain while we would stand by the wagon, shivering in the usually cold air.

When we arrived home with the tree, it was Daddy's job to mount the tree in its holder and to install the lights and the star on top of the tree. We would all pitch in with placing the balls and other decorations on the tree before being ordered off to bed.

(Daddy's tenure as the main tree installer went on for several years until we were living on 45th Street. After World War Two, Daddy worked for the North Shore Fuel Oil Company as a driver delivering oil to private homes. Today, the oil is delivered on a programmed schedule and the homeowner rarely sees the deliveryman. In those days, the oil was delivered on call and the collection was made on the spot after the delivery. It was common practice to invite the deliveryman in for a drink during the holiday season when he knocked on the door to collect.

On one of these Christmas Eves, Daddy must have had quite a few delivery stops to make and came home filled with the Christmas "spirits". Before leaving home, he had promised to bring home that year's tree. When he arrived home after work he did have the tree, but it was about ten to twelve feet tall and our ceiling was less than eight feet. Daddy said that this was no problem; he would simply cut the tree down to size. He cut off the correct amount of tree, but removed it from the top instead of the bottom and we had the strangest looking tree; flat on top and no place to put the star.

All of the children and Mother just stared at this misshapen tree and dared not say a word. Disappointment was written in all of our faces. Daddy in a jovial state inspired by the day's imbibing, was proud of the appearance of the tree. I could not contain myself; I started to roar with laughter at this grotesque sight. Daddy got so pissed off at me that he put his face close to mine, yelled in a loud voice that I could not only clearly hear but also smelled quite foully from the booze. He said, "You smart ass kid. You think you can do better? Well from now on you're going to take care of setting up the tree every Christmas." And he kept to his threat; I had to take care of the tree every year until I left home to join the Navy.)

Many of the presents we exchanged on Christmas Day (never on Christmas Eve) were items that we made ourselves and no matter how simple the gift, we all appreciated what we received, which usually included a homemade Christmas greeting card.

While some of our friends received electric trains for Christmas, we felt lucky when we got a set of trains with a wind up engine. The train would make one to two circuits around the track and then it was time for rewinding for another run.

Soldiers and war toys were popular. The more costly painted lead soldiers were usually beyond the budgetary constraints so we would typically receive cardboard soldiers that were cut or punched out of a book of figures.

Our Christmas Day dinner was always a lively occasion. Mother would make roast chicken, a roast beef, or whatever the resources permitted; and always with all of the trimmings. Between breakfast and dinner we would go to Mass at St.Joseph's and visit Grandma and Pop Schwab before returning home to stay for the rest of the day.

If Christmas was for the children, New Year's Eve was for the adults. In those early days, Mother and Daddy usually stayed home to celebrate with the family. The extent of the festivities for us was to be permitted to stay up until midnight to greet the New Year by going into the streets with any noisemakers available; the most common being a pot banged with a large soup spoon. All of the neighbors would join in for about five minutes of clanging utensils and "Happy New Years" greetings. After this brief interlude outside, most often in the bitter cold, we would be hustled off to bed knowing that tomorrow was the last day of Christmas week holiday before having to return to school.

In later years, Mother and Daddy would go out to celebrate New Year's Eve at a local bar or at the home of a relative or friend. Before leaving for the night's soiree, they would have some friends in for a drink; beer or whisky for the men and a Tom Collins for the ladies made with gin and bottled Tom Collins mix. When they left they would ask us to clean up the glasses for them. We happily obliged by drinking the residual booze left in the glasses and feeling like we were having our own "grown up" party.

The second biggest holiday was Easter Sunday. Besides the religious significance of the holiday, which we were all very sensitive to, we looked forward with eagerness to the baskets of sweets that would be left for us by the Easter Bunny. It was also the end of the Lenten season when all of us had given up "for Lent" something that was especially favored.

On Saturday night, before Easter Sunday we would help with the coloring and decorating of the hard-boiled eggs that Mother would then hide during the night while we slept in preparation for an Easter morning egg hunt.

When we woke up in the morning to find our small basket of goodies left for each of us by the Easter Bunny, which he appropriately marked with each of our names, Mother would always caution us "Don't eat any of the candy before breakfast or you'll get worms."

For the two or three weeks preceding Easter Sunday, Mother would take us to shop for our new Easter outfits one or two at a time. This always seemed like a never-ending chore as we went from store to store looking for the best affordable bargains.

The suit, shirt, tie, shoes, and socks would be the only new outfit that we would get until the following Easter and had to last us for mass every Sunday and any special event that might occur in that time. During the years of our most rapid growth we would find ourselves squeezing into clothes that were one or two sizes too small before the new cycle of Easter finery came.

There were times when Mother found a bargain in shoes that was so irresistible that we were sometimes forced to wear shoes that were so big they would flop on our feet or so small that our feet ached. Mother would say one of two things depending on the problem, "You'll grow into them" or "Don't worry, the shoes will break in."

The most difficult part about Easter was trying to stay clean and well groomed all day; an impossible task for an eight year old boy.

I don't remember the year it started, but at some point along the journey Easter week became the traditional time for us to initiate the swimming season at Rockaway Beach. Whether it was March or April, fair or foul weather, a gang of us would take the Long Island Railroad to Rockaway Beach, if we had the fare, or hitchhike if we didn't, where the bravest of us (or the more foolhardy) would strip to our bathing suits which we wore under our clothes and take the plunge into the always frigid waters.

One year I had to prove my macho by being the one to swim out the furthest. The water was so icy cold that day that when I got out beyond the breakers I got a terrible cramp in the stomach. The tightness spread through my arm and leg muscles and I was soon unable to move my arms or legs and found it difficult to keep afloat. I screamed for help but most of the guys were already headed back to the beach and either didn't hear me or didn't care to come back out into the deep water. I started to pray, feeling that I was about to be dragged under by the roiling waves and the undertow.

I don't know how many times I went under, but I managed each time to float to the surface to get a quick breath of air. I didn't know how long

I could keep this up and my muscles ached with the cold and the cramps. I finally felt a hand reach out to me and someone grabbed me by the arm. It was a young girl who had heard my calls and had taken the plunge to pull me toward the beach. When we finally made it to the shore, I tried to thank her and find out who she was but she just ran down the beach and out of sight; an angel of mercy who I shall never forget for saving my life that day.

Halloween was not a holiday but it was a special day for us nevertheless. We didn't have the day off from school but the following day, November 1st, was a holyday of obligation and those of us who attended the parochial school had that day off, so the evening before was a good time for mischief. During the afternoon of Halloween day the activity most often enjoyed was marking up everyone's clothes with chalk or pounding them with silk stockings filled with flour.

In the evening we would knock over garbage cans, deface store windows with wax candles or crayons or whatever mischief we could conceive. There was no going from door to door to "trick or treat" as became the custom later on; our door-to-door begging then was reserved for Thanksgiving Day (Ragamuffin Day).

One of the neatest pranks we would pull was to fill a paper bag with doggie-doo, which was quite plentiful on the streets in those days before the requirements to clean up after the dog. The bag of excrement would be placed outside the front door or on the front porch (concrete, never wood) of one of the homes. The bag would be set afire and when the flame was at its peak, the doorbell would be rung and we would run to a safe distance to observe the show that was about to begin.

The homeowner would open the door to answer the bell ringing and upon being confronted with a blazing fire, would invariably attempt to put the fire out by stomping on the fire with the shoe.

Just as invariably, the door answerer upon pushing his foot into the fire and the malodorous mass beneath would exclaim,"Oh! Shit!" followed most often by, "You rotten bastards!"

(By the way, it was common knowledge in those days that stepping in horseshit brought good luck, but stepping in dog shit was always a portent for bad luck.)

No matter what kind of deviltry we participated in on Halloween, the following day we would always go to the obligatory mass and, after reciting a "sincere" Act of Contrition, would receive Holy Communion, knowing that our souls were in a state of grace.

Occasionally there would be a small party, either at home or a friend's house, to which we would go in a homemade costume or, less often, with a paper costume which was available at the local candy store for about ten cents. The main activities at the party were bobbing for apples in a basin or tub of water, or bobbing for an apple tied to a string and hung in the center of a doorway. Either game required placing the hands behind the back and using only the mouth to grab the apple and the head to move the apple on the string. If one of the generous parents were supervising the apple bobbing, we would quite often find a coin inside the apple when we ate it.

The Fourth of July, Independence Day, was another day that we all looked forward to for the illegal activity of setting off firecrackers and cherry bombs. Sparklers were permitted and we would light these up after dark under parental supervision but the fireworks were handled more clandestinely.

There was always someone coming around selling firecrackers, cherry bombs, roman candles, rockets, and other explosives out of the trunk of a car. If the traveling salesman wasn't available, we all knew where to go in Brooklyn to purchase the fireworks. (The GG train to Hoyt and Schermerhorn)

We would never waste a firecracker. If a lit firecracker did not detonate, we would pick it up, break it in half to squeeze out the black powder, which would be placed on the ground, fuse lit, and the firecracker stomped with the heel of the shoe to make it explode. One day, after lighting a firecracker that didn't go off, I ran to pick it up. One of the other boys also rushed toward the same firecracker. I was the lucky one to arrive at the firecracker first and grabbed it quickly to pull it from the other boy's grasp. As I pulled my hand back with the firecracker between my fingers, the delayed fuse on the firecracker detonated just as the firecracker was passing by my left ear. The force of the blast went directly at my eardrum and the heat burned my ear and face.

I quickly rushed home, crying of course, and Mother put some salve on it; but it was a long time before the pain abated and my hearing returned to normal. I didn't realize at the time that this incident would come back to haunt me in later years with a chronic ear problem and eventual diminution of the hearing in that ear.

(Many year's after this event, one of the neighborhood boys was attempting to make a "super bomb" by stuffing a huge amount of firecrackers into a metal pipe, closed at one end. While packing the pipe, the explosives went off and he lost his arm.)

Today there are commercial greeting cards for almost every day of the year and for every "special" occasion; occasions which were not yet invented in those early days. (I'm convinced that the greeting card companies devised many of these occasions.) The only days I can remember as being special enough to merit a greeting card, bought or homemade, were Christmas, Mother's Day, Father's Day, and, of course, St. Valentine's Day. The postage for sending Christmas cards in the mail was three cents for a card sent in a sealed envelope. If the envelope was left unsealed and the flap merely tucked into the envelope, the postage was one and a half cents.

WORLD WAR II

One of the most stressful times for the entire family came during World War Two. I don't recall the exact year that it happened but it was around the time that Daddy would have been 35 or 36 (1941 or 1942).

Many young men were being drafted shortly before the attack on Pearl Harbor on December 7th, 1941 and this conscription accelerated after the declaration of war against Japan. It wasn't too long before the draft was expanded to include even men up to 35 or 36 years of age that had large families to support. Mr. Bowman across the street who had a family of about six kids was gone one day and showed up several weeks later in a sailor suit; he had been drafted into the Navy.

Daddy was just short of the maximum age but thought that he would never be called. He did get called down to take the physical and felt confident that he would be rejected because of his age. I remember clearly his coming home after his appointment with the draft board and the look of shock, disbelief, and despair on his face as he told Mother while the rest of us listened about his day. In the end, the draft board said to him, "Well O'Leary what do you prefer, the Army or the Navy?"

Mother was shocked and almost in tears. How would she take care of six children with Daddy away making only twenty-one dollars a month, and more seriously, what would we all do if Daddy were never to return? The family was just starting to see some progress in the family fortunes with Daddy getting a job as a welder in one of the war plants and Mother, herself, taking a nighttime job at the Norden Bombsight plant.

Daddy said he would speak to "some people" to see if they could help him avoid being drafted. I don't know who he spoke to, but they did manage to stall his being called for enough months that he exceeded the age limit which automatically classified him as 4-F, which meant we could keep our father at home for the duration of the war. It was a sad and trying time in all of our lives but it had a happy ending.

Every family was under considerable stress during the war years. It seems that almost every window had a service flag hanging in the window with each star on the flag representing each of the sons or husbands serving in the armed forces. A gold star on the flag indicated that someone had been killed in action. Whenever we passed these flags we would tip our hat, if we were wearing one, or make a sign of the cross in respect for the hero who had given his life for our country.

At our age, we didn't really have a full appreciation of the impact of the war other than that many familiar faces were missing from the neighborhood and were off fighting the war. Many of the women had taken jobs in some of the war plants and the streets seemed very changed; no more crap games on the corner, no more adult ball games at the park where we would go on many a summer evening to watch the men play.

We did spend a lot of time playing war games against the hated Hitler, Tojo, and Mussolini. In the evening, those of us that felt artistically inclined would sketch and color macabre scenes of battle; with planes, cannons, tanks, and bombs ripping apart the bodies of the enemy. We were quite gorily expressive with our depictions of severed limbs and much blood in these "works of art."

On the more positive side, one of our contributions to the war effort was to write to the service men whose names were provided by Sister at school, with the letters used as an English grammar exercise as well as being a morale booster for the guys who would receive them. Some of these letters must have been greatly amusing to the recipients. John Carcia, one of my classmates wrote a letter to Sister Philomene's brother serving in the army and said in the letter that he was a "penis". In her critique of the letter, Sister wanted to know what he meant by that. John said that he played the piano. The men at the front must have had a good laugh at that one.

POTPOURRI

There were still trolleys running in Astoria at that time. Busses would eventually replace them and the tracks paved over with macadam, but until that time the clanging of the trolley bells could still be heard on Steinway Street, Grand Avenue, and Broadway.

The trolley had a two-fold purpose for us, both related to transportation. One was that they provided a convenient and no cost method of transportation for those of us who learned to hitch a ride on the back. A second use we discovered was to place a penny on the track to be flattened when run over by the wheels of the trolley. We would then grind the edge of the flattened penny with a nickel as a template to be used as a slug for entry to the subway.

During the spring of 1941, just shy of nine years of age, I made my first Holy Communion at St. Joseph's Church, after which I was obliged to receive communion every Sunday at mass. It was not too long before I was also attending mass and receiving communion every weekday as well as on Sunday.

Preparation for receiving this holy sacrament included a weekly Saturday afternoon confession and a total fasting from food and water from midnight each time communion was received. Confession was where we would own up to all the horrific sins we had committed since the last confession: failure to say morning and evening prayers, disobeying our Mother and Father, picking on a kid sister, getting angry and, worst of all in later years, having impure thoughts.

Every Sunday after Mass, while Mother was preparing for Sunday Dinner, all of the children would go with Daddy to visit Grandma and Grandpa Schwab, Daddy's mother and her second husband. After the bar was opened after the legal opening time of noon or one o'clock, Daddy would go for a "growler" of beer to share with the grandparents. (A growler was a small, tin container with a handle; about ten inches in diameter by six inches in height with a removable lid.)

It became customary for Grandma to give each of us a dime every Sunday, which we would always use for admission to the local movie theatre, generally the Hobart. If we purchased the ticket for the movie before two in the afternoon on Sunday, the admission was ten cents. After two, the price went to fifteen cents. Many a time, if Grandma was unhurried in proffering the accustomed dime (and we would never ask) we would have to run to get to the theater before two. If we were late, we would beg to be let in at the lower price and most often were successful in our pleas.

A special time for each of us was when Daddy selected one of us to join him at an evening movie during the week. At that time, billboards advertising the week's attractions at a movie were placed in many store windows. The storekeeper was usually given a couple of passes for free admission to the theatre for permitting the billboard placement. Daddy would sometime get two passes from the Chinese Hand Laundry around the corner and this was what prompted our good fortune in joining Daddy for a night out.

When it came to the times that we were sick, Mother was always there to care for us. When the fever became exceptionally high or the illness was very serious, Mother would call the family doctor, Doctor Zoltan Rubin, who would always make a house call to check out the sick child. While he was at the house, he would always insist on checking out all the children that were home. For this Doctor Rubin would charge one or two dollars and if Mother didn't have the money at that time, he would say, "pay me the next visit". When he returned, I quite often heard him telling Mother, "Forget it." How times have changed.

A demonstration of the tough fiber we boys were expected to exhibit was clearly illustrated by my brother Fran when he took on Joe Fox, an oversized bully who lived around the corner. With little or no provocation, Joe rammed a stick, a slat for lathing I believe it was, up Franny's nostril which started to hemorrhage so profusely that the entire length of slat was soon crimson and dripping with blood.

When Franny went to retaliate, Fox ran like the frightened animal he was toward his home on 30th Avenue. Fran dashed after him with the stick hanging out of his nose, undeterred by the discomfort and pain piercing his naval cavity. He caught Fox just as he reached his front door and proceeded to give him a thorough beating with his bare fists; always the preferred and honorable weapon of retribution.

Joe's brother, Billy, attempted to intervene but Franny laid him out flat with a couple of quick punches to the head. Having put both Foxes out, he finally went home to a horrified mother who carefully removed the stick from his bloody nose and tended the wound.

Life on 46th Street was soon coming to an end. With a steadier paycheck coming into the house because of the wartime employment, we could afford a larger apartment and we were about to move to 45th Street just around the corner. It was time to bid goodbye to this modest apartment; a place that introduced me to many adventures and a home in which I found much love and excitement.

1943-1946

OUR NEW DIGS

By early 1943 our family of eight was feeling the constraints of living in four small rooms on 46th Street. There were six children that were rapidly growing. Helen would be nineteen in 1943 and Mother felt it was well past time for a young lady of her age to have more privacy.

Bob, the youngest at the time, was six years old and would be starting first grade at St. Joseph's School that fall. We needed room for all of us to properly do our homework as well as needing more room for sleeping quarters.

We moved into a larger apartment at 30-12-45th Street, just around the corner from our present place. There were four three-story apartment houses on our side of the street. The first three each had six railroad type apartments; two on each floor. Our apartment house, located at the corner of 30th Road across from the recently complete park, had one apartment on each floor that was laid out in what Mother called "box rooms." The Kelly's, the landlords, lived on the first floor, Mr. And Mrs. Ferraro on the second and our apartment was on the top floor.

We had six rooms in our apartment, each more spacious than the four rooms we had grown accustomed to on 46th Street. In the rear of the house overlooking the backyard and with a view of 30th Road and 44th Street, were two rooms; an eat in kitchen on the outside and what would be Mother and Daddy's bedroom on the inside. Adjacent to this bedroom was a complete bathroom with not only a toilet, but also a luxury we had not had for years - a bathtub.

Both the kitchen and the bedroom led to a good-sized dining room that spanned the width of the apartment. The other side of the dining room led through a locked door to the hallway and, adjacent to that a doorway to a bedroom which in turn opened up through a full archway to the "front" room or living room which had windows onto 45th Street.

Next to the living room was a small room with a door that was to serve as a bedroom for the two girls, Helen and Marilyn. The boys would all sleep in two bunk beds in the central bedroom.

With the uncommon amenities we had in this new dwelling, we felt that we had moved into a palace. In addition to the increased space and full bathroom, the house had hot, running water and steam heat in two of the rooms, the bathroom and the dining room.

The kitchen had a coal stove identical to the one that we left in the old place, but this would soon be changed when Daddy decided to "modernize" the stove by having it converted to accommodate two kerosene burners so that we would no longer have to haul coal from the cellar and ashes to the ash can.

Three of the rooms, the bathroom, dining room, and the boys bedroom, had windows opening onto an airshaft between our building and the adjacent building. In the warm weather, these windows were always open to cool the house and everyone could hear what was going on in the six apartments sharing the airshaft.

Directly across the airshaft from us on the third floor were the Kellehers, Harriet and Maurice (pronounced Morris), and their kids, Tommy, Marie, and Jerry.

[On one of those warm days when the windows were wide open, we could all hear Harriet yelling at and badgering Maurice to get up and do something. Without seeing and only hearing Harriet's continuous bellowing, a clear picture was drawn in our minds of Maurice trying to catch a few winks on the sofa while being screamed at so all the neighbor's could hear.

This continued for quite a while until we suddenly heard the sound of flesh against flesh, as if Maurice had risen from the sofa and belted Harriet in the nose. The next thing we heard was the sound of a body hitting the floor.

And after that – silence.

The following morning Harriet was standing in front of the house complaining to the students on their way to the Junior High School, P.S.10, directly up the street from us. She was telling them how terrible her husband was and how he had hit her, without provocation, and she was showing off her "shiner' (a black eye.)]

The kerosene stove that we brought with us from 46th Street heated the front of the house.

In the rear of the house was a fire escape that was often used on some hot summer days as an outdoor bedroom to escape the oppressive heat of the apartment.

One thing we found to be quite a modern innovation in the apartment was the provision in the kitchen of an open pipe in the floor over which the icebox could be placed so that the water dripped down the pipe and a basin was no longer needed, obviating the need to periodically empty the melted ice water from the basin. (Damned clever, these people who devised these home improvements.)

Located on the side of the house and opening onto 30th Road was a multi-car garage. Mr. Kelly, the landlord, had embedded sharply pointed shards of glass in concrete all along the peripheral edge of the roof to discourage the neighborhood boys from climbing the roof to retrieve balls often hit there during the stickball games played in the street.

(The neighborhood we were living in was used as the setting for the movie, "The Bronx Tale, with Robert DeNiro in 1983. Our new apartment house on 45th Street was the location for the scene where a young bicyclist was beat up while passing through the neighborhood. In the movie DeNiro was depicted as living in an apartment house on 30th Avenue where Billy and Pat Griffin lived.)

NEW ADVENTURES

Moving into our new quarters didn't disrupt our way of life at all, other than giving us more room to live at home. My pals continued to be mostly the guys from school, and our old neighborhood cronies were only a block away. The new block gave us a chance to expand our circle of friends as we got to know our new neighbors.

It was shortly after we moved that, at the instigation of Vinny Sheehan, one of my classmates, I joined the Kip's Bay Boys Club on the east side of Manhattan at about 48th Street. For nominal dues of about twenty-five cents a year, which were waived for those that couldn't afford it, a plastic membership card was issued that gave unlimited access to the facilities

Most of the indoor sports were featured and we availed ourselves of all of them while we were members, including, basketball, indoor racquetball, handball, wrestling, tumbling, and the thing that acted as the biggest lure to get us to go that far to join a club, a heated, indoor swimming pool.

The club only admitted boys on the premises so we were not required to wear bathing suits in the pool and every boy would swim B.A. (Bare-ass, if you're not familiar with the nomenclature.) This was fun and gave me a sense of uninhibited freedom, but it did lead to some gross happenings, such as turds floating in the pool from some errant swimmer who couldn't wait for the proper place.

If we had the five cent carfare, we would take the Steinway Bus, which by that time had replaced the trolley along that route, over the Queensboro Bridge (also called the 59th Street Bridge) to the last bus stop that was located underneath the foot of the bridge on the Manhattan side, and from there we would walk down Second Avenue to the clubhouse.

We would usually walk home from the club to save the nickel carfare; walking across the bridge to Long Island City and from there to home in Astoria. This walk would take from two to three hours depending on how many diversions we succumbed to along the way.

A short time after starting my active membership in the boy's club, I was struck with a malady that would take me out of action and out of school for a while. On Ascension Thursday in 1944, a Holyday of Obligation and a day off from school, I awoke in the morning with a slight limp that I had been harboring for the past two or three days and which had now become more pronounced. Mother noticed it and wanted to know what the problem was. I told her that I thought I just had a slight sprain in the ankle.

I attended mass with my class and after lunch Mother gave me the admission fee for the Astoria movie with orders to take Marilyn and Bobby along for the day. Bill Finan, a classmate of mine, joined us. One of the movies at the double feature was "the Lodger" with Laird Cregar.

When the time came to leave, I couldn't stand up. My ankle and my knees had swelled to an enormous size and my legs felt paralyzed. Marilyn and Bobby were both frightened when they saw the size of my swollen joints and started to cry, not knowing what else to do. Bill went for the manager of the theater, who promptly came but said that he couldn't do a thing for me and that my mother should be called.

Not having a phone at home, or the nickel to make the call, Bill ran home to get Mother who must have immediately dropped everything to come to the theater. She enlisted help from some of the men at the movies to carry me out to a taxi that she had summoned.

When I got home she took my temperature which was over 102 Degrees and called Doctor Steiner who came to the house soon after (I don't know when we lost Doctor Rubin as the family physician.) The swelling and pain got increasingly worse and the temperature had gone even higher. I was diagnosed by the doctor with Rheumatic Fever and treated with sulphur drugs. I was bed ridden for over two weeks.

Sister Mida, my sixth grade teacher, sent work assignments home to me through Bill Finan who visited with me every day during my convalescence. This illness hit me right at the end of the term and this homework helped to get me through the final exams that were given as soon as I returned to school.

Mother was certain that the swimming B.A. in a heated pool in the winter and going out into the cold air caused the Rheumatic fever attack. I was forbidden from ever going back to Kip's Bay. This wasn't much of a hardship at this point; summer was upon us and Astoria Pool was open, Rockaway was a short hitchhike away and the East River was always available for anyone who would swim in polluted waters.

Another scourge of the times was the ringworm epidemic that spread through the schools of New York City and effected almost every family with children. All of the kids in our family contracted ringworm in various degrees of severity. The older children had a very moderate form that was quickly cured.

I, myself, had a slightly worse case but Mother quickly brought it under control with her home remedy; shaving the afflicted area on the head and painting it and the other sore areas of the body with iodine. In my case, this seemed to be an effective and permanent treatment.

Brother Bob contracted the worst case in our house, so bad that he had to be removed temporarily from classes at St. Joseph's and was obliged to attend classes at P.S.6 where all of the severe cases of ringworm were sent. We called this the "Ringworm School." When the students lined up for class at the ringworm school, with their shaved heads and sailor caps pulled down around their ears, they would be unmercifully taunted and teased by the students going to the regular schools.

While the epidemic lasted, it wreaked havoc on the lives of the poor kids who were hit badly by it, but the contagion eventually abated and everyone went back to their normal school routine.

Schultz's Delicatessen was located on the corner of 45th Street and 30th Avenue. One of Mr. Schultz's clerks, a young man with a club foot would sometimes open the store early in the morning and be the only one in attendance until later in the day. On more than one occasion a few of us neighborhood boys conspired to get together in the morning while this clerk was alone and hit up the store for whatever booty we could carry away.

The clerk was rather slow because of his impairment, so we would assign one of the guys to place an order for something on the top shelf of a remote section of the store. While the clerk turned to fetch the article, we would stuff our jackets with selected items before hightailing it out the front door of the store. We were always prepared with large billowing jackets with maximum storage capacity for the pilfered items.

On one of these raids on Schultz's deli we carried a fifty-pound bag of walnuts out of the store. (A lot of kids at St. Joseph's were sick that day from eating too many walnuts at school where we distributed the loot.)

When the clerk returned to the counter, the shill would tell him that the item ordered was not the one he wanted and he had changed his mind. He would leave the store and join us outside for his share of the swag.

In later years we would rationalize our larceny by saying that this was a prepayment for a swindle that Mr. Schultz would pull on us.

Mr. Schultz invited me and several of my neighborhood buddies to spend a weekend on his boat out on Long Island. We were delighted and excited; anticipating this holiday on the water. Early on a Saturday morning we piled into Schultz's car; each of us with a small paper bag containing all the necessities for the weekend; our bathing suit, a towel, and a toothbrush. We were all eagerly anticipating the nautical experience we were about to embark on.

When we arrived at the boat landing, we were disappointed to find that the boat was not yet in the water and that we would have to wait for it to be launched. That was not to be on this Saturday.

Schultz told us that before we could put the boat in the water it would have to be scraped and painted and that if we hurry and pitch right in we could complete the work today and launch the boat later on in the day.

As it turned out, the end of the day turned into Sunday morning, which turned into Sunday night. We never got to launch the boat and had instead spent the entire weekend painting and cleaning the boat. Before we knew it we were back in the car headed for home. Schultz had fed us well for the weekend but that was a cheap wage for all of the manual labor we put in getting the boat shipshape.

During the next week as we were hanging around on one of the stoops of the apartment houses, Schultz approached the same group of us who had helped get his boat in shape the previous weekend. He asked us if we would like to go "boating" again. This time we weren't about to spend another weekend as indentured servants and told Schultz to "shove it…"

After Franny won a banjo at one of the matinees at a local theater, no one in the family showed an interest in playing the instrument. When I expressed a desire to play, Daddy made note of it. When he mentioned it to Eddy, one of his fellow ushers at church, who also was a musical instrument teacher, Eddy offered to give me one hour of lessons a week for the unheard of price of twenty-five cents a lesson, a tremendous bargain even in those days.

I started the lessons with great eagerness and was faithfully attending the lessons at Eddy's house and practicing at home during the week, to the dismay of most of my family. The fingers on my left hand that were used to press the banjo strings against the frets started to get extremely sore, especially on the fine strings that cut into the fingertips. Eventually, they started to bleed regularly. Eddy assured me that if I just kept plucking and playing, a callous would develop on my fingers and they would be tough enough not to get sore.

This never happened and my fingertips kept getting more sore. In due course I started to slack off; first by not practicing and finally by skipping lessons and pocketing the quarter for other purposes.

When Eddy mentioned my absences to Daddy at church one Sunday, it marked the beginning of the end of my banjo-plucking career.

Had I a better attention span for the music, academic subjects or any other serious endeavor during those early years instead of my constant predilection for mischief, my life may have taken a much different path than that which I was currently embarked on.

In retrospect, I often have felt that many of us were trying to avoid success. To become successful or affluent meant no longer fitting in with the ne'er do well gang members; and the most important thing in our lives at that age was acceptance by one's peers.

During World War II everyone did their bit for the war effort; even those not serving on the front lines. Mother and Daddy both worked for a time in war plants; Daddy as a welder and Mother stretching quartz crystals for reticles to be used in the famous Norden bombsight.

We kids did what we could as well. Certain materials necessary for the war industries were scarce and we rummaged through garbage cans and the garbage dump for some of these items, such as rubber, zinc, or steel to cash in at the junkyard. Even at our young age we were learning to be war profiteers.

Another wartime home defense endeavor was the planting of victory gardens; an effort to locally assist in relieving some of the scarcity of food products. Directly across from the side of our house was a vacant lot on the corner that one of the neighbors, **Mrs. Green,** organized into a gardening project for any child in the neighborhood who wanted to participate.

She divided the lot into small plots to be assigned to each of the participating victory gardeners. Mrs. **Green** provided the guidance for preparation of the ground, planting, weeding and garden care, and each child would supply his own seed and fertilizer. I was very assiduous in tending my garden and followed Mrs. **Green's** instructions to the letter, but I could get nothing to grow except radishes while all the gardens around me were blooming with lettuce, tomatoes, carrots, peppers, and other vegetables. My gardening expertise was another talent that I carried with me into my later years. Every time I attempted to grow anything, my "black" thumb prevailed and the only things that I was successful in harvesting were more radishes. (I did plant a garden of Chinese vegetables in Plainview one year that I was quite hopeful for. At a cost exceeding fifty dollars and countless hours of labor, I tilled the soil, mulched and fertilized, planted the seeds and watered according to instructions, and tended the garden with loving care. My total yield at harvest time for all of this expenditure and toil was one head of Chinese cabbage.)

Adjacent to the vacant lot used for the victory gardens was a small apartment house where Mrs. **Green** lived on the third floor. The Caperso family occupied a basement apartment. Mr. and Mrs. Caperso were natives of Sicily and had a large brood of children. Mr. Caperso was quite often agitated by the presence of so many kids using the lot for victory gardens and on many occasions would attempt to drive the kids away by throwing rocks at them. This was also his method of reprimanding his own children. Fortunately, I can't recall his ever throwing the rocks accurately enough to hit anyone.

Danny and Franny were both working as stock and delivery boys at Gerlich's Self Service Grocery store, so as the next in line and not currently gainfully employed, it fell upon me to baby sit for Marilyn and Bobby; to take them to the movies on weekends during the day and to watch them at home when Mother and Daddy were going out in the evening.

During the warm weather when the windows were open to let in the evening breeze, I could hear the kids playing outside while I was stuck in the house with my baby-sitting chore. I longed to join my pals in play.

Marilyn and Bobby were not very cooperative about going to bed so that I could slip out to play so I hit upon a scheme that would safely tuck them away for the night. I began to tell them scary stories and described in vivid detail enough frightening things until they got so terrified that they would eventually hide under the bed (at my prompting) to escape the phantoms that had been built up in their minds. Huddling together in fear, they would eventually console each other to sleep, which gave me the opportunity to slip out and play.

This scheme worked pretty well several times and I always managed to get home before Mother and Daddy returned so that I could get Marilyn and Bobby to bed with no one the wiser. Until one night when they came home unexpectedly early and were panic stricken when they found no one at home. They caught up with me on a street several blocks away as they searched the neighborhood for us. They gave me hell for "losing" the younger kids. I thought at that point that they had awakened and left the house and were indeed lost. When we got back home we found the two of them still sound asleep under the bed where I had left them.

That ended my story telling scheme forever.

While returning from the Hobart Theater on one of those Saturday at the movie matinees with Marilyn and Bobby in tow, we were passing a "rock war" being waged by two rival gangs in a vacant lot on 31st Avenue and 49th Street. A group of about a dozen youngsters were in a wide, shallow ditch in the center of the lot, being besieged by a mob of about twenty to thirty boys who surrounded the ditch. The two rival gangs were pelting each other with rocks when we arrived and I decided to enter the fray on the side of what appeared to be the weaker group in the ditch.

I gave Marilyn and Bobby orders to stay put where I left them; out of the range of fire; and ran to join my selected allies in this battle. A short time after I joined the fray, we noticed that we were running out of ammunition. I volunteered to take an empty cardboard box and run through the attacking lines to get more rocks from a vacant lot that was nearby.

As I returned to our embattled trench with the box filled with rocks, all eyes from my chosen buddies were focused on my progress, while the enemy on the other side of the hole advanced without being noticed.

As I jumped in the pit with the box of rocks, one of the opposing boys, who had just arrived at the back edge of the hole, dropped a huge boulder on my head. My scalp split open and the blood gushed out over me, the ditch, and many of the boys around me.

The sight of all that blood frightened everyone on both sides and the "rock war" soon came to a halt. One of the boys on the opposing side took me to his home that was nearby on 49th Street where his mother rinsed off my head with tap water, put a wool cap on my head and sent me home with my two charges who were now in a state of complete fright.

Mother took me on a bus to the emergency room at St. John's Hospital, a familiar place, where they discovered that the hat had become encrusted with the dried blood and could not be removed to uncover the wound. After soaking my head and the hat with water, the hat was removed and my head stitched by the doctor on duty. Before we returned home, we made the customary stop at the Sunshine Biscuit Company store across from the hospital to get an inexpensive bag of broken cookies.

The Boulevard Gardens housing development was, to us, an upscale housing complex located just over the border in Woodside but still within St. Joseph's Parish. Several of my classmates were residents there. On Wednesday afternoons, the Gardens had a showing of films with a sixteen-millimeter sound projector in one of the activity rooms in the basement of one of the buildings. There the resident children were treated to a presentation of cartoons and short comedies such as the Three Stooges, Our Gang, and others, and always ending up with an "educational" travelogue.

Although intended exclusively for the residents, I was often invited by one of my classmates to attend. This was a special treat for me. One day I went to one of the showings while carrying a homemade slingshot that I had fabricated with a Y shaped branch from a tree and rubber cut from the inner tube of an automobile tire.

After the completion of the film program, I lured a group of about eight boys and girls to a nearby room where I held them "hostage" for about two hours with the threat of being shot at with my lethal slingshot. They were thoroughly intimidated and were quite cooperative. While playing this role, I had a sense of power and control but I finally let them go when I couldn't stand their crying and pleas for mercy anymore. This episode ended all further invitations to attend these Wednesday afternoon film showings.

A bit of devilment that was in vogue in our neighborhood was "de-pantsing". When a victim was selected, a usually overwhelming band of boys would jump the selected party, hold him down and pull off his pants to be hung high on a telephone pole, preferably on a main thoroughfare, where he would be obliged to climb the pole bare-ass to retrieve his clothes. In due course all of us had to suffer this humiliation as one of the rites of passage.

Perhaps more serious than these "friendly pranks" were the times strangers accosted us with more malicious purpose in mind.

On a trip to Central Park with a couple of my pals, we were nearing the end of the day and had just arrived at the lake at the foot of the Belvedere Castle in the center of the park. I was alone alongside the lake when I was approached by a gang of seven black youngsters, my age and older.

The smallest of this pack (it seems that every time there is a gang of several on one confrontation like this, the smallest one of the bunch becomes the abrasive spokesman and bully of the group and is always backed up by the biggest and toughest looking crony) asked me to "lend" him a dime. Having lost my change, about thirty-five cents, earlier in the day, I responded negatively. He insisted upon searching me which I resisted until I was restrained by the rest of the group.

Finding nothing in my pockets except a small envelope of postage stamps that was to be the start of my philatelic career, they picked me up and threw me into the lake. A policeman was approaching the lake. I don't know whether he observed what was happening with me in the water, but my attackers saw him coming and quickly departed before I found out what other surprises they might have had in store for me. I was quietly glad at this point that I had lost the little money I had earlier that day.

COUNTDOWN TO GRADUATION

All was not mischief, pranks, and deviltry; there was also time for school, sports, and more benign activities. Much time was spent at 30th Road Park where under the guidance of Mr. Nash, the Park Superintendent, we participated in organized sports and tournaments or took advantage of some of the arts and crafts instructions that were available at the park superintendent's building.

When I was younger, I had played with the 46th Street Thieves (that was only the team name) in the stickball league with the older guys. As the fledgling on the team I was generally given the assignment of steady pitcher or steady catcher, two positions at which one could cause the least amount of damage to the team. The team did have a couple of first place finishes in the park league for which we received a certificate or a maple leaf pin that was the symbol of the New York City Parks Department.

In later years I would play left field for our championship softball team, while leading the league in singles for balls hit over the right field fence (ground rule single.)

In 1944, Danny and Franny along with several other neighborhood boys founded the Astoria Ramblers football team. Bobby and Gerry Kelleher served as water boys for the team. I never played sandlot football with the Ramblers but would later join them as a social member when most of us returned from the service and the organization became the Astoria Ramblers Social and Athletic Club (with the emphasis on the 'social'.)

The Ramblers S & A rented a clubhouse on Grand Avenue near 31st Street; a large room with a private entrance above a saloon. Friday nights were the regular meeting nights; a short meeting followed by a high stakes poker game.

The club would often sponsor fund raising events at the clubhouse which we called stag parties featuring "Football films" that were really black and white silent pornographic films of dubious quality.

One of the most active members of the club was Don "Crazy Legs" Ruddiman who spent a couple of terms as president of the club but who became even more noted for his bank-robbing career. Don was arrested after holding up a bank in Nassau County at gunpoint where, following a high speed car chase by the police, Don's car went off the road and turned over. Don was nearly killed and wound up in the hospital with a fractured skull amongst other injuries and was near death.

This was the latest in a series of bank jobs that Don pulled. None of the club members knew or had any suspicion that Don was in this business. We also found out around this time that he had previously served time for a burglary conviction.

But I'm getting ahead of myself.

The seventh and eighth grades at school were growing up years. Most of us were beginning to feel the onset of adolescence. Boy's voices were changing from the accustomed high pitch to the deeper tones of manhood while during this transition the voice would switch octaves in mid sentence.

Pubic hairs and axillary hairs were beginning to be in evidence and were proudly displayed, particularly the pubic hairs, to the gang when the first hair or two sprouted.

We started about this time to learn about the "birds and the bees" from some of the more worldly wise guys in the neighborhood. It may not have been information that was one hundred percent correct in all the details but the basic facts of man, woman, sex and birth were on the mark. Besides, the street was the only place where we could get this information, accurate or not, as our parents and the schools were reluctant and unwilling to discuss something as "dirty" and controversial as SEX.

Some of our more precocious pals had started to learn the ritual of masturbation; called variously at the time, jerkin' off, beatin' the meat, poundin' the pud or, when reporting this at confession, abusing one's self. They were unhesitant in relating to the rest of us their budding manhood and their newfound carnal pleasures. Some of us could only envy them and long for the day when it was our turn to "grow up".

One of these early 'maturers', who I shall call George, discovered that his genital manipulations were best and most privately accomplished in the shower at home. He did not keep this a secret and we all knew when he was off to pleasure himself. It became routine for him to leave a ballgame in the street in the middle of an inning declaring, "I've got to go take a shower." There were days when this occurred three or four times during the game.

We were told at the time that "abusing one's self" would ultimately lead to blindness. This widespread belief was given great credibility when George was obliged to start wearing glasses shortly after his public announcement of his latest hobby. We knew it couldn't have been from too many showers and anyone who alluded to blurring vision was immediately suspect.

Much of our illustrative educational materials were the small pornographic cartoon books that were widespread at that time and which featured some of our favorite cartoon characters like Joe Palooka, Popeye, and Wimpy in exaggerated sexual activity with well-endowed women.

Other titillating pictures of bare busted women were found in the National Geographic and in some of the proscribed "girlie" magazines of the day"; magazines that depicted no overt nudity, only scantily clad beauties that by today's standard were rather puritanical.

Indicative of the priggish attitude of the nuns at school was an episode in the seventh grade involving four classmates; Eddie Ryan, Kieran Manning, Anthony Rutigliano, and Donald VanMeter, and me. It is true that the five of us were constantly together in those days in what appeared to be a conspiracy of sorts; but we were not a party to any of the accusations that were to be forthcoming. We were at that stage of pre-adolescent curiosity that wanted to know more about this stuff called "sex" and we were finding out that girls were not only the pests that had to be tolerated in class and to have their braids occasionally dipped into inkwells. It was fascinating to us that girls actually had more pedestrian utility.

On Saturday's and Sunday's when we attended the theater, which was a popular meeting place for the neighborhood rogues, we would explore some of these new found verities by pursuing the young ladies in the theater and attempting to do such abominable things as: 'touch them', or pinch them or some other depraved thing that we thought was 'sensual'. We were in a transition between the youthful mischief we always exhibited in our more tender years and the more base activities that were stirring up in our maturing young veins.

Sister Isabel, our seventh grade teacher, called each of the five boys involved in this affair, individually, into the hallway outside the classroom to interrogate us on our behavior outside the classroom. She said at the start of this inquisition that she had a detective following us and knew everything that we were up to outside the classroom and that she had questioned the other boys in the group and that they had confessed to their bad behavior.

Now she wanted me to purge myself of the sins that had been committed by confessing to the things that she alleged all of us were guilty of.

"Have you ever been alone with a girl?"

"Have you ever touched a girl in an indecent way on forbidden parts of her body?"

"Have you ever exposed yourself in front of a girl?"

"Did you let girls touch you on your private parts?"

The answer to each of these questions was, of course, no; I was only twelve years old at the time and had not really began to delve into all these possibilities. (Actually, Sister was stirring up thoughts about things that had never entered our young minds but which we would surely pursue after this business was finished.)

The prodding continued for a long time with the admonition that lying is only going to make it twice as bad for me, both here on earth and in heaven. I wanted to say to her, "Why don't you ask your detective?" but I knew that would only get me a slap across the face and get me deeper into trouble.

"What do you boys talk about when you get into one of your huddles?"

"Nothing," was the reply.

"What do you do when you leave school in the afternoon?"

The queries went on like this for the longest time. Thinking that there may have really been a detective following us, or maybe one of my buddies did, indeed, confess to some malefaction, I felt that I had better own up to some wrongdoing or I would never hear the end of this grilling. I confessed to having broken some streetlights on the Grand Central Parkway, feeling that giving her something as benign as that would get her off my case on the more lewd charges she was intimating. This, however, only whetted her lascivious appetite for more admissions of guilt, particularly in the sexual arena.

At the end, when she had hassled me for all she could get out of me, she said that I was to bring my parents up to the school to see her so that she could inform them of what we boys had been up to.

When I got together with Eddie and Kieran later on and we compared notes, we determined that Don VanMeter's, (who we believed had experienced all of the things that he bragged to us about) braggadocio caught the ear of Sister Isabel and she was convinced that the 'terrible' things that he claimed to have done with girls was something that we were all guilty of because of our close association with him.

The day before our parents were scheduled to see Sister at the school, Eddie, Kieran and I got together to plan a move to avert the need for our parents to come to school. (At this point we still had not informed our parents that they were expected at school the next day.) The plan we decided upon was to go to Sister Isabel at the convent to plead with her for forgiveness (for the things we didn't do) and to beg her not to speak to our parents the next day.

She was steadfast in her determination to get our parents to school for a conference.

Earlier that same day in class, Eddie had been called to the front of the room for some alleged infraction where Sister reprimanded him and slapped him in the face, which was a familiar practice. When Eddie was returning to his seat he muttered to me under his breath, "I didn't do anything"; and he hadn't

Now, Sister accused Eddie of having said something derogatory about her when she scolded him that day. He said that he didn't and indicated what he had said to me, which I was happy to confirm.

However, she wouldn't take that for an answer and kept badgering Eddie until he finally said, "I called you a son of a bitch." This got her so enraged that she immediately terminated the conversation and demanded that we bring our parents to school first thing in the morning before class.

When we left Sister, we were in such a state of fear and apprehension that we agreed amongst the three of us to run away from home together that very night so that we would not have to face the horrendous charges against us tomorrow. We planned for several hours until the sun started to set, the hour grew late, and we all got hungry enough to go home and face the music.

Daddy had to work so Mother went to see Sister the next morning. All day long I lived with dread of the time I had to go home to face what I knew would be the unbridled wrath of my parents. I could feel Daddy's strap on my ass all day and could not concentrate on the schoolwork

I had been ordered home immediately after school with such force that I dared not disobey. When I arrived home with my knees shaking with terror, Mother confronted me with Sister Isabel's accusations of sexual misconduct of the vilest nature. I vociferously denied everything that Sister said, and this time I was not lying. Without even attempting to look at my tongue, Mother gave me a warning not to engage in that kind of activity and I received no further beatings or chastisement. Mother believed me and did not believe Sister Isabel. For the first time in my life, I started to realize that mothers and fathers are really pretty fair and somehow knew when I was telling the truth. I suppose it was difficult for her to believe that I was ready for that kind of behavior at 12 years of age; I wasn't.

There was something else that transpired around this time that may have made Mother more mellow and forgiving with me than she normally would have been. I should have had a hint of this a couple of months prior to all of these events when one of the neighborhood boys said to me, "I see your mother is pregnant." I was affronted by this comment; how dare he say something so terrible about my mother when it wasn't true. (Pregnant was one of the taboo words that gentlemen didn't say.)

I addressed this insult to the family in the usual fashion, by beating up the guy who made this rude remark. Mother was going to the doctor regularly at the time but she said that she had to go to get her blood pressure checked as she was suffering from high blood pressure.

School ended for the term, and on July 2nd, I awoke in the morning to find out that Mother was not home and that they had taken her to the hospital overnight. This time I didn't have to wait for her to come home to find out why she was taken away in the middle of the night. That day she gave birth to twins, our new brothers, Tommy and Billy, raising our household population to ten. Mother's having a baby after more than eight years since the last was a shock for everyone; having twins was a bombshell. Still, life went on as usual; a couple more mouths to feed, that's all. We all welcomed the babies to their new home.

The new additions to the household seemed to be quite hale and hearty until a short time after they arrived home. Tommy was in excellent shape but Billy developed two anomalies that were of grave concern. At six weeks of age, Billy developed a small blood blister on the top of the head that soon grew to the size of a half dollar. He received radium treatments to shrink it; I believe without much success.

More troubling were a lack of muscle coordination on the right side and a retardation of the heel muscles that compelled him to wear a brace on his right leg at night. This didn't prevent him from walking but the deficiency stayed with Billy for his whole life.

When we entered the last year of grade school at St. Joseph's, the eighth grade, the coed classes that we had had for the previous seven years were segregated into two classes, fifty girls in one classroom under Sister Rose Magdalene and fifty boys in the other class with Sister Mary Magdalene as the teacher. Sister Mary Magdalene was a tough mentor but a "lovable tyrant." In addition to her teaching duties, it was her job to instruct us in the church's versions of the "birds and the bees" to prepare us for manhood. She made us aware of some of our own obligations in growing up by such practical advice as, "Keep your hands out of your front pockets. I will have none of my boys playing pocket pool." She also told us all the things that we shouldn't be doing without really telling us in a graphical way that we could understand. She would caution us to, "not have impure thoughts, not to commit impure acts, and to avoid the occasions of sin." (I wish she had given us a better description of the occasions of sin so that we would know where to go to experiment in these newly revealed pleasures of the body.)

It was astonishing how much control Sister had over this class of fifty boys of varying capabilities; especially when I look at today's schools that have a complete lack of discipline in classes one-third the size. The boys had such a great respect for Sister Mary Magdalene that many of them kept in touch with her for many years after graduation, even after she retired and up until the time she died at an age approaching one hundred years.

I was involved in one particularly embarrassing incident with Sister as a major player. Toward the end of the eighth grade school year, we were all obliged to take Regent's Examinations, which were given at St. Sebastian's School in Woodside. On one of those exam days at St. Sebastian's, upon the completion of the tests for the day, I had to go to the bathroom where I discovered, upon completion of an essential function, that the stall I occupied had no toilet paper in it. I asked the group of boys who were loitering in the boy's room to get me some toilet paper from an adjacent booth. Their response to this request was to laugh at and taunt me while all gathering around my stall and peering over the top. I said to them in a loud voice, "Wait until you guys want some paper to wipe your ass."

They suddenly jumped down from their perches where they had been glaring at me, and the next thing I heard through my closed door was the sound of flesh against flesh; palm of the hand against cheek. After several of these slaps there was silence.

The face of George Whiston appeared quietly over the top of the cubicle door and he whispered to me, "Here's some paper, but keep quiet. Sister is right outside the door."

I finished my routine, left the stall, and with cockiness walked out the door. There, leaning against the doorframe with arms akimbo, was Sister with a fierce look on her face. "I've been waiting for you, young man," and with that proceeded to rapidly slap my face about a dozen times with her bony fingers. George wisely held his position inside until Sister had gone.

The next day back in class at St. Joseph's, Sister was relating to the entire class, the disgraceful breakdown in decorum the previous day. "This is the first time I've ever had to enter a boy's lavatory," she complained. She continued to get angrier and worked herself into such lather as her tirade went on, that eventually and unexpectedly, her false teeth fell out of her mouth and onto her desk. Some of the students who observed this could not restrain themselves and roared with laughter. Sister was so mortified that she grabbed her teeth and darted out of the room. She didn't return to the class until the next day.

She must have made note before she left the class of all the boys who laughed at her prior day's embarrassment. Before the day was over she managed to mete out a punishment to many of the boys for any small or large offense they may have committed that day as retribution for yesterday's humiliation.

The eighth grade was a time of transition in many of our lives. Besides the changes in our body chemistry and appearance, we were also realigning some of our fraternal relationships with our regular comrades. While still very friendly with the boys I spent the last seven years with in school, new and growing interests were introducing new "best friends" into my life. During this final year at St. Joseph's I established a circle of close buddies that included Bartholomew "Bart" DeVivo, Jock O'Connor, Eugene "Euch" Fox, and Marty "Mud" Bowman.

Bart was the "Beau Brummell" of our group, always nattily dressed in the latest fashions. His father was a tailor and made all of his suits; "tailor made". He had a tremendous sense of humor and was always ready with a funny quip. Marty was the tall man of the group; about six feet five inches tall and weighing about 160 pounds. The five of us became inseparable during that term.

Marty went on to become a New York City policeman in later years after being discharged from the Air Force after finishing his enlistment there. While in the Air Force he had put on a bit of weight; going up to 350 pounds. He told us at the time that he was putting on weight so fast that they gave him duty requiring civilian clothes so that they wouldn't have to issue him anymore uniform changes. The last time I saw Marty was when he pulled me over for speeding on the Grand Central Parkway. At that time he was a motorcycle patrolman. When I saw this hulk of a man getting off what appeared to be a miniature cycle in the circus compared to his huge and intimidating body, I recognized him. When he approached the car to ask for my license and registration before writing me out a summons, I responded with some nasty remark that made him order me out of the vehicle. When I got out and Marty recognized me, he gave me a hug that must have had the rest of the motorists on the parkway wondering what was going on with that huge cop hugging that frail looking guy.

Marty, Bart, and I eventually wound up going to the same high school together after graduation. I didn't see much of Jock or Euch after grade school. Over the years I've lost track of all of them as we all went our separate ways.

One of our favorite activities was swimming in Oakland Lake in Bayside. A subway ride to Flushing for a nickel and a free transfer to a bus would take us to the lake where we could swim unsupervised and bare ass. The lake was not open for public swimming and there were no lifeguards but we didn't find that to be a deterrence. We would climb the trees around the lake and dive off the highest branches overhanging the water.

That graduation year, one of our classmates, Jack Mahoney, was with us for one of these lake swimming outings. At one point during the day, Jack dove off a tree into the water and when he didn't surface in what we thought was a reasonable time, we became concerned and started to dive under the water to find him. One of the guys found him tangled in some of the weeds near the bottom of the lake and tried to dislodge him without success. When he surfaced and let us know what had happened, we all tried to swim to the bottom to help Jack. In the end, after our futile efforts, we had to call the cops – Jack had drowned.

Warning signs were posted at the lake after that drowning incident prohibiting swimming in the lake. This did not deter any of us from continuing our periodic forays to swim in the lake. The following year, a second drowning of one of our schoolmates from St. Joseph's prompted the authorities to erect a high fence around the lake and to permanently close access to it. We never swam there again. Since that time the lake has become too polluted for swimming.

I sometimes wonder if the carvings of our names in the trees around the lake are still there behind the fence as a memory of many good times and some tragic ones.

It was also in the eighth grade that I got my first crush on a girl. Kay Thomson was not from St. Joseph's and was a cousin to Margie Shearer, one of the girls in Sister Rose Magdalene's class. In fact, Kay was not even a Catholic. Worse than that, she was a Presbyterian who we were led to believe were those "Catholic haters from Scotland." This was an innocent puppy love that never resulted in so much as a kiss but it was a romance that I vigorously pursued while the flame was burning. Meeting at the movie, each paying our own way, was what we considered to be "a date".

I felt so guilty about this relationship with a "Presbyterian" girl that I confessed my association with Kay as a sin to the priest at Confession. His priestly advice to me was to "say ten extra Hail Mary's and in the future try to stick to your own kind'; advice which I ignored after making my Act of Contrition.

One of the girls from our class that attracted the attention of all the boys was Carol Mulligan, an early bloomer who had an exceptionally well-developed bust. One day she entered our class of fifty healthy young male animals with a message for sister Mary Magdalene. She was wearing a tight sweater that revealed her endowments to full advantage. The sight of her had all of the boys ogling, drooling, and sighing. When she left to the disappointment of all, Sister said, "You would think you boys had never seen a girl before. Just remember this; someday they'll all turn into a sack of potatoes."

So many of us have changed since those memorable days at St. Joseph's. In the eighth grade one of the premier femmes fatales was Lorraine Johnson, who even at the tender age of 13 was attracting the attention of not only her male classmates but also many of the older young men. We youngsters were no competition for these more worldly swains and so classy gals like Lorraine were beyond our reach.

On the other hand, there were others in our class who were not the kind to gain the notice of the boys. My partner at the graduation, for instance, was one of these *plain Janes.* The order of pairings was dictated strictly by lining up one hundred boys and girls in alphabetical order, which led to my being lined up alongside of Eileen Petro, a nice girl, but ordinary. For someone like me who considered himself as somewhat of a *swinger,* Eileen was not one I cared to be associated with in any kind of a dating or pairing up situation. When she invited me to be her date at a graduation party, only because we were partners at the graduation ceremony, my initial reaction was to decline; how could I be seen with someone a bit frumpy when, perhaps, a Lorraine Johnson might be available.

However, being unsuccessful in my attempt to date Lorraine; she having chosen to go out with an elderly 17 year old, I accepted the invitation from Eileen so that I would not miss the party. She was a very pleasant date but at that age, in our circle, the superficial aspects of looks and body were more important than the more lasting attributes.

(When I was home on leave from the Navy several years later, I stopped for a libation at one of our favorite watering holes, Coyle's Bar and Grill in Astoria. While sitting at the bar, a dowdy looking woman in a soiled housedress came in to get a container of beer at the bar to take home. I hardly recognized this rather plain and somewhat disheveled looking girl. It was the dazzling Lorraine Johnson from our graduation class. She was now married and living across the street from Coyle's in a small apartment.

She recognized me and immediately started into a fast talking monologue about how she was in Coyle's to pick up some beer for her husband who was home watching television in his underwear while she was doing the household chores. She babbled on like a fishwife. She said that just the previous week she had attended the ordination to the priesthood of Vinnie Keane, another of our classmates from St. Joseph's. I couldn't help but think back to the stunning beauty of not too many years past and wondered how she could have let herself degrade into such a wretched state.

Shortly after this encounter with Lorraine, I ran into another former classmate, Eileen Petro. I almost didn't recognize her. She had blossomed into one of the most beautiful women I have ever seen. She was absolutely stunning; a stately beauty that looked like she just posed for a cover of Vogue Magazine. We talked for a short while and I found her to be totally captivating. If I hadn't just made a commitment to get married I am sure I would have struck at this opportunity to reacquaint myself with Eileen. Alas! How life always changes to surprise us.)

In the last year at St. Joe's, we spent a great deal of time taking entrance examinations for Catholic high schools. I took as many as possible because most of them had an opportunity for a scholarship in addition to being used to qualify for acceptance. I took tests for Rice High, DeLasalle Academy, St.

Francis Xavier, Bishop Loughlin High, and some others. Danny and Franny were both attending LaSalle Academy in Manhattan and because of their matriculation, if I was accepted at Lasalle I would only be required to pay five dollars a month instead of the regular rate of fifteen dollars. I took the test for LaSalle and was accepted; in the end this was my choice.

When graduation came we were all ready with cap and gowns, class rings, autograph books, and eagerly looked forward to the future. I was expecting to receive the school's highest award, the Father Henn Medal, which was named after a former pastor of the church. This medal was given to the student with the highest overall record throughout school and I was certain that my eight years of the highest grades in my class would have qualified me for the honor. Sister Mary Magdalene told me that no student could receive more than one medal and that, although I was the leading candidate for several awards, I was being awarded a medal in Social Studies which at that time included the courses in Geography and History. I did well in the final tests but these were generally not my best subjects.

Patricia Cullen, a good student, was given the Father Henn Medal. Vinnie Keane, who was also an excellent student and slated to go to the seminary after graduation, was given the boy's medal for the highest average in the eighth grade. There was no appeal from these decisions that were probably the consequence of my less than stellar conduct and my readiness to often argue with the teachers when I felt they were wrong.

When I arrived home from the graduation exercises, all of these decisions on awards were soon forgotten. Mother and Daddy, probably at great cost to them, gave me a new Schwinn Bicycle, a dream that I never thought would come true. This was without doubt the most memorable gift I ever received and it served me well every day until the time I joined the Navy four year later.

1946-1950

1946-1950

TEEN YEARS – MEAN YEARS

That first summer after graduation from elementary school, I started working at Gehrlich's Self Service Grocery Store where Danny and Franny were already employed. The store where the three of us worked was located on 30th Avenue near 34th Street.

(There were apartments above the store, one occupied by the Gehrlichs and another by the Gibneys. Agnes Gibney, the daughter, would eventually wind up as Mrs. Daniel O'Leary. I had no idea at the time that she would end up as my sister-in-law.)

The job entailed delivering groceries to customers at their home, a service Mr. Gehrlich provided at no additional cost. The groceries were packed into cardboard boxes and packed into a wooden grocery cart that was pushed by hand through the streets to the points of delivery. A second important part of the job was the restocking of shelves at the store.

Danny and Franny worked a six-day week; stores were closed on Sundays at that time. I worked for five hours on Thursday, and ten hours each on Friday and Saturday. For these twenty five hours of work I was paid a salary of five dollars a week, or twenty cents an hour – plus tips from the customers on delivery if they were so inclined.

Danny and Franny, who were nice enough to arrange the job for me with Mr. Gehrlich, also made sure that each of them started work before me each day. Before I arrived, they would take the pick of the deliveries, knowing from experience who the good and bad tippers were, and left me, of course, with all of the bad tippers, or no tippers. Dan and Fran would be gone all day because they also took the orders that had to be delivered at the furthest locations, some as far as our neighborhood around 45th Street. This presented them quite often with an opportunity before returning to work, to join in with the boys on the block if a ball game was in progress.

In the meantime, my deliveries having been made locally, I would have to return to the store where the bulk of the stocking of the shelves was done by me.

I don't now how many times I had to make deliveries to Mrs. Rosenbaum, who lived just around the corner and was located on the fifth floor of an apartment house with no elevator. She would call in an order about three or four times in a day and never gave a tip. Even if Danny or Franny were in the store, they would make sure that I was given the dubious honor of delivering Mrs. Rosenbaum's order.

One particularly memorable delivery was to an apartment nearby where the mother was not at home when I arrived and the only one in attendance was an older girl, perhaps sixteen or seventeen, who let me in when I knocked on the door. She directed me to put the groceries in the kitchen. She had greeted me at the door wearing only a bathrobe and slippers and when I came out of the kitchen she was semi-reclined on the sofa with her legs up and the robe wide open. Staring at me from between her legs was one of the strangest things I had witnessed up to that point in my fourteen years. I believe this was the first time I ever saw a vagina with hair on it.

She said, "wouldn't you like to stay for a while and talk." Not knowing what to expect from that strange apparition before me, and with my knees shaking with fear, I just said as I rushed out the door that I had to go back to work. I sure had disturbed dreams that night.

That summer passed quickly. We had the usual round of mischief, sports, swimming at the Astoria Pool, Rockaway Beach, and Oakland Lake, fist fights, and just generally hanging around on the corner or on the stoop. In September, I would be attending LaSalle Academy and I was looking forward to this new experience.

LaSalle Academy was a three story Catholic High School located on 2nd Street, just off 2nd Avenue on the lower East Side of Manhattan. It was run by the Christian Brothers and covered the grades from nine to twelve. It was exclusively a boys school which was quite common for the day; coeducational schools in the Catholic High School System were a rarity (if, indeed, they existed at all.)

The surrounding neighborhood was occupied predominantly by first and second generation Italians and Jews each living in low income brownstone tenements clustered within their own ethnic groups. There were other ethnicities represented in the neighborhood as well but it would not be too many years before the burgeoning Hispanic community and the expanding immigration influx from the Middle East and Asia replaced all of them. We didn't get to explore the neighborhood around the school very often because the subway station that we arrived at each morning was located only two blocks from the school.

Along 3rd Avenue, one block from the school was the Third Avenue Elevated transit system which was still in operation then but would soon be torn down to be replaced with the bus line. The stretch of 3rd Avenue in the vicinity of LaSalle was notorious at that time as a haven for unemployed vagabonds that were called variously at that time: hoboes, derelicts, bums, tramps, or vagrants – homeless was not yet the universal appellation assigned to this class of drifter. The street was known for its missions and food kitchens for these men and for its lice infested flop houses where a bed could be rented for the night for a dime. Third Avenue along this section was called *The Bowery.*

Every morning when we left the subway station to walk the short distance to school, most of the route along 2nd Avenue was filled with the local tramps begging for a handout or a cigarette. They would also ask for the lunch that many of us carried to school from home in a brown paper bag. We would occasionally give them our lunch if it was something that we didn't like and if we had the price of lunch at the school cafeteria.

Some of the students that smoked would light up as soon as they left the subway station. After the brief walk to school the smokers would be about half way through the cigarette and the vagrants standing by the school door would hold out their hand to take the remaining butt. Some of the smokers would dowse the cigarette into the filthy, calloused palm with no reaction from the beggar except to take the butt from the hand to put in his pocket to be smoked at a later time.

My first introduction to LaSalle was a happy one. We would soon find out that while most of the Brothers we were to encounter were very stern but fair, many of them would prove to be tyrants and bullies. I lucked out by having Brother John as our freshman homeroom teacher. He was a fine instructor and disciplinarian but had a great rapport with the boys in the school.

At LaSalle, unlike the public high schools, all of the students were required to remain in the homeroom class for the entire day, while the teachers made the change in classrooms. This held true for most of the subjects except for Science labs and, of course, the mandatory Physical Education class in the gymnasium, and as I will relate shortly, the library.

More significant and also in contrast to the public school, there were no choices of curricula at LaSalle; no Shop, no Home Economics, no Commercial courses. Every student took a strictly Academic course consisting of Mathematics, Science, English Grammar and Literature, Latin I, II, and III, French I and II, History (Ancient, World, and United States), and Religion.

Extracurricular activities and sports were encouraged but some, such as myself, had to work after school to pay for the tuition, books, and supplies and found little time to participate in the after school action. I attempted in the freshman year to participate in the band because the lessons were given during the school hours and had decided to play the clarinet. I chose the clarinet over the trombone, the tuba, or one of the other bulkier instruments because it was easier to carry the clarinet on the subway each day; especially after having witnessed one poor soul hauling a bass fiddle in its case each day on the train.

At my first lesson, the music teacher, Mr. Santerammo, discovering that he had a plethora of clarinetists (probably for reasons similar to mine), approached me and asked me to turn in my clarinet saying, "You have *zee* great *leeps* for *zee* trombone, but not for *zee* clarinet." I declined his suggestion to switch to another instrument, turned in the clarinet, and ended my short career as a member of the school band; which I am sure made everyone in my family happy when I didn't come home to play a screeching clarinet every evening; having suffered through my banjo strumming practice.

The most memorable thing about LaSalle, as with most learning institutions, was the variety of personalities on the faculty. Brother Cajitan is a name that all LaSalle alumni will remember if they attended during any of the many years of Brother Cajitan's tenure. He ran the school library and every student had to attend a class in the library once a week under Brother Cajitan's tutelage. There the student would select, or have selected, a book to read within the next week and to present a report on the book read the prior week.

We were required to have three things when we entered Brother Cajitan's domain: Rosary Beads, a scapular, and a notebook containing our written book reports. If any item was missing, or for any breaches of conduct, Brother

Cajitan would place the palms of his open hands across the cheeks of the offending boy, and with the little finger of his left hand crooked into a right angle bend, brother would pull the hands apart and with two swift motions slap the student simultaneously with both hands while saying, "Take two, you old gomb!"(Sounds like bomb) We used to say that Brother Cajitan was the only one that could give you a slap across the cheeks and an ear cleaning at the same time. (We never did find out what an "old gomb" was, but we got the general idea that it was not complimentary.)

Brother Joseph was another one of the faculty that had universal recognition. He was beyond classroom teaching age when I entered the school and his duties primarily consisted of acting as a monitor in the small school cafeteria and in the gymnasium that was used as gathering place during the lunch hour. The cafeteria was very limited, with a small counter where sandwiches or soda could be purchased, and no hot meals. The small room for eating consisted of four narrow tables at a height permitting one to stand and eat; no seats being available. There were two back-to-back tables in the center of the room and one against each sidewall. The students were obliged to not only stand at the tables to eat but were required to constantly move to fill a vacant spot of any student ahead of him who had finished and left a spot. This was continued until they were out the door and into the gym. It was Brother Joseph's job to keep the boys moving along the tables, a task he pursued with due diligence and if you didn't move, you felt the sting of Brother Joseph's wrath. Most of the brothers were known by pet names that the students had collectively adopted for them. Brother Joseph, for instance, was affectionately called, "Creepin' Jesus" because of the slow gait caused by his age.

One day, while I was eating an American cheese sandwich in the cafeteria at lunchtime, I was talking to Jack Egan, a close friend who lived across the street from me in Astoria and was six months ahead of me in school. I had left half of the sandwich behind me on the table while I spoke to Jack.

When I bit into that part of the sandwich, I gagged and nearly threw up. My sandwich was filled with salt that had just been put into the sandwich by one of the other students, Joseph Gildea, who had emptied the entire saltshaker onto the cheese as a practical joke. When this prankster burst out laughing, I became enraged and followed my normal reaction by sending a left hook swiftly to his head. Jack suddenly wrenched my arm to a stop in mid-swing. He warned me not to hit this guy because he had a glass eye that might be damaged if I hit him with the usual gusto. I was still irate but Jack calmed me down enough to avert further hostility and possible injury to the eye. This episode passed, but not to my satisfaction.

A short time after this incident, Brother Phillip, slapped this one-eyed student across the face with such force that the glass eye popped out of his head and onto the floor in front of the brother. When that occurred I quietly thanked Jack for stopping me from slugging this guy that day of the salt caper. I don't know how I would have taken to having to peer into an empty eye socket (more about Brother Phillip, shortly.)

Brother Victor was our first year General Science teacher, a class we had immediately after lunch each day. It was customary to start the first class in the morning and the first class after lunch with a prayer. Brother Victor was a no-nonsense teacher who would quietly direct us to stand for the customary prayer with a snap of his fingers and an upward motion of his forefingers. After the prayer, Brother Victor, standing on a platform that supported his desk, looked down at the class, snapped the fingers of his two hands again followed by a downward motion of the forefingers to indicate that we should be seated. We always obediently responded by promptly sitting in unison at the signal.

One day during lunch, we conspired to remain standing when we returned to Brother Victor's Science class when he gave his usual motion to be seated; after all, we reasoned, he was a short and non-violent man and we students were always ready to test a teacher's forbearance.

Upon return to class, we said the prayers and Brother gave us the hand signal to be seated. More than half the class remained standing, some of the meeker students having lost the nerve to join this *mini-rebellion without purpose.* Brother Victor very coolly glared down at the standing students, staring directly at each of us with an icy eyed gaze that could freeze the heart, and just as patiently, repeated his snapped finger command. At this point half of the standing students lost their courage and sat down.

Brother again motioned us to be seated without saying a word. Again the rebel ranks were halved as more students withered under the stare. Another two or three snaps of the fingers and there was one boy still standing alone against Brother's quiet persistence. That poor soul was I.

Brother Victor never lost that hard, cold stare, nor had he moved from the platform, where from my vantage point he seemed to have grown an additional three feet in height from his normal diminutive stature. He once again repeated his signal. Discretion overcame valor, and common sense prevailed. There was only one option left open for me and that was – to sit down.

Brother Victor had stemmed the mutiny without speaking a word and without losing his control. He had exposed the ringleaders with his cool tactics. Brother proceeded with the class and never mentioned this episode again – and the class never challenged his authority in the classroom again.

Brother George was another one of our classroom teachers that I remember with mirth. He taught us Algebra in our freshman year. Whenever he was writing on the blackboard one could hear the rising crescendo of the students' murmurs behind his back. This chatter would eventually prompt Brother to sternly command silence and attention in the class. If he turned and caught an individual speaking, he would go tearing down the aisle after the offending student where he would either slap him or pick him up bodily and slam him back down into the seat. At times he would start down the aisle in such frenzy that he would find himself in the wrong aisle. At this point he would put his hand on top of one of the desks and do a hand spring over the desks to the next aisle. This was a sight to behold. The brothers wore ankle length cassocks and one had to be quite spry to maneuver this bulky garment over a desk. This happened on numerous occasions and Brother George managed the leap with the agility of a gazelle and without kicking a student at one of the desks.

One day, Brother George was late in arriving at class. In a short time, the restless students were abuzz with frolicking and skylarking. I stood in front of the class doing an imitation of Brother George in one of his paroxysms. I ran down the aisle, put my hand on the edge of a desk, and lifted my legs off the floor and over the desk. As my body was in the air and parallel to the floor and my full weight was on the edge of the desk, Brother George entered the room. At the very instant of his arrival, the desk top split in two pieces; one piece remaining on the desk frame, while the other half dropped to the floor with me close behind. As I sprawled there on the floor, Brother immediately and correctly assessed what was going on. His reproach was immediate, firm, and painful.

Most of the brothers were tough but fair. We respected them even while always testing their patience. Brother Phillip, on the other hand, was one of the few who I would classify as a "real son-of-a-bitch." He was fairly big and strongly built. He didn't hesitate to use his size or his authority to cow the students. He was a first class bully.

My personal run in with Brother Phillip was in our second year French 1 class. Brother told us a story that ended in a punch line that he thought was funny. Most of the students dutifully laughed at Brother's "joke" knowing his penchant for demanding the desired response to his remarks. He noticed that I didn't laugh as expected and zeroed in on me with his usual harsh retribution.

He knew that I was a good student and had no trouble with the assigned French lessons, but he also knew and delighted in how intimidating he could be to the students.

He started on me by asking me some questions on topics that I had no reason to have knowledge of; questions in more advanced studies. Not knowing the answer to these questions was enough reason for Brother to start glaring at me nose to nose while snorting his foul breath into my face. After a short time of unanswerable questions, he started to slap me for "not being prepared."

When he had me suitably shook up and waiting for the next blow, he started to ask me more fundamental question on topics that were currently assigned. I knew the answers but had been so terrorized by Brother that my addled brain refused to function. As these were things that I should have known, Brother felt this was adequate reason to deliver more severe punishment. With the next unanswered question, he closed his fist on the next blows, dropping me to the floor. I got up and was given even more simplistic questions, which unanswered got me a few more punches to the face.

At this point, brother or no, bigger man or no, I had had enough. I raised my fists and lunged forward at Brother Phillip who gave me another straight right to the jaw. I went down again as he grinned an evil self satisfied grin. The other students restrained me when I got up again, with some of them interposing themselves between Brother and me when they realized that I was determined to take Brother on.

Brother Phillip reported my "unprovoked attack" on him to the Principal. I was sternly reprimanded and had to serve some detention time. This episode was not entered into my record and was soon forgotten by everyone – but me.

We also had some lay teachers. Mr. Keker was our freshman English teacher and a former Navy Lieutenant Commander who often digressed from the subject matter to beguile us with stories of his experiences as the Captain of a Navy Patrol Torpedo Boat. The story I remember most fondly was the time that he had his boat tied alongside a battleship in the Pacific, where he was taking on fuel and supplies. In the midst of this operation, an outlet pipe just above his boat started to spew out the excrement from the ship's toilets, which soon decorated the entire deck of the PT boat. Commander Keker started to yell obscenities in a loud voice at the crewmembers on the deck of the battlewagon. One of the officers on the large ship cautioned Keker to quiet down, that the Admiral was on board the ship. Keker replied, "Admiral or no Admiral, no one is going to shit on my boat!" Boy! How heroic that seemed to us.

Mr. Suppe, our sophomore year English teacher, if given his way, would have had all of us memorizing every book, poem, essay, or play written in the English language. I memorized long passages and soliloquies from Shakespeare, countless poems, and such long essays as Cardinal Newman's, "…it shall be my definition of a gentleman that he is one who never inflicts pain…" The readings were quite an exercise for the mind and many of the words I set in the brain over sixty years ago, still echo there. His approach to memorization was: write it down, say it aloud while reading it with the eyes, so that all of the senses would record the impression and make it that much easier to retain; sight, sound, the feel of the hands, and the movement of the lips. Worked for me!

I would meet the local guys that attended LaSalle every school morning at the 46th Street subway station of the IND (Independent subway.) There we would catch the GG train to Queens Plaza where we would change to the F (6th Avenue) train that took us to our final stop at Houston Street in Manhattan. (Pronounced, House – tin)

A typical routine in the morning, when necessary, was to get a copy of the previous night's homework from one of the fellow travelers in the class, to copy on the subway as we made the 50 minute ride downtown.

Most of the time, the F train at Queens Plaza was so packed with passengers that we were obliged to squeeze our way onto the train; a feat which at first glance seemed impossible, but which we always fulfilled. It was also our practice to gather ten or twelve of us at one door to add to the challenge of forcing our way onto the train.

One particularly crowded day, I was the last to force my way into the car by pressing my back into the crowd, which left me facing the door as it closed and unable to move or turn around. There was no room, it seemed, for another person to get on the train at this door. The next station, 23rd Street, was usually sparsely occupied when we arrived so I expected no difficulty at that station. It was my fortune that day, however, to have a very buxom and attractive young lady standing at my door when we arrived at the station. She managed to press herself into the car directly in front of me. When the door closed we were face to face and I was beginning to feel a bit of anxiety. The next stop, Lexington Avenue on the other side of the river, was about three minutes away, and my traveling companion and I were compelled to maintain this intimate bodily contact for that entire time, with nowhere to move or turn.

Being only fourteen or fifteen years old at the time and at the height of sensitivity and unmanageable erectibility, I found myself trying to move away which only led to a heightened consciousness of my growing predicament. The young lady herself was becoming aware of the situation and tried to extricate herself from her growing embarrassment. Each move on either of our parts though, simply increased the tension.

By now, the sweat was pouring down my brow and under my shirt. I could sense every part of her body, as it seemed to burn into mine. Three minutes began to feel like three hours as I wished away this moment, while secretly savoring the agreeable aspects of the occasion.

I felt like I was going to faint with the increasing heat and shortness of breath. When we finally reached Lexington Avenue, enough passengers alighted from the train to give us some space to move but we remained fixed in our current position. It took some time to realize that space had become available and that we could now separate the bodies that were conjoined for the last three minutes.

As we parted and assumed a less restricted position on the train, I knew that this episode would remain in my memory for a long time. As for the young lady, I am certain that she just wanted to quickly forget the encounter with this brash young stranger who had shared three intimate minutes with her on the F Train under the East River.

The New York City subways were an endless source of interesting happenings and amusement. Hardly a day went by without another memorable event. One of the funniest things happened one day as I was traveling home from downtown where I had been working at the time. A middle-aged man was sitting in a seat directly across from me when I sat down upon entering the train. From his working attire, I assumed he was a laborer headed home after a day's work; his head was down and his eyes were closed as he caught a few winks.

A young lady entered the train and took the only remaining empty seat, alongside the sleeping worker. After a short time, she noticed, as did several of the passengers, including myself, that the man's fly was open. He was probably unaware of this as he slept. The young lady tried to ignore this obvious breach of decorum by continuously putting her handkerchief to her face as she purposely averted her gaze in the opposite direction from the open trousers.

As she dabbed at her face, the handkerchief slipped from her hand and landed directly on top of the man's open fly. She looked a bit perplexed and evidently wanted to retrieve the errant handkerchief, but dared not just pick it up as it may have looked like she was reaching into the man's pants.

After a brief time she tapped the man on the shoulder to wake him up, and pointing down at the handkerchief, wordlessly requested him to return her handkerchief. Still a bit disoriented from having been awakened, the man must have thought that his shirttail was hanging out and quickly tucked the handkerchief into his trousers and quickly buttoned up his open fly; unaware of what he had just done.

The young lady turned as red as a beet and knew that the handkerchief was now lost to her. As the few passengers who were aware of the incident were stifling the laughter which we all felt inclined to, the young lady rose from her seat and got off the train at the next stop. I don't know whether this was her final destination or if she just wanted to escape the embarrassment of the moment.

The more interesting question is, how did that man explain to his wife when he removed his trousers at home, how he was in possession of a delicate, lace handkerchief - and in his trousers at that?

During my freshman year at LaSalle, I maintained a good attendance record and a good academic performance, even though I was unable to get to the train on time and was habitually late for the first class. Some of my classmates had picked up the habit of getting halfway to school on the subway and then deciding to take the day off; what we called "playing the hook" (hooky or truancy.) In the second year I would start to fall into some bad attendance habits myself.

Toward the end of that initial year, one of the senior students who would soon be graduating was leaving a part time job that he had at the local agency office of the Connecticut Mutual Life Insurance Company at the Singer Building on Broadway downtown. He put in a word for me and I started to work there after school for five days a week under his tutelage until he left at the end of the term; at which time I took over his position; full time in the summer and after school during the school year.

This was a great opportunity for regular employment. I would do the general duties of an office boy: make deliveries and pick ups, run errands, pick up, deliver, and prepare mail for the Post Office, and any other tasks assigned to me by Mr. LaBelle, the head cashier and my immediate boss.

I held this job at Connecticut Mutual for well over a year; part time during my sophomore year at Lasalle and full time when I quit school in my junior year. I had a good attendance record, did all the jobs I was assigned, and was well treated by the large and friendly staff at the office.

One of my jobs was to go to new insurance clients to get the required signatures on forms and at times, to get a "specimen." I didn't know for a long time what a specimen was and was shocked to find out I was carrying vials of urine around the city subways.

Another task was to collect all of the opened and unopened bottles of liquor left over from the many office parties, and to store them in the large vault to which only the head cashier and myself had the combination to open. As months went by, whoever was in charge of providing these supplies for the next party always purchased new bottles and never used the existing supplies in the vault.

I started to wrap some of the bottles very carefully for mailing and sent them to myself at home. There I was storing the liquor in the cellar of the house inside a seldom-used wheelbarrow under the stairwell. The supplies grew rapidly and it was my intent to throw a party for the neighborhood gang with the accumulated booze when an occasion presented itself.

One evening there was a knock on our apartment door; it was the landlord, Mr. Kelly. Daddy answered the door and Mr. Kelly asked him if that was his stash of booze under the stairs in the cellar. Fortunately I was there at the time because as soon as Daddy answered that he didn't know anything about the liquor hoard, I quickly said that I knew about it and that I had been saving it as a surprise for him. We hauled everything, about two-dozen bottles of scotch, whisky, gin, vodka, and other liquors, up to the apartment where Daddy stored it away. When he inquired, I told him that the liquor was left over from the office, was not being used, and that I was permitted to take it home.

I stopped the shipments of clandestine booze from the office and only took one more bottle that I shared with some friends on New Year's Eve at the Triborough Theatre where we celebrated that occasion, drinking directly from the bottle. It was my first experience with drinking scotch and I got quite drunk and sick before the night was over. I threw up in the theater and the seats around me were soon deserted. This incident turned me off to hard liquor for a long time. For a couple of years after that eye opening night just smelling hard liquor would make me feel sick.

It was while working downtown that I had my first mystical and mysterious occurrence. I had been working late to get out an exceptionally large mailing in the mailroom located across the hall from the main office, which was by this time locked up for the night. I was alone in the mailroom and as the hour grew late the offices throughout the entire building were empty.

I departed our office on the ninth floor, left the building and walked to the subway station nearby. No cashier was on duty at this late hour but I knew I had the fare in my wallet to get me onto the train. When I opened the change purse of the wallet, however, I found that there was no nickel but only my St. Christopher's medal, which I always carried around with me while traveling; St. Christopher being the patron saint of travelers. I went back onto the streets, which by this time were dark and deserted. No stores were open and all buildings seemed to be completely deserted. I walked back to the Singer Building and took the elevator back to the office. All of the doors to the office were locked and there was no way for me to get in. I thought that, if I could get into the main office, I might get some change out of the petty cash box that was never locked up; this being the cash box I normally used to get carfare to make my pickups and deliveries.

I searched my pockets again for some change and took another look in the change purse and there was nothing but the St. Christopher medal. I thought, "Some patron saint you are, here I am stuck in the darkened canyons of downtown New York with no way home and no carfare." I thought that I

136

had one helluva long walk to get home, even if I knew how to get there from here.

I walked back to the subway and paced the streets looking for a cop or anyone else from whom I might beg a nickel to get onto the subway; but without success. I went back to the station one more time and decided to look into my wallet again. Lo and behold! There inside the change purse was a single nickel. I looked in every corner of the wallet and through my pockets for the St. Christopher medal but it was gone. It had miraculously disappeared and there in its place was a nickel and my passage home.

I got on the subway and went home quite baffled about what had transpired. When I arrived home, I told Mother this strange story and she listened politely but was probably thinking that I was losing my marbles or just making up some fanciful story. To convince her, I pulled out my wallet to show her the empty change purse. When I opened the purse, there it was - the St. Christopher medal. I was astounded. I let the matter drop and have just carried this incident with me for these many years as one of life's inexplicable mysteries. I am convinced that, even when the church discredited St. Christopher in later years, he was there when I needed him that dark, lonely night in New York when I needed him.

While returning from one of my rounds one afternoon, I was about to pass in front of a private club on Liberty Street, just up the block from the office, when a limousine pulled up in front of the club and a man with a familiar face exited the vehicle to enter the club. It was General Dwight Eisenhower, at that time a hero to all of us from his role as Supreme Commander in Europe during the recent war. It was 1948 and he had recently taken over as President of Columbia University.

I was thrilled that the "General" was passing right in front of me with that famous grin of his lighting up his face. I stopped to watch him enter the club. He stopped by me and said "Hello young man"; shook my hand and with his other hand tousled my hair. I was speechless then, but I couldn't wait to get back to the office and then home so that I could tell of this thrilling experience to everyone who would listen.

I met other people on the street while making one of my daily forays around downtown. One of the notable encounters took place as I was looking into the window of a bookstore. (It was one of those stores that were having a "going out of business" sale that continued for years.) A man approached me and struck up a conversation. I was somewhat wary of this stranger but remained courteous as he started to ask questions about where I worked.

He started to talk about sports and keeping in shape for them, which was an opening for him to discuss specific muscles that needed development and gave him an excuse to start his exploratory touching, particularly when he mentioned the "love muscle". At that, I artfully dodged his attempt to touch my private parts.

He followed me as I went back to the office building and with each turn said that it was a coincidence that he was going in the same direction as me; all the way to the ninth floor where our office was located. When he saw the large office, he quickly asked where the bathroom was and then disappeared. Evidently he had been hoping that I would wind up in some empty room somewhere or find some other opportunity to make an overt move. This was not my first experience with an aggressive pedophile, nor would it be my last, but I always managed to avoid getting myself boxed into a dangerous situation.

Some of these predators were more blatant in their approach. I was on a subway platform waiting for a train and had just purchased a soda from a vending machine on the platform when a huge man, about six foot six and very heavy, accosted me with the open declaration, "Hey, kid! You want a blow job?" I was frightened out of my wits, dropped the newly poured soda on the platform, and hightailed it out of his reach.

In a couple of years, when I felt more certain of myself, I would just simply punch out any deviate who laid a hand on me.

After the short lived Kay Thomson flirtation, I met a young lady at a picnic who had a name that has always stayed with me; Pauline Grace Stephanie Canuncio. Who could forget a name like that? We started to become better acquainted when I took daily or nightly rides to her house located several miles away in Corona. The house was situated alongside the Roosevelt Avenue elevated train tracks.

The first time I was at the house the whole building started to shake and dishes on the shelves were rattling. No one seemed to notice so I said nothing. After the second or third time that this happened, I said, "My God, what is that?" The response from all in the room was, "What's what?" I mentioned the shaking house and the dishes ready to fall off the shelf and they said, "Oh that. It's only a train passing by. That happens all the time." I guess one can become oblivious to anything.

This romance lasted a good part of the summer and if we kissed, which I can't recall, it had to be the old-fashioned closed mouth peck because I still hadn't met my first mentor in the art of proper osculation. That day was not too far off.

In the fall when we started high school we would attend the Confraternity dances at St. Joseph's on Friday nights. The confraternity was intended primarily for the Public High School Students to provide them with religious instructions for at least one hour a week. These Friday night classes were followed by a dance in the school basement.

At the dances, the boys would ordinarily group together on one side of the room while the girls congregated on the other side. I was typical of most of the boys at that age, a poor dancer who was limited to an occasional Foxtrot. There were a few boys that were good dancers and were not hesitant to ask one of the girls to dance. The girls in this generation were similar to most that

I've observed over the years; they were good dancers and when lacking a male partner, danced with another girl. I recall Jim Kearns and Kieran Manning as two of the guys who knew how to "cut a rug."

It was at one of these dances that I was approached by an attractive young lady, Jane McNamara, who asked me to dance. It was the last dance of the night and a Foxtrot so I felt safe accepting the invitation. The song was the traditional last number of the night, "Twilight Time" by the Three Suns, played on a windup Victrola on a 78-RPM record that was the standard of the day. One student volunteered to change the records on the Victrola that played one record at a time. Later on, the school would get one of the first electric record players.

Jane's brother, she revealed, was in the same class at LaSalle as my brother Franny. As we danced she told me that after the last two Confraternity dances, she was followed home by one of the other students in attendance and that she was afraid that he was going to molest her. She asked me if I would see her home safely to her house, located a short bus ride away in Woodside, near the St. Sebastian School where we had taken our regents exams. Being ever gallant, and in spite of the financial hardship of paying five cents for the bus, I agreed to see her home. (I walked home to save the nickel bus fare and got severely reprimanded for the late hour of arrival home.)

When we arrived at the front door of her apartment house, she asked me to go inside with her to make sure that the "stalker" was not waiting for her there. When I walked her into the vestibule and we found the coast was clear, she said she wanted to thank me for the dance and for seeing her home safely. She gave me a strange feeling kiss that made me think she was trying to bite my mouth.

She asked me, "Where did you learn to kiss? Let me show you how." With that she said that you have to open your mouth so she could stick her tongue in. This was what she called, "a French kiss." I did as I was directed but I found that, other than the taste of licorice when we kissed, it was rather disgusting to be sticking tongues in each other's mouths; as well as being very unsanitary. However, I thought, if this is what you have to do to be grown up, then I'll have to learn to do it. (An acquired tasted; like drinking Scotch)

During our conversation in the hall, she noticed my graduation ring from St. Joseph's and asked if she could try it on. When she had it on, she said she couldn't get it off and that she would get it off with soap upstairs and return the ring to me next week at Confraternity. I left her and thought that I had done a good deed by taking her home safely.

The next week at Confraternity, Jane again searched me out and before the night was over asked me to take her home again. I did.

When we arrived at the door, we again checked the vestibule for stalkers and proceeded with lesson two in tongue kissing or what would become known as, "Swapping spits." She said to me, "I can't believe that we've been *going steady* for a whole week and that this has been our second date." I felt trapped. As for the ring, she said it still wouldn't come off and that I could give it to her as a friendship ring for our *going steady*.

It took me a few weeks of "going steady" before I found the nerve to break up this unwanted romance; but in the meantime, I learned a few things about advanced kissing. I don't know if it was this new "intimacy", but I started to have "impure thoughts" that were dutifully told to the priest in confession.

(I did get the ring back eventually, but lost it soon after.)

At the end of our sophomore year, the school held a Junior Prom in the school gymnasium to which the juniors invited us. It was not a black tie affair; suits were required and the young ladies wore their best cocktail party dresses.

I had my mind set on going to the prom with Jean Sheehan, a pretty little blonde that lived around the corner from me. She was slightly older by about a year but this did not deter me from asking her. It took me a while to get up the nerve to ask and when I finally did my invitation was declined. I had already made a commitment to Jack Egan that I would accompany him and his date, Nancy Dospoy, to the prom.

It was around this time that one of my good friends, Frankie Laurie, was going steady with Marilyn Ryan, a slender and attractive friend who was one of the fun filled members of our local neighborhood circle. The friendship between Frankie and me was so close that the two of us would stand toe to toe boxing each other, bare knuckles, on the corner of the block. We often did this when we had gone a couple of days without having fought someone else; there being hardly a day passing without having a street fight for any of a number of reasons.

We were sitting around on the stoop discussing my present dilemma of not having a date for the prom. Frankie turned to Marilyn and said, "Marilyn, you go with Jack to the prom." Marilyn, being a good friend to Nancy and myself, accepted the challenge.

The four of us went to the prom where we had a great time, drinking warm lemonade, and eating stale sandwiches and cookies. I got pissed off when, after we had promenaded around the dance floor at the climax of the evening, Marilyn was not presented with the Queen of the Prom title, which went to the girl friend of Hugh Reilly, our class's star athlete and leading scholar; *nothing but favoritism.*

It was about a year later when Marilyn and I became an "item". Though we kept steady company, she always had her eyes set on my brother Franny, and didn't hesitate to let me know. She finally collared Fran after going through a round of suitors that included Bill Loes, high school sports star who wound up pitching for the Brooklyn Dodgers, and Pete Gentile, his classmate, who was a "bonus baby" for the New York Yankees. I believe he had one year in the majors before moving on. This year, 2002, Fran and Marilyn will be celebrating their fiftieth wedding anniversary.

Another girl who found an interest in me was Lydia, an attractive young lady but one that I tried to avoid at all costs. She was a weight lifter who could press one hundred and sixty pounds with one arm; something many of my male bodybuilding buddies couldn't do with two arms. When she caught up with me, she would habitually grab me by the bicep, which she would hold onto with an iron grip that I couldn't break away from. This happened every time that I didn't get away on time and I would have to wait for her to release my arm before I could dash away. Fortunately, I could run faster than her.

One day, I got off a subway station in Elmhurst, quite a distance from our home neighborhood. I started to walk down the street and I heard in a strong, piercing voice, a familiar sound. Lydia had spotted me and was running rapidly in my direction. I made a mad dash in the opposite direction and ran in dread fear of being caught again by this Amazon. I got away that time and several other times after that, when I believe that Lydia either moved from the neighborhood or got tired of chasing me around the streets.

In the second year of high school, I started to not only continue my tardiness of the first year, but started to take occasional days off to attend a movie and stage show on Broadway. More often than not, the venue we selected was the Paramount Theater, where for fifty five cents before 1 P.M. we could see a first run movie and a stage show featuring top stars of Hollywood or the music world. I saw more of Louie Prima and Keeley Smith during that term than I saw of Brother Arthur our Geometry teacher. Della Reese, Sarah Vaughan, Mel Torme, and Vic Damone were some of the celebrities of the day that we saw at the Paramount.

One day stands out in my memory as especially amusing. Marty Bowman, Bart DeVivo, a couple of other subway companions, and I, decided on this particular day to "play the hook". We got off at the 42nd Street Station in the City on our way to school and immediately went to the Paramount Theater, which opened early.

That day was another Louis Prima appearance. In the middle of his act, a man came out on the stage, flashed a bright light across the audience, and said,

"I'm the truant officer and I'm here to lock up any truants that may be in the audience." Some were frightened that this was true but most of us laughed. I think the early price reduction was intentional to draw in the thousands of city students that were off on any day.

After the show, we walked to Bryant Park nearby, to eat the lunches that we had carried with us to school in a brown paper bag. When Marty opened his paper bag for the first time since leaving home that morning, he was shocked to find that this was not his lunch; but his sister's girdle. (Worn by most of the women in those days whether they needed it or not.) We had quite a laugh on Marty that day.

When Marty returned home, he found out that his father had discovered Marty's lunch bag at home and, like a good father, took the train ride to the school to give Marty's lunch to Brother Ambrose, the principal, to pass on to Marty. When Brother found out that Marty was not in class, he asked Mr. Bowman if he had signed the other notes to excuse Marty from class that he had on file. Marty had forged his father's signature on all of the notes. Needless to say, that was not a comfortable night at home for Marty; but he never squealed on the rest of us being with him that day.

I picked up another bad habit when I was fifteen years old; one that would stay with me for thirty years before I finally kicked it. Danny had started smoking at fourteen years old with Mother's permission, for which he had asked her. She must have considered the start of smoking as a significant event; it was included in a ledger that she kept to record all of the major events in our lives; sicknesses, graduations, special events… and smoking.

The only bad thing we knew about smoking then was that it would "stunt your growth." I assumed that if Danny had permission at fourteen, I would automatically be given the same consent when I was a year older than that.

I started to smoke and readily flaunted this new mark of growing up even at home. Mother was mad as hell that I hadn't consulted her first and forbade me from smoking in the future. I followed her orders for about a month and then asked for permission, which was readily given; now that I had learned another lesson in who the boss of the house was.

If I could afford a full pack of cigarettes, I would buy them and try to avoid having the grubbers find out about it or they would pester me until I gave them one. If I couldn't' spring for the pack, I could get a "loosie" (one cigarette) at one of the local candy stores that would break open a pack to sell each one for a penny.

I carried the smoking habit with me until April of 1977 at which time I was smoking up to four packs a day. Probably, if I had kept smoking at that rate, I wouldn't be here writing this narrative today.

[I finally quit because of a bet I made with Marion Eckhoff, a good friend and neighbor. We agreed to each of us putting five dollars a week into a common pool with the proviso that the first one to take even one drag of a cigarette would lose the accumulated pool of money. We each faithfully put up the agreed upon amount each week and eventually had about 350 dollars sitting in an account.

Having wanted to spend a weekend in the St.Moritz Hotel overlooking Central Park South in Manhattan ever since attending a party there for Washington State United States Senator, Scoop Jackson, I suggested that we terminate our bet because we were obviously well on our way to having permanently kicked the smoking habit. We would then take the money we had saved and go to the St.Moritz, see a show, and have dinner. Marion was receptive to the idea and said, "Oh! Jean and Chris (Marion's husband) would love to go." My reply was, "who said anything about them; we're the one's that made the bet?'

The *four* of us did go to spend an entertaining weekend in the city at the St. Moritz Hotel with rooms overlooking Central Park; that is, if you stuck your head out the room window to look around the corner,

Neither of us has had a cigarette since that day thirty four years ago.]

When I entered my third year at LaSalle my life started a quick spiral downward; I wanted to get out of LaSalle for reasons that today I can't recall. (It may have been because there were no girls at LaSalle and I was in that age of adolescence where it was quite important to have the opposite sex around.) I started classes at LaSalle but tried to get transferred over to Bryant High School close to home. Because the school term was already underway I was unsuccessful.

I told Mother that I was quitting school to go to work and that I was not going to go back to LaSalle. She was outraged and insisted that I stay in school, but I adamantly refused to go back. She finally relented, but only if I had a job. I approached Mr. LaBelle at Connecticut Mutual for a full time job and although he and most of the office staff were prodding me to stay on at school, they all finally gave up and I was hired for a full time job at the insurance company for twenty five dollars a week. Out of that pay, I had to pay ten dollars into the house for room and board.

As I was only sixteen at the time, I was obliged by law to attend Continuation School for one day a week. Because I was employed in an office, they put me into the commercial course with classes in typing, bookkeeping, stenography and other secretarial skills. Most of the boys who had left school were in unskilled laborer positions in factories and were put into the shop courses.

I would soon be accepted at Bryant for the second half of the year beginning in February and I was expected to be gainfully employed during my time away from school. Before returning to school, I was fired from the office boy position for something that I was not responsible for.

Mrs. Keating, a secretary to one of the nabobs at the company, gave me an assignment one day to pick up a signature and medical report from a client, who was picking up a very large insurance policy and which, I believe, entailed a large commission for her boss. I made the pickup and delivered the items to Mrs. Keating. This was the only assignment that I had on this day because it took me a good part of the day to track down the client and to travel to where I could pick up the items requested.

About a week later, I was called in to see my boss, Mr. LaBelle, who asked me for the papers that Mrs.Keating had sent me for. I told him that I had turned them over to Mrs. Keating and specifically remembered doing it because it was the only task that day. Evidently, Mrs.Keating had lost the papers that I gave to her and would not admit to it. When it came to a decision of who to believe, I lost out and was terminated. I was carrying a lot of chips around on my shoulder, real and imagined, and this injustice only added to my sense of alienation.

The first job opportunity that became available after my dismissal from the employ of the insurance company was as an usher at the Center Theater in Manhattan where a live ice show, "Howdy, Mr. Ice," was being performed on stage for most of the year. In the off-season months, the theater presented ballet and opera performances.

The Center Theater, which later closed to become an NBC Television Studio, was located on Sixth Avenue and 50th Street, one block from the Radio City Music Hall. It was part of the Rockefeller Center complex. All of the buildings in this group were connected through a maze of underground passageways that reminded me of the Catacombs. This complex underground passage was our usual route to the theater and the usher's dressing room. We had to be cleared by a guard at the door before entering.

We were required to wear uniforms and were expected to purchase and provide our own, clean, white gloves at all performances, which were presented every night except Mondays, with matinees on Wednesday, Saturday, and Sunday afternoons. During Christmas week, there were two performances every day and these were always "Standing Room Only". (They actually did sell tickets to patrons to stand in the rear of the orchestra when all the seats were full.)

The wage for this position was one dollar per hour, twice as much as the fifty cents an hour prevailing wage that was being paid for most theater ushering jobs.

Several of my neighborhood and school friends were already working at the Center Theater including; Bill Griffin, who was the Assistant Head Usher at the Center, Marty Bowman who was a doorman because of his six and a half foot height, and a few others from our local gang. Mr. Ward was the Head Usher and ran the staff like a martinet and was very easily disliked. When he was off for a performance, Bill would take his place as headman. When he did, he tried to emulate Mr. Ward and was successful in not only aping his autocratic behavior but also exceeded him in being a real son-of-a-bitch; this did not endear him to his neighborhood buddies.

(Perhaps this was Bill's payback for a practical joke played on him by one of the boys. Bill was noted for being a penny-pinching tightwad who was never willing to share with the boys. If he bought some candy, for instance, he would hide somewhere to eat it alone so he wouldn't have to offer a piece to anyone. Yet, he was always the first one in line to mooch from the rest of us.

One day, one of the guys took an empty Baby Ruth bar wrapper and put an appropriately shaped dog turd from the street into the wrapper. When he pretended to be about to take a bite from the bar, Bill was right there ready to beg a bite, which was readily given. Without hesitation he bit into the bar and was soon running home for some mouthwash. We roared at that one but it still did not deter Bill from further mooching.)

At the theater, before each performance we were required to line up in the locker room in military fashion for an inspection; shined shoes, clean gloves, clean uniform, and no white socks. We were given our assignments for that performance and then were marched up the stairs and into the theater where we would be dispersed to our appointed posts.

The assignments were either as an usher to direct the patrons to their seats or as an elevator operator; there were elevators for the patrons to take them to one of the four levels of seating or a backstage elevator that was used to rapidly move the cast for costume changes between acts. The featured star skaters and performers had dressing rooms on the stage level, the second level was for the female chorus, and the third level for the men's chorus.

Running the backstage elevator was considered one of the plum jobs even though there were no tips to be had. Because of the tight scheduling of acts and the need for quick costume changes, the chorus would be removing their clothes from the time they got off the stage and continue on the elevator. The elevators had no push-button controls to command the desired floor and were manually controlled with a wheel on the sidewall. The speed of the elevator was controlled by the usher/operator and it was not uncommon for the elevator to take a long time to get to the second floor when carrying a carload of beautiful, naked and near naked women.

The ushering job was very active during the time that the patrons were arriving. They would be escorted by the usher to their seats and handed the playbill for that performance. Although tipping was absolutely forbidden and cause for immediate dismissal, we all accepted any tips proffered by the patron, being very careful not to be observed by the Manager, Mr. Ward, or, especially Bill Griffin, who loved to play the part of snitch.

The white gloves we used were buttoned in the palm leaving a small opening. This opening provided an excellent foil for slipping the coins into, to be secreted into a trouser pocket when the opportunity presented itself. We devised a technique of passing the program to the patron and surreptitiously letting the coin drop into the palm of the program passing hand. The tips we received were usually five or ten cents, with a major tip being a quarter and, on rare occasions, a dollar. One night, one of the ushers received a ten-dollar tip, equivalent to ten hours of work. At the end of a week, the tips would often exceed our pay.

After all of the people were seated and the show was underway, we would be required to stand at attention at the exit from the auditorium until intermission time or the end of the show. Mr. Ward would make regular rounds to assure that we were not sitting or slouching on the job. This was the dullest part of the evening. I eventually developed the ability to close my eyes and sleep standing at attention at the door.

A day I will never forget is the day I met Primo Carnera, former Heavyweight boxing champion of the world, who was long retired from the boxing business and was currently a professional wrestler. Carnera had taken the title from Jack Sharkey about ten years before and held it for a year before handing it over to Max Baer.

I was on duty outside one of the doors to the orchestra seats, standing at attention and waiting for the next patrons to usher to their seats. I had a view of the entrance where Marty Bowman was the doorman. Two men and two women were entering the theater, each of them about the same height as Marty, about six and a half feet tall. The unusual height of the five titans at the door didn't register with me because all of them were about the same height, until they came up to me at my station.

The manager joined them as they came into the lobby and after exchanging pleasantries with them for a few minutes brought them to me to be seated. The manager introduced me to the tallest of the group; it was "Da Preem", Primo Carnera himself. I shook his hand, which was the largest hand I have ever seen. The width of his hand from palm to back was about as thick as my own hand was from side to side. He wore size 22 shoes and his shoulders looked like they wouldn't fit through the double doors into the auditorium.

I was surprised when he said to me, "Hey kid, you got any Wop in de orkes'tra?" I didn't know whether he was referring to the band or to the orchestra seats, but I replied, "Oh! We let anyone in if they have a ticket." I showed them to their seats and received no tip.

Another interesting aspect of working at the Center Theater was that I got to meet a lot of homosexuals, or as we called them at the time, 'queers'. Although most of the stars with billing were apparently heterosexual, most of the male chorus was queer (gay at the time meaning happy or merry.) All of the girl's in the chorus were straight, as far as I knew.

Many of the ushers were aspiring young actors, who worked at the theater because it was night work and gave them the opportunity to audition during the day while maintaining some kind of employment. Most of these, I would venture to say, were also attracted to their own sex; it seems endemic to the acting breed.

As a rule they did not bother with any of the rest of the staff at the theater and pretty much kept their activities amongst themselves. One night while I was operating the theater elevator during a performance, Julio, one of the ushers and the younger of two Cuban brothers who worked at the theater while waiting for an acting call, entered the elevator and asked me to take him to one of the other floors. He stood behind me as I turned the wheel to start the elevator up. When we were between floors, he hit a switch on the control panel that immediately stopped the elevator.

As I turned around to confront him, he said in his thick Hispanic accent, "Would you like to eat zees." He had his penis out of his pants and had an erection that appeared to stand rigidly outward about ten to twelve inches. I was appalled. I clenched my left hand into a fist and pushed it into his face and said, "How would you like to eat a knuckle sandwich?" I was tempted to give his protuberance a good whack with the index and middle finger, but I didn't when I realized that he might really enjoy it.

I pushed him back, started the elevator, and told him to get off at the next floor. I didn't relate this episode to anyone at the time because I felt violated and ashamed by Julio's despicable behavior. He never tried it with me again, although I understand he did make advances at some of the other ushers from time to time.

It was during the time that I was ushering at the Center, at the ripe old age of sixteen, that I first started regularly drinking at a neighborhood bar. Ronnie Fisher came to us one day and said that he had discovered a bar on

46th Street at Northern Boulevard where they served youngsters without requiring proof of age; the legal drinking age at the time was eighteen. We started to make a regular thing of the "Dugout" (It was located below ground level and the entry was down about ten steps from the street.)

Although the bar was fully stocked with the usual rotgut liquors, the only thing served was beer at ten cents a glass and an occasional shot of whisky such as Four Roses or Fleischman's.

We spent that New Year's Eve at the Dugout. This was the first time that I saw women at this bar when some of the regulars brought their wives for a *grandiose* night out. I noticed that Bill, the regular bartender, was in a state of confusion when one of the women asked him for a Tom Collins. He was searching frantically for his recipe book to tell him how to make it, never having served anything but a beer or a shot in this joint..

It was at the Dugout that I became proficient at the game of table shuffleboard, which we would play every night for beers. The challenge would be posted on the board and the challenging twosome would play the winner of the previous game. There were too many nights when I did so well at shuffleboard that I was obliged to drink too many beers with the consequence of getting sick and throwing up before going home. When I did get home it took a while to get to sleep. It was difficult sleeping on a bed that was continuously rolling like a ship in a storm.

We introduced "Moose" Massella to the dugout. He was one of our fellow ushers at the Center and lived in The Bronx. (Always "The Bronx" and not just "Bronx.") Moose was a big guy, strong and tough; but was a real gentle soul; or so we thought. After having worked with him for a few months, he asked us if we would like to join him in the Bronx for a gang fight that was about to happen in his neighborhood. We initially accepted his offer and looked forward to a good gang war, which in our neighborhood usually involved fists or nothing more than a baseball bat.

On the day of the planned skirmish, something came up to prevent us from joining Moose in the Bronx. The following day, the front page of the Daily News had a picture of our "gentle" friend Moose being arrested by the police. The 'small' gang fight turned out to be a major war with hundreds of teenagers amassed on each side of the battle. Moose was the leader of one of the largest gangs in the Bronx and was identified by the newspaper as "General" Massella. There were some casualties that night from knife or gun wounds, but I don't think that anyone was killed.

The opposing sides did not only have clubs and bats, but were also carrying knives, chains, and loaded weapons, including "Zip" guns and a few pistols. I never found out the end of that story because Moose never returned to work and we lost track of him. I was so glad that we never did make our appointment that day.

Work and drinking and getting into trouble were not the only things we did. Since our first day at high school and our introduction to basketball, that sport became one of our obsessions; usually half court with three against three. We would play during the day and, at the 30th Road Park where the streetlights partially illuminated the basketball court, we would play into the night.

Another nighttime activity, when the police rousted us from the closed park, was sit-up and pushup contests. We would take turns doing pushups with each guy adding one pushup to the last count when it was his turn. I was often a laggard in the pushup competition but was always a prime contender with the sit-ups, having developed pretty firm *abs*. When we finished our show of muscle development we quite often would sit on the park steps and sing the latest songs, serenading the neighbors who were not always appreciative of our fine singing, as it would grow louder and louder as the night went on; most of us being competitive even in our harmonizing.

(Just before leaving for a hitch in the Navy one of the popular tunes of the day was "Goodnight, Irene". Across the street from my house was a newly married couple and the very attractive bride's name was Irene. We would sit on the stoop across from her house and sing "her song" to her.)

It's a good thing we kept in good physical condition then for hardly a week went by without a good fight. Some of these fights I should have avoided.

The park at 30th Road was built on two levels; the lower level was where the children's playground was located and the upper level was where the ball fields, basketball courts, and handball courts were. One summer day we were playing a game of "o'cat", where two or three players were at bat and the rest of the players were in the field. When a batter made out, he was required to take the field and one player from the field would become a batter. The fielders would then rotate position.

Marilyn Ryan (my someday to be sister-in-law) was on the swings at the lower level talking to a girl friend and a powerful looking young man; large and intimidating. Whoever was playing second base, with a good view of the swings, was hurling insults at Marilyn below. When the remarks became too offensive, Marilyn asked the guy with her to go up to the field and beat up the guy on second base who was taunting her, which he very gallantly proceeded to do.

While he was walking up the steps, a batter made out and the fielders rotated positions; I went to second base. When the avenger reached the field, he immediately came out to second base and confronted me thinking that it was I that was affronting Marilyn. Never being one to avoid a fight when challenged, I immediately jumped at the chance to *teach* this interloper a lesson, even though he had about fifty pounds and a few inches on me. We started to square off and I gave him two quick jabs to the face, which he warded off like pesky flies. I followed up with my best straight right that landed in the middle of his head between the eyes.

He didn't budge an inch, while my right hand felt like it had hit a brick wall and was useless for any more punching that day. He still hadn't thrown a punch. I gave him a left hook to the mid-section with my whole body behind it; he didn't even flinch and just looked at me as my hand sunk a good three inches into his well padded belly.

I then gave it my best shot, a good left hook to the jaw; same reaction - nothing, except another hand put out of action. At this point, I was wishing I was back at third base where I had been just minutes ago. Then I saw it coming and couldn't get out of the way in time; a fist coming right at the center of my face. It caught me on the nose with the full force of nearly two hundred pounds. My knees buckled and I hit the ground with the back of my head as I wondered, "Where's the mule that just kicked me in the face?"

I was carried down to the park house where they called an ambulance. My nose was bleeding profusely and I was completely in a daze. I had attempted to throw myself back into the fight but cooler heads prevailed and I was pulled off. I thought that I was going blind as both eyes started to swell shut.

The emergency crew from a local hospital came and tended me on the spot and sent me home, suggesting that I go to the hospital to be checked out for a broken nose. I ignored the recommendation and the nose eventually healed.

The guy who hit me was Russ Hess, who was known as "Moose" (yes! another Moose) because of his imposing size. Russ was later to marry Kay Manning, sister of Kieran Manning, and I would run into them at a Rambler's weekend celebration in the late 90's. He said he doesn't recall the incident. (Hell! why should he? I never put a dent in him and he nearly killed me with one punch) The later Russ was so gentle and kind that it was hard to believe that he was the guy who trounced me that day in the park with one punch.

Before I returned to school at Bryant High, I determined that some of that fighting energy might be put to better use by participating in some organized boxing activity. I signed up to fight in the Golden Gloves run by the Daily News each year. We had attended several of these tournaments with the finals at Madison Square Garden and I was convinced that with my experience at street brawling (excluding, of course, the Moose Hess fiasco) I had a shot at the title. This met with the usual derision from my buddies who made such comments as, "Ha! If you win even one bout, we'll all be entering next year." Needless to say that after my first win there was no mad rush from any of them to get in the ring.

Even though I weighed about 155 pounds at the time, I decided to enter the 147 pound (Welterweight) Class; Sub-Novice - no sanctioned fights under the A.A.U. auspices (Amateur Athletic Union). Fighters with prior experience were classified in the Open Class. I felt that I could get down to the required weight by the time of the finals. The officials were not too concerned about the weight in the early stages and the tolerance on being over weight was three pounds for the quarterfinals, two pounds for the semi-finals, and one pound for the finals.

The first milestone after filing the application with the Daily News was a physical examination, which was given at the old Daily News Building on 42nd Street in New York. I showed up for this exam in the early evening of one of the coldest days in memory. When we arrived we were directed to strip naked and hang our clothes in the assigned place. The windows were open and the wind was blowing in the ice-cold winter air. All of us had goose pimples where we never had goose pimples before.

We were given the usual checks of the heart, eyes, ears, throat, groin, etc., but the most unforgettable moment came when we were directed to bend over and the next thing we felt, as we stood there with our bare butts shining in the night, was a cold icy finger penetrating the rectum as we all recoiled from the shock of the sudden intrusion.

Having successfully passed the physical, my next task was to obtain my A.A.U. card followed by getting myself properly equipped for our first bout. We were told that we had to have an athletic supporter with a protective cup or we would not be permitted into the ring. (When the contestants get into the ring, I had always noticed that the referee would tap each of them on the crotch. I had thought that referees might be a bit pedophilic but I found out that they were just assuring that the cups were in place.)

I went to Davega's Sporting Goods on Steinway Street to purchase what would be my first athletic supporter, never having felt a need for one in the past, even for some of the other contact sports we were involved in. An attractive young lady waited on me. She was very helpful and unthreatening until she asked me what size "jock" I needed. I stammered a bit and said, "Er, er, Large, I guess." She looked me right in the eyes with those two piercing orbs of hers and replied as she dropped her eyes to my crotch, "Kinda proud of yourself, aren't you, Sonny?"

I must have turned crimson and could only stammer some more, "Well, maybe a medium." She got me the appropriate size and I was happy to get on to less embarrassing items. I purchased a pair of boxing shoes and socks, boxing trunks, and a mouthpiece. With the tournament providing the robe, I was all prepared for the big fight - except, how about training and giving up smoking, and, on fight night, a cornerman.

With my heavy schedule of work, evening activities, and playing shuffleboard at the Dugout, I didn't find any time to start properly training for the first fight that was rapidly approaching. After much procrastination, I went to the Long Island City Athletic Club in Astoria to inquire about using their facilities for training for the upcoming fight. Until this time, I was fighting "unattached"' (to any organization such as the P.A.L. or the C.Y.O.) The manager of the club permitted me to use the facility if I fought under the banner of the Long Island City Athletic Club, which I readily agreed to. A further stipulation was that I provide my own trainer and cornerman for the fight.

I told Daddy about my new attachment and he suggested that I get his friend and co-worker at the North Shore Fuel Oil Company, Al **Minuscolo**, to act as my trainer. Al had some prior experience in the ring and as a trainer and cornerman. Al agreed to handle me and we set a time for going to the gym to start training the next Saturday - two days before my first fight.

I arrived at the gym on Saturday and met Al for the first time. He was very short and small bodied; about five foot two. (Must have fought as a Flyweight) He directed me to get into my gear and meet him in the gym. The gym was small; the width of the building barely accommodated the ring with about a two-foot aisle on each side between the ring and the sidewalls. If you got knocked out of the ring on either side, you would bounce back into the ring off the wall.

The gym was equipped with warm-up weights, heavy punching bags, speed bags, jump ropes, and the necessary gloves and head protectors; not Stillman's Gym but perfectly adequate for our purposes.

There were about twenty boxers of different sizes already in the gym who were also signed up to fight in the "Gloves". In the next few weeks I would spend a lot of time with these boxers - with many of them in the ring.

The first thing that Al asked me to do was to go outside and run around the corner about twenty times to warm up.. I went out into the cold, winter day (It was January of 1949) and did as I was told. By the time I finished twenty laps around the block, I was gasping for breath and freezing my butt off. I made a firm resolution at that point to give up smoking for the rest of my boxing career.

I entered the gym, thankful for the warm air, and was immediately told by Al that he wanted to "work" me on some of the equipment "to see what I could do." He handed me the jump rope and told me to start jumping in three-minute segments. (The usual time for a round of boxing in a professional match; we would be fighting two-minute rounds in the Gloves.) I started to skip rope with my arms spinning like a windmill, hands and arms making a wide circle. Al shot at me, "What the hell are ya? A goil? That's the way goils skip rope, wit' the arms swingin' around like a perpeller. Ya gotta keep ya hands at yer side and just let the wrist do the movin.'"

I tried several times to do as he asked before I finally started to get the technique down. After he thought I had it down, he said to do three rounds without missing a beat. I did this pretty well and even started to do some hand crossovers. Although I was still a little short on the breathing and knew that I needed a lot of conditioning, I was beginning to feel like a boxer.

We did some time on the heavy bag, with Al trying to teach me some of the fundamentals. The first and most important thing was the stance; keeping the hands and arms up to protect the face and body and to have the body aligned and ready to swing or maneuver. I am a natural left-hander and my instinctive posture was always to jab with the right hand with the left hand held back for the coup-de-grace. Al persuaded me that I would be at a big disadvantage to continue fighting this way and had me switch to a right-handed stance. It felt unnatural and I hoped that working on it would help me.

I did some pushups and sit-ups, lifting of some weights, a little shadow boxing, and was then asked to sit and rest for a few minutes while Al found someone to do some live sparring with me in the ring. Nick Gianakis, another Welterweight, and someone I knew from the neighborhood, volunteered. I remembered him as a bit of a bully in the streets as well as being a bit of a strutting peacock; he felt that his "experience" in the ring made him one of the neighborhood toughs.

I was given a head protector and a pair of sixteen-ounce training gloves that I put on after Al taped my hands. I entered the ring, my first time inside a regulation size ring. I began to feel like a real pugilist. I had watched so much boxing on television and at the Long Island Arena and Sunnyside Gardens on amateur night that being in the ring myself gave me a feeling that I had at last arrived at one of my life's goals.

I looked across the ring at Nick, who was flexing his well-defined muscles and doing deep knee bends to loosen up. I was anxious to start the sparring, suddenly realizing that I only had today and tomorrow to get myself into some kind of shape for Monday night's scheduled fight in Brooklyn. Al told me to get ready to go at the bell; someone was keeping the time on the rounds. We would be doing three minute rounds with a one minute break in between.

The bell rang. I quickly moved to the center of the ring with full confidence that I could handle Nick the way I had so often done in the streets. I was on my toes as I was told to do and had my hands and arms set in a right-handed position for the first time in a fight. I rapidly threw two left jabs that Nick bobbed away from with ease, returning several rapid jabs that stopped me in my tracks. I slid to the side and avoided a quick straight right but walked into a sharp left hook that twisted my headgear ninety degrees around my head so that I was now peering with one eye through the ear air hole.

Fortunately for me the headgear was askew because Nick quickly followed with another straight right that caught me right in the middle of the face, now protected with the side of the headgear. I called a quick time out to get a better fitting headgear. When this was done we started anew.

We went three rounds and I managed to slip away from most of Nick's punches but found it difficult to throw the punches while I was cautiously running away. I could hear Al yelling from the side of the ring to get in and mix it up. At the end of each round I was huffing and puffing for air and realized that I was in terrible shape to enter the ring in earnest in only two days.

When the first day's workout was ended, Al gave me a good rubdown with Witch Hazel mixed with a small amount of Oil of Wintergreen. I was so sore from the day's activities that the massage felt like a godsend and made all the work worth the effort. I hadn't done well for the day, but I thought I didn't do too badly. Probably the worst part of the experience was having Nick Gianakis lord it over me. He told me I should hang up the gloves now because I wasn't going anywhere while he was going to make it to the finals at Madison Square Garden. I was too sore and too tired to argue with him.

Early Sunday morning, I followed Al's instructions and ran the streets for about an hour and a half before going to the gym for my second and final workout before my debut. Al showed up again and put me through a pretty rigorous routine, finishing up with about six or seven rounds of sparring with another one of the fighters, this time a middleweight with whom I had a good workout. By the end of the day, I was beginning to feel a return of the confidence that was worked out of me on Saturday.

On Monday I packed up my gear in my gym bag and went to the Church of the Little Flower in Brooklyn where I would fight my first bout. There were sixteen bouts scheduled on the card when I arrived and I was on for the fourteenth bout of the evening. Mother and Daddy both attended the fight with me and, surprisingly, Mother was the biggest rooter and cheered me on from beginning to end, while Daddy sat in the seat and was worried about my performance through the entire bout. When it comes to serious fighting the women are sometimes more bloodthirsty than the men.

My trainer Al advised me to take it slow. He said that in most of these amateur fights, the participants try to throw too many punches in the early part of the first round and become arm weary and have nothing left for the later rounds. He told me to hold back and let my opponent wear himself out and I could make my move in the second round.

I had to sit around for two hours in the dressing room before I was called to enter the arena for my fight. When I did get called, I went down the aisle to ringside and had to sit there until three fights scheduled before me were completed. The first one was Nick Gianakis facing off against an Irish lad representing the Department of Parks. It was a lackluster fight with each of the fighters doing more dancing and side stepping than punching. It lasted for the full three two minute rounds with the decision going to Nick. I said to myself that I couldn't let Nick be a winner and not I.

The next fight was a three round decision followed by an overweight young welterweight who I had been observing in the dressing room. We had been advised to avoid eating anything for several hours prior to the bout, an admonition I followed faithfully. Mr. Chubby, however, was continuously eating while he was waiting for his turn in the ring. He ate at least two hot dogs and a couple of candy bars.

When he entered the ring he played the role as if he had been there a hundred times; being a sub-novice like me this was his first fight. He pranced around on his toes and played to the crowd with what was probably his family rooting him on vociferously. When the bell rang he came out of his corner with such a big grin on his face that you could see his gleaming mouthpiece under the overhead lights. He threw several punches in the air before his opponent hit him with an uppercut that caught him on the jaw as he was slipping off his feet. He landed on his rear but his unbalance took most of the steam out of the blow and he quickly got up before the start of the count.

He and his opponent danced around for a short while before a hard punch caught him in the stomach. At this point, he vomited all over the ring as he tried to back away. Another punch caught him on the side of the head and he fell to the canvas into a pool of half digested frankfurters and candy bars. The referee, trying to avoid slipping on the wet canvas, started the count, but took one look at the poor wretch on the canvas, saw the pallid appearance and blank stare in his eyes and called a halt to the fight in 1:41 of the first round.

I had to wait about fifteen minutes after this fight while they cleaned, washed, and dried the ring. I climbed into the ring and wiped my shoes in the resin box outside the ring before climbing through the ropes. I could feel the adrenalin starting to flow as soon as I entered the ring. I had been very calm up until this point, but when I heard the hungry crowd and could discern Mother's cheers through the din, I asked myself, "What the hell are you doing here, you nut?"

I looked across the ring to size up my opponent, James Smith of the Police Athletic League (P.A.L.). Smith was a well-built black fellow who was apparently well trained. He bounced in his corner while throwing shorts punches into the air. His biceps and triceps were bulging out of his arms and the sheen of his black skin made his whole body seem like a cobra ready to strike. When he turned around I noticed that his stomach was like a washboard and that there was not an ounce of fat on his well-muscled body. I knew I was in for a battle tonight.

We were called to the center of the ring where the referee gave us our last minute instructions while tapping us in the crotch to make sure we both had our protective cup on. We shook hands as directed and went back to our corner to wait for the bell.

Just before the bell for the start of the first round, Al reminded me to reserve my punches and just try to feel out Smith and not to punch myself out. I followed Al's instructions but Smith had other ideas. He came out like a man possessed. I quickly felt multiple left jabs to the face as I tried to dance around while keeping my own left flitting toward his face. Smith followed with a barrage of quick punches, lefts and rights, jabs, hooks, and uppercuts. I bobbed and weaved away from most of these punches but enough hit me that I was beginning to feel the sting of the blows on my stomach, my chest, and most often, on my face.

I was tempted to fight the way I did in the street, just go for broke and give it all you've got, but I kept hearing Al's voice saying, "Take your time, take your time." By the end of the first two minutes, I was grateful to hear the sound of the bell to stop this madman from pummeling me with so many punches. I was beginning to ache and wondering again, "What the hell are you doing here."

Al encouraged me to start punching in the next round. When Smith came off his stool at the sound of the bell for the second round, he didn't seem to have as much bounce as he did at the start of the fight. I danced out quickly and was bouncing on my toes to show him that I was not as fatigued as he was; even though I felt that it might be time to quit. I started to jab quickly and followed up with a left hook and a straight right that caught him off guard. He tried to fight back, but Al's plan obviously had merit. I could notice the sag in his arms and the lack of sting to any of his punches; he was, indeed, arm weary, while I felt raring to go.

I heard Al yelling, "Take your time, take your time." I followed his instructions again and just danced around and threw enough punches to clinch the round, throwing a few into Smith's arms to further weaken them. I felt confident and good when the bell ended the round.

The third round was a repeat of the second round, except I was more aggressive and Smith was more tired. The bell rang ending the third round and the fight. We returned to our corners and awaited the decision. When the emcee announced my victory by a decision, I could hear Mother's loud cheer through the roar of the crowd that had appreciated this hard fought bout.

After a shower in the dressing room, I looked at my naked body in the full-length mirror. My face, my chest, and my stomach were crimson from the many blows I took in the first round. The following day, this would all be black and blue so that I resembled my opponent. I'm sure whatever bruises I may have given him weren't as obvious as my bruised face, chest, stomach and arms. If anyone saw me, they would have thought that it was I who had lost the fight.

Now that I had one successful bout under my belt the attitude of the neighborhood gang took on a different tone. I gained some respect for the fight I put on, especially against someone who was apparently well trained while I was just beginning to go to the gym. I enjoyed the notoriety while it lasted.

The victory in my first foray into the ring gave me the motivation to go on a regular schedule at the gym. I worked hard for the next two weeks before my next scheduled appearance. During this time Al had me doing constantly increasing exercises both in and out of the ring. Before this phase of the training ended, I was sparring up to twenty rounds a session and was doing roadwork at the break of dawn each day for about two hours. My breath control was getting better and I felt the muscles shaping up.

My second round bout was fought at Ridgewood Grove, an arena that was the venue for many professional fights. My opponent was another fighter from the P.A.L., Al Mazzei, who was coming off a win on the same night as my last fight. He stopped his opponent in that fight in 44 seconds of the first round.

I first saw Mazzei while he was warming up in the locker room. He was shorter than me but was built like the proverbial "brick shit-house." I didn't let this bother me and just repeated the routine that I developed before the first fight; while others warmed up and danced around, I sat or lay down to relax in the dressing room to get myself psychologically prepared for the bout. I would do some brief shadow boxing just before entering the arena to loosen up.

I entered the auditorium just as the bell rang for the first round of the next bout being fought at that time. As I walked down the aisle, I recognized one of the fighters in the ring as my new nemesis, Nick Gianakis. His opponent rushed out of the corner and with three quick jabs to the face, a left hook, and a right cross followed by a powerful uppercut to the jaw; put Gianakis on the canvas for a full count of ten and a knockout in 32 seconds. I was stunned (and so was Gianakis, I would wager) by the sudden ending to the fight.

As Gianakis lay on his back in the ring, I thought about the two additional times I sparred with him in the last two weeks. The first time was about five rounds of dancing and light punches with no heavy-duty fisticuffs. The second time, Gianakis tried to rough it up a bit so we both let loose with a barrage of punches. I avoided most of his and managed to get in some solid shots of my own until I knocked him flat on his back, the way he was lying in the ring here at Ridgewood. I was wondering whether he would try to excuse his quick loss tonight as he did the knockdowns in the gym.

The next fight, the last before my turn in the ring, was another fast, first round knockout. I tried not to let this be an omen of the next fight, unless it was I on the delivering end.

My trainer, Al, again advised me to take it easy in the first round and not to punch myself out. He didn't know it at the time, but with very little effort, I didn't get a chance to throw too many punches whether I wanted to or not. When the bell rang for that first round, Mazzei came charging out of his corner like a raging bull. I was ready to start jabbing and dancing around to feel him out, but he came on with such fury that I couldn't stop all of the powerful punches that were pouring in on me and couldn't back off fast enough. Now a punch to the mid-section; next to the chest; left and right fists to the head.

I was dazed almost from the first punch. I tried to dance away but Mazzei kept coming forward with his fists constantly in motion to make contact with my body or face. When I tried to clinch, he pummeled me on the inside. I refused to go down even though common sense dictated a hasty end to this slaughter. I did manage to back off when Mazzei slowed slightly in his attack, but with that short respite he immediately recommenced the barrage.

The bell rang to end the round. I thought that I had been in the ring for ten minutes. I had never experienced such a flurry of keen, hard punching in all of my street battles and my short experience in the ring. However, if Al's theory held, Mazzei would be punched out in the next round and it would be my turn to turn the contest around.

The referee came to my corner between the rounds and said to me as I sat on the stool, "Are you all right, kid?" Al shot back at him, "He's all right, no problem." The ref said, "I'm askin' the kid, not you, let him speak for himself." I told the ref in panting breath, "I'm okay." He asked me my name and I told him. (I hope I gave him the right answer.)

The second round started and Mazzei again came charging out like a bull, and again, his fists came in with as much power as in the first round. Evidently, he was better trained as his arms were still functioning at full capacity. I did manage this time to dance away with a little more finesse. This gave me adequate time to clear my head for a moment. This let-up in the torrent of blows gave me the opportunity to start my own offensive with a couple of quick jabs that took Mazzei by surprise. I crouched forward and brought up a right uppercut to Mazzei's jaw that took his feet off the floor as his mouthpiece went flying directly up into the overhead lights.

He lay there on his back without moving. For an instant, I thought I might have killed him; he was so still. The referee pushed me into a neutral corner as I smiled out at the crowd; I knew this contest was over. The referee counted Mazzei out in 1 minute and 20 seconds of the second round. Mazzei still did not move as his seconds jumped into the ring to help him. When Mazzei still didn't move after what seemed a very long time, the doctor jumped into the ring to help revive him. It was about ten minutes before they brought Mazzei to and were able to proceed with the remaining two or three bouts left on the card. I remained in the ring for the entire time to make sure that Mazzei was okay.

Mother and Daddy were there again to witness this fight, Mother asked me to quit fighting because my father couldn't take the excitement. She told me that he was in a sweat, breathing heavily, and with his heart pounding wildly in his chest as Mazzei mauled me in the first round.

This didn't stop Daddy from taking advantage of his bragging rights when we returned to Astoria after the fight and went to the bar across the street from the Long Island City Athletic clubhouse. The bar was filled with many well-wishers who had been at the fight. Some of the characters who showed up were professional managers, promoters, and other hangers on. They were full of praise and pats on the back, and offers to take me over if I turned professional. I was heady with the mini-glory that evening, as I gloated about Nick Gianakis'

32-second knockout and my own come-from-behind triumph. I was especially proud of all these wonderful newfound "friends" that I made that evening.

I was really on a cloud when the Daily News came out in the morning with a brief description of the fight:

...The most startling performance was turned in by John O'Leary, Long Island City AA. O'Leary took a severe first-round pummeling from Al Mazzei, who kept dishing it out at the start of the second. The referee was ready to step in and stop it when O'Leary launched a right from the floor flush to Mazzei's chin. Mazzei fell flat on his back.

And the Long Island Star-Journal:

John O'Leary of the Long Island City Athletic got by second round of the welterweight division by knocking out Albert Mazzei of the PAL. O'Leary hammered Mazzei into submission with a right and left to the head.

They were the things to swell a young boy's head and make him feel like the cock of the walk. I enjoyed the moment.

My next fight, about a week later, was at a place called Pier Six along the waterfront in Staten Island. This was quite a distance to travel for a fight and I had to attend alone; Mother and Daddy couldn't make it nor could my trusty trainer, Al. I had to rely upon someone at the arena to agree to act as my cornerman that night.

When I finished work downtown at five o'clock, I paid the nickel fare and took the ferry from the Battery to Staten Island. There I caught a bus that left me right outside the arena. I checked in and found out that I was bout number 24 of 26 bouts to be fought that evening. This schedule worked for me because I wasn't too anxious to get right in and fight as I was suffering from three large boils on the back of my neck that Mother had medicated and bandaged before I left home that morning. I didn't feel that the boils would be an impediment to my fighting unless my opponent decided to get me into a headlock.

I found a cot in the dressing area and went through my regular routine as I awaited my turn in the ring; I lay down and tried to get some sleep as it was going to be a long wait for bout number 24.

It was well after midnight when I finally stepped into the ring. My opponent was a guy named Turner Thatcher who was coming off three wins by early round knockouts. He was quite formidable looking and I was convinced that he should have been fighting in the light-heavyweight ranks. He hopped gingerly into the ring and gave me the impression of being very comfortable in this milieu and very businesslike, no stranger to the ring.

The bell brought us both to the center of the ring. I was ready to follow the now familiar pattern of carrying the fight to my opponent to let him punch himself out before I started my lethal onslaught. Tonight, however, would be different. I wouldn't give Thatcher a chance to get arm weary, but not because of any intention of mine.

He rushed out with such speed and started throwing punches with such precision that I was rapidly knocked senseless. I had enough time to throw a half dozen ineffective punches but it was obvious that I was seriously outclassed by this boxing machine. The referee stepped in and halted the fight in 43 seconds of the first round. I didn't object and there was no friendly assistance from my corner to protest this stopping of the fight.

In retrospect, the referee did the right thing to avoid what could have been a permanently damaging night for me.

As I left the ring, I was approached by a young man with a familiar face. It was Al Mazzei, who I had just knocked out at the Ridgewood Grove. He told me that he had come to see me fight because he didn't feel that after standing up to the beating that he had laid on me that I would ever lay down for anyone. I didn't go down, but I did lose in quick time. I was only thankful that it wasn't less than the 32 seconds that Nick Gianakis lasted.

Turner Thatcher made it to the final rounds of the tournament with a couple of additional early round knockouts. He finally lost the decision in a hard fought battle to the eventual Champion, Eppie Alonzo, one of the top amateur fighters of the day. I took some comfort in having lasted three fights against such formidable competition.

I made my way home in the wee hours of the morning, about a two-hour trek by bus, ferry, and subway. I was so engrossed with the solitude and events of the evening that I didn't realize how hungry I was, not having eaten since before noon of the day before. I waited to eat until I returned home with the bad news of tonight's loss in Staten Island.

My biggest disappointment from this experience in the Golden Gloves was not the loss of that one fight, but the realization that many of the relationships in life are only transient and not to be relied upon. This was the first, but not the last time that this aspect of life would be apparent to me, even to this day. The many supporters when I was a winner had suddenly vanished just because I lost one fight.

I continued for quite a while to train at the Long Island City Athletic Club and enjoyed many rounds of sparring with many good fighters in the ring there, but I was never to step into a ring inside a crowded arena again. It was fun for a time, but my exposure to some of the people who had fought too many fights and wound up punch drunk discouraged me from making a career out of boxing. This was a smart move, as I would have wound up rocking on my heels and slurring my speech like most of the pugs in the business.

Street fighting was not only common in Astoria; it had also become a way of life. After my brief foray into the world of organized boxing, three fights in the Golden Gloves, I was marked by some "fast guns" (or fast fists) in the neighborhood as a target of opportunity to be challenged because of the notoriety recently garnered in the newspapers.

One of those confrontations came, not from one, but two boys from 44th Street. They were twins, Billy and Bobby, whose last name I don't recall. Each of them was taller than I, and had about twenty pounds on me. I would not have intentionally entertained fighting either one of them; they were both solidly built and were tough.

Billy confronted me on the street and without reason or provocation started to aggressively poke me in the chest with his forefinger while accusing me of having affronted him in some way. This was just a pretext to goad me into swinging at him and starting a fight that he had calculated would end with my relenting.

Never hesitant to answer a call to defend my reputation, I first asked Billy to back off before he got his ass kicked in, knowing full well that saying this would only antagonize him. His insistent provocation impelled me to haul off with a few rapid punches that caught him so off guard that he fell back on his buttocks. As he attempted to get up, I gave him a few more clouts before he got off the ground.

When his brother, Bobby realized that Billy was about to receive a few more well placed blows and, perhaps, a kick, he jumped on my back as I leaned over to hit Billy again. Before Bobby could clamp a tight grip on me that I may not have been able to break away from, I slipped quickly out of his grasp and turned to deliver a quick left hook to his head. As I went to throw a right hand to his face, I grasped his shirt with my left hand and gave him a right to the face. As he fell away from the force of the blow, his shirt ripped off and I was left holding his shirt in my hand.

I alternately hit Billy and Bobby until they both quit and ran for home, Bobby with his shirt now lying on the ground.

Within the hour, after I had gone home to clean up after this melee, the doorbell rang at the house and Daddy went to the door to see who was there. Billy and Bobby, led by their father, were coming up the stairs where the father started to bellow at Daddy for my "picking on" his sons and ripping the shirt off one of them.

Daddy looked at the swollen and battered faces of the two bullies and told the father that the two boys were big enough to take care of themselves and impatiently asked them all to get out.

When he came back into the house, I thought he was going to lay into me for the scrap with these two mugs, but all he did (and somewhat in jest) was to tell me to stop fighting with the neighborhood kids and that he didn't want anymore of the fathers coming to complain to him. After his gentle scolding, he tapped me gently on the head, which I took as sign of his approval and that he was quietly proud of my having taken on these two brutes. They never bothered me again.

My brother Bob recently recounted an episode that occurred on the street adjacent to the 30th Road Park. Tommy Egan, a young lad, who lived directly across from us, was playing with a Hi-Li on the sidewalk alongside the park. (A Hi-Li was a paddle with a soft, sponge rubber ball attached to it with an elastic rubber band)

While Tommy was hitting the ball with the paddle, a passing car stopped and an enraged driver came storming out accusing Tommy of breaking his car window with the sponge ball as he drove past. He started to jostle Tommy so I interceded and pulled the man away from Tommy and told him to lay off the kid. He repeated his baseless accusations as he started to lace into me.

After a short exchange of blows, we wound up on the street alongside his car with me on top ready to deliver the final shots. His wife, who had been sitting in the car until this time, got out and jumped on my back, screaming and scratching. She clawed at my back until she ripped the tee shirt off my back with her sharp fingernails, which also dug into my back causing it to start bleeding. As I was about to turn around and hit her, the observers jumped in and pulled her off my back. I arose to let the man up, feeling that he was properly chastened. He and his wife got back into the car shrieking at all of us, but significantly humbled.

Whenever I think about the old neighborhood (or anyplace else for that matter) the thing that I recall most is the cast of characters that I met.

Ronnie Fisher was one such character.

Before coming to Astoria, Ronnie had lived his earlier years in Yorkville on the East Side of Uptown Manhattan. I went with him several times to his old neighborhood to meet some of his old buddies or to attend one of the local social events in Yorkville. I have special reason to remember one eventful night at a weekend dance at a local Yorkville school.

I was doing the usual thing, waiting to ask or be asked to dance a foxtrot, which at the time was my sole dancing forte. It was an unspectacular night until I went into the boy's room about midway through the evening.

It was considered very gauche and was the mark of a *wise guy* to walk around with the collar of one's suit jacket turned up. This was normally cause for a little sneering and vocal chiding but never amounted to more than innocent banter. This night a young man came walking into the boy's room with his collar in the proscribed turned up position.

One of the local lads confronted the offending transgressor and going nose to nose with him said, "What are you, a tough guy? Turn that collar down." *Mr. Tough Guy* simply told him what I would have told him, "Blow it out your - - -", or some equivalent demand. What happened next occurred so fast that we were all shocked and helpless. The antagonist pulled a small gun out of his pocket and pulled the trigger once to put a bullet into the chest of the other boy. After what seemed like a long time, but was probably only a matter of a second or two, blood started to pour all over the shirt of the wounded boy, who just stood there for a moment with a bewildered look on his face before he fell onto the tile floor.

All of the boys in the bathroom ran quickly to the door, suspecting that this madman would start opening fire on everyone. Some of the boys were screaming for help as they ran out. The police were called. When I found Ronnie, I said, "Let's beat it out of here before the cops get here, someone was shot in the bathroom and we shouldn't be here when the cops come." We immediately left and didn't look back.

Ronnie called the next day to find out what had happened to the boy who was shot. The boy had been taken to the hospital after the cops and the ambulance arrived and he was in critical condition. The boy eventually survived, and no one ever blew the whistle on the guy who shot him. This must have been a commonplace event in that neighborhood because it never made the newspapers as far as I know. That was the last time I went to a dance in Yorkville.

If there were a contest for sleeping late, Ronnie Fisher would have been the hands down favorite to win the championship. I was no slouch myself when it came to resisting getting up in the morning, particularly on the weekends when we would be out until the wee hours of the morning and not very amenable to rising early in the morning. Mother, however, had her ways of rousting us out of bed in the morning, when she finally lost her patience when we didn't respond to her verbal importuning. One method of arousal was a whack on the butt with a broom stick handle, very effective on most occasions. Often the hapless sleeper would be rolling over from back to front as the broom was swinging toward the body and the blow would fall right in the middle of the crotch, always effective in eliciting the desired response.

The ultimate arousal method never failed to get us awake and out of bed, a glass of ice cold water thrown into the face was always followed by the rapid sound of feet hitting the floor.

Ronnie was immune to all of these stratagems. We would often be calling for him at his house at one or two in the afternoon and he would still be in bed sleeping. One of those days we woke him up and didn't leave the room until he was sitting on the side of the bed where we left him as he had his first sock halfway onto his foot; naively believing that we had him roused to a conscious state.

When he didn't come out of the room for a long time, we went back to the bedroom to find him in exactly the same position we had left him in, one sock on and fast asleep in a sitting position with his hands on the sock. We did the water job on him and then left him to wake up on his own terms while we went to the living room where his father, Mr. Fisher, was demonstrating his ability to tuck his feet and legs behind his neck like the Indian rubber man in the circus.

He was sitting on an old, overstuffed chair into which he had sunk down about twelve inches, nearly sitting on the floor. He did get his legs behind his neck, but couldn't unravel himself as he became frozen in that position. We all attempted to help, but to no avail. After a while, Mr. Fisher became panic stricken while the rest of the family, including Mrs. Fisher, was laughing hilariously at his self imposed predicament.

The police were finally called and before long an emergency crew from the fire department, the police, and an ambulance crew were crowded into the living room. I don't recall how they got Mr. Fisher untangled, but after much pulling and tugging and many pained outcries from the victim, he was finally freed from the chair to much embarrassment.

While all this was going on, Ronnie's brother Bill was in the bathroom cleaning up. He called out to his fiancée, Ann, who was also in the apartment that day, to make a cup of tea for him for when he was finished. Ann was one of the most beautiful girls in the neighborhood; Bill had a lucky catch there.

When Bill finished his grooming he came out and expected his cup of tea to be ready. Ann did not do a thing and said, "I don't know how to make tea." Bill told her, "All you have to do is boil some water."

Ann replied in her sweetest tones, "I don't know how to boil water; I don't know anything about cooking." (I suppose as the only child in her family that she never had to do anything domestic in her house.) We all gave each other a glance as if to say, "Maybe Bill isn't so lucky after all."

175

Ronnie had some amusing idiosyncrasies. He was obsessed with the idea that his head was too small for his body and often said this to me privately. When he said this aloud in the midst of a crowd of boys, they quickly picked up on Ronnie's revelation and teased him unmercifully until one of them suggested that we should henceforth call Ronnie "Pinhead", an epithet that stuck for a long time.

[You had to be careful about letting the crowd seize upon something you said because they were always unmerciful in there riposte. Marty Kelly, our landlord's son, thought of himself as a tough fighter and wanted to be called "Rocky" (as in Rocky Graziano, Middleweight Champion). He wound up walking around with the moniker, "Pebbles" Kelly.]

Ronnie Fisher was always a bit of a dude. Whatever became fashionable in men's wear, Ronnie would always try to go the next step. When peg pants became popular with a narrow cuff and a wide knee, Ronnie had the widest, baggiest knees in his trousers and his cuffs were so tight that he had to have zippers sewn in so that he could get them on.

Ronnie was the first one I knew that had the nerve to wear a cardigan jacket; motivated, I believe, by the incident of the raised collar in Yorkville. Ron and I would expand our wardrobes by sharing clothes, we being the same size. It took a bit of cajoling to get to use his favorite cardigan jacket, but I finally managed to talk him into it for one of the dances that we went to.

One of our favorite hangouts was the Sugar Bowl on 30th Avenue, an ice cream parlor owned and operated by a lady we covertly called "Fat Pat", one of the largest women of the day. (Today, with the growing obesity in the United States, it is not unusual to regularly see people weighing 300 pounds and more, but in the post war years Pat was a rarity.)

One of the favorites at the Sugar Bowl was a wonderfully greasy hamburger smothered with fried onions that cost fifteen cents and that would be washed down with a lemon and lime with water or one of Pat's famous chocolate milk shakes. Here again, "Pinhead" Fisher displayed another of his quirks. He would order a Coke mixed at the fountain and would hover over the Soda Jerk so that he could get the soda fresh out of the spout to be drunk before the head of foam on the drink had a time to settle down. He insisted that this was the best part of the soda.

One last "Ronnie story". There were some nights when we would gather at the home of one of the boys or girls in the neighborhood when the parents were out for the evening. These gatherings would always devolve into a "necking party", with couples finding a quiet part of the house to "make out", which was usually limited to kissing (French, of course) with an occasional exploration into the touching of breasts, if the girl was so endowed and so inclined.

At one of those evenings, I brought a number of my 78 RPM record collection to listen to as we sat around gabbing before the inevitable pairing off to other rooms. The girl's parents were out and weren't expected back until quite late so we had plenty of time for our romantic activities. As the night progressed, the lights dimmed and the music became quieter. I wound up on top of the bed with our hostess and at least one other couple.

Ronnie was alone in the darkened hallway with a young lady who was visiting from out of state.

After some time and with the hour still early, Ronnie and his girl came swiftly and quietly through the door into the apartment. By this time most of the crowd had dispersed and the only two people left in the apartment were my partner and me. Ronnie whispered softly and in a panic, "Your mother and father just came in the door downstairs and are talking to a neighbor in the hall." Knowing that we were not supposed to be in the apartment alone with the girls when the parents weren't home, Ronnie and I quickly sought to escape. Ronnie went out the window of the second floor apartment and went down the fire escape ladder. I grabbed my pile of records and opened the front door to listen. The parents were still talking to the neighbor so I very stealthily slipped out of the apartment while the door was closed quietly behind me.

I went up to the landing on the third floor and waited for them to finish their neighborly talk and come up to the apartment. I was holding the large stack of records in one hand while balancing them with the other. The talking went on and the records felt like they were getting heavier and heavier. I thought they would soon slip out of my hands and go clattering down the stairs. Sweat was pouring from my brow. It would be worse getting caught hiding on the stairs if the falling records announced my presence than it would have been to be caught in the apartment alone with the girls.

The time seemed endless and I didn't know how long I would be able to hold the records in my aching arms or how long I could stand there quietly without sneezing, coughing, or farting to give myself away.

Finally, the conversation ended and the parents returned to the apartment and closed the door. I waited a short period of time to be sure that the coast was clear and then, without a sound, tiptoed down the stairs and out the front door.

I dropped the records off in the hallway of my house and went to see the guys down at "The Modern Age", an all night diner that was a favorite gathering place at the end of an evening's activities or when the bars closed. Most of the guys who were at the party were gathered together at one of the tables recounting the night's action. Shortly after I arrived, Ronnie came in to regale us with his "making out" tonight.

He told us that he got into such a passion with his willing partner that he asked her if she'd "put out" for him. (A popular expression of the day) She declined but he said she "Jerked him off" into his handkerchief. We all scoffed at his imaginative story until he pulled out his handkerchief to show us the evidence of his "conquest". Some of the more incredulous inspected the handkerchief very closely to verify the accuracy of Ronnie's story and upon seeing the semen stains on the handkerchief one of the guys uttered in open admiration, "WOW!"

Anton Lehr was another character from the neighborhood that was more remembered for what he did than who he was. He was one of the burlier guys in the crowd, quite big and very strong, with the appetite of three or four of us combined. He would never turn down something to eat and everything he ate turned to muscle, sometimes in the body but more often in the brain.

He was working for a local delicatessen near his home on 44th Street where he delivered groceries and performed general work around the store. Every Friday, being a day of abstinence, the delicatessen sold homemade clam chowder by the container. On one of those Fridays, a group of us ran into Anton as he was going home for lunch. He told us about a great practical joke he played that day at work; he peed in the clam chowder when no one was around in the kitchen while the soup was being prepared.

After a good laugh at this, he went home for lunch. He passed us again on his way back to work. When he got home, he said, his mother served him his lunch, clam chowder from his store. We asked him, "How did you get out of that predicament?" He said, "I didn't. I had to eat it or my mother would have killed me if I told her." *YUCK!*

Before I left LaSalle, I had my first "real" love. Ethel Cullen was about a year younger than I, lived on 43rd Street near the Six Corners and was attending Bryant High School, which may have been one of the reasons for my quitting LaSalle in my junior year. I was so smitten by this lovely colleen that I would spend hours sitting on the stoop with her outside her house just staring at her while she gazed at the stars in the sky; neither of us saying a word for long intervals at a time. I don't know if the feelings were reciprocated but I really didn't dwell on that, being content that we just had time to spend together.

One day that has always remained etched in my mind is the time that we went on a church sponsored boat ride to Playland at Rye Beach. We had a wonderful day together, sharing the many rides and attractions, swimming at the beach, and dancing on the boat. We took the subway home from the pier in Manhattan at the end of the return cruise and arrived at the station on 31st Street with the rest of the gang that had been on the boat ride. Most of them were taking the 30th Avenue bus for the remainder of the trip home. I only had five cents left in my pocket at the end of this long and, to me, expensive day which was only enough to get one of us on the bus.

I didn't want to tell Ethel that I didn't have the fare but I did ask her if she would like to take the bus home. Happily, she suggested that we walk, an offer that I readily agreed to. Pushing my luck further, I asked her if she would like an ice cream before we move on; an ice cream cost ten cents. Again, she gave the right answer; no. Not pushing my luck any further, the two of us walked home. I sometimes wonder whether she knew that I only had a nickel in my pocket.

This romance lasted as long as most puppy loves do. I don't know how or why it terminated. Ethel would eventually marry Pat Burns, one of the neighborhood guys and a local New York City cop and together they would have six children. I saw her and Pat at a Rambler's reunion not too long ago and she still looked as beautiful as she did about fifty years ago.

Another brief romantic relationship was with Mary Jane Gillis from 34th Street; a beautiful red headed Irish girl with a passion to match the hair. During our brief fling, I never had the opportunity to meet her family. She insisted that she meet me away from her home when we dated and before we turned the corner of her block on our return, she would not permit me to walk her to the door. She said that her three brothers, all professional boxers, were very protective of her and would beat up anyone that she was dating.

I was insisting on taking her home on one of these occasions but before we proceeded, I peered around the corner. At the window of her apartment on the second floor were her mother and one of the brothers sitting at the window while leaning on a pillow on the window sill. Below them on the stoop were the other two pugilists looking like they were itching for a fight. I wasn't about to take a chance against three pugs so I abided by Mary Jane's request. This association couldn't last too long under these conditions, even though she was a hell of a good necker. We eventually went our own way.

[In 1953, I was in a bar in Yokosuka, Japan, sitting beside another sailor from one of the other ships in port at the time. While we were exchanging war stories, I found out that he came from Brooklyn and when I mentioned that I was from Astoria, he told me he was somewhat familiar with the area. Further discussion revealed that he had dated Mary Jane Gillis shortly after she and I broke up, and he also ended the relationship for the same reasons; he didn't like the idea of her three brothers and Mom being overprotective of her chastity. Small world!]

Those middle teenage years were troublesome ones for me. I had no goals other than to join with the gang in whatever mischief or "fun" thing we could do. I had no interest whatsoever in school other than as another opportunity to "make out" with one of the girls. I worked hard at whatever paying job I had but that was only to make enough money to go to the movies or, more likely, to go to drink and play shuffleboard at the Dugout or, later on, the Shillelagh on 30th Avenue.

Most often, though, we just hung around the corner discussing our last and next escapades. When the opportunity presented itself, or we made the opportunity, we would take our latest girl friend for a walk to the park or whatever place was available for "necking". Few of us had automobiles at the time and most traveling was done on foot or by subway and bus. We hadn't yet discovered what a great facilitator of romance a car could be.

(My brother, Danny, was one of the first in the neighborhood to purchase an automobile. I don't recall the make or model, but it was an old used car that spent more time parked at the curbside than on the road. I can still see Danny offering the guys a ride to the Shillelagh to get a "few beers". Invariably, he would put the key in the ignition and find that the battery was dead and the car wouldn't start. He would then ask the guys to get behind the car to push it up to five miles an hour so that he could kick start the engine.

A common neighborhood scene was a gang of four or five boys pushing Danny's old junker down 30th Avenue toward the Shillelagh. By the time the engine turned over and the car was started, if indeed it even started at all, the destination would be arrived at, and the "engine" was ready for a refueling at the bar.

I believe Danny put more miles on that car with manpower than with engine power.)

Our part of Astoria was a great neighborhood; always something interesting happening and always someone to enjoy it with.

I can remember a time when Mother was at the window of our third floor apartment looking out at the activities on the street while leaning on a pillow from one of the beds, having placed the pillow on the window sill for comfort. I heard her yelling down at two of the young neighbor girls who lived across the street from us, "What are you doing with those white balloons?"

They answered with something that I couldn't hear. Mother then said, "You shouldn't be blowing up white balloons; they're poisoned and you'll get sick." She asked, "Where did you get them?"

By this time I had moved closer to the window to see what was going on and one of the little girls replied, "We got them from my father's drawer in the bedroom." I looked out the window and I saw that the white balloons were condoms and the two girls, about 5 or 6 years old, had blown up one of the rubbers to a huge size.

Most of we boys knew what these "rubbers" were used for but I believe the majority of them never had the opportunity to use them although many carried one around in the wallet "just in case." Willie Dooley had one in his wallet for so long that it left a circular impression in the leather. One day, while Willie was napping and his mother was entertaining a couple of lady friends with the usual coffee, tea, and a piece of cake, his young cousin who was also visiting went into his bedroom and took his wallet into the kitchen where the guests were chatting.

She started to pull things out of the wallet and startled the three women when the condom fell to the floor. Mrs. Dooley was embarrassed in front of her friends and immediately went into the bedroom, dragged Willie out of the bed to demand an explanation. All Willie could find to say in his still groggy state was, "Gee, Mom! Would you want me not to use one?" Of course, Willie was duly punished for this transgression.

On weekends, particularly at the beginning of the baseball season in the spring and the football season in the fall, we could expect that there would be at least one "beer racket" thrown by one of the teams at Kneer's Ballroom, Turn Hall, the Steinway Lodge, or some other suitable beer hall, to raise funds for the purchase of team jersey's or equipment. Tickets for these affairs usually went for one dollar apiece and included all the beer or soda you could drink and recorded music. Food, when served, was never more than pretzels or potato chips. The highest price that I can remember for one of these "must" events was $1.25.

On these nights, as most nights, I would be home well beyond the curfew hour set by Mother and Daddy. I knew that I would always get hell from them but was willing to take the consequences as long as I could spend the time with the gang. If I were ordered to stay home on any given night, I would sneak out through the back window and down the fire escape at the first opportunity. I was in constant conflict at home and was always having high volume yelling battles with Mother.

Besides these unpleasant, and unremitting battles at home, there was always a bar room brawl or a street fight to contend with. One of my regular adversaries at the time was a young man from Greece, Demetrios Demetriades, who went by the Anglicized name of Dennis Hariton.

Every time that we met, without exception, we would fight. He would approach me and say in his accented tones, "Hey, Jeckie Bebby, you and me vill fight, eh!"

In our first encounters I fought the way he wanted to fight, wrestling. He always got the best of me, being exceptionally strong and trained to wrestle. It took me a while before I realized that I had better change the rules of engagement or I could never take Denis down. One day I decided to start swinging before he could get a grip on me. After that, I constantly beat him by moving in quickly with jabs, hooks, and straight rights and just as quickly dancing away before the next onslaught. He never got his fight going when I took him on like this and I never let him get me in another stranglehold.

Denis left town for a while when he was sentenced to a boy's detention home, Lincoln Hall, after being designated as an incorrigible problem teenager. At Lincoln Hall he became the elected Mayor of the youth government they had there. The last time I saw him was when he was out on leave for a weekend so that he could appear on a radio edition of "We the People", a popular public events program of the time, to discuss his experiences at Lincoln Hall. This was the first time in our entire association that we met and didn't fight, and the last time that I saw Denis.

In the summer we still continued to take the Long Island Railroad to Rockaway Beach if we had the fare; if not, we would "thumb" a ride there and back.

One of those days we were hitch hiking home along Cross Bay Boulevard with our shirts off, continuing to enjoy the last of the day's sunlight. One of the guys grabbed Jackie Dwyer's shirt and we started to toss it around while

Jackie attempted to retrieve it. In the process of clowning around, Jackie's shirt fell into the bay right into the raw sewage emanating from an outlet into the bay. The water was filled with the usual effluents; garbage, excrement, "white eels" and disease ridden microorganisms.

Jackie jumped into the water and swam underwater to recover his shirt. (I hope he kept his mouth shut while under the water.) When he came ashore after his sewage bath, none of us would go near him and when we finally were successful in getting a ride, we refused to let the foul smelling wretch get into the vehicle. He eventually got a ride on his own and made his way home; much to the chagrin of the Good Samaritan that gave him a lift.

On another occasion, it was my turn to suffer on the return trip home, this time aboard the LIRR. During the day I had fallen asleep on the beach and my fair skin was burned to a crisp in the blistering sun on that hot, clear day. I couldn't stand to be touched by anyone while everything on my body, including the bottom of my feet, was on fire. The only place that wasn't was where the bathing suit covered my butt and other mid body parts. I went into the toilet on the train, locked the door, sat on the edge of the toilet, and stayed there for the entire trip home.

When I arrived at our final destination, Woodside Station, I went into a drug store to get something for the sunburn. The druggist gave me a salve to put on all of the burned parts. I don't think what he gave me was an ointment for sunburn but rather for burns. When I put it all over my body when I got home, I laid on the cool linoleum on the living room floor and tried to find some comfort in the gentle breezes blowing into the open windows. After a while I went to sleep.

When I awoke a few hours later, the salve that the druggist had provided had set into a hard coating around my body, arms, legs, and neck. I couldn't bend any of my joints as they were now encased in a steel like crust. I couldn't wash it off because I was in such pain. I remained in this stiffened position for over a day and could do nothing but lie on the floor and wait until I could bear to start washing off the offending cage of salve. It took a while to get back to normal but I learned my lesson from this heated experience.

I was soon back to the Rockaways, not only to swim, but more important, to join the crowd at the Leitram Castle on 103rd Street or Gildea's across the street where everyone who was anyone would show up to drink beer, dance, be seen, and pick up company for the night. And if romance was not in store for the evening, a good fight was always available.

When I think back to those days, I would feel remiss if I didn't mention some of the many "buddies" we had on the block and at school. Besides Ronnie "Pinhead" Fisher and Marty "Pebbles" Kelly, one of my closest friends in those final years before going into the service was Petey LaMarsh who lived on 48th Street in a three room apartment with his parents and three siblings. Pete's father insisted on being called Jerry by his own kids and when I asked him why, he said, "If I ever meet some nice lookin' woman, I don't want them to know I'm married and have kids." I don't know if he was joking or serious. Mrs. LaMarsh made the greatest lasagna I've ever tasted and I always looked forward to calling for Pete when I knew his mother just made a dish of that delectable pasta. Pete's cousin, Mike Mongelli lived right across from our house on 30th Road and was another member of the gang and the many teams we put together to compete at the 30th Road Park.

Jim Ronacher who was destined to marry Marilyn Ryan's sister Barbara and become part of our family lived a couple of doors down on 45th Street, next door to his Uncles, Bob and Mike Guilfoyle, who also played ball with us.

Jack Egan with whom I still maintain periodic contact with in his Houston home lived directly across the street from me. He, Bart DeVivo, Billy Dwyer, and a few others belonged to a local weight lifting club, which leads me to an incident involving them, me and Bob Dalvano, Marilyn's cousin.

One of the girls in the neighborhood was having a lavish, for the times, "Sweet Sixteen" Party in a room above one of the local gin mills (as we often referred to the bars.) Bob and I were invited but one of the criteria for attendance was to come with a date or "No Entry". Bob and I had dates lined up, but were stood up at the last minute. The two of us were sitting on the stoop all dressed up with no place to go and dwelling on our bad luck in missing this soiree where almost everyone that we knew was in attendance.

While we were agonizing over our plight, Bill Dwyer and Bart DeVivo were walking down the street, returning from their session at the gym and stopped to join us. As we talked, I got a brilliant idea for all four of us to attend the party. We had stored away in our cellar at home all of the costumes that we used on Thanksgiving Day; most of these being women's old clothes. I suggested we dress up Bill and Bart as girls using these garments, I would get Mother's makeup and lipstick to dress them up, and with a couple of the wigs from the costume storage, Bob and I would have our dates.

We dressed them as planned. When we arrived at the party and entered at the bottom of the stairs, Marty "Mud" Bowman was standing at the top step. When he saw our "dates", he laughed so hard that he fell to the bottom of the stairs; fortunately without injury. When we walked into the crowded party, arm in arm with our "girls' who were built like the proverbial brick shit house, all of the boys converged on our companions begging for a dance or suggesting other, more brazen action. What we had observed as a rather sedate party when we entered the room suddenly became a bedlam of noise and activity. We found out later that the party was a big dud in spite of the crowd, until we arrived with our dates. What started out as a joke became the salvation of the party.

At about the time I entered Bryant High in the winter of 1949 I had started keeping steady company with Marilyn Ryan who was also attending that school. As I mentioned before, Marilyn had her eyes on my brother Fran, but in the meantime we had a good relationship until we just drifted apart, remaining good friends. We wound up in at least one class together at school which caused a bit of difficulty for us when the teacher had me transferred to a different class for passing "love notes" to Marilyn in the classroom.

Bryant provided an employment service for the students to help them get part time jobs or temporary jobs through their placement office. I had many temporary jobs doing anything from painting to cleaning cellars and one regular position after school hours. The job was at the Silent Watchman Corporation in Manhattan which provided a service for offices, stores, factories and other businesses that had a need for checking when the premises were opened and closed.

Each of these businesses had a lock on the door equipped with a timing mechanism that recorded when the door was unlocked in the morning and locked at night. A paper chart was placed on a small drum which was rotated by the mechanism over a period of eight days and a stylus recorded the lock position on the chart over a period of a week. Every seven days, the chart was collected to be examined and results reported to the client and a new chart was installed. The manually wound mechanism ran for more than a week to cover up to a day's overrun in case the charts were not picked up on schedule.

My first assignments on this job were to pick up the charts that were not collected on the regular route assignment, which took me to all parts of Manhattan, Brooklyn, Queens and the Bronx. This was an excellent opportunity to ride just about every subway and bus line and see every part of each of these boroughs.

I was finally assigned a regular weekly route which took me from Midtown Madison Avenue on Monday to Harlem on Friday. I serviced everything from Gristede Grocery Stores to some firetrap factories in East Harlem where the working conditions were unfit even for a third world country, no less in cosmopolitan New York.

In one of these garment factories, women were jammed together side by side over machines under the most unsanitary conditions. The toilet was a filthy bowl without a seat, protected only by a small partition that shielded the bowl from the view of the workers on the floor but was open on the front side, exposed to anyone walking down an aisle. This was used by all of the workers, the women and the few men who mainly ran up and down the aisles to supply the women with material. The stench from this latrine and the garlic aroma from the workers were immediately and oppressively evident as soon as I walked in the door. Fortunately, I didn't have to go much past the front door and I attempted to get the chart retrieved and changed as quickly as possible to get out into the fresh air.

This particular "sweat shop", which was typical of many others in the area, was on the third floor of a building with a very narrow and dark staircase and no elevator. If there were ever a fire in this plant, and this was an excellent possibility with the manner in which the flammable materials were stored, or lack of storage would be a better description, the escape route through this single staircase and the lack of windows or fire escapes or exits would guarantee the fiery death of most of these underpaid and overworked employees.

I was surprised in my rounds over the week that the most congenial customers were in the poorer sections on the northern part of my route through Harlem and Spanish Harlem, and that the managers at the stores in the more affluent Madison and Park Avenue facilities were hardly hospitable at all. When I entered the elegant shops along those streets on the hot summer days, and usually I went no further than the front door to pick up the chart, the manager would invariably give me a hard time and insist that I get out with due haste.

In contrast, when I arrived at one of the more friendly establishments in Harlem, the owner or clerk would insist that I take a minute to have a cool drink on such a hot day. I felt more welcome and at home amongst the blacks and Puerto Ricans along the route than the cool snobs in mid-town.

The salary at the Silent Watchman was sixty cents an hour, below the minimum wage at that time, but the company was probably not covered by the minimum wage laws. I stayed at this job until I left school and had to get a full time position.

My attempt to get back into the swing of school was not too successful. I continued in my errant ways and in the first five months at Bryant, I was absent, playing hooky, 43 times. This, in addition to cutting classes, did not put me in good graces with any of the teachers. The Advanced Algebra teacher told me that if I could pass the Regent's exam at the end of the term, she would give me a passing grade, but she didn't expect me to be successful at all on that difficult test. As it turned out, I got 100 percent on that exam and it was the highest grade of all the students taking the test.

When the results were in, the Algebra teacher, **Miss Taiken**, spoke to me and told me that anyone with my brains should be buckling down and studying and that I had a good chance of getting a scholarship to college if I did so. Up to this point in my academic career I had no hope and no encouragement for going to college and had never even contemplated the possibility. All I was ever told by my parents and many teachers was that a "high school diploma" was necessary to get a job after we graduated.

Miss **Taiken** took me by the hand and dragged me into the faculty room where she introduced me to all of the teachers in the room and told them of my academic feat on the Regent's exam and had them all encouraging me to discontinue my truancy and all offered to help me to get a shot at a college scholarship. I was quite flattered by all of the attention and decided that I would, indeed, buckle down and work as they suggested. Before I left school that day, I signed up for summer school to make up for the subjects that I had failed that term because of excess absences and a firm determination to straighten out my wayward lifestyle.

When summer school started, I had myself all psyched up to get a perfect grade in each of the four subjects that I enrolled for; American History, English, French, and Physics. I started to attend every required class, and studied and completed every assignment. I was getting along well with the teachers and my conduct was above reproach.

The summer school History Teacher, **Mr. Homer Secsuill**, had other ideas in mind, other than my academic achievements. He gave us nightly written assignments and daily tests on all the material we were covering. I was prepared with all of the completed assignments and was getting perfect marks in each of the daily tests. In spite of this, Mr. **Secsuill** started to insist that I stay in his class at the end of the day as "punishment" for my failing performance. I adamantly refused to stay after class because I had a job to go to, but primarily because I sensed his real motive in wanting me to stay on at school after everyone else had gone home.

The rumor was around school that Mr. **Secsuill** was queer and that he had made advances on some of the students. In those days no one reported this kind of deviant behavior for fear of being branded as being "one of them" yourself. Mr. **Secsuill**'s demands became more insistent and more threatening as the days went by. I felt that if I did report it, no one would believe me so I just continued to ignore the threats and quickly left class and school at the end of each session.

About halfway through the summer term, he finally gave me an ultimatum one Friday morning, "Stay after school today, or don't bother to come to class on Monday." I decided to avoid any further encounters with Mr. **Secsuill** and did not show up for class on Monday morning. In fact, I didn't show up for any class and quit high school completely for a second time.

I got a job at R.H.Donnelly, a direct mail house in Manhattan, where Ronnie Fisher was in training to be a Dick mailer. Donnelly's sent out millions of copies of mail advertising and paid the minimum wage to most of the employee's. Primarily starting positions were either as a Dick mailer or as a tier and bagger. The Dick mailers placed pre-printed address labels onto the pieces to be mailed with a manually operated device made by the A.B.Dick

Company; hence the title "Dick mailer." This was considered the best job to have because unlike the other positions which were paid a paltry hourly wage, the dick mailers were paid "piece work", for the amount of pieces completed. Their salaries were only limited by the speed at which they worked and the amount of work available.

My job was as a tier and bagger, which entailed taking the addressed pieces, tying them into bundles with common destinations and placing the tied bundles into bags for delivery to the post office. A high ambition at this job was to attain a job as a Dick mailer.

There were absolutely no benefits for employment at Donnelly's as with most of the other laboring positions at the time. There were no paid vacation or holidays, no pension, no medical or dental benefits. The only payment was the salary paid for time worked and the worker was docked for late arrival. When the work load decreased, the workers were immediately laid off without compensation. I knew even then that I would not be at this place too long.

It was around this time that the Wilcox family moved in next door to share the apartment with the Fletchers who had lived there for years. Mr. and Mrs. Fletcher were the parents of Blanche Wilcox who had married Ranseler "Ranny", a former soldier from Winston, Connecticut, who she had met and married in the early thirties when he was stationed in New York while still serving in the Army.

The Wilcoxes had driven in from Detroit with their six kids and all their worldly possessions in an old Buick that looked like it couldn't make it through the city of Detroit, no less carry them all the way to New York. Ranny kept the car together by repairing all of the dents and rust spots by cutting out the offending defect, lathing it with a wire mesh and filling the lathed hole with concrete which he had mixed by hand. (Shortly after arriving in New York and after another dent and cement job on the vehicle, the car was in a collision and all of the concrete was dislodged from the car onto the road, to the astonishment of the other driver and the observing witnesses.)

Gail, at sixteen years (born February 4.1934) was the oldest of the children and was destined to play a brief but key role in my future. The five other children were: Guilford "Busy", Georgiana, Gerald, Gretchen, and Guy who was about four when the family moved to 45ᵗʰ Street. Ranny liked to say that all of the kids had names beginning with G because he felt that although Blanche and he would never have any fortune to speak of; they still would have plenty of G's (Thousand dollar bills.)

Their mode of transportation to travel to New York, the unfamiliar middle west twang in their speech, and their having imposed so many people (8) on the Fletcher's who already had two other daughters living at home in a five room railroad flat, were rather unconventional and gave the neighbors the impression that they were a bunch of hillbillies from the Ozarks.

Ranny was a large, muscular, brute of a man who worked at any job that required raw strength and power. While in the Army, he was a regular participant in inter service boxing tournaments, which combined with his still well conditioned body made him a man that one would hesitate to trifle with.

His wife, Blanche, on the other hand, was born with a congenital malformation in her hips and legs which made her walk with a contorted gait. She was around five feet tall and rather plump. Ranny doted on her to the point where, even when he was later holding down two full time jobs and serving as the janitor for three apartment houses, he would come home tired from one of the jobs and prepare a meal for her. She seemed to take advantage of her physical impairment to induce Ranny to gratify her wishes; and he seemed to be happy to oblige.

Gail and I started to keep company for the last few months before I enlisted in the navy.

Realizing that I had no viable future at Donnelly's as a tier and bagger, I looked around for alternate employment and was encouraged by one of Mother's friends at the Rosary Sodality to apply for a job at Leviton's, the company where she was employed in Brooklyn. Leviton's was the manufacturer of electric components such as light switches, electrical outlets, light fixtures and similar equipments.

I was offered a job in the salvage department at a salary of $32 a week for forty hours work. The compensation was just two dollars more than the prevailing minimum wage of the time, seventy five cents an hour. (I was soon to find out that the mandatory membership in the do-nothing union representing the employees would cost me two dollars a week, which brought me down to the minimum wage that I would have received even if the union didn't exist. This was my first encounter with a "company" union and the experience left a bad impression on me about the benefits of union representation.) There were no other benefits including, no paid holidays, sick time, or vacations, medical or dental benefits, or a retirement pension. At Leviton, as at most of these sweat shop factories, workers were required to punch in on a time clock and were docked fifteen minutes pay for each quarter hour or part thereof that they were late. I readily accepted the post.

On my first day at work, after signing the appropriate papers, including the pledge card to join the union, I was introduced to my new supervisor who took me to the station where I would be working. He led me into a huge warehouse room, about fifty feet square, filled from wall to wall with hundreds of barrels of rejected parts that had either been pulled off the inspection line or returned by the wholesalers and retail stores.

My job would be to separate all of the parts in all of the barrels into similar categories and to place the parts into cardboard boxes which were provided; a daunting task indeed. I started right away with no orientation training. I was told to separate by type, by color, by size, etc. Before the first day was over I was surrounded by dozens of boxes filled with varying quantities of separated parts. I didn't empty one barrel on this first day but estimated that with practice I would be able to empty about one barrel per day. At this rate, I could anticipate enough work in that one room for a number of years. I felt comfortable in the job security.

When a box was filled with parts, they were sent into another part of the shop where the units would be disassembled and the salvaged parts categorized and sent back to the assembly lines. The next step up the corporate ladder for me was to train for one of these disassembler's positions. I could see that I had a promising future ahead of me.

This job didn't seem too bad when I observed one of the worst jobs in the plant. A component of one of the lighting fixtures was a white porcelain base for the electrical bulb receptacle. These were rejected by the thousands because of damage or poor manufacture and could not be salvaged. The porcelain was ground to a powder in a machine located in one of the open areas outside between two of the buildings. There was a crew of men that shoveled the ground porcelain dust into trucks to be carried away for disposal. None of the men wore masks or any kind of protective clothing. I couldn't tell whether the men were white, black, red, or brown; they were all covered from head to foot with so much dust that they were like white ghosts.

I wonder whatever became of all of those poor souls, who for a pittance were subjected to such unhealthy conditions that they probably all died young from *white lung disease.* And where was the union that was supposed to be fighting for a living wage and livable working conditions?

It was 1949 when the first of my siblings, Helen, got married. In her early teen years she had been courted and pursued by a young man by the name of Harry Ivey, who went by the sobriquet Leroy. This relationship didn't sit too well with us boys because of Leroy's propensity to constantly stick his prominent nose into our business and to attempt to order us around. We would usually just tell him to mind his own business or some other more descriptive reply.

When Helen started to go with a soldier named Frank Pitilli, we were ecstatic that, at last we would be rid of her last pesky boyfriend. Helen carried on an extensive and romantic correspondence with Frank while he was at camp and she attempted to always be first to get the mail when expecting a letter from her new swain. When Frank finally returned from the army, however, this romance went quickly on the rocks and Helen was a free agent again.

Leroy, seeing his opportunity reopened, started to pursue Helen again with a consummate passion and determination. Before long Helen and he were engaged and were subsequently married at a mass at St. Joseph's Church. We were not too pleased at first, but we welcomed this new addition to the family.

Leroy came from a small family with whom we soon became quite friendly. His father had died years before and he and his younger brother, Roland, were raised by their working mother. Helen was employed as a clerk at the Metropolitan Life Insurance Company on 23rd Street in Manhattan, while Leroy was accepted for a position as a signalman on the New York City Subway System, a job he would keep until his retirement many years later.

It would be about ten years before they would have their first and only child, Carol. They resided in Astoria until purchasing a Cape Cod house in Hicksville on Long Island, the first in what would eventually be an exodus to the suburbs for the entire family.

[At Helen and Leroy's wedding I met Eileen Bishop, Helen's sixteen year old cousin who lived in Hempstead. She and I hit it off pretty nicely and I made a date with her for the following weekend. Not having learned to drive yet and having no wheels to take me to Eileen's, I had to resort to public transportation at which I was quite accustomed. Little did I realize when I made this date with Eileen that the journey from Astoria to Hempstead would be so long and tortuous; the subway to the last stop in Jamaica, a bus from Jamaica to the central bus terminal in the Village of Hempstead, and then another bus out to the farm area where the Bishop's lived in a large, well appointed house.

The Hempstead area was very rural with many large farms and a very small population. (This would soon be changing. With the opening of the Levittown housing development, the population of Hempstead, less than four hundred thousand, would more than double in the next twenty years.)

Although Eileen was one of the most beautiful and classy girls I had the pleasure of dating (she would soon be accepted as a member of the famous Rockettes dance troupe), this relationship was doomed from the start because of the geographical isolation of Hempstead from Astoria, and the expense of getting to this *remote* part of the world. After a half dozen treks to Hempstead, I called it quits. Eileen and I did have some memorable days together, but I soon found that, in addition to the tedium of the long trip, a good part of my time soon became a regular session of shooting pool with her older brother, Howard on the regulation size pool table that he had in the basement of the house; a game at which he always took me to the cleaners.

I didn't see or communicate with Eileen after that brief interlude and only saw her one more time, at Helen's wake in 1982. She still retained much of the old glamour then, even at fifty years of age.]

In 1948, before Helen's wedding, I had my first experience with the death of someone in the family close to me. My grandfather and Mother's father, Herman Beiser, died and was laid out at Farley's Funeral Home around the corner from us. He had just turned sixty on July 4th, but this was not an unusually young age to die in that era. I didn't get a chance to attend the funeral, having been designated the baby sitter for Marilyn, Bobby, and the twins.

I remember the many good times we had at Pop (as we called him) and Grandma Beiser's house in Hell's Kitchen in the city, and later in an apartment above a millinery shop on Steinway Street in Astoria. We particularly loved

197

the fun we had on his July 4th birthday which was always cause for a dual celebration.

Grandpa Beiser was noted in the family for his exceptional potato salad and he would always make it for our July 4th festivities. He was greatly loved by all of the grandchildren and would often play roughhouse games with them. He was quite good natured; I can remember that on one of these occasions he permitted us to paint a face on the top of his bald head with his halo of hair emulating a beard as he walked around backwards with his face toward the ceiling. The children were running as if frightened to get into the spirit of the masquerade, and Pop Beiser laughed heartily as we ran through the rooms to *escape the monster.*

On another occasion, Pop was giving us a demonstration of his ability to do hand stands. On one attempt he fell so hard on the wooden floor that he cut himself across the top of his head. With the violent flow of blood that started to gush from his head, we were all afraid that he had hurt himself badly, but he quickly recovered and cleaned it up in time to finish making another batch of potato salad.

Pop Beiser was also the family carpenter, known in the neighborhood for his skills in cabinet making. One of my last memories of him was shortly before his death when he made a beautiful end table for us and brought it over to the house.

Several days after the funeral, Grandma gave my Brother Bob the locks and keys that Pop had accumulated over the years. There must have been hundreds of keys and a like number of locks with none of the keys matched with any of the locks. (Pop Beiser was also a noted collector of "good junk" discarded in the local garbage pails, and keys and locks were especially welcome finds.) Bob spent countless hours trying to match up "a" key with any lock. After days spent at this long and tedious task, I can recall Bob's finding only one matching pair.

Before, after, and between weddings, wakes, and whatever, life went on as usual. I continued to work at Leviton's salvage department and spent the nights doing what had become the highest priority in my life; hanging out with the boys on the corner or on one of the stoops, that is when we weren't down at the Shillelagh Bar drinking beer, and playing shuffleboard, or participating in a barroom brawl.. We would often be at the closing of the bar at 4 A.M. but would always be up in time to make it to work in the morning. (There was, however, many a day when I would fall asleep at work while I was lost amongst the hundreds of barrels while sorting the salvageable electrical parts.)

Mother was always reading the riot act to me after these nightly episodes and we would often have loud quarrels. These were not my proudest days; not when my greatest ambition was to score a shutout in a shuffleboard game or to be able to down more beers in a night than my barroom buddies. When not carousing with the boys, I would pass the time courting the new girl, Gail Wilcox, attempting to do what all red blooded boys are supposed to be attempting. Although neither she nor I could drive a car at that time, we did have her father's well fortified car available to us for a modicum of privacy when parked on the street at night out of the glare of the streetlights. The back seat of the car was especially conducive to quiet and personal 'conversation.'

My aimless life went on with the same lack of purpose; work five days at a meaningless job, spend the night boozing it up at one of the local gin mills or at a bar that we discovered in Elmhurst, where we could get a sixteen ounce glass of beer for ten cents, sleeping late on the weekends, or taking advantage of romantic opportunities when they arose – until – tragedy struck.

MOTHER AND DADDY

At the start of 1950, Mother was only forty-two years old and had spent most of her years bearing and raising children; eight of us. As the center and heart of the family, she shouldered the burden of keeping the household functioning smoothly; from feeding and clothing us to making sure there was a roof over our head; from assuring that we all went to school or to work to caring for us when we were sick. Life wasn't easy for her but she accepted the drudgery with a glorious spirit and never complained.

Mother was born Florence Beiser in Hell's Kitchen on the upper west side of Manhattan on July 9, 1907 to Herman and Lena Beiser (nee Kessler), the first of seven children, four girls and three boys. The three boys died at an early age, one from blood poisoning after being cut on the sharp edge of a tin can and a second during a flu epidemic. I never did find out how the third boy died nor do I know their names. The girls, "Florey", Lillian, Ruth, and Frances all survived to marry and produce healthy families.

Mother often delighted us as children with her tales of growing up on the west side. We were always fascinated with the visions of her playing as a young girl on the streets of New York. Many of the games she played were the same street games that our generation played in Astoria; potsy, jump rope, doubly Dutch, and other sidewalk games. She grew up at a time when milk was purchased from a street vendor's wagon out of a large vat of milk. The customers provided their own carrying can or pitcher and the vendor ladled the milk into the vessel. By the time we were born the milk was being bottled and pasteurized and sold in the local grocery stores or delivered directly to the home for those who could afford the additional pennies for the home delivery.

Just as in our day, the neighborhood was divided into different competitive gangs depending on the street one lived on. Mother lived on a street called "The Sissy Block" because they were always getting the worst of any street fight that might have occurred, and the boys on her block were not as aggressive as some of the others. Daddy, who lived not too far from "The Sissy Block", on the other hand, came from the toughest block in the area; called "One Arm Block" because there were tenement houses on only one side of the street and a vacant lot on the other side.

From all the stories that were told to us by and about Mother, we learned that she was very smart in school and very popular. She loved to sing and dance and as a young single girl would often enter and win the local dance contests where the prize was a "Loving Cup" which gained for Mother that nickname amongst her many friends.

She was raised in the brownstone tenements in the city and from her own descriptions of the times; she seemed to have had a fairly happy and normal childhood. She did finish grade school. I don't know if she attended high school, but by the time she was sixteen she was married to Ed Roepke. The following year she was blessed with her first child, Helen.

I don't know the timing of the events of the next five years, but in that interval Mother was divorced from Ed Roepke, married Daniel O'Leary, and had the first born son, Daniel, Junior on August 9, 1929. (We called Danny,

"Junior", until he reached his teen years when he insisted that we call him Danny.) This second wedding took place in the Catholic Church, permission having been granted by the Church allowing them to get married in church because the ecclesiastical authorities did not recognize Mother's first marriage, it not having been performed in a Catholic Church.

Her new husband, Daniel O'Leary, Senior, was born on the West Side of New York on November 12, 1906 to John O'Leary and Susan Nodine. Dan never had a chance to finish his formal education and had to leave school in the seventh grade to join his only sibling, an older brother, Joe, in getting a job to help support their small family.

The only position he could find without schooling or a trade was as an unskilled laborer. Shortly after the passing of the Prohibition Amendment and the Volstead Act, he would put his skill and love of driving to profitable use when he entered the field of transportation and sale of alcoholic beverages. In later years he would be reticent about talking about this period in his life that ended when Prohibition was repealed in 1933, but from what little he told us, he worked for a guy by the name of Owen "Ownie" Madden who, I understand, was part of the organization that produced the infamous "Dutch" Shultz. It was "Ownie" who got Dad released from jail when he was picked up for running liquor in from Canada.

(I remember my reaction the first time I heard this story about Daddy's bootlegging days. Then attending St. Joseph's Parochial School and having been thoroughly indoctrinated in good and evil by the good Sisters and Priests, I self righteously asked Daddy how he could have been a part of such an evil and illegal activity and his only reply was, "Well! I delivered to the priests." - this of course, justified everything in my eyes; priests being incapable of wrong doing per the teachings of the church.)

At first, life wasn't too bad for the newlyweds, Dan and Flory, with his illicit but adequate income; Dan owned a car, a dapper wardrobe and seemed to be doing quite well for a young man in his early twenties. This was soon to end, however, with the Great Depression with its massive unemployment, and the Prohibition repeal which put Dad back into the worsening job market where there were hundreds of applicants for every job. The family's economic fortunes quickly declined. They moved to Astoria and after a series of moves to ever more humble dwellings, wound up in four rooms in an unheated apartment on 46th Street.

The financial plight did not stop them, however, from continuing the growth of the family, with Fran and me following Danny within three years, Marilyn and Bobby joining us within another five years, and the twins, Tommy and Billy coming at the end of the war after the family's luck had improved to some extent.

Through all of this, Mother was always there to do what needed to be done. She cooked on the antique stoves that we had been forced to live with, but always managed to make our often meager fare seem like a banquet. Ready to cook foods were not yet in vogue to any great measure and all of the preparations for meals had to be done tediously by hand.

Keeping a large family of active children properly clothed was another big problem. The only time we got new, "store bought" clothes was for Easter Sunday, and these clothes had to last the year, whether or not they fit the growing body. In addition to having to wash and hand iron the clothes, the garments were constantly in need of repair which Mother would usually do in the evening while listening to the late night radio shows after the rest of us were in bed. Daddy was always an early retirer and an early riser, going to bed around 7:30 P.M. and getting up at the crack of dawn. I can still hear the voice of Arthur Godfrey on his early morning radio show that Daddy always listened to while eating his breakfast of leftovers from the previous night's dinner.

Daddy would do the patching of holes in the soles of our shoes with a patch kit available from the five and dime store; we had three of those on Steinway Street; Woolworth's, Kresge's, and McClellan's. Until the shoes were repaired Mother would cut out cardboard insoles to the inside shape of the shoe for a temporary repair. This patchwork was especially ineffective on rainy days.

Shopping was another major chore that Mother handled with aplomb. It was not just a matter of going into a store to select and pay for a needed item but it was first, a walking search from store to store for the best bargain and then when the store was selected, negotiating the price down to an agreeable level. (This was widely called, "Jewing down the price.")

With all of these jobs that Mother held; cook, laundress, seamstress, shoemaker, nurse, housecleaner, and a host of other things, she still had time to help us with our homework, give us advice on every aspect of life, and wipe away our tears when we were in pain. I thought Mother knew everything and that, with her additional set of eyes in the back of her head, she saw everything. (Remember! She could even tell if we were lying by the white streak down the center of our tongues that only she could see.)

For a period of time she added to her burdens by working at Bob's Florist around the corner and, during the war, at the Norden Bombsight Factory in Manhattan. (Fifteen years later, Norden would be the company that would hire me for my first engineering position.) While Mother took this evening job at Norden's, Daddy did his part for the war effort as a welder in a war plant after taking a short course in Arc Welding offered by the government.

Mother managed to fill in her "spare" time as an active member of the Mother's Club at the school and the Rosary Sodality at the Church. As part of these organizations she played the lead role in several of their theatrical productions which were put on for the parishioners. She did black face in a Minstrel Show, when it was not politically incorrect. She had a powerful singing style that was comparable to Ethel Merman; I can still hear her singing on the stage, or at home as she often did, powerfully rich melodies like, "There'll be a Change in the Weather" or, one of her favorites, "It Had to Be You." She was quite a talented lady both on the stage and in life.

She would sometimes supplement the family income by crocheting customized purses and handbags to be sold to friends and neighbors. She was a beautiful lady with a beautiful soul and was much loved by everyone she came in contact with, but even with her lovely disposition she knew how to control her youngsters. She was a practitioner of "tough love" before it became a fashionable phrase.

For as long as I could remember she was plagued by a serious case of psoriasis, a skin ailment that covered her arms and legs with a thick scale and that constantly itched her. She would sit for long periods of time scratching away while the scales fell on old newspapers that she would place on the floor alongside her to catch the flakes. This itching would sometimes abate but the ailment seemed to have no cure and always would return. Psoriasis has been suspected at times of being caused by emotional stress. This may have been true in Mother's case in spite of her usually unflappable demeanor; she may have been internalizing her concerns so as not to get us worried.

In 1950 she seemed to have the psoriasis under control. She was getting out more with her friends and seemed to be on the way to expanding her outside activities. When the skin was clear Mother was able to put aside some of the long sleeved blouses that she felt obliged to use to cover her arms and at these times was able to wear short sleeves.

Things were going fairly well for her as far as I can recall, and I don't believe that she had any outstanding medical problems. Most of the children could fend for themselves and Marilyn was always eager to mind the twins if Mother wanted to go out to one of her social groups. With her recent marriage, Helen was out of the house; and Franny had joined the Navy in April of 1949 and was scheduled to be discharged, having served the one year hitch that he had signed up for; to be followed by four or five years of time in the Naval Reserve. With Danny and I both working, Mother had more freedom than she had for the past twenty years.

Then, on the morning of March 25, 1950, I was awakened to be told that Mother had collapsed last night and had been taken to the hospital. Before the morning was over, word came from the hospital that Mother had died of a cerebral hemorrhage, before she reached the age of forty-three.

The family was devastated by the news of Mother's death, and no one more so than Daddy. Mother was the axis upon which the whole family revolved. Daddy was a hard worker and brought home the paycheck when he was on a payroll, and he was the one who did all the heavy "men's jobs" around the house, but Mother tracked and paid all the bills, budgeted the small income to meet our needs, kept us physically and spiritually fit, and did all of the things that a household needs done; things that Daddy didn't know the first thing about. He did dabble from time to time with cooking some simple meals and was noted for his very tasty meatloaf, but "man can't survive on meatloaf alone."

Mother's wake was held at Farley's Funeral Home around the corner and the next three days were like a nightmare for most of us. I couldn't believe that Mother was gone and my mind refused to accept that she wouldn't be coming home again.

A burial mass was held at St. Joseph's Church. Every seat in the Church seemed to be filled, with standing room only, as the whole neighborhood joined family and friends in showing an outpouring of love and affection that I've rarely seen. The one thing that stands out in my mind at the mass was the organist playing and singing a hymn that was dedicated to … "Mother, dear Mother…" and the words filled the church with sorrow and pain.

I didn't, or couldn't, cry when I first heard the sad news of Mother's death, and I didn't cry at Church even though the pain of the loss was beyond my comprehension. It wasn't until the funeral procession passed down 45th Street on the way to Calvary Cemetery that the full import of the loss struck me. Passing the house I realized that Mother would no longer be walking up that stoop into the front door and no longer would she be there when we came home. There would be no one there to soothe the wounds or to give advice. There would be a void in my life that would never be filled. As everyone else's tears started to muffle into quiet sobs, I broke down completely and couldn't stop the painful wailing.

(I realize now why it took me so long to get to this part of the narrative. I had been writing at a fairly nice pace, not rushed but a constant output; until this point. I believe that subconsciously I had been fighting the need to go through Mother's death a second time. Even now, as I type this onto my laptop computer, I can't restrain the tears as they fall onto the keyboard. I find it hard to write about and have tried to steer clear of a memory that had left such emptiness in my soul. Although she died over fifty years ago, she has lived these many years in all of our minds and hearts. I suppose that this is our real immortality, living on in the minds of our loved ones. Her memory has been, and will continue to be, burning in our hearts.)

A NEW LIFE

The next four months were very difficult. I returned to work and started to fall into the same old pattern; working, drinking, keeping late hours, and finding some solace necking in the back seat of the Wilcox car.

In June, the North Koreans invaded South Korea; two countries on the other side of the world that most of us were unfamiliar with. President Harry Truman declared a state of emergency and along with the United Nations opened up a "Police Action" in Korea to repel the North Korean invaders. This action would eventually cost more than 54,000 American lives before a truce was finally called in 1953.

Around that time, I was transferred from the salvage department at Leviton's to work as a helper on a truck delivering to stores and warehouses in New Jersey. This was another job without a decent future.

One day in July, after my eighteenth birthday, while traveling to work at the factory in Brooklyn, I decided to take the day off and visit some of the people I remembered at the Connecticut Mutual Company at the downtown office where I had worked a couple of years before. Instead of getting off the train in Brooklyn, I continued on to Manhattan. I got off the subway at Chambers Street in downtown Manhattan and while walking to the office, after calling in sick at Leviton's, I passed the Navy recruiting station.

I went in and talked to the recruiting officer and decided on the spot that the life I was leading wasn't going anywhere and joined the Navy for a four year enlistment. They gave me a physical examination before I left and told me that I would be sworn into the Navy on August 2nd, about three weeks time.

I have often been credited with having enlisted in the service as a response to my country's call for men to fight the Korean War, or from other quarters, for enlisting to relieve the burden at home now that Mother was gone and Daddy had his hands full coping with the young ones at home. The plain truth is that I signed up on impulse with no prior soul searching about what my motivation was. It was just to get out, and get on.

For some unfathomable reason, I found it difficult to tell Daddy that I was going into the Navy and delayed telling him until the beginning of August. When he asked me when I was leaving, I said simply, "Tomorrow!"

I packed a small paper bag with my toiletries and after saying goodbye to the gang on the night of August 1, and saying my last farewell to Gail with promises of writing to each other while I was away, with about thirty dollars in my pocket, I took the subway to downtown New York in the morning to start this new adventure.

On the day before I left, I ran across Gus the Butcher as he was leaving Coffey's Bar and Grill after having his usual few brews. He stopped me and with slurred speech wished me luck in the Navy and tried to give me some money as a going away token. I declined his offer but he kept insisting and finally pushed two dollar bills into my shirt pocket and refused to take it back. At this point, I didn't feel like arguing anymore with his drunken persistence.

When I came home on my first weekend pass a few months later, I would again run across Gus as he was leaving Coffey's in his accustomed inebriated state. He started to berate me in a voice loud enough to bring some of the neighbors to their windows to see what was going on. In harsh and deafening tones he let all the neighbors know that I was so thoughtless to not even send him a post card while I was away after he had been so generous with me before I left.

1950-1954

1950-1954

THE UNITED STATES NAVY

I arrived at the recruiting station in downtown Manhattan where I was to be sworn into the Navy and shipped off to the Great Lakes Naval Training Center in Illinois for thirteen weeks of Boot Camp and basic training. There was a group of about thirty young men from different parts of the metropolitan area being sworn in that day. It was a hot August day so no one had to bring along a sweater or a jacket. Most of the guys were dressed in casual clothing; some were in jeans and sweat shirts while others were in linen trousers and tee shirts. We were told that everything we had on would be packed up and shipped home after we were issued uniforms.

One nattily dressed character stood out amongst the rest of us. He came dressed in a suit with shirt and tie and the top of his head was covered with a thick mop of flaming red hair. He was rather plump compared to the rest of us who all seemed to be in trim condition. He was accompanied by his mother, father, and a sister who might have been attractive except for a terrible case of acne and a scowling face that would turn off even the least selective of the boys preparing to be sworn in.

They lived on Park Avenue in the city and had been driven to the recruiting station in the family's chauffeur driven limousine. This was a new experience for me, having known few people who owned cars, no less someone who had a chauffeur to drive them around. This boy, I'll call him "Red", was the only one to be accompanied by anyone to the station and his family entourage was soon asked by the Chief Petty Officer in charge to leave the station so that the proceedings could begin.

Before leaving, the father pulled an enormous roll of bills from his pocket, peeled off three C notes ($100) and, with a great flourish so everyone was aware of his benevolence, gave them to "Red". With tears flowing from all eyes, they bade their farewells and Junior was finally let go as if he were going to a children's summer camp.

Most of us had already started to introduce ourselves to each other and were starting to establish relationships with those we felt a compatibility with. Some of us reached out to welcome this well dressed newcomer, but his haughty attitude seemed to say, "I don't associate with the riff-raff; just leave me alone," and we happily did.

[Red's naval career was to be short lived. Before two weeks were up in Boot Camp he was removed from our company to a disciplinary company. We didn't see any more of him until weeks later when we were in the Outgoing Unit Barracks waiting to be shipped to our new assignments after graduation. He was dressed in civilian clothing and was being discharged from the Navy with a Medical Discharge.

We asked him what happened to his finger; the tip of his forefinger was missing and covered with a bandage. He said that he was so harassed by the drill instructors in the disciplinary company that he started chewing on his nails and when the nails grew too short, he chewed on his fingers. They became infected and eventually Red got a bad case of gangrene and the last two joints of his index finger had to be amputated.

He told us that his father had pulled some strings in Washington to get him out of the Navy with the Medical discharge. Most of the other rejects that were being discharged with him, identified by the same black suits, were being released with General Discharges.

Red probably wound up heading up the family firm when he got home, and would eventually raise kids like himself to carry on the family tradition of *hard work, industry, and adaptability.*]

I had expected some hard nosed petty officer to greet us upon our arrival that day with a snarl, a bellicose voice, and a commanding presence and that we would be subjected from day one to a rigid discipline. I was somewhat disappointed when we were greeted by a soft spoken Chief Petty Officer who welcomed us to the Navy and swore us in with humor and patience. We were told what to expect over the next day until we arrived at Great Lakes and were introduced to our new Company Commander.

After a brief final physical examination, we were sworn in and taken by bus to the train station and boarded a Pullman car where we were assigned our staterooms. There were four of us assigned to each stateroom and we were told when the meals would be served in the Dining Car.

There was a First Class Petty Officer in charge of our group who held our papers which were to be turned over to the Great Lakes Command upon our checking in at the boot camp. He was another soft spoken guy and after making sure we all had our room and meal assignments, retired to his private stateroom where he spent the next twenty four hours sleeping and drinking; we didn't see him again until we arrived in Chicago for transfer to a bus that would take us to Great Lakes.

What a wonderful introduction to the Navy; luxury Pullman accommodations, free meals, no one badgering us or ordering us around. This was not what I had expected; I thought, "This is going to be a piece of cake, this Navy life." I looked forward with eager anticipation to my first trip outside of New York State, except for the few times I was on the Leviton truck making deliveries in New Jersey. I didn't know what would be coming next but the journey started off on a high note.

It took about twenty four hours to get to Illinois with many stops along the way. We spent our waking hours getting acquainted with the other new sailors on the train as no one had thought to bring along a deck of cards or some other diversion. It didn't take too long to find out how quickly I would establish friendly relationships with guys who were in the same boat as me. This would be characteristic of every assignment I had while in the Navy; make good friends, leave the post, and make new friends.

I slept well that night, not realizing that tomorrow my life would change forever.

BOOT CAMP AT GREAT LAKES

We arrived at the Naval Training Center at Great Lakes, Illinois late the next day, Thursday, August 3rd. After checking our papers in at the base office, our escort from New York turned us over to a First Class Bos'ns Mate (Boatswain's Mate) who immediately impressed upon us that life was not going to be the easy time we had led ourselves to believe we would have from our first leisurely day in the Navy.

In a loud, commanding voice that demanded our instant obedience, we were instructed to line up into formation with a host of other recruits who had also arrived that day from different parts of the country. The Bos'n then walked in front of each of us and stuck his face into ours so close that we could smell the foulness of his breath as he sprayed spittle at us as he bellowed his commands.

He spoke with a rough Southern accent that was at times difficult to understand, although we all were fully aware of the import of his words.

"Okay, you mangy curs line up and shut up. Now that y'all are here under my command, I want y'all to know that from now on you skinheads are in the

Navy and when you're told to do anything, you just do it. If I tell you to shit, I just want y'all to squat and say nothin' except how much and how deep."

"From now on you're nothing but a number and y'all better remember it. (He was referring to the service number we had all been assigned when we were sworn in. My number was 719-52-69.)

He continued his harsh tirade in this fashion while giving each of us an unwanted shower of sputum. "And you," he sprayed at me, "Wipe that grin off yo' face or I'll wipe it off for you." Although most, if not all, of us were frightened by this menacing presence in front of us, and although I was beginning to feel that I had made a terrible mistake to put my future into the hands of this maniac, I was trying to maintain my sense of humor and was gleefully enjoying the reactions of my fellow recruits.

The Bos'n at last came upon the only black recruit of this entire contingent of about a hundred. (I would soon learn that the blacks were in most cases separated from the white sailors. They were usually assigned at that time to all black groups, most commonly as Stewards working in the kitchen or mess halls.)

The Bos'n came down unmercifully on this young man who was visibly trembling with his eyes looking like two spotlights of fear. "And how the hell did y'all get in the Navy, nigger?" the Bos'n shouted into his face with obvious disdain. "Y'all gonna find out that this ain't a place for the likes o'you. We gonna work your ass off so hard, boy, that you gonna wish yo' momma were here to wipe the shit outta yo' pants when we get through with you. Y'all gonna be lucky, boy, if y'all make it outta here on yo' black feet."

We couldn't believe that this son of a bitch was beating up so unmercifully on this poor sailor whose shaking had now become so violent that his knees buckled and he would have fallen to the floor if the sailor alongside him hadn't caught him first. The Bos'n screamed at this sailor, "Get yo hands off'n that nigger, boy or you'll be bunkin' with him tonight."

None of us dared speak up; we were all petrified.

When we were assigned our sleeping accommodations for the night in a large empty barracks, this black sailor was told by the Bos'n to get his ass down to the far end by himself and not to mix with the "white boys". He was reminded again and again about how miserable life was going to be for him and that there was no escape. If he tried to run away, he would be thrown in the brig and his life would be made even more wretched. We were ordered not to fraternize with this *boy*, that he had to be taught his proper "place." We felt sorry for the poor recruit but, again failed to do anything for him.

During the night, the poor guy got up and went to the washroom alone where he took a razor blade and cut his throat from ear to ear. When he was discovered, he was rushed to the base hospital but it was too late. We learned in the morning that he had bled to death in the ambulance. We were not too eager to find out what the next few weeks would bring and many of us were already longing for home.

COMPANY 243

After the sounding of Reveille on a bugle played over the barracks loudspeaker system, a sound which we would come to deplore over the next thirteen weeks, we were rousted from our temporary bunks by the same Bos'n who greeted us the previous day. We were lined up, still in the same civilian clothes that we had been wearing for the previous two days, and marched off to a huge mess hall where we experienced our first Navy breakfast. A few of the new sailors complained about the quality of the food but most of us thought it was fairly adequate and wholesome.

After breakfast, thousands of new recruits were assembled in a huge drill hall building where we waited for our names to be called and a company number assigned. We were told that after our orientation, medical examination, issuance of uniforms, haircuts and showers, we were to assemble again in the drill hall to be introduced to our Company Commander. We were praying that we would not be assigned last night's Bos'n as our Company Commander.

We were then taken by company assignment to our first stop of the day. We were told to remove all of our clothing, an order to which we immediately complied. Our civilian clothes (Civvies) were to be packaged and sent home to the address we provided and our toiletries and shaving gear were placed in boxes to be retrieved after our processing. Then our newly formed company, Company 243, one hundred and twenty bare assed sailors, marched off for the start of our day's indoctrination.

Our first stop was to get our medical examination and inoculations. We were given the usual tests; blood pressure and heart check, hernia ("turn your head and cough"), eyes, ears, etc. We were given our first "Short arm inspection". We stepped up to a Medical Corpsman sitting on a low bench and were ordered to take our penis and "skin it back, and milk it down." This was an examination for any venereal disease secretions and would be a test that we would become very familiar with especially when we traveled to ports of call that were particularly noted for their sexually transmitted diseases. When it was my turn to be examined by the corpsman, I pushed up so close to his face that he pushed me back and said, "Not so close, I don't want to eat it, I just have to look at it."

The next stop was the dentist where everyone was given a thorough checkup of the teeth. There were several of the new recruits who had very bad teeth, decayed enough so that every tooth in the mouth was extracted on the spot; some needing stitches to stem the bleeding. I observed that all of the sailors requiring this radical extraction procedure were from south of the Mason-Dixon Line.

We were then taken, still stark naked, to the barber shop where we were given our "regulation" haircut and found out for the first time why the Bos'n last night called us skinheads. The barbers spotted "Red", our soon to be reject, and argued amongst themselves about who would get the pleasure of cutting off that large mop of curly red hair. All work stopped for the 30 seconds it took the chosen barber to clip "Red's" head down to the roots. When he was finished, the rest of the barber's cheered.

Many of the shorn sailors revealed heads that when shorn of hair, were filthy, as if they had never been washed in a lifetime. This was soon remedied when we were herded into a shower and ordered to clean every spot of dirt off the body and particularly those grubby heads.

These bald and naked, but clean, sailors were then marched off to be issued our new uniforms, bedding, and other necessities. We queued up first to be measured and then were handed a list of all the necessary measurements. We were issued the allotted amounts of equipments; underwear (skivvies), navy blue and white uniforms, hats, dress and work shoes, socks, pea coat, dungarees, our bedding: a blanket, and mattress cover ("fart sack"), other sundry items, and a canvas sea bag to hold all of our worldly goods while in the Navy. Every item of clothing and bedding was then stenciled with permanent washable ink with our names and service numbers.

Some of the clothing items did not fit as well as we would have liked but we would have the opportunity before leaving boot camp of having all of our clothing tailored to fit. In the meantime, after we dressed in the dungarees and other items as directed, our ragtag naked company now looked like a ragtag baggy pants outfit.

With arms full of our new issues, we returned to the drill hall where we had left our personal items, recovered them, and were introduced for the first time to our new company commander, Chief Petty Officer Bailiff, a veteran of over sixteen years at sea, training his first company of recruits.

My first impression of Chief Bailiff was not too positive. He spoke with a definite Texan drawl, and I was thinking, "Oh my God! Another bigoted southern red-neck!" As it turned out, compared to the other Company Commanders, Bailiff made Boot Camp a pleasant experience. He was tough but fair and had a great sense of humor. It was Chief Bailiff who introduced us to the term "Open Bottom Navy". When we were out on the drill field for Saturday morning Assembly and the WAVES (Women sailors) came marching by, he would turn to us and say, "Here comes the Open Bottom Navy," and when they would be lined up at attention near our Company, Bailiff would have our entire company snap a finger in our mouth to make a popping sound with the cheek, as the WAVE company went from a stance of *Attention* with the legs together to a position of *Parade Rest,* a rapid parting of the legs to move the feet about twelve inches apart.

Now that we had our official company family together under our new leader, Company 243 was led by Chief Bailiff to our home for the next thirteen weeks, a two story wooden barracks that was outfitted with thirty double bunk beds on each level. I was assigned an upper bunk on the first level. There were no lockers in the barracks and all of our clothes were to be kept in the sea bags which were lashed or tied to a steel rack running down the center of the barracks. We were provided with small combination lock footlockers for our small personal items.

There was a community toilet and shower room on each floor. We would learn very quickly to live without privacy in these conditions. We would also learn that the Navy had a unique language and we would be calling the toilet the "head". (This goes back to the old sailing days when the toilet was located on the front or "head" of the ship.)

Most of the barracks that were then being used had not been occupied since World War II. With the outbreak of the Korean War and the stepping up of enlistments, many joining the Navy to avoid being drafted into the army, these barracks were now being opened and many had not yet been cleaned and fumigated. The smell of years of neglect was clearly evident when we entered the barracks. One of our first jobs would be to get the barracks into habitable shape.

The next thirteen weeks would be busy ones.

Day one and every day thereafter, we were subjected to daily marching drills. At the beginning we were terrible; no one could keep step, as a group we couldn't make a straight line. I never thought that we would shape up to be anything and Chief Bailiff constantly confirmed this assessment. Eventually we did start to catch on and before graduation we were the equals of any other company on the base. In fact, toward the end of the training period our company won the award given weekly to the company who showed the best overall performance, including how we marched, classroom performance, and overall seamanship; the Bluejacket's Manual became our bible.

One of the first things we were taught was the Navy nomenclature. We soon learned that a floor was a deck, a door was a hatch, right was starboard and left was port, upstairs was topside and downstairs was below, the refreshment stand was the gedunk (which also meant ice cream), a ceiling was the overhead.

When it came to meals we used some very descriptive and sometimes gross phrases. For breakfast we would have SOS or Shit on a Shingle (minced beef on toast) or Foreskins on Toast (chipped beef on toast). Every Sunday evening we would be served cold cuts which were, in Navy parlance, "Horse Cock".

Fore and aft, abaft, and amidships, and climbing ladders instead of stairs - we had to learn a whole new vocabulary.

We were issued Springfield bolt action rifles that we were expected to carry wherever we went from reveille in the morning to taps at night. If a recruit dropped his rifle for any reason he was directed to sleep with the rifle at night. We used these rifles for drills and for dry rifle range practice (without ammunition). I was sure that if we ever tried to fire real ammo from these rifles they would have blown up in our hands.

Between drills and meals, we attended classes that covered everything from seamanship to the Uniform Code of Military Justice. One of the first training sessions was learning how to roll and tie every item of clothes that we were issued so that they could be packed neatly into our sea bag. The clothes were precisely rolled in a very specific way so that the stenciled name appeared on the observable edge of the garment after folding and tying.

Every Saturday morning there would be an inspection in the barracks to check out the cleanliness of the barracks and the individual recruits. All of our rolled garments would be laid out in a dictated pattern on the floor at the foot of our bunks and we would be required to stand at attention alongside our billets until the inspection was completed. Demerits would be given for any infraction; dust balls on the floor under the bed, unshined shoes, rack (bed) improperly made; and even dirt on the bottom of the shoes.

Recruits who accumulated demerits were obliged to march these off in the evening on the drill field during the sparse time that was free for private activities. I managed to avoid the demerits until boot camp was almost completed and then I got gigged for dirt on the bottom of my shoes.

Every recruit was required to pass a minimum swimming abilities test. We were taken to a large Olympic sized indoor pool for this occasion. We were told to strip bare and then were ordered to take a thorough shower before entering the pool. Each recruit was inspected by the petty officer in charge to see how well they had cleaned themselves. The inspector rubbed his finger across the chest and shoulders to loosen any residual dirt. If the recruit was deemed unclean, he would be sent back to the shower to try again until he was body rubbing clean. A short arm inspection was also given to each of the sailors.

One hundred and twenty naked bodies strong, we entered the pool area where we were directed to climb a diving tower that was approximately ten feet off the water. Every one of us had to jump off the tower into the water even those that couldn't swim. After hitting the water, we had to swim the length of the pool, about 100 feet to meet the minimum qualification. Every sailor had to be prepared, in case his ship was sinking, to get off the ship and to swim far enough from the ship so as not to get sucked in with the downwash of the vessel as it went under the water. There were sailors with long poles alongside the pool to assist the non-swimmers out of the water. Those who hesitated to jump into the pool were pushed off; no one was left dry that day.

The ones who failed to meet the swimming requirements were given lessons on their own time after regular drill and class hours until everyone was qualified.

There was continuous hazing of the new recruits by the sailors in the more senior companies. The new recruits or "skinheads" were easily spotted. With the fresh haircuts down to the scalp, all of our hats tended to fall over the ears. That and the baggy clothes which had not yet been altered for a decent fit, all of the "skinheads" were prey to the "old salts". As the hair grew and we learned to cock the white hats into a jauntier, though non-regulation position, we became the senior company and had our turn at taunting the incoming recruits.

Marching and rifle drills, calisthenics, and class work went on every day except Sunday. Sundays were a time to do the laundry, write letters do guard duty, clean the barracks, spit shine the shoes to a mirror like finish, and enjoy some free time off. Everyone was also required to attend religious services on Sunday, whether one was a member of a formal religion or not. We had a choice of three services to attend; Catholic, Jewish, or Protestant.

Saturday's were usually reserved for a morning Call to Quarters of the entire Battalion followed by the inter-company athletic competitions. The company winning the highest point total in these competitions was entitled to carry the Athletic Awards flag for a week until the next competition.

In the indoor and outdoor classes we learned everything from general seamanship, such as knot tying, launching and rowing whale boats to fighting fires and firing large guns. In thirteen weeks we may not have been ready to carry on our naval duties but we were given all of the tools to start learning in the real world at our next assignments, be they aboard ship or on a land base.

During our off hours (actually we were on duty 24 hours a day) we were required to do sentry duty in or around the barracks.

About halfway through the boot camp training, every recruit had a break from the daily drills, exercises, and classes. This "Service Week" was required of everyone and for that week we were assigned to some general duty to serve the rest of the ten thousand sailors on the base. My job was as a "hot shell" man in the scullery. For a week I worked there pulling racks of dishes out of a huge industrial washing machine at each meal. After all of the sailors were fed and out of the cafeteria, I had to haul the filled garbage cans to be dumped; but before they were dumped, the garbage to be taken to a local farm to feed the farm animals, each garbage can had to be hand searched for any tableware, cups, or trays that may have been dropped into the pails by some careless recruit. This was the most disgusting job I've ever had. I was ordered to stretch the arm to the bottom of the garbage up to the shoulder and feel around the bottom of the pail while my cheek was lying in the raw garbage.

After the completion of service week, we were given our first pay and the following weekend we were granted our first liberty and our first opportunity to wear our dress blue uniforms. With a choice of destinations of Waukegan to the north or Chicago in the south, Chicago was the choice of 99 percent of the recruits on liberty. We were permitted off base after breakfast and were ordered to return by midnight.

I boarded the train for Chicago with my white hat worn on the back of my head although the regulations specified that the hat was to be worn on the front of the head over the center of the brow. When I got off the train in the center of Chicago we were greeted by the Shore Patrol who greeted us with the admonition to "Square that hat, Sailor"; an order which we of course immediately obeyed.

Our group of now "asshole" buddies, as good friends were nautically described, spent the day exploring Chicago around the Loop. Nothing I saw that day stands out as particularly memorable; Chicago was just New York City with different street names.

In the evening, we went to the local USO where we got a free meal and had the company of some of the local young lady volunteers. We danced to a record player and drank soft drinks; no hard liquor being permitted in the club. The hostesses were not permitted to leave with or fraternize outside the club with the servicemen. I singled out, or was singled out by, a very attractive, but shy gal named Kate. She was twenty one and I was flattered that this "older woman" seemed attracted to me.

I invited her to leave so that we could be alone and perhaps take a walk in the park along the waterfront before I had to catch the train back to Great Lakes. After some hesitation she agreed to meet me at the park as soon as she could leave without arousing suspicions. We spent the next couple of hours lying in the grass alongside the moonlit lake to get better "acquainted" until I had to leave to get back to the base before curfew.

I had one more opportunity to get together with Kate before graduation and we carried on a correspondence for the next several months, but this eventually ended shortly after I was assigned to the Naval Radio Station in Panama.

I was also writing to several other lady friends in New York at the time. These letters were usually pretty similar and, of course, professed my undying devotion and remembrance. I would often plagiarize some romantic poetry and include that in the letters. Most of these contacts were soon ended and the only continuous correspondence was with Gail; we never lost touch with each other.

(Speaking about writing; there was one recruit in our company who was assigned to the bunk next to me. He was carrying on a fan writing correspondence with Margaret Truman, the President's daughter, with whom he claimed he was madly in love. He had a picture of her that he would moon over every night while lying in his bunk.)

As graduation day approached and our thirteen weeks of basic training would be coming to an end; we were all anxious to find out what our next assignment would be and where we would be assigned. When I enlisted I was asked if I would like to take an assignment in Electronics. I readily accepted, thinking that this would be good training in a trade that I could use when I finished my hitch in the Navy. They designated me as an EFSR (Seaman Recruit, Electronic Field). I thought that I would be learning about Electronics and how to build and repair radios, sonar, radar, etc.

Included in the EFSR designation was a Radioman rating which was primarily a communications job which included working with Morse code and teletype. When the assignments were posted, I found out for the first time that I was selected to go to the Navy Radio School at Norfolk, Virginia.

We graduated on a cold windy day in November and were immediately transferred to the Outgoing Unit barracks to await our orders to proceed to the next post. It wasn't long before I found myself on another Pullman car on my way to Norfolk, Virginia. I was sorry to leave the many new friends I had made in our company but I was eager to move out into the "real navy."

RADIO SCHOOL, NORFOLK, VIRGINIA

I arrived at the Norfolk Naval Station and embarked upon a life that was much different than the harrowing and pressured thirteen weeks that I had spent in Boot Camp. The following twelve weeks would be primarily class room work interspersed with cleaning duties and guard duty (the guard duty was either watching the clothesline at night or, preferably as the barracks watch.)

The best part of being out into the "real Navy" was that now we would be getting regular liberties; evenings or entire weekends from Friday afternoon until Monday mornings, if not on the duty watch.

Norfolk itself was not the ideal place to pull liberty; it was popularly known in the fleet as "Shit City", a very appropriate description. The residents were not too cordial to the thousands of sailors stationed at the Naval Station or the additional thousands who arrived regularly in the ships from the Atlantic Fleet. The Norfolk Naval Station was the largest on the East Coast.

There were not too many diversions or entertainments in Norfolk and most of the time there was spent in one of the many sleazy bars that lined the main streets. These bars were not paragons of cleanliness and the décor was nonexistent. No hard liquor or wine was sold in the public bars and one had to have access to one of the private clubs to get these kinds of drinks; a luxury we sailors were not socially or financially equipped to participate in.

The service in the bars was invariably provided by a surly, redneck bartender who openly despised all Yankees, Catholics, Jews, Irish, Italians, and Blacks. In their bigoted minds they were still fighting the Civil War. The barmaids who assisted them and were always on the make to have the sailors buy them the watered down swill that they called *beer*, were also poured from the same mold; I don't believe there was a barmaid in Norfolk that weighed less than two hundred pounds. The thing that always amazed me was how some of the "old salts" were prey to the wiles of these damsels.

One incident that happened at a bar immediately outside the main gate of the base still stands out in my mind and gives me a chuckle. Two sailors who were getting intoxicated on what we called "three two" beer (low alcohol content), the only alcoholic beverage at our disposal, were vying for the attentions of a young lady sitting on a stool at the bar, one on each side of the girl and each clearly hoping that tonight they would get lucky and take the target of their attentions home.

I don't know how the girl sat there all night without having to go to the ladies room and if she had the ending would not have been so amusing. When it came time for her to leave, she accepted the invitation of one of the sailors to escort her home. She summoned the bartender and asked him to pass her the crutches she had left behind the bar. When she stood, it was on one leg, the other one having been amputated above the knee. It wasn't funny that the poor girl had lost a leg; the thing that had us all in stitches after the couple left was the look of consternation on the 'lucky' sailor's face and our own imaginings of how he would handle the night's activity.

In 1950 segregation of whites and blacks was in full force. There were separate black and white facilities for just about everything from public bars to public toilets. Buses were segregated with blacks relegated to the back of the bus.

One day I boarded the bus that took us from the Naval Station to the heart of town. The front of the bus was about half full with plenty of seats for the sailors traveling to Norfolk who now occupied the remaining seats. Meanwhile, the rear of the bus was crowded with black passengers and all of the available seats were taken while a large number of the rest of the passengers remained standing.

An elderly and frail black woman entered the bus at the first stop after we left the base and was dutifully headed for the back of the bus as the law dictated. As there were no more seats available anywhere else on the bus, I rose from my seat on the aisle and offered it to her. She declined but I insisted that she should accept the seat.

The bus driver saw through the rear view mirror what I was attempting to do and yelled back at me to "...let the nigger git to the back of bus. Ah haint movin' this bus 'til she gits where she belongs." This only stiffened my resolve to give the poor woman my seat and most of the sailors on board loudly supported my attempts and told the driver to move on.

The old woman looked at me with eyes wide with fear and said, "Please don't cause me no trouble." I looked to the rear of the bus and that same fear was in every face back there; it was like looking at a field of bright stars in a black velvet sky; all waiting for the Nova to explode. The bus driver kept ranting on about 'gittin' the pol-leese', and 'damn Yankees' while adamantly refusing to put the bus in motion.

Seeing how frightened these folks were made me back off for their sake. While I wanted to punch out the driver and confident I would have the support of the sailors on the bus, I let the woman go to the rear and sat down.

I realized that further confrontation would only make their life miserable while this 'Damn Yankee' could go back to the safety of the base.

At last, we were finally away from the daily military drills and exercises that had become our routine in boot camp. We now spent our days learning the Navy communications business with most of the day being dedicated to learning to copy the Morse code on a telegraphic typewriter which was operated without a shift key to go from lower case to upper case letters. The typewriter only had capital letters.

The remainder of the day would be used to learn the telegraphic procedures and the special language of the radio operator, with a small amount of radio theory thrown in.

I caught onto the academic portion of the curriculum with ease, but the code copying came a little harder. I struggled to keep up with the required speed that was increased each week by about another two words per minute; a copying speed of a minimum of 18 words per minute was mandatory to qualify for graduation. I was held back for two weeks at one point for not meeting that week's standard, which was all that one was allowed before removal from the program and assignment to the fleet as an ordinary deck hand. I managed to squeak by and graduated two weeks later than expected; but I did attain the new rank of RMSN (Radioman-Seaman) which entitled me to henceforth be called "Sparks".

About every other week while in radio school we were granted a full weekend pass from Friday afternoon until muster on Monday morning, sufficient time to get to New York and return, a trip of nearly 400 miles each way. As students in one of the service schools we were not permitted to keep automobiles on the base so we had to rely upon the sailors permanently stationed at the Norfolk facility to provide us with the transportation home.

There was a seaman who was assigned to a private room in our barracks who would take five of us to New York for a fee and drive us back to the base on Sunday night. (This guy was supposedly doing clerical work on the base but had no office to report to. The Commanding Officer was a baseball fan and kept this sailor on board to pitch for the base team along with any good ball players that he could get from the fleet. The C.O. also kept a stable of boxers for fleet competition and who were also given special treatment in assignments of jobs or quarters.)

We would leave Norfolk late Friday afternoon and arrive in Manhattan in the wee hours of Saturday morning to take the subway home. I would usually go home first to see the family and then go on to my other commitments. The Wilcox family had moved to an apartment in Williamsburg, Brooklyn after I left for boot camp and it soon became my routine to spend my Saturday night there while on a weekend pass. My relationship with Gail was becoming more serious; serious enough that her father took me aside one day and asked me my intentions toward his daughter; to which I confidently answered, "Strictly honorable, sir. Strictly honorable!"

These truncated weekends went very quickly and we were soon meeting again on Sunday night with our driver in Manhattan to take us back to Norfolk. It was a grueling trip and not too comfortable with six good sized sailors crammed into a small vehicle. The New Jersey Turnpike and the Chesapeake Bay Causeway were not opened until later years so we had to travel the overcrowded roads between New York and Norfolk, with a ferry ride across the Chesapeake from Kiptopeke Beach in Virginia.

As we didn't get much sleep on Saturday nights, all of the passengers would try to sleep during the long eight or nine hour ride back to the base and rely upon the driver to get us there safely. One weekend the weather was so bad that the driver found it difficult to see the road as the rain poured down unrelentingly. He decided to follow a large truck that was apparently headed south in our direction to help him in keeping on the road. It wasn't until a couple of hours later that he realized, when he had better visibility, the truck had led us not south, but southwest, and we wound up miles off our course somewhere in Pennsylvania.

It took us a while to get back onto the correct road to Norfolk and we were lucky to get back to the base with only minutes to spare before we would be Absent Over Leave (AOL).

Instead of going to New York one weekend, I took a trip to nearby Washington, D.C. with one of my shipmates, "Ski" Rydzewski from Milwaukee, Wisconsin. We picked a great weekend for the journey by Greyhound bus. The spring weather was beautiful and it was "Cherry Blossom Time" in the city. Hundreds of flowering Cherry trees lined the avenues in an array of radiant color. We spent the day sightseeing and in the evening we went to a dance that was being held at the YWCA.

We ended the night in a room in a flea bag hotel that cost us three dollars. There was one bed in the room and the bathroom was at the other end of the hall and shared by the rest of the occupants on that floor. We were too tired and had participated in the usual bit of over imbibing during the evening, so we didn't object to the arrangements. It was not too long after we hit the sheets that we were fast asleep. (Today, if two young sailors were to share a room and bed the way Ski and I did, the world would look on it very askance and would probably assume that there was some kind of homosexual relationship going on. To us however it was just a place to sleep at a cheap price.)

I was awakened sometime during the night by some very heavy vibrations in the bed. At first I thought that it was the booze getting to me; there had been many a night when I felt as if the bed was going to roll right out from under me from drinking too much. As I adjusted to the dim glow in the room emanating from a street light through the yellowed window shades, I realized that Ski was thrusting up and down beside me and there was the heavy breathing of, not one, but two people beside me.

I focused in on an overweight older woman beneath Ski and noticed that she was still wearing a dank looking chenille robe that was opened in the front. She may have been in her late twenties or thirties, but to an eighteen year old she looked like she was well into her dotage.

In the course of the grunts, groans, and gasping breaths, I heard Ski mumble, "Jesus Christ, you've got hair all over your back." At this point, Ski must have had his fill of the lady and gently kicked her out of the bed. As she left, I didn't say a word nor did I give any sign of being awake.

In the morning Ski mentioned that he went to the bathroom down the hall during the night and had encountered a "beautiful, young" lady coming out of the head and invited her to join him in the room. I laughed and told him that I woke up during his encounter and had a good look at the "hairy backed" beauty that he had expended himself on.

We spent the rest of that Sunday recovering from a terrible hangover while seeing some more of the Washington sights. However, we didn't have the energy to climb the equivalent of the Washington Monument as we did the day before with the encouragement of the guard at the monument. We arrived safely back on the base and I didn't waste too much time in relating Ski's adventures in the hotel with what had become the ugliest woman in creation, not only with a hairy back but a mustache, warts, and hair under the arms.

We took a second trip to Washington on another liberty weekend to take further advantage of the large ratio of single women to men in that town and to do what had now become our custom of overindulging in the spirits. This time we stopped at a night club called the "Casablanca" that featured a swinging jazz group whose sound attracted us in. The dimly lit club seemed to be filled to capacity but the waiter managed to find us a booth. After a short time I realized that the place was filled with only men and it was not too long before two gentlemen approached our table and asked if they could join us because of the lack of available seats. We said "Okay!" and they sat down, one alongside Ski and the other on my side.

The conversation was very general and congenial and related primarily to the excellent jazz band that was performing. When the conversation turned to more intimate things and the guy next to me started to touch me on the leg, I looked around and suddenly recognized that we had stumbled onto a "Queer" bar or what today would be called a "Gay" bar, and that the two mugs at our table were "on the make" for these two tender young sailors.

I tried to ignore the first time that he touched my leg, but when he attempted to do it a second time and more aggressively, I pushed him out of the booth onto the floor and stood up. As he turned over and started to get up, I gave him a swift kick in the butt and he sprawled across the floor on his face. He rapidly crawled away on all fours as Ski was about to join the fray by pushing his companion out of the booth. This guy didn't wait and just scurried away before Ski hit him.

We left the Casablanca shortly after this episode and looked for a more congenial place.

(A few years after this episode when I was back in Astoria at one of the local bars, I ran into Pat Larkin, an older brother to one of my elementary school classmates. We were exchanging "war stories" with most of his occurring in Washington where he was stationed while in the Army. He mentioned at one point a 'terrific' night club in Washington that he always went to where they had good jam sessions. When he mentioned that the name of this place was the 'Casablanca', I told him that I was familiar with this place and knew that it was a 'queer bar'. I don't know if Pat was a participant in any of the regular activities in that establishment but he did turn a deep shade of red when I revealed that I had been to that joint.)

Most of my weekends in New York were spent at the Wilcoxes where I avidly pursued Gail. On my last night in New York after successful completion of Radio School, I didn't go to Brooklyn for the farewell and instead went out with a bunch of the old buddies including Marty Bowman and Bart DeVivo. On Sunday night, a carload of us went to the City in Marty's old junk heap and after sharing a few more drinks, they saw me off at the Greyhound Bus station on the West Side.

(I found out subsequently that Marty's vehicle wouldn't start; not a new phenomenon. The guys pushed and pushed to get it started but the car would not cooperate. Marty reportedly got so mad at the car's eccentricities that he had the guys push him to the dock where they pushed the car into the Hudson River.)

I took the bus back to Norfolk where, in the early spring of 1951, I would be shipped out to my next Station in Panama; my first time on foreign soil. In the meantime, Franny was called back into the Navy as an active Reservist, and Danny had been drafted into the Army. Now three of the brothers were out of the house and off to the War.

(For my last leave in New York before leaving for Panama, I got a 'hop' from a Navy plane that was leaving the Norfolk Naval Air Station for Westover, Massachusetts. There were many sailors that wanted to be dropped off in New York so the pilot got permission to land at the Grumman airfield in Bethpage, Long Island. This was my first time in the air and I was very excited about the experience. We were issued parachutes which we were obliged to wear for the entire trip and boarded a C-47, a propeller driven military workhorse.

We landed at Grumman's field where we were left on our own to find our way home. I hitched a ride from a friendly stranger outside the Grumman property that eventually took me along Hempstead Turnpike past large farms. I saw few private homes other than the farm houses and no housing developments. We passed the old Mitchell Field, which at the time was still being occupied by the Air Force and I eventually wound up at the Hempstead Bus Terminal. I was very familiar with the area from the times I was dating Eileen Bishop so the rest of the trip home was a *piece of cake*.

PANAMA

When the assignments were posted for the graduates of the Radio School, I was to be sent to a place called Farfan Radio Station in Panama by the "first available" transportation. The U.S.S. New Jersey, a battleship and the largest vessel in the Navy, was in port at the time finishing an overhaul before going to the Far East by way of the Panama Canal. This was to be my transport to Panama, so I packed up my gear in my sea bag and reported to the New Jersey where I was assigned a bunk in a below decks compartment directly adjacent to the barbette for one of the sixteen inch guns, which were the largest naval guns aboard any ship. The barbette was the protective steel cylinder that surrounded the gun turret. I shared this compartment with approximately 60 crew members and about a half dozen other sailors being assigned to duty in Panama.

The first thing I became aware of after checking out our bunks, was the community toilet; a long metal trough the length of the head, with sea water rapidly and continuously flushing the entire trough from one end to be discharged through the other end. The trough was provided with slats, so close together that the crew would sit cheek to cheek when defecating while having a full consciousness of the expansion and contraction of the neighbor's buttocks while relieving themselves.

A favorite trick for the crew was to light a crumpled newspaper with a match and to drop it into the trough at the water entry side. The paper would float down to the other end under the toilet seats, singing pubic hair and burning the protrusions hanging beneath the seats.

The cruise on the battlewagon down to Panama across the Caribbean Sea took about seven days as the ship went through some battle exercises while enroute. While the crew went to their stations for general quarters drill during these exercises, the passengers, having no part to play aboard the ship, were ordered to stay in the assigned compartment for the duration of the drills. The hatches were secured for watertight integrity and there was not much for us to do but sit, read, and wait for the end of the drill.

The compartment was without air conditioning and was hot as hell in those searing tropical climes. It was quiet and eerie in the quarters until the crew started to shoot off the sixteen inch guns. The sound of the tremendous impact from the gun reverberated through the compartment. I never heard such loud noise and our ears were in pain with every fresh burst of the gun. This happened on two separate days and we were glad when they finished the gunnery drills and we finally headed south for Panama.

We arrived at Limon Bay at the Atlantic end of the Panama Canal Zone early on a clear, hot spring morning. Someone pointed out to us the small town of Colon in the distance. It was then we learned that the passengers to be disembarked in Panama would not leave the ship until it had traversed the Canal to the Pacific Side. This was a lucky and exciting opportunity for us. The transit through the Canal would take the entire day because the New Jersey had a beam that just barely made it between the walls of the locks which made the process especially time-consuming.

The ship slowly entered the first of three chambers in the Gatun Locks which would raise the ship to 85 feet above sea level to the Gatun Lake which was made by the building of a dam along the Chagres River. The gates of the lock closed behind us and valves at the bottom of the lock were opened to permit the ship to rise until the water in the first chamber was at the same level as the second. A set of gates between the first and second chamber were then opened and the ship was pulled by "mules" (electric locomotives along the side of the locks) into the second chamber.

The ship was raised twice more in the locks until it reached the level of the man made Gatun Lake. The ship sailed about 22 miles across the lake to the Gaillard Cut, a channel cut through the rocks for about 8 miles. Violet flowers and the green leaves of hyacinths floated in the lake and we could see the tops of trees that were covered when the lake was built. We learned that there was a special hyacinth patrol that destroyed about 40 million plants each year to make sure that the ship's sailing channel was clear.

The Gaillard Cut was being continuously dredged to clear it of earth slides as we went through the small channel. At that time only one way traffic could be accommodated in the Cut and we had to wait our turn to go through until the Atlantic bound ships were cleared. (I understand that the Cut was widened and finally opened to two way traffic last year in 2001.)

The ship next went through the locks to take us down to the level of the Pacific Ocean. The Pedro Miguel Lock with a single chamber was first, followed by the Mira Flores Locks that took us down the last two steps to the Pacific.

After about fifty miles and a long day, we finally reached the terminus at Balboa in the early evening. The ship moored at a dock and we disembarked with our gear with orders to report to the officer of the day at the Headquarters of the Caribbean Command. As it was too late for transfer to our final destination, we spent the night in temporary quarters until our departure the following day.

We were not permitted off the base but we were allowed to explore the facility and to enjoy some tropical drinks at the base PX. The weather was balmy - we were to soon find out that that was the only kind of weather in Panama; relieved at times only by a daily rain during the rainy season.

For now, we thought we had been assigned to a tropical paradise as we sipped our Rum and Cokes and sat on an open veranda covered with a thatched roof watching the large tropic moon shed its rays across the bay.

In the morning the two of us who were to be stationed at the Farfan Radio Station were taken in a small bus to our new assignment. We drove inland from the ocean on a highway that paralleled the canal until we came to a bridge that took us over the Mira Flores Locks to a paved road that seemed to lead us into the middle of the jungle. We arrived at the gate of the Fort Clayton Army Base where we presented our papers to the sentry at the gate, who directed us to a side road which led us to what would be our home for the next several months.

As we drove down the road there were several houses along the right side of the road which I would soon find out were the quarters for the enlisted married personnel who had their families with them on base. On the opposite side of the street was a small building which served as a lecture hall and movie theatre for the small contingent stationed here. Alongside this building was a baseball field and on the other side was a tennis court.

On a hill overlooking the compound was a large residence which housed the commanding officer. The one thing all of these buildings had in common, and that included our barracks, was the lack of glass windows. All windows were open and screened and were protected from the rain by large overhanging eaves.

The barracks for the unmarried enlisted men and those with no dependents living on the base was a three story building situated at the end of the road at the bottom of the hill where the C.O.'s home was located. Between these two buildings alongside the barracks was an Olympic sized swimming pool which was used by both the officers and enlisted men. A long staircase led from the pool to the Captain's quarters.

The living quarters for the crew were located on the top floor of the barracks. There was an aisle along the front and rear of the third floor of the building with a door leading from each of the aisles into each of the five rooms located on opposite ends of the building. The head, staircase and a "dry room" for storing our winter uniforms were located in the center of the building separating the two pairs of five rooms.

The rooms for housing four crew members each were furnished with two double bunk beds and four six foot high lockers. (The inside of my locker door would become a bulletin board for Marilyn Monroe pictures cut from fan magazines, starting with her famous nude calendar photo. I have a picture of this collection of pinups in a photo album at home.) I took the upper bunk in a room that already had two occupants. It would not be too long before we were joined by a fourth room mate to fill the room.

Our room would become the gathering place for most of the off duty crew. There was always some action going on there even if at times it was only lively discussions of everything from women to philosophy (and usually back to women again.)

The crew's mess hall (dining room) and sick bay were on the second floor. There were no doctors or nurses on the station but we did have a Corpsman assigned to the base to tend to our everyday medical needs. If we required care for serious ailments, we would have to go to the hospital in Balboa.

Half of the first floor was a reading and game room and lounge where we would often gather for a "high stakes" poker game; the other half was the PX and bar, which opened everyday to serve the crewmembers not on watch.

The road to the crew's quarters took a sharp turn to the right onto a road that led to the radio shack located in what we called the "Bomb Proof Building", which held all of the communications equipment. This is where I would be spending most of my time on duty watch for the next year and a half.

The building was about one hundred feet square and was constructed of double concrete walls with the outer wall being two feet thick and steel reinforced. The 'bomb proof' radio shack also housed an extensive armory of weapons and ammunition of all types. We were permitted to check out any weapon; B.A.R., Carbine, M-1 rifle, etc. at any time we were off duty to practice on the firing range located in an open area in the jungle a few hundred yards behind the radio shack. At one point during my tour of duty in Panama, we were given classes in the care and firing of every weapon in the armory by a Marine instructor.

Entry to the radio shack was through a locked steel door that was guarded twenty-four hours a day by an armed Marine sentry. There were no Marines stationed at Farfan and the relief guards were driven in for their watch from Headquarters in Balboa. We all got to know the guards pretty well and established a good relationship with them. On the late night watches, when the guards were left alone outside in the dark with no lights, we would often bring them some refreshments or when things were not too busy, keep them company for a time.

It was quite a boring job, watching a building in the dark while hearing rustlings in the adjacent jungle, whether real or imagined. I can remember one occasion when I was on the midnight to 7 A.M. watch and was swabbing the decks, which was one of the jobs assigned to that relatively quiet tour of duty. While cleaning the swab (mop) in the deep sink, a scorpion came out of the damp swab and was within striking distance of my hand. (When the scorpion's tail is cocked in the upright position, it's an indication that they are ready to strike and inject their venomous serum into the victim.)

I jumped back and looked for something with which to kill the scorpion. Not having anything suitable for the purpose, I went to the entrance and asked the Marine on duty to come with me and to bring his rifle; we had a scorpion to get rid of. He eagerly brought his M-1 rifle into the washroom, pointed it at the scorpion which was now lying dormant on the handle of the swab, and was ready to shoot. I stopped him and said, "No, don't shoot the bastard, just crush him with the butt." He was very disappointed that he couldn't shoot the scorpion, which would have blown a hole in the deep sink as well but did as I requested and squashed the scorpion with his gun.

The radio shack was about a half mile from the barracks and the relief watch would usually walk there from the barracks, whether it was daytime or the middle of the night. I always felt a great feeling of trepidation when I was walking down that road at midnight while either relieving or being relieved from the evening watch. One never knew what was walking across the dark road at night.

Poisonous snakes, from bushmasters to fer-de-lances, were very prevalent in the area. There were reports from time to time of large felines in the vicinity and very often while walking the road we would trip on a sloth lying in the road or beside the road.

Midway between the crew's quarters and the radio shack was the base maintenance building and garage. The upper level of this building was set aside as quarters for the Chief Petty Officers and First Class Petty Officers. They were provided with private rooms and toilet facilities.

One of the first class petty officers was an 'old salt' with about twenty years of service who was a top notch radio operator, whether sober or drunk; a state he was in most of the time. His room was filled with many cases of Ron Carta Vieja, a local clear rum drink that could be purchased for a dollar a quart or less, and was so potent that it would have made an excellent paint remover.

"Whiskey Bill" as he was known secretly to most of us, would consume a quart of rum between reveille in the morning and lunch. No matter how much he consumed, he always managed to be on the job when required and could out communicate anyone else on the base for speed and accuracy. I believe if he had remained sober long enough, he might have achieved a higher rank than first class petty officer; by the normal progression of promotions he should have been at least a Chief Petty Officer many years before. He didn't spend any time with the rest of the crew and occupied most of his time in his room drinking, and on occasion would sit for hours at the barracks bar.

Panama had only one kind of weather – hot! Actually, there were two seasons; wet and dry; but the temperature was always 80 degrees or higher during the day. In the dry season, it never rained and during the wet season, it rained every day at some time. At times the rain would come down in torrents that were so localized that you could be sitting in a bar on one side of the street where the sun was shining and the streets were dry, while on the other side the rain came pouring down. Even when one got caught in the rain and got drenched, the only thing necessary to do after the rain ended was to remain in the sun for a short time to dry off.

What seemed at first like paradise soon became a tiresome repetition of one hot day after another. While the blood naturally thinned as we grew more accustomed to the heat, there was no relief from the hot and humid jungle air. Most of us soon developed terrible cases of fungus which no medical care seemed to relieve. At one point I had such a bad incidence of this 'jungle rot' that I would awake in the middle of the night and find myself sitting up in the bed scratching a pernicious itch that wouldn't abate. I had this terrible fungus without letup for about six months prior to my departure for my next assignment in the States. Interestingly, as soon as I received my orders to ship out, the fungus started clearing up immediately and was completely gone by the time I left Panama. This might lead to a conclusion that there was a certain psychological component to the rash.

Spread across a grassy field abutting the radio shack was a pole antenna field of several acres surrounded by the thick tropical jungle. Up the road a short drive into that jungle was our storage house for cables and other equipment.

During the dry season there were often forest fires generated by some careless natives wandering through the jungle or spontaneous combustion caused by the excessive heat and the relentless aridness at that period. At these times the entire crew would be enlisted to help fight the fires, all of us having been briefly trained in these skills while in boot camp. Our primary goal was to protect the antennas and the store house.

Much of the fire fighting had to be done by hand as it was impossible to get the mobile fire equipment through the thick jungle foliage. We would fill back carried water cans outfitted with a hand pump and carry these into the fire. No one was ever burned in any of the many fires I was involved in but just about all of us at one time or another got surrounded by the quickly spreading flames and had to be rescued by the rest of the fire fighting crew. It happened to me on one occasion and I thought that I was going to be consumed in the fire.

These fires often went for several days at a time before we finally got them under control. There were no liberty passes during these times and we were expected to go directly from our watch in the radio shack to the front line of the fire fight. After a particularly bad and long fire, the C.O., Commander Morrison would open the bar at the barracks with free drinks for the crew. No matter how tired we were from the lack of sleep and the constant battle to save the equipment from the blaze, we always managed to take full advantage of the Captain's generosity and drank our fill.

The working area inside the radio shack consisted of about 8 to 10 stations for the operators. Each station served a different purpose; from communicating with the fleet or commercial vessels to copying the one way broadcasts of correspondence out of Washington.

On the other side of the room was a bank of teletype machines, while the Watch Officer's desk to oversee the entire activity was located in the center of the room.

Our communications were with both Navy ship and land stations and commercial vessels heading in and out of the Canal Zone. We sent out daily weather conditions to the entire fleet over the wireless in Morse code. In those days, all ships were equipped for CW (Morse code) operation, but not all were into teletype or other advanced techniques. We therefore, had to take the weather reports we received from the meteorological station in Washington, transpose the reports onto special tapes which would subsequently be run through a keying machine to convert them into radio signals for transmission.

The newest members of the crew would be given this simple but tedious task that entailed typing groups of numerically coded reports and monitoring them as they automatically were transmitted to the ships at sea. It was a particularly boring chore and the temptation was always there to doze off while listening to the constant drone of the dits and dahs.

The importance of constant and careful monitoring of these reports was brought home to us very dramatically when complaints started coming in from our fleet and the commercial vessels that were relying on our accurately transmitted weather reports. The decoding of some of our weather transmissions by the ships at sea had snow falling in Costa Rica and non-existent hurricanes threatening some sea lanes; needless to say that these errors could have caused grave safety problems for the ships.

As we had to personally sign off on all communication in and out of the station that we were responsible for and were required to keep files of all of the tapes, the Executive Officer assigned some of the senior crew members to go over all the records and listen to all of the tapes to determine who was at fault for the botched up broadcasts. It was determined that one of the junior staff had been typing bad tapes and sending them out without monitoring. He was summarily transferred overnight to another post outside the Canal Zone and we never heard of him again. This overnight and quick transfer was a common way to deal with people with problems.

One duty that was quite interesting was communicating with the Columbian Navy in Bogotá and the Peruvian Navy in Lima. We had a short program of official correspondence, most often from the State Department to and from our Embassies in those cities, at a regularly scheduled hour each day. After our exchange of messages, we would often carry on a brief conversation (in Morse code) with our counterparts on the other end.

As a diversion, and not being seen or heard at the other end, I started to carry on a regular conversation with one of the Peruvian sailors when we both had the same watch in which I pretended to be a WAVE (woman sailor) by the name of Seaman Mary Bratcher. One of the crew and a room mate of mine was Howie Bratcher. The Peruvian sailor and I (as Mary) had as torrid a romance as possible over the many miles without having voice or visual contact. During one of these sessions, I invited him to visit me at our Farfan station if he ever got to Panama.

After some time I didn't hear anything more from "Mary's swain" and assumed he had been assigned to other duty. A short time after this, Howie received a call from the Army sentry at the front gate informing him that there was a visitor at the gate for "Seaman" Bratcher. Howie went out and - you guessed it - it was the Peruvian sailor who had been transferred to a ship that was now stopping in Panama.

I would like to say at this point that Howie and the Peruvian hit it off immediately, that it was love at first sight, and that they got together and lived happily ever after. But instead the Peruvian was disappointed and went back to his ship and Howie was pissed off but never did find out who pulled this prank on him.

[Shortly after this incident Howie, who slept in the lower tier of my bunk bed, fell in 'love' with a Panamanian girl who worked in one of the local bars in Panama City. He got quite serious about this relationship and couldn't stop talking to me about her every time he came back from liberty in the city. However, if the stories that some of the crew related were true, she had been bedded by half the guys at Farfan and lord knows how many from the other stations in the area.

Howie was in love and blind to any of these insinuations. He told me that he planned to marry her as soon as he could get permission from the Navy; which was required at the time in the Caribbean Command area.

One night Howie came back to the barracks and, knowing that he was not one of the big drinkers on the base, I was surprised that he was stewed to the gills. He plopped into his rack with his uniform still on and started to cry. He said that he had gone home with his girl (I forget her name but I think it was Pearl) as he frequently did and she asked him if he wanted to go to bed with her. He had always told me that he knew she was a virgin. At first he was disappointed but then realized that she could no longer constrain her love and need for him so he told her he would like that. When she wanted to charge him for the privilege, he suddenly became aware that the stories about her were probably true.

Howie didn't continue to drink after that disappointment but he did start to sleep almost continuously every time he was not on duty. I particularly remember him coming down to the radio shack one night while I was on duty, claiming that he must have insomnia because he couldn't sleep; this after having slept for more than 24 hours straight.]

MISSION IMPALPABLE

We worked on a four day cycle with two days on duty and two days off. The first watch was from Noon to 5 P.M. followed by a Midnight to 7 A.M. shift. After sleeping in during the day (provided there was no fire to fight or special duties) we would return to the radio shack from 5 P.M. until Midnight and return again at 7 A.M. until the finish of the two day tour at Noon. During the times we had special operations with the Fleet, we went on more but shorter shifts for a two day period with one day off.

During one of these special operations, I was summoned to the Captain's office. The Captain asked the orderly to leave the room and close the door as he wanted to speak to me privately. I was a bit concerned when he did this because anytime this was done in the past whether it was at work or in school; it was because I was going to be called on the carpet for some malefaction. It wasn't long before I found out the real purpose of this private meeting with the C.O. and relieved to find out that I was not about to be "reamed out."

251

As part of our preparations for this latest fleet operation all of the radiomen on the station were required by order of the Executive Officer, a Chief Warrant Officer, to practice our communicating skills to improve both our sending and receiving speed and accuracy. Every day both on watch and off watch we were pushed to the limits by the Exec. The automatic keyer that we practiced on had an adjustable speed that the Exec kept pushing faster and faster. Although I was a laggard in radio school in meeting the speed requirements, I soon became one of the most proficient operators in the crew; approaching the copying speed of our top telegrapher, the Exec himself, who had a top speed in excess of 55 words per minute.

This proficiency along with my demonstrated knowledge of communications procedures and equipment maintenance was the reason I was summoned to the Captain's office. The Captain asked me if I wanted to volunteer for a special mission off the base to a destination that would never be revealed to me. This mission had an element of danger to it, but the C.O. said that he thought this risk would be minimal. He said he would lay out the entire project for me if I accepted, but that I was to reveal absolutely none of this to anyone either before or after the completion of the mission. No one on the base was to be told a thing about this and there would be a cover story to account for my absence.

It sounded intriguing and as I was already falling into a state of boredom with the everyday routine on the base, I gladly accepted the challenge.

I was then briefed personally and privately by the C.O. That night I was to awaken the Corpsman in his room to complain of severe pains in the lower abdomen. The Corpsman, by standard procedure for this type of ailment, would call for an ambulance to take me to the hospital. The ambulance would by prearrangement pick me up, but would deliver me to a pier where I would be taken by small boat in the dark of night to a submarine anchored off shore. I was to board the sub where I would be given further orders and told then only as much as I needed to know. I was to bring no personal gear as everything I would require would be provided.

Everyone on the base with the exception of the Captain would be left with the impression that for the next week I was in the hospital and was not permitted any visitors because of my condition. Later, I was to claim that I was hospitalized with an infected liver and could not have guests for fear of further contamination.

On board the submarine, I was introduced to an Army Major who was to be in charge of the mission and who would prepare me for my part. I was to be part of a group of ten servicemen including the Major in charge, a Marine Lieutenant who I soon learned was fluent in Spanish and who would be in charge of six enlisted Marines, a Navy Ensign who in addition to being an expert cryptographer could speak Russian, and me. My function would be, first of all to ask absolutely no questions and to follow all directions explicitly, and to communicate on a fixed frequency at three set times each day with a station on the other end that would be identified by a preset signal and would only acknowledge its readiness to receive and acknowledge receipt of any communications. The objective, I was told, was to get on the air quickly, send out as rapidly as possible a coded message that would be provided by the Ensign, verify the receipt of the transmission, and get off the air. There was a short window of opportunity to complete all this and I realized I had been selected for this mission because of my recently acquired speed and accuracy as a radioman.

Other than these basic instructions, the only thing I was told was that we would be landing in possibly hostile territory and would be traveling mostly at night through the jungle and would be trying to avoid detection. If we were to be discovered, we were to avoid any kind of conflict unless overtly threatened and that if we were to be taken into custody by anyone we were to say that we were part of the ongoing fleet operation and had gone off course and outside the operating area and then washed ashore during an outburst of bad weather.

I was given a set of camouflaged fatigues, a backpack which contained a small radio transmitter/receiver, and about a week's supply of K rations. I was to soon find out that I would not be shaving (no great loss for my fair face at that time) or bathing for about a week. When submerged and underway we were assigned bunks that were shared with the regular submarine crew and were told, during what I thought must have been daylight hours, to get some sleep in preparation for a landing that night at our destination.

We arose toward evening, donned our new outfits, had our last decent meal for a while, and waited to be called up to the deck to board the rubber rafts that would take us ashore. When the word was quietly passed that the time was at hand, I suddenly began to feel a bit frightened about what was ahead. I began to feel in a modest way, the fear and uncertainty that surely must have been on the minds of those young men huddled in the landing crafts as the D Day invasion was about to be launched in Normandy. I did what I had to and climbed down into the raft under the dim light of the stars on a moonless night.

It seemed like forever before we hit shore even though I knew it was a short trip in from the sub. The crewmen that took us in on the three rafts pulled the rafts onto a small beach and we got out and watched the boats start the return trip to the sub, leaving us standing on the sand waiting for the Major to give the order to leave. It was the Marine Lieutenant however that gave us the quiet signal to follow him into the brush.

I don't know if I was the only one to be tethered but someone quietly tied a line of light nylon cord to my waist and I was told to follow the marine at the other end of the line. This tether was no doubt to assure that I didn't get lost in the dark jungle at night and that our party would not get separated. They were particularly protective of me and I assumed that it was to protect the radio gear.

I still didn't know where we were going, or why, or how long we would be here in this godforsaken thicket of heat, humidity, and insects; and who knows what other crawling things were slithering around under our feet. We traveled what must have been inland for the next two nights; moving after sunset and bedding down on the ground during the day while the marines did sentry duty. As I lay on a home made bed of leaves and greenery, my imagination as to what would be crawling on me as I slept hindered my sleep each day. Nothing untoward happened however, except for one day as we slept when one of the marines killed a fer-de-lance, a highly poisonous snake, by quietly crushing its skull with the butt of his rifle.

Whether by design or by accident, we didn't come across any inhabited areas or see any two legged animals until the end of the second day in the jungle just prior to our departure for the night's journey. There was a group of men traversing the jungle in our vicinity and we were alerted by the marine who was acting as the lead scout for our detachment. We crouched down in the brush and were told to keep quiet. I couldn't see if the group was a military patrol or just a group of locals and I couldn't ask as we were told to limit our talking. If anyone were ever nearby there would be less chance of being detected if we kept silent.

The Ensign prepared brief coded messages for each of the scheduled broadcasts with what I later decided was probably the submarine. I assumed these messages were reporting the progress of our mission. I still didn't know what we were looking for or why we were here. Each day, as most of us rested for the next evening's trek, the accompanying Marines would take turns scouting the area around us and reporting back to the Major.

Late on the third day out, with about three hours of daylight remaining, one of the Marine scouts returned to our bivouac and spoke briefly with the Major. When the last of the scouts returned shortly after, we were told we would be moving out immediately and would not be waiting for sunset. We were admonished to keep absolutely quiet and to stay close together as we cut our way through the jungle in the direction that the first marine had returned from.

For the past two days we had been climbing higher into the mountainous jungle and now we were approaching what appeared to be the crest of the mountain ridge. As we neared the top, we stopped and we all looked curiously down into a valley that seemed to be cleared of foliage, and there before us was what appeared to be a long aircraft runway and several hanger sized Quonset huts.

Then we all saw it at about the same time. One of the hangers opened up and a sleek looking jet aircraft was being towed toward the runway. Not being an experienced plane spotter, I couldn't identify the type of plane in the valley but I did recognize the bright red star painted on the wings and on the side of the fuselage.

This was what we were here for! The Russians had established a presence somewhere in Central America. I assumed it was Central America or Northern South America because we hadn't been traveling long enough in the submarine to have gone further.

The sun was getting ready to set soon. The Major took out a small camera and started to shoot pictures before the sun went down. We then retreated back into the jungle and the Ensign prepared his usual message; this time longer than most, and it took me about ten minutes to complete the transmission.

The Captain said that we would camp in the jungle that night and return to the site of the airfield in the morning. It was bad enough sleeping in that morass during the day, but at night it was a horror for me. I couldn't sleep not only because of the queasiness I felt for this place but with the knowledge that something big was going on here and I was not privy to it – until now.

At daylight, the Captain, the Lieutenant and two of his marines took off again toward our discovery of the previous evening; doubtless to take more pictures and more notes. Upon their return about four hours later, we broke camp and started back in the direction that we had come from. I was hoping we were headed back to the coast where we could be taken back to the sub.

We spent another two nights in the jungle and finally reached the coast early on the third night. I had my last scheduled message to send out this time, and even though it was coded, I knew that it was instructing the submarine to pick us up; I just didn't know when.

It wasn't long before we spotted the rafts from the sub pulling onto the beach a few hundred feet from where we were waiting. It was now a moonlit night and we had to move fast to get to the boats before we were discovered. When we finally reached the sub, closed the hatches and submerged one last time under the ocean, I felt like I could breathe freely for the first time in a week.

On our return to Panama, I said goodbye to all of my unnamed companions and was taken off to the hospital where I would spend the night before returning to Farfan in the morning. I never breathed a word of this to anyone until now, but it still remains a clear memory in my mind.

Subsequent events helped me to put together the only possible scenario for this strange journey. Shortly after my return to normal duty, I was monitoring some of the messages that often crossed our desks. One communication between Washington and one of the embassies mentioned the existence of an airfield in the middle of Guatemala that was equipped with a squadron of Russian MIG's. It was not too long after noting this memo that the then current government of Guatemala, which had been considered sympathetic to the Russians, was overthrown by an internal cabal that was suspected in some newspapers of being secretly assisted by the United States Central Intelligence Agency. This was well before Castro had turned Cuba to Communism and was a time the Soviets were trying to get a foothold somewhere in our hemisphere.

I don't know for sure if our mission and this Guatemalan government overthrow were related but from what I had seen in the place that we scouted, it's the only scenario that makes sense.

By the way, as a result of the fleet operation that was going on while we were on our little escapade in the jungles of Guatemala, our command received a unit citation and a letter of commendation from the Secretary of the Navy that entitled us to wear the "Letter of Commendation" service ribbon. I have always privately thought of that particular award as a tribute to the group of ten that spent a week together on that special mission in the jungle.

A NEW COMMANDER

When I first arrived at Farfan in early 1951, the Commanding Officer of the base with a crew of about fifty was Navy Lieutenant-Commander Bennett, a Naval Academy graduate. Commander Bennett was a stickler for regulations in performance and in dress. He, himself, was always nattily dressed and a model for the well dressed naval officer; trousers always neatly pressed with a razor sharp crease, shoes that reflected like a mirror, and hat worn squarely on the head. He expected no less from the crew.

However, when I came aboard, I sensed that behind the drill like operation of the station there was a low state of morale. There was animosity amongst certain crew members and an undercurrent of hostility between the men and the Captain and Executive Officer.

I had not been there more than about three months when it was announced that Commander Bennett was to be transferred and would leave as soon as his replacement, a Lieutenant-Commander Morrison, arrived in Panama. On the morning of Commander Morrison's arrival, the entire crew that was not on watch was summoned to an assembly outside the barrack's at which the formal change of command would take place.

As we stood at attention in formation in our dress white uniforms, the only time we were required to wear our dress uniforms during my service in Panama, Bennett as usual was well groomed, erect, and in full command of the situation. He came to attention and in a loud and clear voice he read his official orders turning command over to his replacement who stood at his side. When he finished, he smartly closed the folder he had been reading from and briskly passed it to the Yeoman and just as sharply turned and gave Morrison a crisp salute.

This was our first glimpse of our new Commanding Officer and the crew was anxious to hear his response; up to now we had no information on him or where he had served before. Morrison was not attired in his dress uniform, but rather a set of oversized fatigues that appeared wrinkled from sleeping in all night. As he stepped forward to the lectern that had been set up for this ceremony, he tripped on a crack in the cement and grabbed the lectern to stop from falling on his face.

He started to search through his pockets for something and finally pulled out a wrinkled piece of paper which he dropped on the deck. After scrambling to pick it up he placed the paper on the lectern to smooth out. He started to read from what we assumed were his orders in a voice that was barely audible and which would get him his first nickname by the crew; "Mumbles."

The stark contrast between Bennett and Morrison was not lost on the crew. After the reading of the orders Morrison turned to Bennett and gave him a quick flip of the hand to the brim of his cap which substituted for a salute. Bennett congratulated Morrison, wished him luck, and just as quickly and sharply as he did everything, boarded a waiting vehicle and left Farfan in the hands of this apparent bumpkin.

Instead of turning the crew over to the Chief Petty Officer for dismissal, Morrison announced himself that he was opening up the bar early and that the drinks were on him to celebrate the day. I thought that he would retire to his quarters but he joined the enlisted men at the bar; a fraternization that was frowned upon by the Navy and made many of the crew uncomfortable, particularly the senior members who were not used to this.

We soon found out some of Morrison's background which started to alleviate some of the misgivings all of us had from that first day's performance. First and foremost, and perhaps an explanation for his garbled speech (but not garbled thoughts), he was captured by the Japanese early in the war and had spent most of the war years as a prisoner of war in a Japanese prison camp where he was starved, tortured, and constantly abused. He had been an enlisted man at that time but, in spite of his terrible ordeal, decided to stay in the Navy after the war and received his commission as an officer.

Life on the base changed dramatically after Morrison's appearance on the scene. Although he neglected the grooming aspects of the job that had been such a fetish with Commander Bennett, he focused his attention on the crew's performance of their duties and made the hard life in the tropics, a lot better. There was a vast improvement in the morale on the base and much of the petty quarreling that had become endemic in the barracks had diminished. We began to work together as a team and "Mumbles" became an affectionate term for the C.O. rather than the disparaging characterization it had on that first day.

Even the food started to improve, but I don't think this was because of Morrison's presence. There were two Chief Commissary Officers to administer our kitchen; one supervised the actual cooking and the other handled the ordering of supplies and administrative functions. There were three First Class Cooks (That's First Class Petty Officer, not cook) who shared the kitchen duty; each working two days with four days off; and not one of them could produce a decent meal even though there were never more than about thirty crew members to be fed at any given meal. The only saving grace from the kitchen was a young seaman who was learning to bake and did a terrific job on breads and desserts.

As a result of the outbreak of hostilities in Korea many veterans who had decided to stay in the Naval Reserve were called up for duty. One of these was a former ship's cook that had become a chef at the Waldorf Astoria Hotel in New York where he was gaining a reputation as one of the cities top Chefs. He was assigned to our base to replace one of the cooks who was being discharged. From the day that he arrived, the meals started to improve immensely. He was put in charge of all food processing and made sure that the other cooks started to produce as well.

The crew hired two local young Panamanians to assist in the kitchen as 'mess cooks'. Chipping in a couple of dollars every payday for the mess cooks obviated the need for us to share in the kitchen duty and gave the youngsters a chance to make a few dollars in a job that was sought by many of the local unemployed workers. They would supplement their income by shining shoes and doing other jobs for the sailors living in the barracks. We also shared in the hiring of a man to clean the barracks.

One of the mess cooks from the small nearby town of LaChorrera invited some of us crew members to his wedding held in his local church with a reception outside his house. It seemed that the entire town attended the reception. It was a grand party and a lot of fun dancing, singing, and drinking with the locals and the half dozen of us from Farfan that attended got thoroughly soused before the long night was over. We were asked to sleep over by the groom's father; an invitation we readily accepted. I think some of the family gave up their beds for me and my drunken shipmates.

Three of us shared beds in the same room as the bride and groom. Two of us fell asleep shortly after hitting the sack while the third one stayed awake long enough to eavesdrop on the newlyweds who shared a bed nearby. In the morning he reported the activity to us on our way back to the barracks. According to this report, the two lovers pulled a blanket over them while the young man banged away. Every once in a while he would peak his head out from under the blanket, assure himself that everyone was asleep, and then go back to the business at hand. This kept up until dawn before the two of them finally went to sleep and our snoop could get some rest himself.

Commander Morrison added to our sense of comradeship by encouraging us to participate in team sports against some of the other military units in the Canal Zone. One of our most successful endeavors was the formation of the Farfan Basketball Team to compete in the Canal Zone Inter-service league. There was some pretty stiff competition out there but we put together a good squad. The tallest guy on our team was six foot two inch Tom "Bull" Burgess and the next tallest were Radioman Chief Hobbs and me at six feet. The only team members who ever played organized ball were the Chief who played some college freshman ball and Harry Bishop who at five foot ten inches played varsity ball at the Cape May High School in New Jersey. The rest of us played some 'sand lot' basketball in the local parks or the high school gym but no prior experience at organized basketball.

With the Chief acting as coach, because he was the senior rank, we practiced for a couple of weeks when we could get the team together, which was usually impossible with the varied tours of duty. We were invited to play some of the teams before the first game of league play. We accepted and had an opportunity to play about six games against some pretty tough competition.

Typical of the teams we would be facing was the local Air Force team. The first team was composed of five players who were selected as All-State Players in their respective states while in High School and some while playing college ball. Each of these five was taller than our 'Bull'. The other teams had rosters that were equally threatening but we eagerly accepted the challenge. We felt what we lacked in size and experience we could make up in speed, hustle, and just plain guts.

Happily, our six practice games went fairly well. We beat four of the teams by a slight margin and lost the other two by only a couple of points.

The league season was about twenty games for each team and usually played in the Balboa High School gym. We did have a fast, hustling team and finished every first half in the lead or trailing by no more than four points. During half time, however, when the other team went to their locker room to rest or for a pep talk, our team would retire to the locker room to pop down a few cool beers and to congratulate ourselves for bearing up under the pace of play.

At the end of the season we surprised everyone; our team was the only team with a perfect record – 0 wins and 20 losses. We were beaten but unbowed. Our efforts on the court turned the guys on the base, both players and rooters, into a smooth working unit which proved to be very helpful during some of the stressful operations that we would later participate in; and we did have a hell of a lot of fun.

Speaking about fun, our leisure time on the base was limited to swimming in the pool, attending outdated films at the base theatre, or drinking at the base bar that was usually sparsely patronized except for one or two base 'sots' who seldom went into town. There was an occasional card game in the lounge and reading was a popular pastime.

Most of the time however, when we were not on watch, we would opt to don our civilian clothes (civvies) and head for Panama City. All of the servicemen and American Citizens (Zonians) in the Canal Zone had open access to Panama at all times except during those not infrequent times when the Panamanians were in the midst of an overthrow of the then ruling government and the country would be declared 'Off Limits' to the servicemen.

The normal liberty routine in Panama City was to buy a bottle of the local rum (Ron Carta Vieja could be purchased for one dollar a quart) and to gather in one of the local bars where we could buy setups of ice and soda and were permitted to bring in our own bottles of booze. The 'in' drink at the time was Rum and club soda with a squeeze of lemon. The alternative was to drink the local cerveza (beer) which was also quite inexpensive.

When the booze started to work its evil upon us someone would invariably suggest that we grab a cab and go out to Rio Abajo, the local red light district to get a woman. This district was "Out of Bounds" for the servicemen but they still patronized them and were rarely bothered by the Shore Patrol or Military Police. (These in service policemen would later to be merged into a full time "Armed Service Police" force.)

Prostitution was very flagrant in Panama City and women were always available to service the Americans from the Canal Zone. They ranged from the girls who worked in the "Houses of Love" in the red light district, to the bar maids, most of whom were available for a price, to the lowest priced whores who stood on the streets or in the alleys trying to lure in the passing guys with what we termed the "Panamanian Love Call"... "Pst! Pst! Hey sailor, want to get laid? Want a good blow job? I give you 'round the world, Heh?" This latter selection was sure to have you reporting to sick bay with one of the rampant venereal diseases.

We were paid twice a month, on the first and the fifteenth but the Army was paid only once a month. The Army was such a huge presence in the Canal Zone that their payday determined the prices charged by the prostitutes in town. As the end of the month approached and most of the soldiers were broke, the price of a woman dipped to ridiculously low levels. Many of the sailors and the more prudent soldiers would save a few dollars and wait until the end of the month to avail themselves of the lower cost.

A taxi could be hired for one dollar to take one or more customers or fellow travelers out to the brothels and the driver would wait for the participating passengers to conduct their business and then return them downtown.

When I first pulled liberty in Panama City, we were forewarned about the pandemic venereal diseases that prevailed in the area. We were given lectures and shown "V.D." films that were so frightening that one was tempted to take a vow of celibacy. Unfortunately, in most cases, the loins won out over the brain. Initially we were directed to use the public "Pro" Stations which were situated in strategic locations around the city and in Balboa. At the station, a serviceman who participated in the local body sports would be given a supply of Prophylactic cleaners and instructions in their use. He would use one of the private cubicles to clean up and apply the cleaners to the effected areas. I don't think this was too effective as we still had a high venereal infection rate across the Canal Zone. Continence proved to be the most effective defense against the Syphilis, Gonorrhea ('clap'), or one of the other common 'social' diseases raging in Panama.

Before I left Panama, our base became part of the Navy's experiment with new penicillin pills which were to be used as venereal disease preventatives. Anyone who engaged in sexual relations with any of the natives was to go to sick bay upon return to the barracks, take one penicillin tablet and record the name and date of exposure into a log that was kept there.

After some time, it was discovered that the pills were being used at a rate higher than was recorded in the log and, in fact, at a rate higher than the number of personnel on the base. The mystery of the disappearing penicillin was solved when the base Medical corpsman couldn't get out of his bed one morning. His crotch was swollen to gigantic proportions. He had contracted a case of what was variously called Buboes (or 'Blue balls'), or Elephantiasis (or Elephantitis as we said it).

The corpsman was carried off to the hospital where he confessed to having used all of the missing penicillin pills in the hopes of curing his venereal disease with a super dose of the medicine. He was another case of an overnight transfer that we never heard from again and a new corpsman was sent over to replace him.

I was sitting at the bar at one of the Panama cantinas one night drinking beer with one of my shipmates when a huge black man took the seat alongside me and started to knock down straight shots of the fire water they called 'rum'. He was a giant of a man; about six feet ten inches tall with shoulders as wide as a desk. He was solidly built and the muscles seemed to be straining to tear open his shirt. His hands were larger than Primo Carnera's huge mitts that I had the honor of shaking as an usher at the Center Theater a couple of years before.

After a time, and a few drinks, he turned to me and said, "Why they callin' me a nigger. I ain't no nigger, I'm an Indian." I don't know who 'they' were.

I looked into his dark ebony face and discretion prompted me to vociferously agree with him. He accused me of not believing him and I was reluctant to argue with him. If he wanted to be an Indian or an Eskimo or anything, it was alright with me.

When I had to go to the men's room, I started to get up and he grabbed my arm. "Where you goin'?", he wanted to know. I told him, "The head."

He said, "You jus' tryin' to get away from me 'cause you think I'm a nigger."

He held my arm in such a steel like grip that he was cutting off the circulation of blood. His hand was so big that it encompassed the whole of my upper arm. I could feel my hand going numb but I didn't want to say anything to enrage this madman.

I finally convinced him that I was not leaving, that I knew he was an Indian, and that I would be right back. I did go to the head, but I slipped out the back door and didn't look back. I left my shipmate to figure out his own way to get away from that nut. When he realized I wasn't coming back, he rushed out of the bar without finishing the fresh drink that he had just paid for.

These encounters were not unusual. On another occasion I was in the same bar with Jim Gallagher, one of our crew and one who often liked to provoke fights when he had a bit too much to drink. Jim was a good sized fellow and was quite capable of handling himself in most fights. On this night, however, he bit off more than he could chew.

Two short and slightly built Indians (these were 'real' Indians from the San Blas Island) came into the bar for a few drinks. They sat at the bar drinking and were bothering no one when Jim decided to start poking fun at them and trying to start a fight with these two "shrimps" sitting at the end of the bar. When he finally went over to one of them obviously intent on starting a ruckus, the Indian swiftly pulled a large knife out of a sheath on his belt, and pushed the point of the glistening blade into Jim's neck. Having the courage that only a few drinks could give (and the stupidity to match) I walked over and was ready to wrest the knife from this little guy.

His friend had other ideas. Before I knew it, there was the blade of a long sharp knife now resting across my throat. These guys were quick. Thankfully the bartender intervened and in Spanish talked the Indian's into putting down their knives and asked us to leave, which we very quickly and gratefully did.

(Panama's society was basically divided into three classes; the upper class that was composed of the Military, Politicians, Clergy, Businessmen, and Bankers; the lower class that included the laborers, bar maids, whores, and farm workers; and the Indians; in that order. The upper class still lived under many of the old time Spanish rules of behavior.

One of the enlisted men in our crew initiated a romance with the daughter of one of the local Panamanian bigwigs and was surprised to find the restrictions that he had to live under while courting this lovely young senorita. He could not see the girl alone and when he went on a date with her, he had to take along a duenna or chaperone to monitor the activities of the couple. They courted for about a year before he finally married her at a lavish wedding and reception at the parent's estate that was attended by most of the 'who's who' of Panama City. None of our crew was invited to the wedding; probably for fear that we would get too raucous.)

I played my first round of golf in Panama at the Naval Ammunition Depot (NAD) Golf Course, a nine hole course in Balboa. I still have the score card of that game of nine holes as a testament to not only my first game, but also my first birdie on a 140 yard Par 3 hole. My final score on the card was 47; although I don't know how many rules of golf I violated to attain it. Actually I have over the years called that birdie, "my first hole-in-one that I missed by only one stroke." As I swung at the teed up ball on that hole I topped the ball and it simply rolled off a couple of inches from the tee. Without re-teeing the ball, I hit the ball a second time. The ball went straight as an arrow to hit the green and roll straight into the cup.

Before I leave my reminiscences about my tour of duty in Panama I should mention some of the characters that colored my days in that God forsaken jungle of snakes, bugs, heat, and fungus; many of their names long forgotten.

First there was one of my room mates and close associates during my stay at Farfan, "Bull" Burgess of Boston, Massachusetts and the 'star' center of our basketball team. Besides the many times we spent in barracks philosophizing and on liberty together, the thing that stands out most in my mind was Bull's appetite for the Panamanian women. There was more than one night when, after a bout of drinking rum and soda at one of the local haunts, Bull would insist upon hopping a cab out to one of the local whore houses.

After making his selection of a playmate at the first establishment and completion of his activity, he would invariably come out of the room into the bar area where the rest of us were waiting and tell us that the girl he had just bedded was completely unsatisfactory. We would then get back into the taxi to be driven to another *house of love* where Bull would repeat the ritual. This continued until we found a place where he was satisfied, gave up finding the woman of his dreams, or ran out of money. On one occasion, we went to five different places and he serviced five different girls before he called it a night.

Another character was Seaman Potts from Flushing, New York, who we called "Potsy". He was another of our crew who fell in love with one of the local Panamanian bar maids and was so smitten that he had her name, "Star", tattooed on his forearm with an elaborate heart and scroll. This was another romance that eventually soured when it became evident that she was also for sale. In this case, poor Potsy was left with that large, gaudy reminder on his arm. (When I later went to the Prep School for the Naval Academy, one of the sailors that was attempting to be accepted into the academy also had a tattoo on his upper arm. When I met him he was in the process of having the tattoo removed, one square inch at a time, by removing the tattoo and grafting skin over the arm. Tattoos were cause for rejection at the Academy at that time.)

Bill Page, a third class Radioman, occupied a room at the opposite end of the barracks from me and I never did get to know him too well. Although we all shared the showers that were located in the center of the barracks and, in typical Navy fashion, the crew members walked stark naked through the halls with a towel tossed over the shoulders to take a shower, I never noticed any unusual endowments on any of the men.

One night while sitting at one of the city bars, the barmaid asked me where I was from and when I told her that I was stationed at Farfan, she asked if I knew "Three-legged" Page. When I said, "Yes, I know Page, but what is this "Three-Legged?" she filled me in on his special attributes.

She told me that Page was well known amongst the barmaids and hookers in town and that most of them wouldn't take him on as a client because he was so hugely endowed that he was noted for the damage he wreaked on the girls because of this. The next time Page was headed for the shower I made it a point to witness myself this legendary protuberance. The bar maid was not exaggerating and I was surprised that I had never noticed this phenomenon before.

His penis was a contender for the Guinness' Book of World Records. In the flaccid state it had to be a good eight inches in length and nearly stretched to the bottom of his thigh. I could understand why the women in town avoided him; in the erected state he surely would be yielding a weapon that could disrupt their business. (I would have thought that when he got gorged with blood that a sudden erection would make him pass out from the rush of blood from the brain.)

Page started to have an affair with the wife of one of the Commissary Chief's that lived in one of the houses down the road from our barracks. It seems that everyone on the base was aware of this situation except the husband. It was a match up that was difficult to comprehend by those of us who were aware of Page's physical abnormality. She was a small, thin lady; not more than five feet tall and about one hundred pounds. (Page had one member that was almost as long as she was tall)

One night, I entered a bar in Panama City with two of my mates. Sitting at the bar was Petty Officer Page and his paramour. They joined us in our trivial bar room palaver and no mention was made of their being out together. Until this point they had been somewhat discreet about the relationship and had not been seen together in a public place.

We weren't at the bar too long when the Chief came into the bar alone. When he saw his wife and Page at the bar he must have verified what he no doubt suspected. He wasted no time to approach the couple, order his wife to leave with him and then without a word to Page, punched him across the cheek before Page could get off his stool. Page was a ponderous size (not only below the belt) and was hardly fazed by the Chief's blow.

Page moved like a shot off the stool and just as quickly threw a succession of punches at the Chief that had him on the deck. We jumped in to hold Page and to break up this fight before it progressed any further; it was obvious that the Chief would be no match for Page. Two of us hustled Page and the girl out of the bar and escorted them to her car and suggested that they return to the base. There was suddenly a pall over the evening so we asked the lovers to take us back to the base in the car.

We arrived at the Chief's house a short time later. The living quarters were on the second floor above an open garage where we pulled in to park the car. We stood there together for a while talking and trying to ease some of the tension. As we talked, the Chief arrived home and walked stridently up the stairs to the apartment and we figured it was time to leave to return to the barracks.

We were saying goodnight when the Chief came down the stairs with a 45 caliber pistol in his hand and started to fire recklessly into the midst of the group. Everyone, including me, panicked and ran as hastily as we could to get away from the lunatic with the gun.

Whether intentional or not, every shot went wild and missed all of us, but came close enough to scare the daylights out of us. Someone must have heard the shots because as we cowered in the nearby brush to which we had retreated, two jeeps with the Army sentries pulled up in front of the house. We didn't know it until later but the Chief had gone back to the apartment. We stayed in our hideaway and didn't reveal our presence.

Page and the girl came out to speak to the sentries and the entire group went up to confront the Chief. We did the most prudent thing and quietly walked up the road to the barracks.

The next morning we awoke to find out that during the night, the Chief and his wife and "Three-legged" Page had been transferred off the base to parts unknown. The Navy evidently had made the decision not to permit this scandal to be publicized and the episode was soon forgotten.

All of the romances with the local senoritas did not end in frustrated desires. One of the petty officers fell for one of the local ladies who had a young child and, from appearances, seemed to be quite a few years older than he; he was about twenty three and was on his second hitch in the Navy and looking forward to making it a career.

He applied to the Navy for permission to marry, which was the required procedure. It took a long time but the go-ahead was finally approved and he did marry the lady, got one of the married quarters on the base, and moved out of the barracks and into the house with his new bride and her child.

They seemed to be happy about their marriage even though she was shunned by the rest of the sailor's wives on the base. When the couple attended the base movie, the other wives would conspicuously move to avoid having to be near her. The sailor's all accepted this relationship as none of their business but the women were merciless. There was a pecking order amongst the women and they would fawn over the commanding officer's wife who presided over this pack like a queen bee.

Patty Gannon from Ohio was a tender, young innocent that found his first real "love" in the tropics. He was not too worldly wise and evidently came from a very proper Ohio family. He related to us his experience with his high school girl friend, who was waiting for his return to Ohio for their planned marriage.

One day while they were in their senior year awaiting graduation, the girl came to Patty and told him that she was pregnant. The frightened young couple didn't want to tell anyone about their dilemma and were planning on running away from home; until the young lady got cold feet and revealed her condition to her parents. There was the expected anger and recriminations but eventually after a doctor's examination it was determined that she wasn't pregnant at all.

The interesting part of this story is that Patty and his girl had never had intercourse and the most they ever did was kiss. They thought that was enough to get a girl pregnant. Patty would soon learn the 'rest of the story'.

He lost his virginity on the streets of Panama City to one of the side alley whores described earlier, who solicited business from the men in the street with their infamous "Panamanian Love Call". These ladies were the bottom of the prostitute hierarchy and were considered the dregs of the city. They were physically (as well as morally) unsanitary and rampant with venereal disease; a sorry way for a young man to lose his innocence.

TIME TO MOVE ON

All was not duty watches alternating with play; I spent a good deal of my free time reading or taking one of the many Navy correspondence courses that were available. The first such course that I took was in preparation for the promotional test for Radioman 3rd Class. I successfully completed the course and the test and before I left Panama, I was promoted to that petty officer rank on April 16, 1952.

One of the most significant things that I accomplished while assigned to Farfan was successful completion of the requirements for a High School equivalency diploma; I had only two complete years in high school and this certification would assure my later acceptance into college. A more immediate use for the equivalency diploma was as the vehicle that would permit me to get out of Panama.

After Franny got called back into the Navy, he took the fleet examination open to all sailors and marines for the Naval Academy Preparatory School (NAPS) in Bainbridge, Maryland. Fran was accepted to NAPS while I was still stationed in Panama where I learned in a letter from home that he had started his one year of preparation for admission to the Naval Academy at Annapolis.

I was getting bored with duty in Panama and was tired of the constant heat, the case of fungus that I had contracted, and especially missed the company of the girls at home, having nothing of interest in Panama beyond the prostitutes, rum, and cerveza. My winter clothes that were stored in the so called 'dry room' were rapidly deteriorating from the jungle rot even though they were in dry storage.

The thing that I enjoyed the most was the regular correspondence that I kept up with Gail Wilcox back in New York. What had started out as very friendly letters had turned into a torrid romance by mail as each of us grew closer though thousands of miles apart. I had entered the Navy writing to several people and now, other than a letter home to Daddy every month or so, my communications were mostly with Gail.

After two years in the Navy, I had come to the conclusion that the Navy life was not for me and that I would not reenlist when my hitch was up in 1954. In spite of this decision, I decided that I would apply for the fleet test for the next year's class which started in August of 1952 as my only hope of getting out of Panama and onto a ship. I attempted to file the required papers and was initially turned down by Commander Morrison at the recommendation of the Executive Officer. Their reason was that I had become too valuable to the operation of the station and they could not afford to lose me. I appealed directly to the Admiral at Headquarters in Balboa and with the intercession and recommendation of our Radioman Chief Petty Officer managed to get the application accepted and now only had to pass the difficult test to be accepted.

I not only passed the test, but I was told that I was the only serviceman in the entire Caribbean Command to be accepted to that year's NAPS class. When my orders came to report to the Naval Station at Bainbridge, I was ecstatic. I was so happy about getting out of the tropics that just the anticipation of leaving must have played a part in curing the jungle rot fungus that I had for several months; as soon as I received the notice the fungus started to clear up and other than a small residual rash on the instep of one foot, it was cleared up by the time I arrived in the States.

I flew by Navy plane (I don't remember the type) from Coco Solo to the Naval Air Station at Guantanamo ("Gitmo"), Cuba with a second stopover in Miami, Florida. We finally made our last stop outside Washington, D.C. where I was permitted to travel the rest of the way to New York by bus for a week's liberty before having to report in to the school at Bainbridge. The entire trip with the layovers took about forty-eight hours and I was tired from the journey and looking forward to a good meal after two days of box lunches on the planes; but I was glad to be back home.

HOME AND MARRIAGE

When I left home two years before, Daddy and the family were still living at the apartment on 45th Street; familiar haunts where I had spent half my life. In the interim, while I was frolicking in the tropics, Daddy had met a widow, Marianthe Gregoreadis, from Astoria and after a brief courtship, married 'Mary' at St. Joseph's Church. Mary had four adult children herself, each one older than me; Mike, Lillian, Alice, and Teddy.

Mary had been married to Leon, an Astoria barber and lived in an attached (on two sides) one family house on 19th Street directly across the street from Astoria Park and Pool. Leon had died a couple of years prior to Dad and Mary's meeting and Mary had gone into mourning and rarely, if ever, left the house.

Mary was born in Constantinople (before it became Istanbul) and had been living in Istanbul at the time she met Leon. It is my understanding that she was the daughter of a Roumanian merchant who lived in Turkey. Mary met and fell in love with Leon, a Greek merchant sailor, eloped with him against the wishes of her parents (which reportedly cut her off from a rich inheritance) and went to the United States to set up house in a strange land.

[One of the stories Mary told about those early days was how she had left home in Turkey with nothing but some valuable jewels that had been given to her as gifts. She was a young girl of about sixteen in an unfamiliar land and was reluctant to leave her small apartment on the fourth floor of a tenement apartment house unless she was with Leon.

She was fluent in several European languages, but was only then learning to speak English. One day, while Leon was out of the house, Mary leaned out the window to look into the street and while doing so a diamond necklace (ostensibly worth about ten thousand dollars at the time) fell from her neck to the street below. Mary was too frightened to leave the apartment and decided to wait for Leon's return to retrieve the necklace. By the time Leon returned, the necklace was gone and was never recovered.]

As Mary and Leon struggled to make ends meet and provide for their young growing family, Mary would try to supplement the family income by distilling home made Ouzo, a Greek anise based liqueur, at night while the family slept. On many a sleepless night, Mary would monitor the dripping of the Ouzo as it was distilled into the waiting container. It was critical that the flow of crystal clear liquid be stopped as soon as it exhibited any clouding. This, according to Mary, was the key to her high quality Ouzo that was in great demand in the growing Greek community in Astoria.

Mary and Leon were very close and his death left the bereaved widow with a sense of grief that seemed to have no end. Her son Mike had married Yvonne and was now out of the house raising his own family; as was Lily who married Dieter Moog. Alice and Jimmy Dixon had not yet taken the vows, so Alice was still at home with Teddy and Mary.

At the time that Daddy first met Mary, he was driving a truck, delivering domestic fuel oil for the North Shore Fuel Oil Company. In those days there was no computerized, automatic delivery of heating oil to the homes and deliveries were made on call and were paid for upon delivery directly to the truck driver.

Some time after Mother's death, Daddy was called upon to deliver oil to the Gregoreadis' house on 19th Street.

Shortly before this delivery, Mary had had a dream one night in which she was sitting at the kitchen table in her house with a strange man who she didn't recognize and didn't know. As they sipped coffee, Leon came into the room, took Mary's hand and placed it into the hand of this stranger. She said that she didn't know the significance of the dream but it was very vivid and had been haunting her, as if Leon had wanted to tell her something.

When Mary answered the door that day, she immediately recognized the man in front of her, the man who was there to collect for the oil delivery, as the man who was in her dream. She knew then, the message that Leon was passing on to her.

For the first time in many months; months of grieving and being cut off from the outside world; Mary asked Dad into the house and offered him a cup of coffee; which he graciously accepted. In the course of the ensuing conversation, they both learned about the other's recent loss and found a sympathetic partner. (Daddy's destiny was sealed from the moment Mary pegged him as the man in her dream.)

They kept company for a time and eventually tied the knot while I was away in the Navy. Daddy moved into the house on 19th Street with Marilyn, Bobby, and the twins to join Mary, Alice, and Teddy. This was a second marriage for Daddy and Mary and the union endured for nearly 35 years until Daddy died in his eightieth year; followed within a year by Mary's demise.

When I arrived in New York one day in that August month of 1952, I went immediately to the new home by Astoria Park. When I arrived that afternoon, the only one there to greet me was Mary, a lady I was meeting for the first time. She was very gracious and very friendly and though I found it difficult to understand her very pronounced accent, I instantly took a liking to her. She showed me the room that I was to occupy during my short stay and prepared me some lunch.

The first thing I did after lunch was to call Gail in Astoria; since I had left, the Wilcox family had moved from Brooklyn back to the apartment house next door to our old digs on 45th Street where Ranny became the janitor in addition to the two jobs he already had; as a laborer on the Long Island Railroad in the evening and a day job cleaning chimneys, coal burners, and large industrial boilers. Gail was not at home and wasn't expected until late in the evening. I told Mary that I was going to go into the city to see some old friends, hopped on a bus and subway and went into Manhattan to go to one of the bars we used to hang out in whose name I can't recall.

I didn't meet anyone that I had hoped would be there; probably all of the boys had gone off into the service. I spent some time drinking and gabbing with some of the strangers sitting at the bar. A night of drinking after not having slept for over twenty four hours resulted in a long night on the subway; always waking up beyond my stop and having to backtrack while falling asleep again.

I finally got home in the wee hours of the morning and had to wake Mary who let me into the house. (Mary, I would later learn, had a thing about letting anyone have a house key. Even when the twins, Tom and Bill, were finished with school and working were not permitted to have keys to the house.)

Daddy woke up and came down to greet me and talk for a while before going back to bed. I finally got to sleep and felt that I could sleep forever.

In the morning, I woke up briefly to the sweet aroma of coffee brewing downstairs in the kitchen. I looked at the clock and saw that it was 9:30 A.M. (I assumed it was morning and that I hadn't slept around the clock.) I dozed off until I re-awoke at about 12:30 P.M. and smelled again the wonderful scent of that freshly brewed coffee. I got up, showered and shaved, dressed, and went downstairs where Mary was again the only one on the scene to greet me.

She said in her accented English, which was often difficult to understand, "Would you like a cup of coffee." I responded that I would love it and she replied, "It vill be ready soon." I learned later that the coffee that had been brewing earlier was still 'not ready'.

After another short wait, Mary finally poured me a cup of her extraordinary brew. I had never seen coffee like this. It was so thick that one could literally stand a spoon straight up in the middle of the cup. As hard as I tried, and I did try, I couldn't drink more than the first sip of this powerful swill. When Mary left the room for a short time, I took the opportunity to dump the coffee down the drain in the sink.

When Mary returned to the kitchen, I again called Gail and made arrangements to get together with her that evening.

In the course of that first week at home, I spent most of my time with Gail; she had taken off from work and we pursued in person the romance that had been growing in our correspondence over the last two years. I asked her to marry me and told her I was going to resign from NAPS as soon as I reported into the school the following week. We set a date for October, went to St. Joseph's Church to talk to a priest and start the process, and made arrangements for an old fashioned "football wedding" reception at the Long Island City Athletic Club for whom I fought in the Golden Gloves.

Because Gail was not a Catholic, we had to arrange to get a dispensation from the Bishop to be married in the Church. We paid the required fee for the application and with Gail's signed agreement to raise any offspring of the marriage in the Catholic Church, there was no difficulty getting the necessary permission from the Diocese as well as a dispensation from the usual reading of the banns of marriage. The only other proviso was that we could not be married at the altar but would have the ceremony at the altar rail.

NAPS – A SHORT INTERLUDE

At the end of that short week, I took a train to Bainbridge and reported into the Naval Academy Prep School (NAPS) command. I was assigned temporary quarters pending my signing in the following day. I had been feeling ill just before I left New York and was feeling even worse when I arrived in Bainbridge. My throat was so badly swollen and sore that I couldn't swallow anything more solid than water.

I asked to go to sick bay but was told that I couldn't do that until I signed in at all the appropriate offices; the last of which was my assigned company, followed by a quick physical at the sick bay. It took about four hours to go through most of the check-in process until I got to sick bay. There I was told that I had such a severe case of tonsillitis that I should have reported to them first thing upon arrival and that they were transferring me over immediately to the base hospital; but before I was taken to the hospital, I had to sign into the Company office, be assigned my billet, and store my gear.

I spent about a week in the hospital and was fearful during that time that I would never be released. I had a wedding pending in a couple of months

282

and I had to get my release from NAPS before then. While in the hospital, I was sharing the ward with a bunch of recruits who looked upon me as an 'old salt' because I already had my Petty Officer stripe and had over two years of service under my belt. I had no sea duty up to this point (except a cruise to Panama on the battlewagon) but I beguiled all these young sailors with tales of my experiences in Panama.

When I got out of the hospital, the first thing I had to do was report to my new company commander, Lieutenant Lundine. I was instructed to enter his office, snap to attention, and to "sound off" (shout out name, rank, and serial number, followed by a very obeisant 'SIR'.)

Having spent the last months in an atmosphere of reduced military discipline in Panama, I was not properly prepared for this formal appearance before Lieutenant Lundine. I slouched into the office, raised my hand in a gesture of greeting instead of a salute and said, "Hi!"

With an apoplectic look of disbelief, the Company Commander said, "Don't you know how to sound off, sailor?" I replied, "No, sir."

With this, Lundine jumped up from his desk and was spitting into my face as he turned a deep shade of red, "Snap to attention, sailor, and give your name, rank, and service number."

I followed his orders, snapped to attention and said in a loud voice that could be heard outside the door, "John O'Leary, Radioman Third, 719 52 69".

I didn't think it possible, but he turned even more red in the face and his veins seemed ready to burst from his temples as he glared at me and said, "I might have known, are you any relation to a Francis O'Leary that was here last year?"

I proudly pulled my shoulders back, thrust my chest out and replied in stentorian tones, "YES, SIR! THAT'S MY BROTHER!"

It looked like he was ready to leap over the desk at that point and said, "Your brother gave me nothing but trouble and I'm not going to let you do the same. You'd better straighten out, mister, or you won't make it to the Academy."

I told him that I was not intending to go to the Academy and that all I wanted to do was to check out and to get assigned to the fleet in some combat role.

He jumped at this and said, "Getting out of here is harder than getting in and we are not going to make it easy for you." I could see he took a dislike for me and was not going to be very supportive in my efforts to get out of NAPS.

I was dismissed, returned to my barracks and started my routine as a prep student. The routine was a microcosm of the treatment that was expected as a plebe, or freshman, at the Naval Academy itself. I found out that to get out of NAPS, I would be required to personally get five approval signatures on a release request, with each signature in a specific order.

First I had to get the Company Commander to sign off before I could move on to the next signer, the Brigade Commander. The last one to sign off was the Secretary of the Navy, and I was told that this process could take weeks, if not months.

All of these signatures except the Navy Secretary's had to be attained while carrying on a full schedule of classes, drills, and watches. It was difficult to do but I was in a hurry to get out of there before our wedding that was scheduled for October. I persevered and managed to get the four signatures on base including the Commanding Officer of the entire complex. When the papers went to the Secretary of the Navy, they sent a letter to Daddy to get his approval of my release.

Everyone was surprised when I managed to get this final approval in record breaking time. I was released from NAPS and sent to the OGU (Outgoing unit) to await further orders for my transfer.

Before my release from NAPS and my impending marriage, I thought that I was going to be the first of the brothers to get married; Danny was over in Germany in the Army, Franny was in Annapolis where marriage was cause for dismissal, and the other three had not yet come of age. This was not to be.

Franny 'went over the hill' (took unofficial leave from the Academy) and married Marilyn Ryan on September 11th at St. Joseph's Church without fanfare or a big reception. On his return to Annapolis he announced his intention to resign because he was married but was encouraged by his Company Commander at the Academy to keep quiet about his recent wedding as there were many cadets who were married but were keeping it under wraps and he could do the same and get his commission in four years.

Franny however felt as I did, and did not want a Naval Career and his acknowledgment of his marriage led to his release from the Academy and the service.

(Jack Egan, a good friend from 45th Street and fellow student at LaSalle Academy was also a NAPS graduate and was admitted to the same class as Franny. Jack stayed on at the Academy and graduated as a Second Lieutenant in the Marine Corps. Jack served his required four years as a regular Marine, eventually married and settled down in Houston, Texas. We are still in periodic communication.

Jack had a heart transplant while in Houston and subsequently dedicated over ten years to a campaign to encourage voluntary organ donations for transplant as the result of a personal pact he made with God for pulling him from the brink of death before his transplant.)

While waiting in OGU, I got a pass for the weekend of the wedding and got married in a ceremony at St. Joseph's Church on Sunday, October 12th with Father John O'Rourke presiding and Gail's brother 'Busy' and my sister Marilyn performing the witness duties. (We had wanted to get married on a Saturday but the Church did not permit Saturday weddings without a Mass.) I got married in my dress blue uniform while the bride wore the traditional white gown.

A reception followed at the Long Island City Athletic Club with beer and shots of whiskey and a cold cut sandwich and potato salad buffet that was prepared by Gail's mother and friends. Music was provided by changing the 78 R.P.M. records on a record player.

For our honeymoon, Gail returned to Bainbridge with me where we rented a room at a rooming house until I received my orders to ship out to my new assignment. This was not too long in coming. I was to be transferred to the U.S.S. Yorktown, CVA10, the famous "Fighting Lady" aircraft carrier that had been in mothballs since after the war in the Pacific and was getting ready to be re-commissioned for service with the Seventh Fleet in the Far East and was presently in dry-dock at the Navy Shipyard in Bremerton, Washington.

Within a week of our wedding day, I had my orders in hand and a short leave to go back to New York from where I was to fly out to the Yorktown. On the first day back in New York we got a small apartment on 43rd Street in the basement of a two family house. We planned this to be Gail's home until I returned home from my duty in the Orient. The apartment was 'cute'. The ceiling was less than seven feet from the floor and water and drain pipes were hanging down into the room so that I was often banging my head on them; but the rent was cheap. As newly weds we hardly noticed the surroundings. (After I left for Washington, Gail stayed at the apartment only long enough to run out the first month's rent before moving back in with her family on 45th Street.)

U.S.S.YORKTOWN CVA10

In late November I landed at the Seattle-Tacoma Airport and upon arrival in Washington was taken directly to the Puget Sound Naval Shipyard where the Yorktown was being modernized to handle the new jet aircraft. The few early crew arrivals such as me were put up in temporary barracks for a short time until the ship was ready to start receiving the crew. When we moved on board the Yorktown several days later, I was the senior enlisted man in the OR Division to which I was assigned and had to assume the responsibility of getting our quarters and the radio shacks into ship shape condition; it had been six years since the ship had seen life on it, which together with the mess that the shipyard workers had made, presented a formidable task.

We were well along with the required work before some more senior men started to come aboard. The first officers assigned to our division were Ensign Clark, a former enlisted Radioman, who had been recently commissioned after about twenty years in the Navy, and four young Ensigns fresh out of an R.O.T.C class in their respective colleges. Other than Ensign Clark, the new officers were wet behind the ears and were as strange to the Navy as I was to serving on a ship. Before long, however, they would all be promoted to Lieutenant Junior Grade while Clark remained an Ensign for the duration of our tour of duty on the Yorktown.

Ensign Clark was busy with administrative tasks and coordinating with the Department Heads and the ship's Executive Officer, as the novice ensigns attempted to organize our radio shack; something they were completely unequipped to do. Fortunately, until we put the ship in the water and went to sea all communications with the ship were done through a daily pickup of correspondence at the Headquarters building on base. There was a low volume of traffic at this time but the four greenhorns still managed to screw up the filing system so badly that it didn't get organized properly until Chief Kittredge and some of the 'old salts' came on board to set them straight.

As the crew took shape the OR Division took on a large number of personnel from the U.S.S. Kearsarge, an aircraft carrier that returned from Korean waters in early 1953. We also took on a number of recruits fresh out of boot camp and others who had just graduated from the Navy Radio School on the West Coast.

The recommissioning ceremony took place on the hanger deck of the carrier on December 15, 1952 with Captain William Nation taking command as the captain of the ship. The next couple of months were busy times, finishing the last changes to modernize the ship, accepting the ship from the Navy Yard workers, and readying ourselves for the first sailing.

After the recommissioning ceremony many of us were granted leaves to go home for the Christmas holidays. I was offered a chance to join one of the mates in my division in his new Mercury that he would be driving to North Carolina; five of us would be making the trip and sharing the expenses along the way. We got our leave papers and after piling our bags in the trunk of the Mercury, we left Bremerton for the long journey to the east coast. My plan after North Carolina was to hitch hike (or thumb a ride) up to New York.

ON THE ROAD

We left the ship early on Thursday and had to travel south toward California as there was a blizzard in Idaho that had all the state roads closed. We drove through the day and night with two or three of the passengers taking a turn at the wheel; I still had never driven a car and was not licensed.

Early on Friday morning as we were approaching Klamath Falls, Oregon, I was sitting in the front seat on the passenger side and had just dozed off. I heard someone shout and was suddenly awakened from my short lived sleep. We were on a straight road approaching an intersection and we must have been doing 80 to 90 miles an hour. A pickup truck, doing about the same speed, was on a collision course with us as it drove down a road on our left toward the intersection. It was immediately obvious to me as I shook the sleep from my head that the truck was going to hit us even if our driver tried to avoid the impending crash.

The truck broad-sided us across the front quarter of the car and we went into a spin until finally we came to a halt a hundred feet up the road from the intersection when we hit a large tree. Miraculously, no one in either vehicle was hurt but the car was extremely damaged and not fit to drive. We were towed to a Mercury dealer in Klamath Falls where we were given an estimate on the costs of repair and a lay-up time of nearly two weeks.

The choice before me was to either wait for the car to be repaired, which would have left me with at best only two or three days in New York, or to return to the ship in Washington and try to cancel the remainder of the leave. As fate would have it, a third alternative presented itself.

A black man and his sister were traveling with her young daughter to South Carolina and two weeks before had been in a similar accident as we were with the same model and year of Mercury that we were traveling in. They had the vehicle repaired and were in to pick it up and were getting ready to hit the road, traveling south to Sacramento, California and then heading east.

While speaking to them the brother offered me a ride as far east as I wanted to go. I figured that South Carolina was not much different than North Carolina so I gratefully accepted. Our other riders decided to stay on and wait for the completion of the repairs on our car. (Only two of the four eventually made it to their final destinations for leave, which made me glad I accepted the alternative transportation.)

We were traveling south without incident in spite of a continuous snow storm. Just before we reached Sacramento, we stopped on the northern outskirts of the city to pick up some food and drinks. I purchased a sandwich and a quart container of milk which I would eat in the car as we continued our drive.

The car was moving south at a pace well above the speed limit as I opened the container of milk. At the moment I raised the container to my mouth, the car hit a slick spot in the road and skidded into an endless turn; banging into mounds on both sides of the road until we finally came to a stop. During the twisting turns, I was so astounded that I kept drinking the milk; when the car came to a halt, the quart container was empty.

We were towed to a gas station outside of Sacramento where I knew this car, too, would be laid up for repairs again. Someone at the station upon hearing of my attempts to get to the east coast and being in two accidents since leaving Washington, suggested that I go out to McClellan Air Force Base outside Sacramento and try to get a 'hop' (free passage) on one of the planes flying out of that field. I thanked him and said I would give it a try, got directions to the Air Base and hit the road to thumb a ride to the field.

As I was standing on the road headed out to the Air Base a car with a young man at the wheel stopped and he said, "Where are you headed, sailor?" I was wearing my dress blue uniform and pea coat, which I wore without changing for the entire trip to New York so my military status was immediately apparent.

I told him I was looking for a ride to McClellan and he said he was headed out there himself. I hopped into the passenger's seat, looked at the driver and said, "Well, I'll be a son-of-a-bitch, if it ain't **Sam Aritan**." It was one of the neighborhood boys from back home. He was in the Air Force and was heading for McClellan. This was not only a strange meeting so far from home, but it was to prove my ticket out of Sacramento.

Along the way he told me that there were quite a few servicemen waiting for hops at the base, many for as long as five or six days. When we arrived at McClellan, he escorted me to the terminal where I had to sign up for a flight and found out that he was not exaggerating, the terminal was filled with waiting servicemen, some sleeping on the floor as they were hanging around.

Reports were still coming in about the terrible blizzard that was coming down from the northern plains states toward the Middle West. I was hoping to get a hop that would bypass most of the severe weather.

At the check-in desk I was told that there was nothing going out except one C-47 that was headed only as far as Hill Air Force Base in Ogden, Utah, just north of Salt Lake City. It may as well have been in Rio de Janeiro for all my familiarization with this part of the world. **Sam** knew the sergeant on duty at the desk and talked him into giving me a spot on the plane to Utah, bypassing many eager guys that had been there before me. I accepted the favor, thanked him gratefully, was handed a parachute to take on the plane (a parachute was required of all passengers), and I was directed to the aircraft.

I intentionally got on the back of the line of guys waiting to board, so that I could be the last one on the plane, figuring that when we arrived in Ogden, the last on would be the first off and I could beat the rest of the passengers to the waiting list there. We got on the plane which was fitted with seats along the walls of the fuselage on each side. As the last on board I did get the seat by the door. I fastened the seat belt as directed and settled down for the short flight.

We weren't in the air too long after take-off when we realized that there was no heat in the cabin. It had been over 48 hours since I left the Yorktown and other than the brief nap in the car on the first lap of the journey, I had not slept since that morning of departure. I was hoping that I could catch some sleep on this flight, but it was so cold, well below freezing, that all most of us could do is complain and try to stomp our feet to keep the blood circulating.

As we flew off over the mountains in the dark of night, the plane suddenly listed toward one side and there was a change in the sound of the engines. The co-pilot opened the cockpit door and yelled back to the passengers, "We're having trouble with one of the engines, but don't worry, the captain can keep this in the air on one engine if he has to."

We accepted the reassurances but griped loudly as a group about the freezing cold. We were told that with the engine out we shouldn't expect any heat.

After another short interval, the co-pilot again opened the door and this time came out to tell us that we were in deep trouble but that if the Captain couldn't handle it, we would all be given ample time to jump. We were

directed to tighten up our parachutes and to line up at the door in the event
we have to jump in the next few minutes.

Lucky me! I was first in line at the door. I was scared out of my wits. The
last thing I wanted to do on a warm day was jump out of a plane, no less being
asked to jump out of a plane in the dark of night over strange and probably
uninhabited mountains.

Some of the guys joked that they were looking forward to the plane
crashing so that we could all warm up around the flames from the burning
plane.

We stood in the queue waiting for the command to jump for quite some
time. With the thought of jumping going on in my head getting me more
frightened, I was relieved when the plane attendant came out of the cockpit
and told us all to sit and relax, the Captain felt he would be able to land the
plan in Ogden as planned.

We hobbled onto the airfield in a feat of fine flying by the captain; one
engine gone and the other on the way out. When the wheels hit the ground
there was a loud cheer from all the passengers, and none louder than me. I
was happy to get off that plane but was still hoping that I could get a decent
hop, perhaps all the way to the east coast.

When I entered the waiting room at the terminal, the situation in Ogden
was worse than it was at McClellan, and here I had no patron to help get me
on board a plane. There was not too much flying out in any case because of
the weather conditions that were spreading across the country.

Having never traveled across the country in this manner before, I had very
little appreciation of the magnitude of the journey I had undertaken. I had a
map of the country that I was using to guide me, but it was hard for the mind
to translate a few inches on the map into thousands of miles. Had I known
what I had undertaken, I may not have come even this far; but undaunted
because of my ignorance, I moved on.

John J. O'Leary

I had come this far from Seattle and I was determined to make it all the way to New York. Realizing that it would be days before I may get something out of Ogden, I took my small travel bag and hit the road.

(One nice thing about the base at Ogden was that they fed me a good breakfast; I didn't know it at the time but that would be my last meal for about five days. Along the road for the remainder of the trip, I limited myself to coffee, an occasional donut, and a daily chocolate bar. I was trying to preserve what little cash I had taken with me for what might become a real and unexpected emergency.)

I headed first to the south toward Salt Lake City and then headed east on Route 40 toward Denver. The storm had not yet hit Utah and Colorado with its full fury but the snow was falling more and more heavily as I moved further east.

I moved along toward Denver by virtue of several rides along the road. I never did have to wait too long and just after entering Colorado, I was picked up by a driver in an old 'bullet nose' Studebaker. As we drove, we picked up another sailor who was headed toward the east. The driver was headed right to Denver and said he would drop us off at Lowry Air Force Base when we arrived.

We stopped at Steamboat Springs, a busy skiing town, for a cup of coffee and snack before we moved on. The town was really jumping with young, beautiful college girls and very few men. We learned that they were college girls on Christmas holiday and that they probably outnumbered the men in town by about 10 to 1. Had I not been newly married and traveling home to the anxious bride, it would have been very tempting to end the trip there in Steamboat Springs to finish off my leave; instead, I continued on the trek.

Not too far out of Steamboat Springs, we started to climb toward the summit at Rabbit Ears Pass. The snow had started to come down in earnest now and it was getting difficult to hold the car on the road with the wind and the snow getting ever stronger. We were quite a way up the pass and had not reached the summit when the driver said that he was having difficulty moving the car forward up the hill; perhaps if we would get out and walk a bit, he could drive the car to the top and would wait for us there. Having no choice, we agreed and wrapped our scarves around our ears and covered our faces and followed the car as it slowly made its way ahead.

The weather was getting worse and we found ourselves in the middle of a terrible blizzard. We lost sight of the Studebaker as he pulled ahead of us a little more quickly now that we were out of the vehicle. After a time without seeing the car, we were wondering whether we had made a terrible mistake by leaving the vehicle and even started speculating that when, and if, we did reach the top of the pass, that the car would not be there.

We finally came to a point in the road where we could see the top of the pass several hundred feet in front of us; and there waiting for us at the top was the Studebaker; the driver had kept his word.

As we approached the car, another vehicle stopped and the driver opened his window and asked if we needed a lift. I said, "No thanks! We prefer to walk," (Of course, knowing that our ride was just steps ahead.)

He inquired further, "Where are you headed for?"

I replied, "New York."

He gave me a strange look and said, "Where are you coming from?"

I told him, "Seattle!"

He shook his head in bewilderment, thinking perhaps that he had met two lunatics on the road, closed his window, and moved on.

We got back into the warm vehicle when we reached it and were happy to be warmly on our way to Denver. Although there was still plenty of snow and the blizzard kept up, the driver did manage to get us into Denver safely and took us out to the air base.

Denver was relatively clear compared to the rest of the state and had not yet been hit with the full force of the storm that was racking the country. No planes were leaving Lowry for any points in the Middle West or to the East Coast. Most of the servicemen who had been waiting for flights had given up and moved on to other means of transportation or just gave up the trip.

When we arrived there was only one flight going out and that was going south to a non-military airfield in Amarillo, Texas. I was offered a seat on the plane and grabbed at the opportunity. With the entire country under storm watch and States such as Nebraska and Missouri closing all of the highways, my best chance of making it to New York by Christmas was to head south away from the storms and then up the East Coast.

When I arrived at Amarillo, I was told that there would probably be no flights out of that small field for several days and that my best chance of catching anything was out of Tinker Air Force Base about 260 miles east in Oklahoma City; so again, I lifted the thumb and hit the road for Oklahoma.

I was having reasonably good success picking up rides toward Oklahoma City and was moving along at a fairly good pace through a lot of small towns. At one point I paired up with a soldier who was also trying to hitch hike his was to Oklahoma City. We were at the outskirts of a small town somewhere in Texas waiting for our next benefactor as the sun was starting to set. We were not in the path of the storm that was hitting the plains and the last few hours had been relatively warm; warm enough so that I took my pea coat off and carried it.

As we watched a beautiful Texas sunset in the western sky, a kindly gentleman in a pickup truck offered us a ride to a town that was along our route and would take us within a short distance of Oklahoma City. We both jumped into the front seat alongside the driver and we were on our way.

As night fell and we moved at a good speed along the road, I felt that we were well on our way to our destination. It must have been about ten o'clock when the driver suddenly stopped along a road that was pitch black on that moonless night. He told us that he had to drop something off at a place down a side road and that we should get out and take the next ride along into the town as he may not return for an hour or more and that there were many cars coming this way. The town was the place that he had originally told us he was headed for.

Having no choice, we got out of the car and watched him drive down the side road until his lights disappeared in the distance. Somewhere down that road the only thing we could see were lights in a farmhouse that could have been several miles away.

We stood by the side of the road as the night started to get colder. Soon, the lights in the house that we saw were extinguished. With no further sighting of the car lights the night turned blacker. The only illumination that we had was the packet of matches to light our cigarettes. We waited patiently for a ride, any ride. We trusted that if we couldn't get a ride the kindly gentleman who got us this far would return as promised.

There was nowhere to go and we dared not wander too far. It was so black that if we left the road or attempted to walk the road, we would definitely get lost; so we waited. Talking about the possibility of snakes or other wild things approaching us in the night did not help our mental attitude.

Through the entire cold night we didn't see one vehicle, and that son-of-a-bitch who left us on that dark road never returned.

At the first break of light, we started to walk in the direction that we thought would take us to town. At about seven o'clock a broken down truck loaded with some kind of manure came by and we stopped him to ask for directions and a ride. He told us that there was no room in the cab, but we were welcome to jump into the back and he'd take us to the next town. At this point we were willing to take anything to get us back to civilization where we could get a good cup of coffee and a little heat. We jumped into the back of the truck, sitting on the side, and attempting to avoid as much contact with the manure as possible. We held our noses but were happy to be on the road.

John J. O'Leary

After this, it was pretty straightforward; get a ride, move on and get another ride, eventually making my way to Lowry Air Force Base where again I had to head further south for lack of any flights headed east. This time I got a hop from Oklahoma City to Lake Charles, Louisiana, in the deep, Deep South.

When I arrived at Lake Charles it was early evening and the sun was just setting. I saw a sight that looked like it was out of a science fiction movie. There alongside the runway were huge numbers of B-52 Bombers. This was the first time I had seen them and seeing so many lined up in the fading sun was awesome. I stood gaping at this scene until I was directed to move on into the terminal.

At last I was completely away from the threat of the snow storm and could head east and north on the road. It was getting close to Christmas Day and I wanted to get home by then. There were no flights to be had at Lake Charles and too many people waiting for hops; I made a decision to go the rest of the way to New York by thumb.

The rest of the trip to New York was a blur in my mind. I hadn't slept since Seattle and wouldn't until I got to my destination, but something was driving me on. It was one car after another and one town after another. I remember just a few places: Mobile and Montgomery in Alabama, Atlanta in Georgia, and the Blue Ridge Mountains through Virginia.

Along that latter route, I was picked up by a gentleman who drove the car at speeds sometimes exceeding 100 miles per hour on his speedometer as he drove in the dark through the winding turns of that treacherous road. I thought that here I could sleep at last, but I couldn't get my eyes off the speedometer and the road and thought for sure that I would be taking part in another accident before the end of the trip. Having been in two collisions since leaving Seattle and having been driven by drivers of questionable abilities, it was understandable why I couldn't sleep, even though I was fatigued to the point of hallucination.

Somewhere along the way, after leaving the Mountains, the driver reached the end of his trip and I moved on to the next ride with great relief that I had survived the worst driving experience of the entire trip.

I finally reached Astoria late in the day on December 24th, Christmas Eve; to my amazement, I had not only made it home by Christmas but I made it home in one piece. I went directly to the Wilcox home where Gail was staying and arrived looking like I had already been through the war; I hadn't shaved, bathed, or changed my clothes since I left Washington. The neckline of my tee shirt was dirty and drooping out the front of my blouse. There were black circles around eyes that were sunken into my head like a corpse.

Gail had just arrived home to change clothes for an office party and said that she would stay home. I hadn't told her that I was coming home and she wasn't expecting me. I insisted that she go to the party as all I wanted to do was to go to sleep; even before eating – or anything else. She went off to the party and I dropped onto the bed and instantly fell into a deep sleep.

We had a good couple of weeks together before I had to return to the ship on the west coast. I spent the week visiting old friends and family. Gail was getting a military allowance by this time of 138 dollars a month and would not be joining me on the west coast as we would be shipping out shortly after I returned. She would be staying on with the family on 45th Street.

I had originally planned on meeting my original driver in North Carolina but those plans went out the window in Oregon. As things turned out, I got a better deal.

One of the neighbors on 45th Street was an executive with TransAmerican Airlines, a non-scheduled carrier that flew cross continent. He arranged for me to get aboard one of their planes at half-price off the current fare of 99 dollars one way. This was the price they gave to kids under 12 years old. The only trouble with these flights was that they didn't take off at a scheduled time and you couldn't plan on when to be there and may have had to wait for hours.

Secondly, the flights went to destinations that were decided at the last minute before takeoff but the ultimate destination would eventually be reached. The trip that I took had us in Buffalo, Baltimore, Pittsburgh, St. Louis, Sioux Falls, Boise, Walla Walla, and a couple of other places before finally getting to Seattle nearly 48 hours after I first got to LaGuardia Airport. I did make it back to the ship in time.

PREPARING FOR WAR

The ship was now out of dry dock and was going through dock trials before we finally took her out to sea. By early February 1953 the ship was ready for our maiden voyage to the Navy Base at Alameda, California where we took on Aviation stores, fuel and gasoline. After a short stay and liberty in Oakland and San Francisco, we sailed south to San Diego where we would be going through extensive underway training (UTE) in preparation for our tour of duty in the Far East.

While on liberty in Oakland I was engaging in one of the customary pastimes, drinking at a local bar with some of my shipmates, when out of the blue (a pun) another of our shipmates came running down the street and past the bar. We noticed something unusual about him as he hurriedly passed the bar; he was stark naked except for the hat on his head and was carrying what appeared to be his uniform and shoes.

Later on, back on the ship, we got the story behind the 'streaker'. He had met a girl earlier in the day and had taken her home to her apartment which was on the first floor of a building not very far from the bar that we were at. Her husband, another sailor who was supposed to be at sea, had come home unexpectedly. As he opened the front door, our pal had no alternative except to grab all of his clothes and 'haul his ass' out of there. Without saying goodbye, he hopped out of the bedroom window and just headed for what he thought would be a safe harbor.

I don't know if the husband ever found out about his wife's indiscretion, nor was it ever revealed whether or not our shipmate consummated his liaison with the young lady before the untimely intrusion of her husband.

Before we left that bar in Oakland, on that same day a man took a seat alongside me at the bar and for a time just sipped his drink and did not intrude on our small group's conversation. After a time he started to make a lewd move on me; by this time I had been sufficiently exposed to aggressive homosexuals to immediately read his intentions. I suggested to him that, if he didn't make tracks and leave me alone; he would find himself on the floor. He laughed and persisted in pursuing his lewd intent.

At this last brazen move, a woman came charging out of the back room; we would find out later that she was the owner-manager. She was about five feet ten inches tall and must have weighed about 300 pounds; all solid muscle. She picked the masher off the seat by grabbing him on the neck and the belt of his pants. She lifted him off the floor and walked him to the door as his arms and legs were flailing helplessly in the air. As she tossed his limp body onto the sidewalk outside the door of the bar, she said, "I told you before to leave my customers alone, and don't let me catch you back in here again."

She returned to the back room and as she passed us she said, "That fag will never bother you again; bartender, give the boy's here a drink on the house."

When we returned to the ship, I decided to play a joke on the crew of about 40 men in our sleeping quarters. I went to the head and filled a bucket with water and returned to the compartment. It was pitch black except for the red night lights by the hatches on each side and the visibility was near zero in the darkness.

I walked up and down the aisles alongside the bunks which were stacked in tiers of three, and started to make loud retching sounds as if I were about to throw up. When I had made sufficient noises to arouse the sleepers, I poured the bucket of water in the dark at strategic locations around the compartment.

The entire crew was growling while moving to the back of their bunks to avoid getting hit with the copious amounts of vomit that were inundating the room. Upon hearing me stifling a laugh, which must have sounded like an attempt to hold down any more of the discharge, and my saying to my crew mate, accomplice, "Better get another bucket, Dan" (meaning, filled with water); some wag said loudly in the darkness, "Another bucket? My god, he must be sick; call the corpsman."

After a good laugh, things finally quieted down, and the crew, in spite of what was presumed laying on the deck, went back to sleep. Except for one crew member, who was scheduled to go on watch in the radio shack at 3 A.M.; it was now only about 1 A.M. He got up from the rack, dressed and went up and relieved the previous watch. When asked why he was there so early, he told them, "That damned O'Leary came back drunk as a skunk tonight and threw up all over the compartment. I couldn't sleep for the smell and I ain't going to spend the rest of the night down there."

The final laugh, however, was on me. When I awoke in the morning, the bare metal decks were already starting to rust from the seawater that I had spewed across the entire compartment the night before. I spent the greater part of the day cleaning and polishing the deck.

We operated in the waters of the Pacific off the San Diego coast. The flight wings were flown in with their modern Navy jets, Banshees, Cougars, and the Grumman F9F-5 Panthers. We also brought on board some AJ's, a rotary engine plane, and the support helicopters.

While at sea we were under constant training; fire drills, General Quarter's drills, and particularly flight operations where we would be constantly launching and retrieving aircraft. Drills could be at any time of the day or night and sleep was a luxury that we would try to grab at any available time; even on the cold metal deck of the ship, using a metal pipe for a pillow and a flight jacket for a blanket. (During the day, at all times, the bunks were folded up and it was forbidden to sleep in them during daylight hours unless you had a sick pass or a special duty pass.)

I enjoyed watching our replenishment exercises where, while underway, we would bring on stores, ammunition, fuel, or personnel from the supply ships, or act as the feed ship for some of our destroyer escorts. I never tired of observing these maneuvers even while sailing the Sea of Japan later on.

For the next few months we were in and out of San Diego while every day the crew began to work together better and better until we all finally felt that we were working as a well oiled machine and were prepared for the real thing.

San Diego in 1953 was a great place for liberty. San Diego was a jazz town and almost every street had a night club or bar that featured some great Jazz musicians. (I was disappointed about ten year later when I returned to San Diego and found that all of the Jazz bars had lost out to the proliferation of topless bars. While seeing a well formed female body is not without its gratification, looking at a breast is a transient enjoyment while one could listen to good jazz all night.)

While we were operating out of San Diego, many of the crew members joined one of the local 'locker clubs' where a locker could be rented at a reasonable monthly rate to store civilian clothes ("civvies"). In large Navy ports there has always been an intolerance on the part of the local natives toward the enlisted sailor; wearing 'civvies' while on liberty seemed to open more doors without the notorious discrimination.

One day on liberty, Bill Marshall, Rick Hennessy, and I donned our on shore costumes and rented a car for the day with the intention of eventually traveling across the border in the south to spend the night in Tijuana, Mexico. We picked up a case of beer, a bottle of Smirnoff's Vodka, and some grapefruit juice to mix with the vodka. (I always have been partial to California grapefruit juice.)

We spent the day driving around town to view the sights, while drinking our beer and grapefruit 'Screwdrivers'. As evening approached, and our stores started to deplete, we decided it was time to head for the border. Along the way we got stopped by a California Highway Patrolman, who pulled us over for speeding. When the window was opened and he looked at the three of us in the car, he said, "Have you guys been drinking"; to which we innocently replied, "No, sir we haven't been drinking.'

He asked us to step out of the car, at which point the driver opened the door on his side and all of the beer cans that we had not thrown out and had accumulated behind his seat, came pouring out at the cop's feet. He looked startled but amused. In today's anti-drinking and driving society we would have been hauled off immediately to jail but the cop, after checking our identification and finding out that we were sailors stationed on a ship getting ready for the orient, gave us only a verbal reprimand and warning and advised us to go directly back to the ship. With great relief we said that we would return posthaste, but when he was out of sight we pointed the car to Tijuana and were on our way.

We spent the night 'bar hopping' in Tijuana drinking tequila with salt and lemon until the wee hours of the morning before we decided that we had to get back to the ship; our liberty was up at 7:45 A.M. and we had a personal crew inspection at 8.

On the trip back Rick and I fell asleep while Bill drove. I was awakened from my sleep by the sounds of blaring automobile horns. I opened my eyes and saw that our car was stopped at a red light in a busy intersection in the middle of San Diego. Alongside me, Bill, the driver was fast asleep while Rick was snoring away in the back seat. Bill had pulled up to the light at some point and just dozed off while we sat there. As the morning traffic started to build up we were blocking the flow of cars by not moving from the intersection.

I looked at my watch and realized that we only had about 45 minutes to get back on board or we would be AOL (Absent over leave). I poked Bill and with great difficulty managed to arouse him. When he realized the situation, he immediately started the car, which had stalled, and high-tailed it back to the locker club where we had to quickly change into our uniforms before getting back onto the landing craft which was used to shuttle us from the shore to the ship.

I don't know how we did it, but we managed to get all of this done and get the last boat back to make it past the officer of the deck by the curfew time. It was our luck that the Executive Officer picked our Division to inspect that day. When he saw the three of us looking like we couldn't stand at attention, he made some remarks that got us the wrath of our own Division Commanders but, other than that, there were no further rebukes.

Before we went to the Far East there were a few more liberties to pull while the ship was anchored in San Diego; on a couple of these weekends I went to Los Angeles with one of my shipmates whose home was in El Monte. One Saturday night we attended a dance at a place that was called "The Okie Stomp" by the locals, where Tennessee Ernie Ford ("Sixteen Tons) was the featured singer.

The ship stopped in San Francisco for a short stay for some shipyard repairs and then returned to Seattle where some of the crew had one last chance for a leave at home before going on the line. This time I was not going to thumb my way across the continent. Somehow, I found out that there was a military transfer office at the city airport where there was a possibility of getting a flight across the country, if an opportunity presented itself.

I applied for and was granted a short leave to go to New York and I went to the airport and arrived at a perfect time; an Army unit was being transferred from Korea to Camp Kilmer in New Jersey and there was one opening for me because one of the soldiers had "gone over the hill". I took flight and knew that after last Christmas' journey, that hitch hiking from New Jersey to Astoria would be a 'piece of cake'. Without this flight, I would have never made it to New York.

After a short leave in New York, my new found friend at TransAmerican airlines arranged for my flight back to Seattle.

In July, Captain Arnold McKechnie, a former submarine commander and pilot, relieved Captain Nation of command of the Yorktown. In August Rear Admiral Robert Hickey took over command of Carrier Division 5 (CarDiv 5) and brought the flag aboard the Yorktown. We now had to integrate our OR Division operation with the communications arm of CarDiv 5; a combination that went very smoothly. (When we reached the Far East, Admiral Hickey would take over command of Task Force 77.) Admiral Hickey would be relieved by Rear Admiral John Whitney in February of 1954 while we were on line in Korea.

ON THE LINE

On August 3, 1953, the U.S.S Yorktown was ready to meet the enemy as we sailed out of Puget Sound and headed west toward Hawaii. It took about five days before we spotted Diamond Head and steamed into Pearl Harbor. We could see the flag staff of the U.S.S. Arizona, a grim reminder of the December 7th, 1941 sneak attack by the Japanese which put us into World War II.

The waters around Hawaii were beautiful, the clearest and bluest blue waters I'd ever seen. For many of the crew, who had joined us after we left San Diego, it was the first time that they saw palm trees. The tallest building on the island of Oahu was the Royal Hawaiian Hotel at Waikiki Beach. (Since that time, Honolulu and the entire Hawaiian Islands have expanded with the addition of towering hotels for the tourists and other high rise buildings. The once low expanse of buildings which provided such a beautiful vista from the high points around the city has now become another American City downtown with large, high rise, concrete structures dominating the scene.)

We didn't spend much time in Hawaii but did have time to explore the Island of Oahu during one liberty day and to attend an evening of tropical drinks and Hula Dancers at the night club at the Royal Hawaiian Hotel.

Five of us chipped in to rent a car to drive around Oahu to see the sights and to take pictures. (While in Panama I purchased an Argus C3 Camera at the PX which I had used exclusively to take 35 millimeter slides; colored prints being prohibitively costly for me in those days.) I took a picture of Honolulu with Diamond Head Mountain in the background from atop the National Cemetery where the famous reporter and war correspondent Ernie Pyle is buried. (Ernie Pyle was the coiner of the title "G.I. Joe", which was also the title of a movie produced during the war of his war time experiences.) I compared the picture of this vista with one taken recently from the same vantage point by a friend who was visiting Hawaii and I was disappointed to see that Honolulu had become just another boring metropolis.

Along the road we came upon a beautiful deserted lagoon where we all stripped to swim B.A. in the Pacific and to explore the beautiful underwater world of coral, vegetation, and fish.

We left Hawaii to steam full speed ahead to our next stop, Japan. Along the way we were subjected to an Operational Readiness Inspection (ORI) to verify for the Commander of the Seventh Fleet that we were prepared for the duty ahead.

Along the way we crossed the 180 degree Meridian where we lost a day and where all members of the crew who had not previously done so, became members of the Order of the Golden Dragon for which we all received written certification. Unlike the initiation that was performed on sailors crossing the equator for the first time, we were not subjected to any kind of initiation ceremony.

On September 5, 1953 the U.S.S. Yorktown entered Tokyo Bay headed for Yokosuka (pronounced Ya koo ska), which was to be our home port for the next six months.

As we sailed closer to the dock at the Navy Shipyard at Yokosuka, there was a strong, pungent odor in the air. We would soon discover that this was not only characteristic of this Japanese city but also many others we would later visit. It was the open air fish and food markets and the open sewage system that combined to give this aroma that we found offensive upon our first arrival. (Later we would learn to appreciate this characteristic smell as a sign that we were about to step on terra firma again after a long stint at sea.)

The World War had only been concluded eight years before and Japan had not yet unleashed the great growth in trade and industry that would make it one of the world's leading economic players. The country was still under an occupation economy and mentality and this was soon evident to us in our dealings with the people. One of the first things I noticed was that upon our arrival and the dumping of our garbage into the large dumpsters along the pier, many of the peasant workers who had been hired to work on the base and the ships as they were moored there, rummaged through the garbage to find whatever useful things they could find.

I must admit that my reaction to this human tragedy was not very charitable or Christian. After being hit with so much wartime propaganda as well as some of the realities; the Bataan Death March, the Japanese prisoner of war camps, and the many atrocities of the barbaric Japanese; it was a case of "Chinky chose always shows" (One of the common phrases used on the streets of New York City that indicated, "You're finally getting your comeuppance.")

As a member of the "Radio Gang", I had the privilege of an open gangway, which meant I could get a liberty pass to go ashore anytime that I was not on watch. When we were in port, we closed down all of the radio circuits and got all of our communications from the base office, if there was one in the port we were currently in. This gave me and the guys in our division a great opportunity to see more of the places we traveled to than most of the crew.

While in Japan and the Far East, except for Hong Kong, we were not paid in American dollars, but instead were paid with Military Scrip (MPC) that was as good as cash to us and was readily exchanged into the local currency; at the time the exchange rate in Japan was 1 dollar for 360 yen.

When we pulled our first liberty one of the first things we did was to go to the PX where we were issued a liquor card that entitled us to purchase from the PX one bottle of booze each day for a month. The price of an average good liquor such as Canadian Club Whiskey, Jack Daniels Bourbon or Johnny Walker Scotch, was one dollar a fifth; a price that encouraged us to drink even if we didn't previously have such inclinations.

After exploring the city of Yokosuka and partaking of many of the Japanese foods and sights, one of the first things that most of us did, by recommendation of many of the old salts who had already spent some time in Japan, was to get a Japanese massage. I went to one of the many Japanese massage parlors to submit myself to this obligatory initiation into an important part of Japanese culture.

Upon entering the massage salon, after removing my shoes, leaving them at the door, and putting on the house slippers provided to all of the customers, I was escorted to a private room where I was told to strip myself down to the bare flesh, after which I was to go to a small room where I was to sit on a short stool about eight inches off the floor and wait for the service to begin. A charming and petit Japanese girl came into this small tiled room and was herself in the 'all together'.

In businesslike fashion she proceeded to wash me down with a warm sudsy solution of water, from head to foot; not missing a part of the body. Upon completion of this wonderful and surprising ablution, by body sign language she directed me to rinse off in the nearby shower. After the shower, I had to submerge myself in a small tub of steaming hot water that covered me to my neck. I learned that night that this procedure should not be sought out after having several drinks; I started to hyperventilate and found it difficult to breath. The girl pushed me back in when I started to get out of the tub, and I obediently followed her directions.

Finally, I was permitted to get out of the scalding hot water that was cooking me alive. I felt great on getting out and my body was completely relaxed. I moved on to the next room where another petit and naked young lady waited to give me a massage. She was small but had strong hands that knew precisely how to relax and renew each muscle. Partway through the massage, a part of which included her walking across my back while I was lying on my stomach, a huge Japanese man, perhaps a Sumo wrestler, came into the room. I was motioned to sit up on the end of the massage table. The Sumo wrestler got behind me, put his knee into the small of my back, and grabbing my shoulders, pulled until I heard my spine snap.

After another short interval of the more gentle massage by my masseuse, I was finished, dressed, and went out feeling like a new and revived man. This was to become a regular stop on most of my liberties in Yokosuka with the later ones taken upon the start of my liberty and not after drinking.

For most of us Yokosuka was the most exotic place we had ever been to; the culture of the Japanese was so foreign to us that we knew we were in a different world. There were so many new things to see and do and we resolved to do them all.

Shopping was an enterprise every crew member was obliged to participate in. There were so many bargains to be had at outrageously low prices that everyone had to buy something. I wound up with a cultured pearl necklace, a 93 piece set of Noritake China for a serving of 12, Kimonos and Smoking jackets, carved figurines, including one carving of the seven gods of good fortune inside a small gingko nut, and a grain of rice carved into a figure of the Buddha, and several of the locally made 'Zippo' cigarette lighters that were fabricated from inverted beer cans and sold on the streets for about ten cents apiece.

Thirty-five dollars must have been the 'magic number'; I paid that for the string of cultured pearls that I later had appraised in New York at two hundred dollars, and that was the cost of the Noritake china, including shipment back to New York.

The next months were spent alternating between a long time on line in the Sea of Japan and a short time in each of the ports that we stopped at; primarily Yokosuka and occasionally at Sasebo and Kobe, and often at ports where we simply took on stores or accomplished some other mission with no liberty for the crew.

While at sea we followed a constant routine; watches in the Radio shack followed by filling in the waking hours with reading, talking, writing letters home or, most often, playing 'pay day stakes' poker. We trusted that the players would not exceed the amount of money that they could draw at the next payday. The payroll was always posted just before the twice-a-month payday indicating how much each crew member could draw from the paymaster. If a player lost more than he could pay out on payday, he would be black-balled from the game until he got his accounts up to date.

As I was most often a winner, I paid particular attention to who owed money at the end of a 'poker period' and usually wound up being the collector and disburser of the proceeds. (Although I probably made more in poker winnings than I did in salary, I was such a profligate spender and poor saver that I never did salt away any of the money I won into a savings account; a practice that would someday come back to haunt me.)

While we were not launching and retrieving aircraft, which was only a small fraction of the time, movies were shown on the hanger deck or we could participate in some basketball on the same deck; otherwise, we were pretty limited in our off duty activities. In addition to the card games and reading historical novels (I must have read every one of Frank Slaughter's novels), one of my favorite enjoyments aboard ship was the unofficial competition I had with Bluford "Lee" Herion to see who could memorize the most passages from Shakespeare's plays. We would beguile our mates with our dramatic performances until they started to throw things at us, such as their dirty underwear (or 'skivvies' in nautical jargon).

While docked in Yokosuka on one of our several stops there, I took a train to see the imposing Buddha at Kamakura. It was worth the trip and I took a series of photos of the Buddha and the surrounding shrine. Before I mailed the film for developing the ship had put out to sea and we were caught in one of the worst storms I've ever witnessed at sea. There was a typhoon in the Pacific and, even though we were on the outer fringes of the weather system and not subjected to the full force of the tempest, the ship was being tossed about like a helpless cork bobbing on the water. The waves were so intense that the water was washing over the flight deck; sixty-five feet above the water line.

I still had a couple of pictures left in the camera from the Kamakura trip and wanted to finish the roll to get it out in the mail. This storm gave me an excellent opportunity to get some dramatic pictures. I borrowed a foul weather jacket from one of my mates and climbed up to the gun tub located near the bow just below flight deck level. As I entered the gun tub, the ship's prow dipped into a particularly large wave and the water came in a huge rush to fill the gun tub.

At the last moment, I wrapped my arm around a steel post on the chair of the five inch gun and held tightly. I managed to hold on again a second time as another colossal wave washed across the flight deck and filled the gun tub where the water from the first wave had still not drained out through the gunnels.

I managed to get some pictures taken to finish the roll of film and at the first chance left the gun tub.

I removed the roll of film and put it in the pocket of the borrowed jacket. Later in the day the owner of the jacket put it on to go up on deck, found the film in the pocket and asked, "What is this?" I was about to tell him that it was my film when he tapped it on the table and it opened, exposing the entire role of film. My Kamakura pictures and the photos I took of the storm were lost to me and posterity.

The Navy was very solicitous toward the enlisted men serving on the line. As part of their paternal benevolence, they provided select individuals with an opportunity to participate in a rest and rehabilitation (R & R) program. For a nominal sum, the participants were granted leave to a luxury hotel in the country for a few days at a rate of one dollar per day for meals and another dollar a day for the room.

I was chosen and accepted a chance to spend my R & R in the Fuji New Grand Hotel set alongside Lake Yamanaki in the Japanese Prefecture of Yamanashi. My room overlooked the famous Mount Fuji and the view was spectacular; I never knew such luxury.

Three lavish meals were served daily with no limit on what could be eaten. The service was impeccable and, in fact, was overly solicitous. Every time I took a cigarette out of my pocket to smoke, before I could strike a match, the staff was there in twos and threes with a light for the cigarette. The challenge for us became one of trying to light the cigarette before the staff could react; I was never successful and they were always there.

The days were filled with hikes through the woods at the foot of Mount Fuji, hot baths, massage, chess, card games or other diversions. Each evening there was a dance in the main ballroom and local girls were provided for our dancing pleasure.

When our train had arrived at the small town of Asahiagoyoka, a short distance from the hotel, I noticed that there was a small bar and a gingko parlor where the locals played a strange game that seemed to me to have no purpose. My shipmate and I took some time out from all of the planned R & R activities (you might say we were taking an R&R break from the R&R) to have a few drinks at the town bar and to play the 'strange game' at the parlor next door.

315

The entire center of town was the bar, the game parlor and a small general store. (The town was so small that over the years I have not been able to locate it on even the most detailed map of Japan but the name has been etched into my brain, never to be forgotten.) We were the only customers at the bar but there were about five girls in attendance to wait on us and tend bar. The bar maid was opening our beer bottles with her teeth. Most of the Japanese women were not renowned for the size of their busts, but this bar maid in addition to having a fine set of teeth was also well endowed in the bust department. I note that only because of its rarity.

(In Japan the boobs were called 'chi-chi bans', while falsies were branded as 'PX chi-chis'.)

After our sojourn at the bar, we went to the game parlor and played the local game, not knowing what the purpose was, but it only cost one yen (at an exchange rate of 360 yen to the U.S. Dollar.) The game was played by pulling a plunger to drive a ball to the top of the machine, and the ball would then roll down hitting a series of symmetrically arranged pins and eventually wind up going through a hole at the bottom of the machine. There was no indication of the score or even how the scoring was done.

As I continued to play the game, a crowd of the local townspeople (probably all of them) started to gather around my machine as I played and periodically would cheer or giggle as I stood watching the ball fall from the top to the bottom of the machine. I didn't know why they were cheering but they seemed like such a happy bunch that I kept playing just to witness their enthusiasm as I did something good and their disappointment when I did something wrong. (There were no controls on the machine so all one could do is start the ball and observe.)

Before I finished and was ready to return to our hotel, there was a crowd of observers so deep that they were spilling out onto the wooden walkway that served as the town's sidewalk. When they saw that I was quitting, they all sighed with disapproval and must have been pleading with me to continue but I couldn't understand a word of Japanese other than Ichi-ban (Number one), Chi-chi ban, Origatto, Sayonara, and Mama-san.

It was a great holiday that came to an end too soon.

The night that I returned to the ship, I followed one of my shipmates up the gangplank to report in. The normal routine was to stop at the top of the gangplank, face the stern of the ship and salute the flag (during the day) and then to salute the officer of the deck (O.D.) and announce your return to the ship while presenting the liberty pass. The shipmate I was walking behind presented a strange appearance; he was naked except for a white hat on his head and shoes and socks on his feet and a pair of skivvies shorts. He reeled from side to side; the obvious effects of too much Sake or too much of the inexpensive booze.

He saluted the O.D. with a quick flip of the hand that knocked him in the head and staggered him momentarily. The O.D. said, "Where the hell is your uniform sailor?"

The sailor looked down at himself and slurred, "I doe' know, zir;" after which he was led off by the Marine Sentry to spend the night in the brig, until he could be properly identified by his division Chief in the morning. This was not atypical of some of the things that the returning sailors presented the O.D. during our tour of the Far East.

There was a policy established on the Yorktown for the returning sailors who had participated in any sexual activity while in port (not while out at sea, which was obviously ignored) to take one of the venereal disease preventative tablets that had been tested in Panama. The actual practice however was that every returning sailor had to take the pill whether or not participating in any of the local body sports. As the crew members returned to the ship, the Corpsman on duty would simply direct each individual to open his mouth and would pop the pill into it.

This didn't stop the widespread occurrence of the many varieties of venereal diseases (VD) that were reported after each stop at one of these oriental ports. The most common problem accounted for in Japan was NGU, non-gonorrheal urethritis, with some cases of Gonorrhea and a small number of cases of buboes.

Later on, when we would leave Hong Kong from our one short visit there, in our OR Division alone there were reportedly more than fifty percent of the sailors who came down with a case of syphilis. I am happy to report that I did not succumb to the beautiful temptresses in Hong Kong and stayed healthily in the minority.

Although we never heard a shot fired in anger while we were on our Far East tour as part of Task Force 77, these maladies were an ever present danger when we pulled liberty in these less than sanitary ports and were the main source of our casualties.

While in Yokosuka one night, four of us went to a small bar in town; so small that there was only one table with four seats and a bar with one stool. When we arrived our only concern was that they serve us the mixes for the bottles we had purchased at the PX. This was done, but we were to soon learn that this particular establishment had a dual purpose when the young girls started to come into the bar from a room in the rear in order to solicit our attention with the obvious purpose of selling their wares.

We didn't show any interest in the girls at first and they eventually returned to the back room through a door that was dutifully watched by a fairly good sized Japanese man. The room was off limits without the entry fee.

George Sterman, the largest one of our group and perhaps the strongest, started to feel the effects of too much hard liquor. He got louder, meaner and more rambunctious. We attempted to quiet him down but he only became more antagonistic until he decided that he wanted one of the girls in the back room. The proprietor told him in his stilted English that he was not welcome in the back with the girls because he had had too much to drink.

George insisted on having his way and broke down the paper thin locked door and tried to impose himself on the ladies (without compensation).

The proprietor having sensed that George would be causing this trouble had earlier called the Japanese Police. After George broke down the door, it was not long before about a half dozen policemen were in the room, positioning themselves around the periphery of the small quarters. None of them were taller than five feet tall or weighed more than 120 pounds. They were unarmed except for some lethal looking leather clubs wielded by each of them.

The leader of the group approached George who was just inside the door to the back room which was hanging limply by one broken hinge (as was George). He motioned George, who towered over him by over 14 inches, to come out of the back room and to follow him; none of the cops could, or would, speak English so all directions were given in pantomime.

George was ready to take on this 'squirt' and our initial reaction was to back him up; after all there were only six of them against four of us and we did whip them in the war. Fortunately, the drink had still not clouded my mind and instead of joining in the fray that was about to begin, I interposed myself between George and the lead cop and restrained him from hitting George on the head with his club.

I did some fast talking and gave some gestures to indicate that we were willing to pay for the damage that George had done and would calm him down. "No hit! We pay! Make sailor quiet! No trouble!" The proprietor understood what I was saying and convinced the cop in Japanese that he would be happy to be paid for the damage and for us to leave.

The policeman relented and we did manage to get George to cease his belligerence. We all kicked in a share to pay off the barman, probably well in excess of its replacement cost, but the police insisted on taking George down to the station. George wisely decided to go along; for when we walked outside, parked in front of the bar was a truck with about another two dozen Japanese policemen sitting inside the back. At this point I was so glad that we didn't wind up in a donnybrook with the cops inside.

George was taken down to the jail and locked up until released to the shore patrol in the morning. The Japanese took no further action against him, but the Navy put him up on charges. I don't remember the punishment he received except that it was rather mild and did not include brig time; probably just restriction to the ship for a short period. I made it a point of avoiding making any liberty stops with George in the future. Although I had spent most of the early part of my life never avoiding a fight, I was gradually changing this physical way of dealing with problems, and liberty with Sterman always ended in a fight.

All sections of the country were represented in our division; from New England to the West Coast; from the Deep South to the Great Plains. One of the representatives from the south was "Buzz" Steiner, a Seaman from Georgia. Buzz was about five feet two inches tall and couldn't have weighed in at more than one hundred and ten pounds. He resembled Pa Kettle (Percy Kilbride) from the movies and had a permanent look of bewilderment on his face.

Buzz was such a sad sack that he would be the last one to be suspected of being the "Don Juan" of the division; but whatever port we hit, he was always the one to be searched out by the most desirable looking girls in town. He received a constant stream of letters from a bevy of girls back home in Atlanta, which from their pictures were quite stunning. One can imagine the speculation that went on amongst the crewmembers as to what special 'charm' Buzz had to attract so many beautiful women.

Another 'charmer' from the south, Arkansas in this case (and no doubt, the Ozarks), was "Booger" Bailey a Third Class Teleman (Teletype rating). We called him "Booger" because while serving on watch in the Teletype room he would be constantly picking his nose and sticking the 'boogers' underneath the shelves holding the equipment. When the Chief came around inspecting one day, he asked Bailey, "What the hell is this stuff under the shelves?" To which Bailey replied, "Those are stalactites, Chief."

Bailey was not too keen on hygiene and often was ordered to shower and clean his clothes by the lead Petty Officer because he was smelling up the quarters for the crew. When getting ready for liberty in port, instead of showering, particularly after coming off a sweaty work assignment, Booger would just take off the work clothes, douse himself with talcum powder and put his grungy dress uniform on. With all of this, he was another one who had an affinity for attracting the best looking women. Perhaps the women went for the more 'earthy' types.

A STOPOVER IN HONG KONG

In November, instead of heading back to Japan, we sailed for Hong Kong where we would spend enough time to pull liberty and visit one of the many tailors to get one of the custom made suits for which Hong Kong was famous. On the trip south every sailor was given extensive exposure to some frightening oriental V.D. films to warn us about the dangers we were about to embark on in this port. (As I mentioned earlier, a majority of the sailors ignored these cautions and a large part of the crew was infected with a 'social disease' while in Hong Kong.)

We were also advised that before we hit Hong Kong, we would have an opportunity to change our military scrip to American Dollars because the scrip was not exchangeable for Hong Kong dollars (at a rate of 6 Dollars Hong Kong for 1 Dollar U.S.) and that we should only exchange as much as we expected to spend because there would be no exchange of Hong Kong dollars back to American currency upon our departure from port. From discussions with some of the experienced Hong Kong travelers, I had a pretty good idea of what to expect in Hong Kong so I took enough to buy myself a tailor made suit and topcoat, some jade, which was also another Hong Kong bargain, and entertainment expenses.

We anchored in the bay and took the small liberty boats onto shore, with a final caveat being given to not drink the local water. (With the cheap price of beer and booze, I don't believe anyone had any intentions of drinking any of the local water.) As we pulled into the bay, the horizon was filled with junks, bumboats, and sampans. The junks were the larger wooden boats with a single sail; the bumboats were the floating merchant boats that had merchandise for sale, and the sampans were small craft manually propelled by the owner.

The sampans moved in droves toward the ship and would be attempting to board except that the Captain had teams of crewmembers standing by with high pressure water hoses to fend off any attempts of this type. The sampans came at us by the hundreds, but no one got close enough to get on board. Many of the crew members on deck were throwing coins to the peasants in the sampans who were successfully diving to retrieve them in the putrid waters of the bay. (I understand that many of the native Chinese lived aboard these sampans with some of them spending their entire lives aboard the boats without stepping onto dry land.)

The first stop I made was at a tailor shop that was recommended by one of my shipmates. We wouldn't be too long in Hong Kong and the tailor needed a couple of days to make the clothes. I selected the style and materials and was fitted for a suit and a topcoat to be picked up in a couple of days.

After a short walk around town to get a taste of the local scenery, I went to a large beer hall called 'The Metropole' where a great number of the sailors went to drink or to acquire a companion for the day. The Metropole was like a large German Brauhaus and was filled to capacity with sailors from the visiting ships; American, English, and Australian; and a bevy of beautiful

Chinese girls with the customary slit skirts. One distinguishing characteristic of all of these ladies was that they all had beautiful legs.

For a fee of as little as ten dollars Hong Kong money (less than two U.S. dollars) a girl would accompany a sailor for the day; with the sailor being responsible for any additional expenditure such as drinks, food, or more personal services; from the casualty list after we left Hong Kong, it was evident that many took advantage of these 'personal services'.

I joined a table occupied by several of my shipmates, who had invited some sailors from a visiting Australian ship to join them for drinks. It was quite an interesting afternoon, sharing stories with the Australian sailors about our homes and exchanging cigarettes. The Australians were very fond of American cigarettes and I welcomed the chance to try their native brands. I gave one of the Aussies my Pall Malls, the brand I was smoking at that time, and I accepted his Craven A's (which he pronounced, "Cry-vin eyes". One drag of the 'Cryvin eyes' and I understood why they liked our cigarettes; they were powerfully strong.

As we were drinking and sharing small talk with our new found international buddies, one of the Australian's said, "Hey! There goes Salty Rick;" (one of their shipmates.) "Ya know, Salty Rick's got Mickey Mouse tattooed on his dick." One of our boys replied, "Oh come off it, yer only bullshittin' us."

"No, I'm not, might (mate)" he shot back. Calling out to 'Salty Rick' in a loud voice that could be heard over the din in the beer hall, he said, "Salty Rick, come on over here and show these swabs your Mickey Mouse." Rick very accommodatingly came right over, unbuttoned the front flap on his uniform and whipped out a quite sizeable tool that brought immediate stares of envy from some of my companions.

Sure enough, there on the body of his shaft was a full color, detailed rendition of Mickey Mouse. Of course this brought forth comments speculating on how Mickey looked when he reached full stature. This was not to be demonstrated for us on that day, however.

It was a grand afternoon and probably did a lot for international relations, this camaraderie between our two navies.

As the crowd thinned, with many of the sailors leaving with their leased 'escorts', a group of us left to do some more sightseeing of this crowded and dynamic city. Along the way we stopped to watch a cricket game being played by some British teams as we stood outside the private club where the game was being held.

We hit some of the local bars before returning to the ship before the midnight curfew.

I returned to Hong Kong two days later for the final fitting and finishing of my suit and topcoat and to arrange to have them shipped back home. After trying on the clothes, the tailor asked me to wait while he made the final adjustments.

A group of about five Chinese men were playing a game of poker at the tailor shop. I had been observing the game and saw that the stakes were well within my limits, so as I waited I asked if I could join them in the game. They all spoke some Pidgin English and happily moved aside to let me join them.

The game they played was the poker I was used to playing without all the weird variations. We played either five card stud or draw poker. The only strange custom was that the deal was not passed around in any set order, and whoever grabbed the deck would deal the hand. I didn't know how this would effect the odds in the game but I calculated that I didn't have too much to lose and that whatever I had left over couldn't be changed back into usable currency after we left Hong Kong.

I spent a good part of the afternoon playing with these gentlemen, some of whom were replaced with substitutes during the course of play. I started to win as soon as I entered the game and continued to add to my stack of cash as the day progressed. At about 2 o'clock, the tailor's wife (or assistant; I assumed it was his wife) brought all of the players a dish of fish heads and rice. The other players avidly dug in to start eating with their chopsticks. I was repulsed by the three or four eyes staring up from me from the plate but I didn't want to insult our host so I reluctantly and tentatively picked up a small portion to eat. To my surprise and delight, the food was delicious and I ended up devouring every morsel, even as the pile of cash in front of me kept growing. I had learned very quickly to gather up the cards to deal at every opportunity to put myself in a more favorable betting position.

Toward late afternoon, I looked at the pile of cash in front of me and realized that I was going to find it very difficult to spend all of that Hong Kong money before having to report back to the ship at midnight. We would be leaving Hong Kong the next day and would not be returning. I decided to quit the game, take my winnings, go back to the ship to pick up anyone hanging around and to take them on a night on the town.

I returned to the city with three of my shipmates and a pocketful of cash. We ran over to the Metropole, acquired four 'escorts' and the eight of us went off to paint the town. The first stop was dinner at one of Hong Kong's finest restaurants (I don't recall the name.) It was a snooty affair and the Maitre'd' balked at our entering until I slipped him a large Hong Kong bill, which gesture immediately got the eight of us a table up front near the dance floor. All eyes in the restaurant were on us as we were escorted to our seats. None of those blue blood snobs expected to see four "White hats" (as the enlisted sailor was often referred to) in such a pretentious place, especially escorting four lovely Chinese ladies of the evening.

We had a fine dinner and left the club with plenty of time before having to return to the ship. I approached a group of jinrikisha drivers on a nearby street and asked them how much they wanted for the rickshaws. One of the men answered that they wanted ten cents each (Hong Kong). I gave the man a dollar and told the girls to get into the rickshaws and then picked up the pulling end of one and started to run with the rickshaw while telling my mates to follow suit.

Each of them grabbed a rickshaw and we ran away pulling the girls in the 'purchased' rickshaws while laughing heartily at this great joke. The drivers were chasing us alongside the rickshaws saying, "No takey rickshaw. We pully sailor. You no takey."

We ran a short distance before stopping. We had had our fun and were ready to move on. I suggested that we end the night with a cup of coffee before returning to the ship.

The four 'escorts' went along with our loud and boorish behavior and probably got some pleasure out of dining in that restaurant where they were usually not welcome.

After a cup of coffee at a local coffee shop, it was nearly time to head back for the ship and I still had a pocketful of my poker winnings burning a hole in my pocket. There were some dirty faced young kids in the street begging for a handout and I tossed them some of the coins that I had collected during the day. It seemed that this opened up every door in the neighborhood because before long there was a crowd of not only kids but older women with babies in arms.

I found it was great sport to toss some coins in the street and watch the crowd race into the street to pick them up. When I ran out of coins I started to throw the remainder of the bills that I had into the street. At this point, many of the men who were standing by joined the fray and started to push the women and children out of the way.

The crowd grew so big and disorderly that we soon attracted the attention of the police; four of whom came to the scene to tell me to leave as the crowd growled at them in disapproval. The police were holding the crowd back on the sidewalk as I walked away across the street with my mates and our companions. As we did so, I took most of the money I had left and tossed it up in the air. The cops could not constrain the mob; they rushed through the police line while pushing each other; all trying to get some of the bills that were now blowing about in the slight breeze. I walked away and didn't look back any further.

We got back to the landing to pick up the boat to take us out to the Yorktown and we bade farewell to our lovely companions of the night; not having availed ourselves fully of the wonderful opportunity that we had with these ladies. I split up the remainder of the money that I had amongst the four women, keeping only a few souvenir samples of the currency. We bid the ladies and Hong Kong goodbye as we hopped into the Landing Craft that served as a ferry to the ship.

BACK ON THE LINE

In the morning we lifted anchor and headed for the waters near Formosa (Taiwan) where we spent a couple of days conducting Air exercises with the Chinese National Air Force before returning to the Sea of Japan off Korea.

One of the sailors who joined me on that final night in Hong Kong was a rather unique individual whose family 'owned' a town in Pennsylvania that was named after his mother's side of the family. We thought that he was making up the stories he told but we tolerated him because he was a key guy in the division, smart as a whip, and disrespectful of most authority.

(When we finally arrived back in the states after our tour of duty in the orient, our friend, "Ike" Eichler, was met at the dock by his mother and the family chauffeur in a large Rolls-Royce sedan. She had come all the way from Pennsylvania to greet Ike. Ike had other plans though. When he saw his mother waiting at the end of the dock, he sneaked out through a side gate after leaving the ship to avoid her. He had orders to report to Treasure Island for discharge and told us before he left that he was going to avoid seeing his smothering mother and not return to Pennsylvania. That was the last we heard about Ike.)

By the time Ike left the ship, he had almost five years in service and never rose above the rank of seaman. He had many opportunities to be promoted but he declined every one of the offers. He said that he may have to obey orders but he doesn't have to accept the promotions. His initial enlistment was for a four year period but he extended for an extra year. For someone so adamantly opposed to life in the Navy it was surprising that he extended for the additional time.

My most vivid recollection of Ike's eccentricity was an episode that occurred shortly after the Flag came aboard the Yorktown. (The Commanding Admiral was referred to as "The Flag" because "flag ranked" officers were required to fly their flag over the ship or base for which they were responsible.)

When I first arrived aboard the Yorktown, our division was responsible for sending out radio 'homing' signals for the incoming planes to guide them into the ship. This was done by a sailor manually transmitting the ships call sign which would be detected by the aircraft. Ike designed an automatic keying system for this purpose and built it himself from parts that were scavenged from the trash. This keyer relieved the necessity to have a man manually present to accomplish the task.

When the 'Flag" came aboard, the Chief in Charge of the Flag radio room staff was inspecting the Flag Center compartment where Ike's keyer was in operation and sarcastically said to Ike, who was on duty at the time, "What the hell is this piece of shit, get it out of my Radio Room." Without hesitation, Ike picked up the keyer assembly, opened the port hole and dumped it into the ocean.

The Chief was livid and put Ike on report for destroying Navy property. After an investigation, Ike got off the hook because no Navy parts were used in the manufacture of the device.

As 1954 approached, we were visited by Francis Cardinal Spellman, Archbishop of the Diocese of New York on New Year's Eve. It was a big occasion for everyone on board, especially the Catholics, when the Cardinal said mass on the hanger deck of the ship as we sailed the Sea of Japan off Korea.

The new year would bring to an end my four year enlistment in the Navy. For some time I had been giving serious thought to what I would do after being discharged. There was much discussion amongst many of us in the crew about this subject which led to having called to my attention a college in Angola, Indiana that offered the equivalent of a four year college degree that could be attained in twenty-seven months. Tri-State College (eventually to be Tri-State University) not only had an accelerated curriculum leading to a Bachelor of Science Degree in Engineering, but accepted students who had not graduated from high school but did have an equivalency diploma.

Having completed only two years of high school, there were some prerequisite high school subjects that were offered at Tri-State prior to the start of the college curriculum. Should I be accepted at Tri-State, I would have the opportunity to make up these subjects; Physics I and II, Chemistry, Mechanical Drawing; in the first three months at the school. These considerations and the availability of tuition assistance under the G.I. Bill for my wartime service prompted me to write for further information on the school and I eventually applied for and was accepted for the term beginning in September 1954, after my discharge.

In the meantime, we finished a few more tours off Korea and some more liberty time in Japan before heading back to the United States around March of 1954. Just before leaving Japan, the Navy announced that anyone whose enlistment was ending in 1954 could take an option to be honorably discharged two or three months earlier. I opted for the early discharge which meant I would be out of the navy and home before summer.

GOING HOME

We sailed at top speed, non-stop from Yokosuka to San Francisco. Cruising into port under the Golden Gate Bridge on our way to the Navy Base at Alameda was a sensation that I shall always recall with fond memories. We had a wonderful experience in the Far East and got a good taste of an alien culture, but it felt so good to be back home in the United States.

Upon our arrival we were greeted by many members of the crew's families and a large contingent of Shriners. In the last months before returning to the United States, the Yorktown ran many fund raising events on board for the Crippled Children's Fund that was sponsored largely by the Shriners' organization. As a result of this fund raising, the Shriners were presented upon our arrival with a check for twenty-five thousand dollars.

The first sailor to be granted liberty was the winner of a new car that was raffled off as part of this fund raiser. Interestingly, the winner of the vehicle had also won a six thousand dollar anchor pool. (Every time we hit a port there were many anchor pools with the prize given to the sailor who had the exact minute that the anchor was dropped or the first line was secured to the dock; as registered in the official log of the ship. The return to the states was particularly auspicious and the pools became quite expensive.) We all envied the winner as he drove off in his new car with six thousand dollars in his pocket.

Because I was being discharged within the next couple of months, I was not granted a leave to go back to New York, but I would over this time have many opportunities to enjoy liberty around the San Francisco area. One of my first stops upon leaving the ship was at a diner where I got several orders of fresh toast and a few glasses of fresh milk. These were two of the things I missed most dearly while we were out at sea and out of the country. The only milk I had been offered since leaving the states several months before was the tasteless powdered milk that we had on board the ship or, while in port in Japan, reconstituted milk which was a step up from the powdered stuff, but was still terrible. One never knows the things that will be missed when not available for a long period of time, and surprisingly it's the simple things that stand out.

Lee Herion and I, who had been vying for division thespian of the year with our informal Shakespearean performances, spent our first day back in San Francisco at a movie that was off the beaten path for most of our shipmates, viewing Shakespeare's "Julius Caesar" with Marlon Brando and John Geilgud. After the show, we discovered a wonderful bar where the beer sold for the unbelievably low price of twenty-five cents a bottle; and hot dogs were provided gratis by the bartender, to be grilled over the fire in the open fireplace that stood in the center of the room. When we spread the word about this discovery, it was not long before this remotely located bar was filled from wall to wall with sailors from the Yorktown.

We had the ship in dry-dock in San Francisco for a short time before going out to sea off the coast of California. We alternated between a short time at sea and liberty in Oakland or San Francisco. Shipboard life went on as usual as I awaited orders for my discharge from the service. As we approached that day, something happened on the ship that threatened to thwart all of my plans for terminating my enlistment in the Navy.

One of my jobs as a Radioman Second Class, a rank I had been promoted to shortly after starting my tour of duty aboard the Yorktown, was as the 'Police Petty Officer' for my division. One of the duties entailed in that position was to make sure that the entire crew of enlisted men in our division were out of their racks after reveille in the morning. With three remotely located sleeping quarters on the ship, it took about fifteen minutes to make the circuit from the main compartment at mid-ships, to one all the way forward at the bow, and, finally, the third one which was all the way aft.

One morning as we cruised the Pacific Ocean, I entered the final compartment where one of the men was just easing his way out of his bunk. I entered through one hatch and, after determining that everyone was up except this last straggler who now had his feet on the floor, exited through the hatch at the other end of the compartment. As I did so (as I was later to learn) the Sergeant-at-Arms entered the compartment where I had come in just as I stepped out.

Within the hour, I received a call from the Sergeant-at-Arms, directing me to put my mate on report (that is, report him to the ship's Executive Officer for disciplinary action) for 'being in bed after reveille." This was a relatively trivial infraction, had it been true, and as a matter of principle I told the Sergeant-at-Arms that as far as I was concerned, the presumed miscreant was out of bed and should not be put on report and that I would not accede to his request and that if he felt the need, he should do the reporting.

He told me, "You put him on report, Sailor, or I'm putting you on report." This got my hackles up enough to shoot back at him, "Well then, you're going to have to put me on report", and blithely adding, "I don't have too long to go in this man's Navy, so I don't give a shit if you do or not"; (words that would come back to haunt me in a very short time.)

I was notified by the Sergeant-at-Arms office that I had, indeed, been put on report and was to present myself at "Exec's Mast" in just a couple of days. I was not too concerned because of the pettiness of the charges against me. Typically for a violation of this nature, the worst that would be imposed would be a reprimand by the Executive Officer with a notation in the record; surely nothing to be concerned about at this stage of my naval career.

The procedure in matters of discipline was to first have a hearing before the Executive Officer, where he would hear the facts of the case and make a determination to settle it at that level or, in more serious infractions, to pass it on to the Captain at 'Captain's Mast' with a recommendation for disposition. Normally, the Captain would go along with the recommendation of the Exec and mete out punishment accordingly.

I attended Exec's Mast fully confident that he would at most give me a tongue lashing to save some face for the Sergeant-at-Arms and dismiss the whole matter. After the Sergeant-at-Arms presented his view of the facts, I was further convinced that the Exec would close the case immediately. I was about to give my version of the episode but the Exec focused in on only one thing; not the failure to report my mate for anything but rather on my comment that, "...I don't have too long in this man's Navy..."

The Exec started to dress me down for my 'short timer's attitude' and wound up recommending to the Captain that I be given a court martial for failure to obey the legitimate order of the Sergeant-at-Arms, while underway at sea. He stared at me with steely eyes and said, "You think you have a short time to go. How do you think you'll feel after six months in the brig on hard duty?" I couldn't believe what I was hearing and I was dismissed without an opportunity to defend myself or give another version of events.

Knowing the proclivity of the Captain to go along with the recommendations of the Executive Officer, I suddenly became aware of the fact that I could be facing months of time in the ship's brig; not a happy thought. However, if the Exec thought that he was going to frighten me with his threats of the brig, he was absolutely on the mark.

As soon as I returned to the radio shack, I called upon Ensign Clark, who had become a good friend and mentor to me since my first day on the Yorktown. After filling him in on the course of events of the past few days, I asked if he would be my advocate before the Captain at the upcoming mast. Through his personal relations with some of the officers who had an 'in' with the Captain, he managed to prepare the Captain for my defense at the hearing.

When I finally appeared at Captain's Mast while we were at sea with Ensign Clark by my side, I acted as I was directed by Clark; very contrite and sorry for the flippancy of my comments. The Captain made a big show of reaming me out and keeping me on edge waiting for him to throw me in the brig. When he got finished with the dressing down, he found me guilty of the charges as brought by the Sergeant-at-Arms, who grinned from ear to ear expecting that the Captain was now going to hit me with the full recommendation of the Executive Officer to put me before a court martial or throw me into the brig directly.

After tense moments of waiting, I was convinced that the worst was about to happen. The Captain finally gave his recommendation for punishment; no court martial but only five days restriction to the ship. This penalty started immediately. Because we were out at sea at the time and would not be in port until more than five days had passed, it was no punishment at all. I thanked Ensign Clark for his help and swore to myself that I would keep my mouth shut and avoid any punishable actions until I received my discharge.

It was also around this time that I made another resolution that I was determined to adhere to.

For my entire life I had walked around with a 'chip on my shoulder' and would often find myself in a fistfight for the smallest provocation. I suppose it was another step in the maturing process that finally made me realize that this was not the way to solve disputes. I made a promise to myself that henceforth I would avoid fights no matter what provoked it or who was the antagonist.

I was sticking to this resolution very well, walking away from several incidents that ordinarily would have resulted in a donnybrook. One night I was out on liberty and sitting in a club in Oakland, sitting on a stool at the bar and drinking with Bob McCauley, one of my shipmates who had previously served on the U.S.S. Kearsarge. Bob had a similar disposition to my own when it came to fighting and we had on several occasions joined together in a bar room brawl, both in the United States and overseas. That night I was relating to Bob my determination to avoid these scraps in the future.

There were four Marines at the opposite end of the bar who started throwing some verbal barbs at us with the obvious intention of trying to goad us into a brawl. We ignored them for the most part until they asked us what ship we were on. We answered, "The Yorktown". One of the Marines must have recognized Bob and said, "I recognize you, what ship were you on before?"

Bob said, "The Kearsarge." With a scowl on his face, the marine said in a malicious tone, "Oh! The Queer Barge?"

Bob had a short fuse and it was only seconds before Bob and this marine were in a fight with Bob throwing the first punch.

I kept to my resolve and did not join the fray; I assumed that Bob would make short shrift of the marine and we could go back to our quiet private conversation. One of the other Marines had other thoughts in mind. I found myself being grabbed by the shoulder and turned around in the swivel stool. A fist came flying into my face and hit me square on the cheekbone. I turned around in the stool, picked up my drink, and tried to ignore this attack.

I was turned around on the seat again and another blow caught me on the other cheek. Again, I turned around, feeling proud that I could restrain my temper and avoid a needless fight.

A third time, the Marine repeated his assault. This time, resolve or no, I kicked him swiftly in the groin and followed up with a sharp left hook to the head that sent him sprawling to the floor in the front vestibule of the bar. I stepped out alongside him as he was about to get up from the floor and kicked him in the face, which seemed to put him out for the duration of the fight.

The other two marines jumped me just as Bob was putting his adversary out when he dumped the contents of a spittoon onto the marine's head and banged the spittoon itself onto his skull. Bob jumped the two marines who were about to swing at me and in a swift turn of events, all four marines were on the floor as we beat a hasty retreat out of the bar before they regained their composure and renewed the battle. This was a wise move as I don't think we could have prevailed against the four of them and that we were just lucky in what had just ensued.

After this tussle with the four Marines, I renewed my resolution to quit fighting. I thought I had remained quite cool and controlled as I sat at the bar, but there's only so much abuse one can take before retaliating.

**JACK ON 49TH STREET
ASTORIA, 1932**

**JACK IN BACKYARD OF
HOUSE ON 46TH STREET
1939**

**DAN, FRAN & JACK
EASTER SUNDAY IN ASTORIA
Ca. 1941**

**FIRST HOLY COMMUNION
1941**

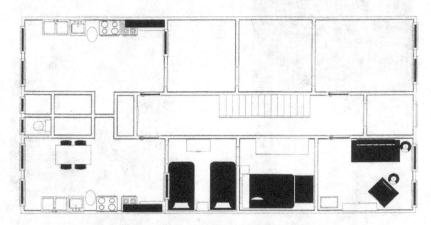

**Our Apartment at 28-44-46th Street, Astoria
1936-1943**

**Our House at 28-44-46th Street
(downstairs, left)**

**Daddy, Mother, and the
Twins, Billy & Tommy
ca. 1946**

MOTHER AND JACK
GRADUATION 1946

MARILYN, JACK, BOB
1944

MOTHER ON 43RD STREET

FRAN, HELEN, DAN, JACK
1951

341

The Recruit, 1950

Outside the Barracks
Panama, 1952

Letter from Home, Panama

"Hello, Washington"

R&R in a Panama Cantina

Jack's Locker

**Daddy & Mother (center)
Helen (at the wheel)
and friends, ca. 1927**

**Grandpa John O'Leary (r.)
and friend, ca. 1910**

Jack, Panama, 1952   **Jack aboard USS Yorktown, 1953**

Landing on the USS Yorktown   Jack in Hong Kong, 1953

Jack at the Blowhole in Hawaii   Honolulu & Diamond Head, 1953

1954-1958

१९५४-१९५८

DISCHARGE AND HOME

In May, I received my orders to report for discharge to the Naval Receiving Station at Treasure Island in San Francisco Bay. I was honorably discharged on May 24, 1954 after serving 3 years, 9 months and 22 days in the United States Navy with a final payout of $498.85 including $190.26 for travel pay home. As I left the Navy Base and Government property for the last time, I took my sea-bag which was packed with all of my navy gear and tossed the whole conglomeration into the San Francisco Bay. I had no commitment to serve in the Naval Reserve as required by some of the shorter enlistments and I felt free for the first time in nearly four years.

I was looking forward to seeing Gail whom I had only seen for a maximum of three or four weeks out of the past nineteen months that we had been married. I would join her for a couple of days upon my arrival in New York at the family apartment on 45th Street in Astoria, but my plan was to immediately find a furnished apartment to rent until I would start school in September.

Two additional top priorities in the interim before school were to get a job and to purchase a car, which I would need to get us to Indiana. My plans were not to work out as smoothly as I had hoped for.

I had written to Gail and informed her of my impending early discharge but I thought it would be a nice surprise if I flew home and just popped in on her after I was released at Treasure Island. If I had let her know the exact time of arrival, the next weeks may not have been as unsettled as they were to be.

When I landed at LaGuardia it was mid-week; Wednesday, I believe. I splurged and took a cab to Astoria; arriving at the house by mid-afternoon. I didn't expect Gail to be home from work until later in the day but was told by her mother that she wasn't expected home from work until late that night. I called Gail to tell her that I was home and that she should come right home from work.

She insisted that she had an engagement with a very 'special' friend and that she wouldn't be able to break it. I asked her who the friend was and, when she told me it was a guy who was having marital problems and needed her counsel, I controlled my temper and suggested that if she didn't want to have marital problems of her own, she should break the engagement and come home where she belongs. She demurred and insisted that she would be keeping the appointment.

I showered and put on my clean set of civilian clothes. (I had purchased three changes of casual clothes at the PX on Treasure Island before leaving San Francisco and would supplement this small wardrobe before going to Indiana in September.) I decided to meet her at the office to short circuit her intentions to go out that important homecoming evening.

When I met her outside the door, she was stunned; as I was stunned when I saw how she was dressed to go out to "counsel" a friend. She was dressed to the nines; Attire hardly suitable to business and surely not for a casual evening with a 'friend'. She continued to insist that she had to keep this appointment for this 'poor soul' whose wife didn't understand him and who had all kinds of emotional problems.

I told her that if he has that many problems, he should be seeing a priest or a psychologist; not another man's wife. When she said she had no way to contact him as he was scheduled to pick her up, I agreed to wait for him, not to take her out but to tell him what I had just told her; he should go home to his wife and get counseling, and that his relationship with Gail was ended.

When he arrived and was introduced as **Nick DePravato**, it didn't take me too long to realize that he was nothing but a Lothario on the make. He was about six foot two, muscular, and swarthy. I didn't waste any time to let him know what the situation was and that now that I was home he should stay out of our lives.

He got a bit snide and aggressive and tried to get Gail to go with him. I held her back and didn't give her a chance to make a decision. She was wordless when he asked her what she was going to do. I simply yanked on her hand and pulled her away with a final word to Nick that this was the end of this friendship.

Gail followed me home where my first evening at home was unexpectedly strained. Not only did I get greeted with this unwelcome suitor but she told me that evening that she didn't want to accompany me in September when I was starting college as we had agreed in our correspondence while I was away. We did agree, however, to rent an apartment as our first order of business the next day. While she was at work, I would look through the ads and inspect any likely places in Astoria to meet our needs for the next four months.

I didn't want to spend any more time in the Wilcox household than was absolutely necessary; Blanche was not the world's best housekeeper and the apartment was surely not a "Fanny Farmer" home (a farmer's fanny was more descriptive of the environs.)

While Gail worked the following day, I found a small furnished apartment on Steinway Street, one block north of the Grand Central Parkway. It was a store that had been converted into a two room apartment. The front room was used as a bedroom and the front wall was a locked glass door and two large plate glass windows from the former usage that had been painted on the inside with an opaque green color. The other room which was previously the back room of the store served as the kitchen/dining/living room, behind which was a small bathroom. The furnishings were simple and minimal but were adequate for our short stay; besides which, the rent was well within our price range.

There was no requirement for security deposits or any extra charges so we paid the first month's rent and moved in immediately; which was rather easy, as we had no major possessions to move in with us.

Before the first week was over, I had also landed a job which I would start the following Monday. I would be working in the deburring department of the Ledkote Aircraft Manufacturing Company on Vernon Boulevard in Long Island City along the waterfront of the East River. Ledkote was the manufacturer of forged aluminum parts for the aircraft industry and it would be my job to file or sand off the burrs on the parts after they had been forged and trimmed; another dead end job but adequate to start earning a pay check. The pay was 54 dollars a week to start.

We quickly established a routine of getting up in the morning, preparing lunch to carry to work in a brown paper bag, and catching a bus to take us to our respective jobs; in those days I had not yet acquired the habit of eating breakfast in the morning and a container of coffee before work was the only semblance of food that I would have before a coffee break at mid-morning. Mr. **DePravato** was out of our lives, or so I was convinced, and we had started to re-establish the relationship that we had before I left for the Far East.

We had not resolved Gail's insistence on not going to Indiana with me; she said that she didn't want to leave the job she had and could be of more help working in New York while I attended school. I didn't push at the time and decided to wait for the passage of some more time to convince her otherwise.

350

We were also searching for a suitable car at a price we could afford and which was in good enough condition to take us to Indiana. I still had not learned to drive but knew that I would learn very quickly; Gail told me that she was an experienced driver and would teach me when we got a vehicle.

About two weeks after returning home, I finished work and came back to our humble apartment. Gail was unusually late and I became concerned. We had no phone in the apartment so I went to a local store to call her at the office from a public telephone. There was no answer at her office. After waiting a short period of time, I decided to walk down Steinway Street and would then decide whether I would hop a bus to see if she was still at work.

It was about 9 P.M. and darkness had just set on Astoria. As I was walking down Steinway Street I saw Gail walking in my direction arm in arm with that son-of-a-bitch, **Nick DePravato**. I was fuming and rushed to confront the two of them on the street.

I told Gail to get home, while in a rage I prepared to flatten this punk. Before I could get my hands up **DePravato** hurled a couple of quick punches into my face and after a fast barrage of further punches, I found myself flat on my back on the ground, banging the back of my head into the concrete sidewalk as I fell.

I was stunned and was ready to get up to continue the battle, when Gail knelt down beside me and urged **Nick** to leave as he might have hurt me badly. I was too out of it at this point to say a word. Reluctantly, **Nick** left.

Gail and I had a battle royal that night, with me insisting that she don't see **Nick** again and that she was going with me to Indiana. I decided also, to take some time off the next morning to go to the Courthouse in Long Island City to file assault charges against **Nick** for his attack on me that night. I got a subpoena for **DePravato** to show up in court the following week and the option was to either hire a summons server for a fee or to present the papers to **Nick** myself. I decided to save the money and do the job personally.

I found out where **Nick** lived and staked out the apartment house for a couple of evenings after work until on the second night, I saw him nearing the building. I approached him as he walked to the front steps and he unexpectedly ran into the house and up the stairs toward the second floor. (I realized only later that Gail must have told him about my visit to the courthouse and was running to avoid being served with the summons to court.)

I quickly ran after him and grabbed him by the ankle as he hit the top of the stairs on the second floor. This time, before he could get himself oriented, I gave him two quick straight rights to the face, a left hook, and another right. I grabbed him by his unruly head of black hair and pulled his face into my uplifted knee. While he was still reeling from this sudden onslaught, I pushed him down the flight of stairs where he landed at the bottom on his butt.

I jumped down the stairs and finished him off with a kick in the ribs and one in the face. I stuffed the summons down the neck of his shirt and walked out; satisfied that I had my revenge for the other night's 'sneak attack'. Having gotten physical satisfaction, I decided that I would not go to court the following week to follow up on the complaint. **Nick** didn't show up either so I believe the court just dropped the whole matter.

After this episode, Gail seemed to settle down again; I think there was a certain ego stroking satisfaction on her part that two men would be not only vying for her attention but were ready to fight for her. We both continued to work and I was eagerly looking forward to getting out of New York and on with school.

Working at Ledkote was an enlightening and motivating experience. It was the kind of working environment that made me doubly inspired to get my college degree; I didn't want to spend the rest of my life in these dead-end laboring positions.

(My initial job as a deburrer was to take a drill bit that was attached to a knurled handle and remove the burrs from the holes that were drilled into the parts. The edge trimming was done by the more experienced men on the line. One of these senior fellows who had been doing the edge trimming on the emery wheels tried to encourage me to strive very hard so that someday I, too, could be elevated to the lofty position of doing the edge trimming.)

When I first started to work at Ledkote, the noise from the forges and machines in the shop were deafening; it was difficult to hear anyone speak. It didn't take too long to naturally filter out the noises to a point where I was able to hear ordinary conversation. The only problem remaining was that every time the machines stopped suddenly, at break time or quitting time, the abrupt cessation of the noise always caused extreme auricular pain; I never did get used to that in the short time I was to be at Ledkote.

It was only a couple of days after my last confrontation with **Nick DePravato** that I was outside the Ledkote plant on Vernon Boulevard taking the morning break and chatting with Ben, one of my co-workers. Ben was a large black man, about six feet five inches tall and close to three hundred pounds of solid muscle. He was big and strong but as gentle as a lamb.

As we talked, I saw **Nick** pull up in his car. He got out of the car, opened the trunk and took something out, and after slamming the trunk shut came walking across the street toward me. From the snarling expression on his face, I knew that he was about to continue the conflict with me. I stood up; ready to accept the challenge. It was then that I noticed that he had a tire iron in his right hand and as he neared he rushed at me and raised the tire iron to smash into my head.

I didn't have time to dodge the blow and as the iron was ready to make contact with my skull, a hand suddenly and swiftly reached out and stopped the blow just before the iron hit me. It was gentle Ben, who seeing what was about to happen, jumped in to grab the tire iron in flight and save me for the moment. He took the iron out of **Nick's** hand and said, "If there's going to be any fighting around here, it will be with fists, not with clubs."

With the sudden relief, I realized that I had a small kitchen knife in my pocket that I had taken in to sharpen that morning before the whistle blew to start work. I pulled the knife out and was ready to plunge it into **Nick** when Ben grabbed my arm and took the knife from me.

Nick came charging at me in a rage. I knew by now that he was a sucker for a straight right, so I shot two quick punches right into the middle of his face. This did not stop his assault; he grabbed me and soon had me in a headlock. He had a tight grip around my throat and I was down on my knees while he straddled across my body.

As I started to lose my breath with his stranglehold on my neck, in desperation I reached behind me and felt my hand on his face. I tried to gouge his eye hoping that this would break his hold. I felt the moistness of his eyeball and pushed my finger inside and pulled to the side.

I noticed a spreading pool of blood running off my shoulders and onto the ground. I thought that he had cut me somehow and that although I couldn't feel or sense where the blood was coming from, that I was bleeding profusely. The pool of blood became so widespread as we rolled around on the ground that Ben jumped in again and pulled us apart.

As I arose I saw the blood pouring out like Niagara Falls from **Nick's** face. When I struck him with those two earlier straight right hands to the face, I evidently had split his nose open and when I reached into what I thought was his eye, I had dug into his slashed nose and had pulled it open with my fingers.

Someone gave **Nick** a towel or an old rag that was lying around and the group that had gathered stepped between us to break up the fight. **Nick** headed for his car with the compress on his face and promptly drove away; I assume to get medical care. That pretty face that was trying to encroach itself upon my marriage would not look as appealing in the future.

That proved to be quite a significant day. Earlier, prior to the conflict with **Nick**, I was visited at my work station by the President of the company himself. When I was first hired they had given me a card to fill out agreeing to join the union within the first thirty days on the job. I never signed the paper and was now holding out from joining the union until I was shown what advantages it held for me; there really were none. Having had previous experience with "sweetheart" unions, I was not going to join one again, if I could avoid it.

The President said that I had to join but I still adamantly refused. Nothing further was said but I knew that some retribution was going to come down. For now, they were stumped as to what action to take because no one had ever refused to join the union when ordered to do so.

After the row with **Nick**, I was covered with blood and was in no emotional state to go back to work. I took off for the rest of the day and told them I would be back tomorrow. (This was the last time that I raised my fists in anger and managed to hold to my no fighting resolve until today. One never knows what tomorrow will bring but at seventy years of age, I don't believe that I will have resort to physical solutions for relational problems.)

When I arrived home, a letter was in the mail notifying me that I had been accepted for a position as a 'platform-man' at the Railway Express Company and if I accepted I could start work at the beginning of the next work week. The starting pay was 75 dollars a week; 21 dollars more than I was making at Ledkote. With the situation at my current job after the union episode and the fight outside the plant I figured that the prudent thing to do would be to resign forthwith from Ledkote and accept the job at the Railway Express. I immediately called Railway Express to let them know of my availability and would notify Ledkote in the morning that I would be leaving. I would be starting at the Railway Express on the Midnight to 8 A.M. shift the following week.

After **Nick** had his face put back together, he went to see Gail at work and got her terrified with a tale that whatever I did to him, I would be doing to her when she got home. He convinced her that she shouldn't go home and the two of them hopped in his car and headed to Findley, Ohio, where they hoped to seek refuge at the home of her Aunt **Maude,** Blanche's sister.

(**Maude** was married to John McCann, a former all-star basketball player at St. John's University and the general manager of Findley's largest department store.)

After a call and consultation with Blanche in New York, **Maude** let them stay long enough to rest up for the trip home after convincing Gail that the right thing to do would be to return home and do what has to be done to repair the faltering marriage.

ALMOST FATAL

While they were out of the state and I was between jobs, another nearly fatal problem arose in my life. With all of the things going on in my life, I had been ignoring a sore that had developed on the back of my foot from the poorly fitting shoes that I was wearing every day.

During this Ohio interval I was alone in the house and at a loss as to what to do next. I was so angry after realizing that Gail had taken off with **Nick** that I came home and slashed apart with a sharp knife, a large oil painting of her that I had had made in Japan from a photograph. I also destroyed all of the letters that each of us had written over the past four years; a great loss of the everyday occurrences, feeling, and events. I consoled myself with some Early Times Bourbon and beer and continued to ignore the now festering wound on my feet.

During the night, I awoke with a terrible pain along the whole left side of my body, the side where the shoe had irritated the back of my foot. I went to get out of bed to go to the bathroom for an aspirin for the pain, when I fell on the floor. In the dark, I felt my left leg; it was greatly swollen. I crept over to turn on the light and with great difficulty pulled myself up to the lamp on the night table and switched it on.

Not only was my leg swollen but the ankle was larger than the leg and I could see that the entire leg had become infected. Without a telephone, I didn't know what to do. I crawled again with great pain to the door to the hall. I pulled it open and yelled into the hall for help without getting any response.

I was beginning to feel groggy and dizzy. I had a burning fever and felt like I would pass out at any moment. I had heard about people dying of blood poisoning from infections and recalled that one of Mother's brothers had died from that very cause when he was a child.

In desperation, I dragged myself across the floor into the bathroom and looked in the almost bare medicine cabinet for something to help my situation. The only things in there were a bottle of aspirin (or maybe it was Midol) and a bottle of iodine.

At this point, I felt that I would pass out and no one would know and that I would be found dead only when the next month's rent was due. Neither my old employer nor my soon to be employer would care if I didn't show up.

Before I passed out, I took a fresh double edge razor out of the pack and slashed the back of the offending foot. A gush of yellow fluid came pouring out over the floor. I didn't worry about where it fell; I felt that this was the right thing to do and did begin to feel somewhat better. Having had lots of experience with squeezing boils a few years prior, I squeezed the flesh in my ankle, foot, and leg until I felt that every drop of the poisonous liquid was out of my body.

I washed up the blood with hot water and poured the entire bottle of iodine into the wound and over the inflamed foot and ankle. I crawled back into the living room and I don't know whether I fell asleep or just passed out on the floor. It was not until late the next afternoon that I woke up to find myself still lying in the middle of the room. The infection seems to have subsided and my leg and foot looked close to normal.

I managed to get myself dressed and went to the nearby drugstore in the rubber clogs that most of us had purchased in Japan to get some more iodine and some bandages to tend to my own wounds. (I remember Mother always using iodine on cuts and it always seemed to do the job. It was also her personal, successful cure for ringworm when it was endemic in the neighborhood.)

Mother's cure worked and I was soon on my way back to normal health. Before I started the new job, I was able to get my shoes and socks on. I had thrown away the shoes that had caused my problem.

STARTING OVER

When Gail returned from Ohio in a repentant mood, she went to her Mother's house on 45th Street. Ranny, my father-in-law drove over to talk to me. Up to this point we had managed to keep this entire incident to ourselves but now that Gail's parents were involved, they wanted to play a part in reconciling our disagreement.

With Ranny acting as the intermediary, Gail and I got together and came to terms; she would cut off the relationship with **Nick** while continuing to assert that nothing untoward had happened between them; their not being caught *flagrante delicto* and my desire to believe her and get on with a normal life convinced me to accept, no matter how incredulously, her protestations.

She agreed to go to Indiana with me in September. Ranny and Blanche offered to let us stay at their house for the two months remaining until our departure and that they would give up their bedroom so we could have the maximum of privacy. Without it being said, it was understood by all that this accommodation would be helpful in assuring that Gail was not seeing **Nick** while I was on the night shift at Railway Express. This sad incident in our lives was never mentioned again as we settled into a more normal relationship.

I also renewed my resolution to not attempt to solve future problems by fisticuffs and have managed to maintain the resolve until today, where at my advanced age I doubt that I could effectively prevail in any case.

I started the new job at the Railway Express at the railroad yard at Steinway Street and Northern Boulevard. The work was continuous but not difficult. It was the job of the platform-man to unload the trucks as they arrived at the terminal and to load those outgoing packages onto the appropriate trains when separated and marked by one of the senior men. The next half of the shift would be unloading incoming packages from the trains and transferring them to the trucks for local delivery; not too much excitement but it was a job with a steady paycheck for the employees.

As a Railway Express worker, I was part of the Railroad Retirement System and paid eight percent of my salary (six dollars) toward that pension. Although the Railway Express would eventually go out of business, my contributions to the retirement fund were carried on the books and gave me a modest increase in my Social Security pension when I applied for it a couple of years ago; no more than one dollar a month.

One of my co-workers was Jack Egan's father who I had always thought had a job as a white collar worker; accountant, stock broker, or something along that line. Whenever I saw him going to work, he always was dressed to the nines, with suit, white shirt, and tie, and carried a briefcase. The briefcase I was to discover was his lunch pail, and he changed to his 'business attire' at the locker room at work. I had always admired him and working with him only increased my admiration for his warmth, intelligence, and sense of humor.

There was one man who worked beside me who was paid the same salary and held the same position as I, but who had worked at the Railway Express since 1901; fifty-three years. I soon discovered that the only advantage to having seniority on the job was that when the holidays came around the senior men would be permitted to work overtime with the time and a half pay differential, while we junior guys would be laid off so that we wouldn't have to be paid for the holiday; usually to be called back to work sometime after the holiday..

I enjoyed this job because it had no stress and only required the lifting and moving of small packages, rarely anything too heavy for one man to lift. It also gave me a chance to observe what the women of the neighborhood did while I was off during the normal work day because I was on the midnight shift. While the men were working, most of the neighborhood women would gather outside the apartment houses on 45th Street and sit around in their housedresses (which was the established uniform for married women in the neighborhood) on their aluminum beach chairs while they were ostensibly watching the children. I got this sedentary gaggle of women angry one day when I suggested that it would be nice if their husbands came home to find some food on the table after a hard days work instead of finding them all still sitting outside on their butts. (My father-in-law, for instance, held two full time jobs; one was as a mechanic on the Long Island Railroad where he lifted heavy equipment all night. The second was as a boiler and chimney cleaner which he worked at six days a week during the day. In addition to these two jobs, he was the Janitor for three apartment houses which required cleaning and maintenance daily. When he came home in the evening, he would normally have to prepare his own dinner while Blanche exclaimed, "My Ranny loves to cook!")

I called this coterie of sidewalk surfers, "The Beach Chair Brigade."

An important order of business for us before returning to school was the purchase of an automobile. A friend of Ranny's was selling a 1946 Dodge with Fluid Drive Transmission for 100 dollars; well within our budget. The transmission was one of the newer semi-automatic transmissions that also accommodated a standard shift. It ran pretty well, so it was a good buy. The only difficulty I had with the car before leaving for Indiana was a broken starter. I soon learned to repair the car myself with the help of Ranny, who had extensive experience trying to hold together all the old hunkers that he was used to.

Gail, as promised, undertook the task of teaching me how to drive. I didn't realize at the time that she had almost as little experience as I had driving a car and only learned her driving 'skills' from observing her father. I was soon getting the knack for driving, however, and felt I was ready to take the driving test.

The first week I had the car, I was driving at all opportunities. One of those nights I took the car, with Gail as a passenger, on an evening drive that found us in Garden City in Nassau County shortly after nightfall. As I was approaching a street where I was going to make a left turn, I noticed flashing lights behind me and I realized that it was a police car and that I was being motioned to pull over to the side of the road.

A Garden City policeman asked for my license and registration and told me that he had pulled me over for failing to give him the right of way. I showed him the registration but, not having yet taken the driving test, all I had to show was a learner's permit which did not allow me to drive after dark and certainly not without a licensed driver in the car. The summons that was issued was for 'Driving without a license' and I was to appear in the Garden City Village Court in about two weeks. Surprisingly, the cop permitted me to drive the car back to Astoria.

I showed up at the court not knowing what to expect. Judge George Wildermuth, an old gentleman who looked like he should have retired years before, was presiding. He was a tough jurist. Most of the people who were pleading guilty to the lesser offenses had done so in the mail and had sent in the specified fines. Some, such as me, didn't have this opportunity and had been ordered in the summons to appear in person, with or without an Attorney. Those who were in court on this night were those who, like myself, were pleading for the first time, or were there to be tried on a previous plea.

Those pleading not guilty were given a date at some future court session. Those pleading 'Guilty with an explanation' were heard, but from the expression on Judge Wildermuth's face, not listened to. When they finished theirs explanation, they were hit with fines or jail time as bad as those handed out to the people who were found guilty after a hearing or a plea. The fines, I thought, were outlandish, with a typical fine being 150 dollars for driving without a license. I trembled at the thought of what was going to happen to me when I got before the judge; I didn't have that kind of money and would most likely wind up in jail.

When it was my turn, I was somewhat relieved when Judge Wildermuth postponed my hearing until I applied for and got my license with an order to return before him in court at a date in late August. I knew that I would be hit with an insurmountable fine in August but felt that, for now, I had some breathing space.

I applied for my road test, which I took and failed. Not having attained the license as directed by Judge Wildermuth, I decided it would be wise to just ignore the new hearing date in August and proceed to Indiana in September as planned. I assumed that they would not track me down in Indiana. I was right for the time being, but it would be twenty years later when this delinquency would pop up to bite me in the behind when I was least prepared for it (more about that much later.)

OFF TO TRI-STATE COLLEGE

I don't know how we had the balls to do it and in retrospect I think that we were quite out of our minds to pack up to travel to Indiana so ill prepared for what was ahead. With all of the expenses of settling down into civilian life; buying clothes, purchasing an automobile, and other things; we did not save much money from the small salary that we were bringing home. Gail had lost her job when she took off for Ohio without informing her boss of her absence and she didn't find another position before we departed.

We packed up the few worldly goods we had and, with neither of us having a valid drivers license or too much experience driving, we headed west for Indiana in September, leaving plenty of time to register for school after our arrival. We started off with seventy-five dollars in our pockets; I anticipated taking advantage of the advertised loan programs at school to cover my initial tuition until I started receiving a check from the government under the G.I. Bill. Tri-State College had a local employment service to assist the students in getting part-time and odd jobs around the town and I assumed that this would help to meet our everyday needs.

We sure displayed the impetuosity of youth at its most blatant. We had little cash, no health or life insurance and no source of income. The mandatory insuring of vehicles had not as yet become law in New York State, so our vehicle was not covered for liability or collision.

We used twenty-five dollars of our *fortune* for gas and tolls across the Pennsylvania Turnpike getting to our destination. The Ohio Turnpike and the Indiana Turnpike had not been built yet, so about half of the trip was not on super highways.

Blanche had packed us a large package of food for the 700 mile trip and to save money we only stopped for drinks or to make a pit stop, arriving in Angola late Saturday afternoon, the day after we had left.

Upon our arrival, the first thing we did was to survey the local motels so that we could get the cheapest quarters until Monday when the school office was open to give us the anticipated assistance in finding living quarters in or around town. We settled on a small motel just outside of town that had cabins with no toilet or bathing facilities in the room, but instead had shared facilities in a building attached to the main office. It was not the Presidential suite at the Waldorf-Astoria but it served its purpose for the weekend stay and the total cost of the room for the entire weekend was only three dollars.

We used the free time over the weekend to explore the town and its environs.

Angola was the County Seat of Steuben County with a population of about four thousand inhabitants plus the approximately 1000 students at the college. Neither of these populations was to change significantly over the next fifty years even after the college became a four year University.

The town was at the intersection of two major truck routes; US 20, an east-west road and Rte. 827 a north-south thoroughfare. There were several truck stops on the outskirts of town in all directions to service the large volume of traffic that passed through Angola. This traffic would diminish greatly after the building of the Indiana Turnpike in later years. The turnpike was built about eight miles north of Angola and the diversion of the trucking which was part of the life's blood of the community would contribute greatly to the diminishing growth of the town. Other than the transient business from the truckers and the town's college, there was no significant commerce or industry in or around Angola. Summers were witness to an influx of tourists during July and August because of the large number of lakes in the region but, other than that, it was a quiet, rural, college town.

The farmers, who dominated the surrounding lands, were serviced by the Farmer's Cooperative which had its headquarters in Angola. I would spend many hours over the next two years working on these farms.

The main part of town was the square which was at the intersection of the two major arteries. The center of the square was a traffic circle with a statue in the middle commemorating the servicemen lost in the wars. Most of the stores in town were located around the town square with a few on the side streets directly adjacent. The two town movies, the Brokaw and the Strand were located in the square.

The area around the town was primarily farms and there were many lakes dedicated mostly to summer vacation homes.

I reported to the school on Monday morning and my first inquiry was to get a place to rent. The school had a listing of a small two room apartment in a private home on Lake James, about ten miles out of town. We drove out to the lake, talked to the owners and decided to rent the apartment for thirty dollars a month. We paid the first month's rent after which I returned to the college while Gail got us settled into our new quarters.

The apartment was built in the basement of a two story log cabin that faced the driveway from the main road. The apartment was built into the side of the hill and overlooked Lake James; a beautiful vista. In the middle of the lake was a small island which provided just enough property for the house that was built there. This house remained vacant most of the year and could only be reached by boat. (During our stay on Lake James, someone got arrested for tapping into the electric lines out to this island house; bypassing the meter which was located at waterside at the foot of our property.)

The owners of the house who we always called, "The Mister" and "The Missus" occupied the upper part of the house when they were in residence there. They owned a farm elsewhere in the county and the Mister would often spend a lot of time at their house on the farm.

I reported to the registrar at the school to sign up for my first term (September to December) which would not include any college courses but only the four High School subjects that I would have to make up before actually entering the college for matriculation. When I inquired about the loan program that I had intended to use to pay my first quarter's tuition, I was informed that the loans were only available to those who had already been attending school. This revelation put me in a real quandary. I asked to see the President of the school.

President Wood agreed to speak to me and I presented him with my sad tale of woe. I had driven from New York with the intention of attending school through borrowing from the college loan fund. We had rented an apartment on Lake James after which we were left with barely enough money to eke it out for about a week. I pleaded my case with him with the promise that all payments would be made as soon as I started receiving my checks from the federal government under the G.I. Bill. In any case, I did not have the funds to return to New York. After an hour's pleading, I must have made my case because President Wood agreed to accept me into the curriculum and informed the Registrar to allow me to enter the college with the tuition to be paid by me at a future date.

The student employment office was not open that day and I had to wait until classes started the following week to find employment. In the meantime, we got a copy of the local Angola weekly newspaper and looked through their classified ads for a position for either or both of us; without success. We reviewed our financial situation and by frugal planning we decided we could stretch out our meager dollars for a few extra days.

When classes commenced the following week another reality of college life became immediately apparent; tuition was only the start of the school expenses; there were books to be purchased and tools for the Mechanical Drawing class were also required. There was a used book sale being conducted on the campus sponsored by the Tau Sigma Eta Honorary Engineering Society which I searched out. I managed to get some used drawing instruments to meet my starting needs and the text books I needed for the other courses. I would later discover that the text books for the college level courses were even more expensive so I was fortunate that I was only taking the prep courses. I bartered with the book sale sponsors and they permitted me to purchase the books with the proviso that I pay for them within the week; a stipulation to which I readily agreed.

I would soon learn that a slide rule (this was before the advent of hand calculators) was another necessity. A typewriter would also be helpful but in the meantime I settled on writing by hand all of the required laboratory reports; of the four subjects I would take in the first quarter, three had mandatory laboratory experiments and reports every week.

As for the slide rule, I had to be content for the first two quarters at school making all of my calculation long hand until Art Fletcher, Gail's grandfather, sent me an 'antique' slide rule that he got from one of his co-workers at Norden Laboratories who was retiring; he had used that slide rule since his own days in college more than forty years before.

ODD JOBS

My first stop after classes was to the employment office to inquire about available jobs in and around the town. The only thing currently open was an opening for apple pickers. I was desperate and would have taken anything that was available. I went to a local farm and spent as much time as I could during the daylight hours picking as many apples as possible at a pay rate of twenty cents per bushel.

My initial speed was only getting me about two bushels or forty cents per hour but I soon learned to increase the rate to over five bushels or more than one dollar per hour. The farmer expected the pickers to strip an entire tree bare before moving on to the next tree. Picking from the lower branches was rather fast but when it came time to strip the upper branches, the maximum rate slowed down to as low as one bushel per hour.

I worked diligently and continuously every day after classes until dark and slowly was saving enough to pay for the books I had purchased on a promise to pay. About the third day, it was raining and the farmer said that we would not have to pick apples in the rain. I insisted on continuing to pick over his objections because I needed every penny that I could make. This turned out to be a fortuitous decision because without the farmer monitoring the work, I could pick the apples off only the lower branches of the trees and double my usual output. The farmer was pleasantly surprised that I had been so productive and never questioned how I accomplished such a prodigious yield.

I attended classes every day and reported to the employment office just as regularly. As it turned out, there was plenty of work to be had in the community but every job paid only one dollar per hour. This low wage was the reason for so many jobs; every homeowner had odd jobs that they gladly farmed out for those coolie wages. As for me, I couldn't complain because I needed any work I could get.

I found out during registration that my first government check would not be in my hand until December, three months after classes started; after that they would be coming in regularly every month. The amount I was to receive would only be 120 dollars a month for the first three months because I was not taking college level courses. After I started with those courses the monthly stipend would increase to 135 dollars per month. Fortunately, the tuition when I started at Tri-State was 140 dollars per quarter. As is quite evident, even with working a maximum schedule to supplement the G.I. check, there was a tight budget.

Through the next two years, I would attend class, do homework and work as many hours as I could on sundry jobs. A lot of the work was on the county farms and every one of the farm jobs entailed heavy and tiring manual labor. Beside picking apples, I helped in harvesting things like hay that would be automatically tied into bundles and would then have to be manually stacked on carts and hauled into the barn for storage; backbreaking labor. My body soon became keenly aware that every job that the farmers would hire us for was a backbreaker.

I worked on a chicken farm doing all of the chores necessary to maintain thousands of chickens that were being raised for the dinner table. Typical of the jobs to be done was the inoculation of each chicken with a serum that was carried in a back pack and connected by a tube to a single needle that was used to inject the serum into each bird. This work all had to be done in the dark so that the chickens would not stampede if frightened by us while we were working in the chicken house. The chickens when excited would pile up on top of each other and smother to death the ones on the bottom of the heap.

To prevent this mass chicken hysteria, we would enter at one end the darkened coop which housed thousands of chickens. We wore a helmet which was provided with a dim lantern which barely provided enough light to assist us in the chore. A small fence no more than eighteen inches off the floor was used to separate the inoculated chickens from the rest of the flock. As a chicken was injected he would be put on the other side of the fence. As we quietly progressed, we slowly moved the fence forward as necessary until all of the chickens were inoculated.

Another interesting chore was the 'debeaking' of the chickens. Using the same separation technique as before, we would take the chickens one at a time and cut off one beak with a clipper. This was to prevent the chickens from pecking holes in each other and bruising their flesh.

After the chickens reached maturity and were ready for market, we would scoop them up in the dark to place in crates of about twelve chickens each to send to the market. With very little experience we soon learned to grab about six chickens in each hand to fill the crates.

There seemed to be no end to the variety of work that I was called upon to do over the next two years. I worked in many private households doing such things as scrubbing the scrollwork on an old Victorian porch with a toothbrush, cleaning out rat infested attics and basements; one of the oddest jobs was painting a kitchen for one of the local widows.

When I arrived at her house, she told me that she wanted me to repaint her aged yellow kitchen walls with another shade of yellow paint; for this she gave me a half-pint can of yellow paint, which I told her was insufficient for the magnitude of the job. She told me that I should thin it out and it would cover the walls. It was her one dollar an hour and I didn't feel obliged to offer further resistance.

When I asked her for the thinner, she gave me a can of gasoline and said that that was what her late husband always used. I did as the lady requested and managed to spread the watery mixture across the entire kitchen; fortunately the kitchen was already yellow and the paint just acted as a wash on the walls. I suggested to her that she not light any matches or the stove in the kitchen until the fumes from the gas were dissipated.

She was so delighted with the job being done with so little paint, so little time, and so little expense, that she said that she had been planning to paint the outside of her house and would ask for me when she called the school employment office for that job. I made a mental note to myself to be previously occupied when that request came through; I would leave the problem of painting the entire outside of the house with a pint of paint to one of the other more resourceful students.

From time to time, I found regular employment for short periods of time. I worked in a local self service grocery, the Model Market, doing general chores around the store. One of the main tasks that I can remember was the revitalizing of the wilted vegetables by soaking them in ice water for a couple of hours; this would keep the food in a crisp enough state to permit sale and would retard further wilting until the customer served the greens at home.

I worked for a time at the Strand Theatre, the smaller of the town's two downtown movie houses. I worked at the candy and popcorn counter where I was paid a commission based on sales. I got five percent of the gross on the candy sales which sold for five cents a bar, and ten percent of the popcorn sales at ten cents a box. It was my responsibility to clean the vending area and the popcorn machine, as well as to purchase the goods at a local wholesaler;

none of these chores were compensated for and the only income was the sales commissions. There were nights when the movie was so sparsely attended that the total sales were less than a dollar and the commission was less than ten cents; for a four hour double feature this came to about three cents an hour. I only stayed on this job until I could land another.

The manager of the theatre was very attentive to how much butter I used in the making of the popcorn but I soon found out that if I surreptitiously doubled the amount of butter, the popcorn sales would increase significantly. Soon the reputation for my 'buttery' popcorn spread widely enough in the community that the people who were going to the neighboring Brokaw Theater would stop off to buy their popcorn from me before attending the other movie.

I worked for a time at a local gas station for the owner, Warren Schenkel, who was a cousin to Chris Schenkel, a Channel Nine television sportscaster back in New York City. The gas station was located on one of the back streets away from the main thoroughfares and relied upon its business by charging significantly less than the prices that were set by the major oil companies in town. The gas that was sold was unbranded and was actually a conglomeration of all the major oil company gasoline and was delivered to our station by the major company drivers at the end of their normal routes to empty their tanks (and perhaps make themselves a few dollars *off the books*.)

The oil we sold, at various grades, was sold 'loose' from fifty gallon drums of used oil that had been re-filtered and reconditioned. We also had a single car bay where Warren would do repairs on the vehicles.

My job was to pump the gas, clean the windshields, and check and change the oil. In the winter time, I would also drain and flush the radiators and fill them with the *expensive* anti-freeze or more often with a cheaper alcohol which was added to the cooling water until the hydrometer indicated the desired level of protection. Unlike the permanent anti-freeze, the alcohol would evaporate with time and have to be periodically checked.

For this work, I was paid less than one dollar an hour, but at least it was steady work for a while, and occasionally someone would drop a dime or so on me as a tip.

The first time I changed oil, Warren simply told me to put the car on the lift, remove the drain plug on the oil pan, and let the oil drain into the rollaway tank which was provided with a funnel on top. I followed the instructions; put the car up on the lift, rolled the used oil tank under the oil pan, and removed the plug from the pan. The black, hot oil spouted out in a steady stream right into my face and over my head; Warren neglected to tell me that the funnel on the tank was to be extended up to the oil pan before removing the plug. It was a lesson learned and would not be repeated.

The job at Schenkel's gas station was another position that would end shortly because of circumstances beyond my control. Warren attracted the locals to the station by keeping the prices lower than the other stations. The other stations were either in collusion to maintain higher prices or were dictated to by the parent oil companies. When Warren started pulling too much business from the other stations, they ganged up on him and threatened him with 'retaliation' if he didn't bring his prices in line with the rest of the stations along the main arteries. He refused to change his prices and the other stations dropped their prices below his until he agreed to get in line with them.

With the changed prices, Warren had to lower his overhead which meant laying off some of the workers, including me, and picking up the slack himself.

The loss of this job came at a very fortuitous time. One of my classmates had been working at the Lakes James Machine and Tool Company and was leaving the job. I found out from him later on that he was let go by Harry the owner because he complained when Harry tried to stiff him out of some hours that he had worked.

In the meantime, I went out to the shop and applied for the opening. Harry was in his peak season, installing wooden piers along the many lakes in the area and the first job I was to work on was the construction of a large sea wall for a homeowner on Lake James.

The wall was being installed in a location that was inaccessible to cement trucks or other construction vehicles so all the work had to be done by hand. We did have mobile rotary cement mixers and all of the cement, gravel, and sand had to be hauled by hand to the site down a long steep hill. We constructed the wooden form for the sea wall and after sealing it and pumping out the lake water; we were ready to start pouring. Once the pouring was started we were obliged to continue mixing and pouring until the job was completed. I don't know how many tons of cement we poured but we started early on a Saturday morning and continued until it was nearly dark before finished.

It was hard work but I enjoyed it even if it only paid the customary one dollar an hour. (It was interesting that the unskilled laborers who were working on the Indiana Turnpike which was being constructed in that year, 1956, were making close to five dollars an hour. We often passed them as we were being driven to a worksite while standing in the back of a pickup truck like a bunch of itinerant farm workers. The Turnpike laborers would more often than not, be leaning on their shovels, while we were expected to put out a maximum effort at all times.)

When pouring the sea wall, I was carrying one 94 pound bag of cement per trip from the top of the hill to the mixers at the waterside. Harry browbeat us into taking two bags on each trip and alternating with loads of sand and gravel that were equally as heavy. As tough as the work was, I tried to get the maximum number of hours in from the ending of the last class of the day until nightfall and all day Saturday and Sunday from sunup to sunset. I did manage to get the studying done during the few off hours I had.

The classmate who touted me onto this job had warned me that, if I wanted to keep the job, I shouldn't say anything to Harry when and if he shorted me on the pay. I worked for three months during the summer from June until August and had no problems with Harry and getting paid for the hours that I worked. Toward the end of the summer, he did short me on one of the paydays and I called it to his attention; I sure as hell was not going to let him beat me out of even one dollar at that coolie rate of pay. Harry objected but did wind up paying me. The following week, he cut down on my hours and at the end of the week told me that my services were no longer required because business was off. By this time I was one of the senior guys on the job and really produced for him. Harry did hire another student in my place.

I warned the student about Harry's pay shorting practice and passed on the same advice that was passed on to me; if you want to keep the job, don't complain about being cheated out of some of your pay. Harry shorted my replacement after a couple of weeks; he did not complain and he did not lose the job.

I had many other odd jobs during my time at Tri State; Gail, in the meantime, pitched in to do her part to keep our head above water. Shortly after I started classes she applied for and got a position at the local Farmer's Cooperative as a bookkeeper to maintain and balance their books; they evidently believed that one term of Bookkeeping I in high school was adequate preparation for the job. She held this position for about six months and worked very diligently every day, arriving early for work and staying late when necessary without overtime pay.

At the end of this time she was let go from the job. After six months, the books didn't balance and they had to bring in an accountant to try to unravel and straighten out the six months of erroneous entries. We felt blessed that we had at least one steady paycheck coming in each week for those six months.

During the time that Gail was employed at the Farmer's Co-op, I was usually working at another job, or at home doing my studies, cleaning the house, or preparing a meal. During one of the coldest days of winter, I was at home and had just taken a shower and put on a robe. While still attired in nothing but the robe, I swept the floor of the apartment with a dust mop.

After completing my sweeping chore, I went to the front door to shake the mop outside. At this point our two dogs made a move to run out through the opened door. I instinctively pulled the door shut to prevent the dogs from getting out; realizing too late that I had locked myself out of the house.

I had nothing on but the robe and the cold winter air bit at my naked body beneath the robe. The temperature was close to zero degrees Fahrenheit and with the blustery wind, the effective temperature was well below zero.

The dogs were still inside the house and were jumping up on the glass in the door, thinking I was playing a game. (We had adopted two cocker spaniels that we named "Dawn" and "Dusk". Dawn was white with light brown rings around the eyes and on the torso; Dusk was similarly spotted but with black rings.)

There was no way to get back into the house. The windows were sealed, the doors were locked, and no one was home upstairs. The lakeside was desolate in the winter and just about all of the neighboring houses were sealed up for the winter. There was, however, one occupied house about a quarter of a mile up the road. I had no choice but to walk there to see if I could prevail upon the residents to call Gail at her office to come home with the key to get me out of my dilemma.

There were still a few inches of snow on the ground from a recent storm, and I was obliged to walk the short distance to the neighbor's house with my feet covered with nothing but a pair of rubber clogs that I still had from my tour of duty in Japan. I knocked on the door of the house rather impatiently and, perhaps, a bit too lustily; but I was cold and was hoping to be asked into this warm shelter.

After what seemed like an interminable wait, I heard a barely perceptible woman's voice on the other side of the unopened door ask, "Who is it?" I answered the unseen questioner, "I'm your neighbor from down the road. I've locked myself out of the house. Could I use your phone to get some help?"

The door opened a crack and I could see that there was a safety chain in place on the door preventing it from opening more than a couple of inches. The wizened face of a woman, who must have been about ninety years old, peered out through the small aperture in the doorway. Her eyes could not mask the apprehension she must have felt when she observed this strange character that was standing on her porch; a wild-man in a robe with his hair blown asunder by the wind, and wearing snow crusted slippers which were topped by a pair of bony, white legs that were shaking with every gust of the wind.

I realized that I had better do some fast talking before she slammed the door shut and left me there to freeze to death. My pleas must have finally convinced her to at least open the door and let me in to make the phone call to Gail, who said she would leave work immediately to come home. The old lady, being alone in the house, was still uneasy about my presence there, but in spite of her hesitation, permitted me to sit in the hallway by the door until my savior arrived. When Gail arrived from town about thirty minutes later, I was just beginning to thaw out and was enjoying the crackling sounds of the blazing logs in the wood burning stove in the parlor.

We returned to the house and were happy to see the dogs sleeping on the mat at the door and that they had not been up to any mischief in our absence.

In the rest of the two years that Gail spent in Indiana, she had other jobs, including; waiting on tables at a local beanery and cashier at the local drug store.

LIFE IN INDIANA

We soon settled down in our little two room home on Lake James. The intensive pace of the accelerated classes and the necessity to work at every available opportunity left us with little time for recreational activities; and if we had the time, we didn't have money to spend for such frivolous purposes.

The "Mrs." spent most of her time during the warm months of the year in her quarters above us and we often stopped in to talk with her and get informed about the local area and the neighbors around us. Next door to us was a summer camp run by the Church of Christ. In the off season, it was closed and boarded up, adding to the isolation and quiet in the winter months.

During the summer when the camp was in full swing, there was a continuous buzz of activity. It didn't bother me and didn't interfere with my concentration while I was studying but the "Mrs." was always provoked by the din. One day, she told me that she was tired of the Minister and the female counselors "Jazzing it up in the bushes" (her expression.)

[Thirty years after graduation I returned to this location and found that the camp was still in active use and that they had purchased the log cabin from the "Mrs." and had turned it into a storehouse for the camp equipment.]

I remember one particularly inspirational story that the "Mrs." told me during one of our many conversations. During the Second World War, her son was a bomber pilot in the Army Air Corps, flying in the South Pacific. One night she had a dream about her son and saw him piloting his plane on a bombing mission. The plane was hit by anti-aircraft fire and was going down into the jungle on one of the islands. The "Mrs." said that she awoke with a start and immediately got out of bed and knelt beside the bed to pray to the Blessed Virgin Mary to protect her son, wherever he was.

Some time after this disturbing night, the "Mrs." received a letter from her son describing an incident that occurred to him on one of his flight missions. He was flying his bomber back to the base after completing a mission in which the aircraft had been hit by the enemy and he was having difficulty controlling it and keeping it in the air. The plane started to lose altitude and was nearing the tops of the trees. He was glad that he had most of the crew bail out when he realized the plane was going down. Only he and the co-pilot stayed on board to try to restart one of the engines that had stalled. By the time they were about to hit the trees, it was too late to bail out.

The pilot fingered the Miraculous Medal that was hanging from his neck and said a quick prayer. As the aircraft was about to hit the trees, the co-pilot tried once again to restart the engine.

Then all of a sudden, appearing before them in the windscreen was a smiling face that they knew was the Blessed Mother; they both felt that she was there to greet them into heaven. Just then, the engine kicked in, the pilot pulled back on the control stick and the aircraft started to rise as the belly of the plane brushed across the tops of the trees.

When mother and son eventually coordinated the timing of this event, they realized that the vision appeared in the windshield of the bomber at the exact moment that the "Mrs." was making her plea to Mary. I shiver whenever I recall the "Mrs." and her sincerity when she told me this amazing tale.

The "Mr." spent most of his time at the farm and would occasionally show up early in the morning to take his small dinghy with the two horsepower outboard motor onto the lake to do some fishing. He was an astute fisherman and always knew where the fish could be located. Within an hour he would arrive back at the house to prepare the fish for his breakfast; on a couple of occasions he invited me to join him for breakfast. It was a real treat to have just caught fresh water fish fried over a wood burning stove for breakfast.

I was permitted to use the "Mr.'s" boat, but not with the outboard motor and only with the oars. Having arrived in Indiana at the beginning of September there was still a period of warm weather where I would take the boat out to the middle of the lake to swim 'with the fishes'.

The weather was beautiful along the lake at this time of the year. I got in the habit of doing my studying while wearing my swimming trunks and, when the temperature got too high, I would take a break from the work, run down to the lake and dive in to cool off.

We were always short on cash and our meals were minimal; we were learning to live on corn meal mush, the cheapest ground *meat*, and without any niceties unless the "Mrs." gave us some of the always great food that she prepared in abundance. We still thought that this was an idyllic life; the weather was great, we had a large lake right out our front door, and we were in good health. When Gail got her *steady* job at the co-op, we thought that we couldn't have it better.

As winter approached, things began to change.

The old Dodge got very temperamental; any time it rained, or even in damp weather, the car would not start. It probably needed a change of ignition wires; but at the time I didn't know much about the repair of cars. When the battery stopped kicking over the starter, I would give up my attempts to start the car and would head for the road and attempt to thumb a ride into school; a distance of about ten miles. There was not too much traffic along our back road and I would often have to wait longer than thirty minutes before a car came along. Fortunately, the first car that came along always picked me up and dropped me off at the school, but I was invariably late for the first class.

If one of the other students didn't give me a lift after the last class of the day, I would have to hitchhike home again. I was lucky that the professor in my first class, Mechanical Drawing, was an understanding guy and did not penalize me for the lateness as long as I made up the missed classroom work. It added to my study time at home but I had no other choice.

When we were in the heart of winter, it became difficult keeping the two rooms warm with the one kerosene burner that we had to heat the apartment, especially when the wind was roaring out of the north where our front door and window faced.

The local fishermen would park outside our log cabin to spend the day on the frozen lake fishing through a hole that they would chop in the ice. The lake was often frozen to such a thickness that it would support the weight of many cars and some of the youngsters would drive their cars onto the lake, run them up to high speed and jam on the brakes to slide uncontrolled across the barren ice.

One night as we were sleeping, we were awakened by a loud, eerie sound that echoed across the lake. We lay in bed and listened as the terrible screeching continued; we didn't know what was happening and thought something was ready to attack us from off the frozen lake. It wouldn't be long before we became used to this ghostlike sound. It was the expansion and cracking of the ice in the lake and would continue every night through the winter.

That first winter we spent in Indiana gave us our first out of town visitors. The curiosity of my Mother-in-law, Blanche, couldn't keep her from coming to visit us at our small apartment on the Lake. From what Gail had been relating to her mother in her letters home that we were in sumptuous quarters prompted her to come out to Indiana for a visit. Blanche decided to come during the worst cold spell of winter, with Gretchen and Guy as accompaniment. She took the train with the two children from New York to Fort Wayne, which was about forty miles from Angola, where we picked them up to drive to our place on Lake James.

When our guests arrived, the temperature was nine degrees below zero. Our car's eccentric heater was not working that day and we traveled to the station in Fort Wayne without the benefit of heat. We picked up our visitors and started the drive north to Angola. Along the way, it started to rain such that the rain was immediately freezing on the windshield. The defroster wasn't working so I had to drive the fifty miles to Angola with my right hand on the wheel and my left hand out the open window to scrape a small hole in the ice on the windshield as it froze.

Our three passengers were wrapped in a blanket in the back seat wondering, I am sure, why they came to this god forsaken frozen wilderness. My arm was soon coated with a layer of ice that grew thicker and heavier as we drove on, but if I didn't continue scraping the ice off the windshield, I would have had to pull over to the side of the road where we no doubt would have all frozen to death in that frigid and windy weather. I don't know how we made it to our home but when we got there I turned the heater in the house up to maximum and sat alongside it for about two hours before the ice completely thawed and dried off my left arm.

Blanche and the kids spent about a week with us. Gail and I gave up our double bed to our guests and slept on the floor during their visit.

Gail continued working every day and I continued to attend my classes and do my assignments at home and working whenever an odd job was available, so we had very little time to entertain Blanche and the kids. We managed to make it through the week even though we both wound up with sore bodies from sleeping on the floor. We enjoyed the visit but were happy after we dropped our guests off at the train station in Fort Wayne and to reclaim our bed and the privacy that we were getting used to.

We managed to make it through the winter on Lake James even with our difficulties with the old Dodge; there was a time when we were without the car completely when I let the car run out of oil and burned out the rings and valves. I had the car repaired by a man working out of the garage at his house who did the valve and ring job for an unbelievably low sixty four dollars, which he permitted us to pay him off in irregular installments as we could afford it. It took about a year to finally retire this debt in full.

We enjoyed the spring and summer at the lake but when winter was looming on the horizon, we decided to seek out new quarters in town and close to the school so that we wouldn't have to deal with the problems of unreliable transportation or the hardships of the cold weather so far from school. Before the fall term began an opportunity arose that we immediately jumped at.

One of the local nabobs had an elderly mother, about 95 years of age, who was really in need of a skilled nursing home but wanted to remain in her own house, located directly across the street from the campus. (I believe that the son and his wife only hired us to save on the cost of institutionalizing his mother.) We left our cozy little nest in Lake James and moved to Angola to take care of Grandma (as I will call her).

The house we moved into was a large two-story Victorian home with a large center hall and a wrap around roofed porch. To the left of the entry to the house was a parlor accessible through double glass doors. Grandma's room was directly off the parlor with the kitchen abutting the bedroom in the rear of the house. Our room would be in the rear of the front hall with access to the kitchen. There were three bedrooms upstairs that were occupied by students who rented by the week.

For taking care of the old lady for twenty-four hours a day; feeding her, bathing her, and emptying out her chamber pot; we were to be given free rent and a stipend of thirty dollars a month. We collected the weekly rent from the student boarders and took care of the general maintenance of the house. We didn't have to clean the students' rooms but we did have to change the bed linen every week and had to clean the halls and the rest of the house.

The house was heated by an old coal burning furnace in the basement and it was also our responsibility to keep the furnace going in the winter and to dispose of the ashes. The furnace was equipped with an *"up to date"* automatic feed system so that I wasn't required to shovel any coal. The main problem we had with the furnace was the accumulation of 'clinkers' that often caused the fire to be smothered and go out, causing a rapid chilling of the entire house.

Gail took care of most of the personal care of our charge and one of us had to be on the premises most of the time. The son and daughter-in-law showed up about once a week and I believe this was primarily to pick up the students' rent payments. At these times we would slip out to accomplish any tasks that we had to jointly take care of.

We didn't find this too much of a hardship or a burden as I spent most of my time either working a job or on class assignments at home. The convenience of having to walk across the street to get to the campus was priceless after having spent a year never knowing when I would have to hitch-hike to school.

Grandma was not too much of a burden and was not too demanding in her needs. Emptying her chamber pot a few times a day took a while to get used to. Grandma was also quite interesting when she had her lucid moments.

She was most often in contact with the world but there were many times when her mind would wander and she would believe she was in a different era. She listened to the radio quite regularly; most often a religious program such as Billy Graham and at other times the news so that upon my arrival home, she would apprise me of the latest happenings in the world.

One day I returned to the house and she called me into her room. "Sonny," as she always referred to me, "The President was just shot." Knowing that she was quite up on all the news, I was stunned, thinking that President Eisenhower had been the victim of an assassination attempt. I soon realized, however, that the poor lady was in one of her mentally distracted states and I questioned her about her report about the President. Upon questioning it became evident that she was not talking about our current President but was reliving the assassination of President William McKinley who had been shot fifty-four years before in 1901.

It's interesting to note that Grandma was born just after the Civil War in the nineteenth century and as a young girl traveled with her family across the Great Plains in a covered wagon. She remembered quite vividly those days and having her wagon train attacked by Plains Indians. I always said that someday I would tell this story to my grandson so that he could relate it to his grandchildren to make this trivial, but fascinating personal link across three centuries.

Shortly after moving to our new home and our position as caretaker and nurse, the old Dodge finally gave up the ghost. We had no choice but to buy a used car, which we did at a used car dealer in a nearby town. (Grandma's son owned an Oldsmobile dealership in another town and when approached for assistance said there was nothing he could do to help us.) We didn't think we could get a loan even for the paltry amount we were able to pay but out of necessity we made the attempt.

We picked out a four door Hudson Sedan (about a 1950) that was on sale for three hundred dollars and with a surprising one hundred dollar trade-in on the Dodge and a dealer arranged loan payable in twelve months, we went into the first contractual debt of our marriage; that is not counting the other bills we were carrying on faith and a hand shake alone.

About seventy percent of the students enrolled at Tri-State at this time were, like me, veterans attending under the G.I. Bill. We established a few friendships during these two years together at the college; most of them married couples.

There was Dewey and Nettie-Mae Currier who were living, like many of the married students, in a trailer near the campus. Nettie-Mae worked at one of the truck stops outside of town as a 'waitress' to supplement the family income. Dewey was quite proud of the large 'tips' that she brought home from the restaurant. The restaurant served a dual function that was quite well known by nearly everyone in town; the upstairs had several rooms to accommodate the transient truck drivers and some of the local men with the services of the waitresses in more amorous pursuits than slinging hash.

I often suspected that Dewey was aware of the source of Nettie-Mae's 'tips' that far exceeded what was customary at the other truck stops around town, but that he feigned ignorance to assure the extra household income.

There was a time when I had occasion to drop some papers off for Dewey at his trailer when he wasn't home. When I arrived Nettie-Mae was sprawled across the small sofa in the combination living/dining room area of the trailer wearing a diaphanous negligee with all the mysteries of her womanly body on display. The invitation was obvious and we both knew that Dewey was not expected home for several hours.

Being a man of honor, however, prompted me to make a swift departure. (Nettie-Mae was built like a scarecrow; scrawny and flat busted, and had a terrible case of acne. She was hardly attractive and I wondered who she appealed to at the truck stop. I like to convince myself that even had she been more alluring, I still would have avoided this 'occasion of sin'.

THE HALLS OF ACADEMIA

From my first day in college, I pursued my studies with enthusiasm, diligence, and great success. I was a leader in most subjects and would eventually graduate at the top of the Engineering class. Although I had spent my earlier days in avoiding homework and study and relying instead upon my innate intelligence to get through the school year, in college, I rapidly developed good study habits. This new found diligence paid off in good grades.

My primary approach to successful scholarship was to buckle down early in the term to get a firm understanding of the subject matter at an early stage. I realized that if I didn't do this, each day would be more difficult until the entire subject matter became incomprehensible. This paid off; especially in the final year when I had plenty of time at the end of the quarter to participate in the end of quarter fraternity parties while most of the other students were cramming to catch up.

In the winter of 1956 I received a letter from the Tau Sigma Eta Honorary Engineering Society that I was elected to that august group; an invitation that I readily accepted. My induction into Tau Sigma Eta was soon followed in June of the same year with exceeding the requirements for the Gold Scholastic key, which was presented to students who maintained the highest grade average. In August of 1958, upon graduation, I again maintained a grade average to qualify for a second Gold Key. Instead of a key, the second awarding of this recognition entitled the student to a listing of the name on the Gold Plaque which was on permanent display in the Administration Building. I was the only student in my graduation class to qualify for this honor.

(I left school immediately after graduation and did not get to see my name on the plaque. The first time I revisited Tri-State was in 1988, thirty years after leaving. One of the first things I did upon my return was to visit the Administration Building to see for the first time my name engraved on one of the brass plates on the plaque. Imagine my chagrin when I found that my name was not on the plaque.

I had told my wife, Jean, who accompanied me on this trip, about my inclusion on this plaque for years before this trip, so it was especially embarrassing to have her think that I had been making up this story for these many years. I inquired at the office and they assured me that they would review my situation. Three years later, I was notified by the college officials that I was, indeed, entitled to be placed on the plaque. I received a revised copy of my transcript which indicated this entitlement as being in effect as of July 1991 but retroactive to August of 1958.

My new brass commemorative inscription, if placed in chronological order on the plaque should be a standout amongst all the aged and darkened name plates of the same era. Someday, I shall return to inspect the addition.)

As we approached the end of the summer term in 1956, I was looking forward to only six more months of college before graduating with my degree in Mechanical Engineering. In anticipation of that time, I started to float my credentials around the industry for my first engineering position.

One application that I made was with Westinghouse in Pittsburgh, Pennsylvania, for a fellowship in Nuclear Reactor Engineering. If accepted and successfully completing this work/study program, I would eventually wind up with a Doctorate degree in Nuclear Engineering. I was one of the finalists for the fellowship and was anticipating my approval when we were unexpectedly confronted with a serious problem that would put all of our plans on the backburner for a while.

GATHERING CLOUDS

When Gail and I returned by train to New York in 1954 from our brief and unconventional honeymoon in Bainbridge, we arrived at Grand Central Station in the late afternoon. As we walked through the crowded terminal, planning to take the subway to Astoria, Gail suddenly and tightly gripped my arm while with a downward wave of her eyes she signaled me to look toward her feet. Her feet were covered with a blanket of blood that poured down her leg from under her skirt. I was terror stricken; I thought that she had been surreptitiously stabbed as we walked through the terminal.

She said to me, "I believe I'm hemorrhaging." Confused, I asked her, "From what?"

She said, "I think I'm having my period."

I was not conversant with this aspect of a woman's physiology, but I maintained my composure as I quickly sized up the situation and responded with the first thought that came to my mind; get her Mother here to help. I rushed Gail into the nearest telephone booth, put a coin in the phone and told her to call her Mother. Her mother, Blanche, told her to stay put and

392

that she would be there as soon as she could get a ride to the station. In the meantime, I opened our suitcase and selected some suitable garments to use to stem the flow of blood.

Being rescued by Blanche, we returned to the Wilcox apartment on 45th Street where Gail was helped into bed and I was delegated to go to Sugar's Pharmacy on the corner to purchase a box of Kotex Sanitary Napkins; an item with which I was not familiar. I only knew that, in that era, it was something that was not discussed in mixed company.

At the drug store, the cashier was a young girl and I was reluctant and embarrassed to let her know the nature of my errand. I saw that the druggist, Mr. Sugar, was on duty in the back and told the young lady that I wanted to speak to him. When Mr. Sugar came to the counter, I indicated to him in a low whisper that I needed a box of sanitary napkins, hoping that the cashier would not hear.

Mr. Sugar immediately yelled in a loud voice that penetrated me to the core and made me turn a deep crimson, "Mary, get this young man a box of Super Kotex" - so much for discretion.

We made it through this minor crisis, but it was not long before I found out that this was a common occurrence with Gail and was most often accompanied by menstrual cramps that would sometimes lay her up with pain for a day or two at a time; with some relief from Midol or another pain killer. The periods were very irregular in duration and were also erratic in their rate of recurrence. I soon learned that this was to be an integral part of our life and that Gail would be incapacitated at random times.

We lived with this sporadic difficulty until the fall of 1955 when Gail became so debilitated that we had to seek out a local doctor even though we had no medical insurance and could not afford this *luxury*. The doctor recommended a surgical procedure which entailed opening up the abdomen and burning the pain causing nerves with an acid. We told the doctor that we could not afford the fee but he permitted us to pay him off in installments and performed the operation in his office to eliminate the hospital costs.

The doctor told us, after a successful surgery, that while inside he had found some constrictions or kinks in the fallopian tubes which he corrected. It was not too long after this that Gail became pregnant; no doubt a result of removing this impediment

In the spring, Gail began to have more of these 'female problems' and we returned to the same doctor who we had been paying off sporadically for last year's surgery. He was reluctant to see Gail again because of our apparent inability to make timely payments, although we were sending him what little residue of cash we had. In the end he consented to see her, took a biopsy and sent it to a laboratory in Chicago.

The doctor reported to us that the lab analysis was negative and that we had nothing to worry about. He gave a prescription for some mild pain killers and added our visits to the unpaid bill.

As Gail became conspicuously larger with child, we decided that it was time to move from our present quarters as the caring for Grandma and the boarding house was becoming too much for Gail and I could not be of much help because of the ever increasing classroom and lab work. We rented a small furnished apartment in town within walking distance of the school and moved into it in August.

It was about this time that Gail really started to become ill, with strong indications that the pregnancy was in danger. There was staining and other signs that all was not right. The doctor didn't seem to be helping nor offering solutions; I had the feeling that he was pissed off because we had so much difficulty paying him off for the last operation and the subsequent lab work.

Gail spoke to her mother in New York who suggested that we take the four week recess time in September to come home for consultation at the New

York Hospital. We learned that we could be taken care of at that hospital as indigent residents.

We drove to New York and I took Gail to the New York Hospital where they admitted her for tests. It was suggested by the doctor that Gail finish off these last weeks of her pregnancy in New York and to not subject herself to the long return trip to Indiana. We both thought this was an excellent idea because we had lost faith in the abilities of the Angola doctor and were happy to be getting good care at no cost.

Having only two more quarters of study to complete before getting my degree, it was agreed that I would return to Indiana to continue my studies while Gail stayed in New York to have the baby and await the results of the hospital tests. The doctor at the New York Hospital had also requested a copy of the previous report from the laboratory in Chicago. I was later to learn that the report from the lab had indicated a positive result for the cancer and which the Angola doctor had not told us about.

(Later, upon my return to Indiana after learning about this criminal neglect by the doctor, I found out that the doctor had left his practice in town and no one knew where he went. He had other complaints from residents and I believe he beat it out of town before he got hit with too many malpractice suits or even criminal charges. In my case, I held him responsible for willingly withholding the positive lab results which, if caught at an earlier stage, may have been curable.)

I was back in Angola for about a week when I came home from school one day to find a telegram from Blanche waiting for me and asking me to give her a call as soon as I got the message. We didn't have a telephone so I called from a public booth. My mother-in-law told me that I would have to return home immediately, that Gail had to undergo surgery and that I would get the details when I got there.

I had to leave school, to return sometime in the future when it became feasible. I withdrew from school, packed up all of our worldly goods (not a big job), and returned home.

Upon my arrival, I was shocked at the news that was to greet me. Gail had been diagnosed with an advanced case of uterine cancer which had spread fairly widely. The doctors had induced the childbirth and I found that in my absence I had become the father of a very healthy boy.

Gail was to be operated on the next day after my return. I was happy to learn that the surgeon that would be performing the procedure was one of the most respected surgeons in the city, so I felt hopeful that all would come out okay. I didn't realize then the extent of the cutting that the surgeon would have to do. Gail was cut from just above the right knee to a point above the naval. The cut was about six inches wide at the center and required a second surgery in an attempt to apply a skin graft to the cancerous areas. The pain of such extensive removal of organs and skin must have been excruciating.

Gail was to be in the hospital for about three weeks before they permitted her to come home. In the meantime, I took my newborn son home to the Wilcox house where we were staying to await the return of the new mother from the hospital. We were very hopeful and encouraged by the doctor and staff to expect an eventual recovery from the extensive surgery.

While I was in New York in September before my last trip back to Indiana, I had arranged for a job interview with the Norden-Ketay Corporation, the maker of the famous World War II Norden Bombsight and the employer of Gail's grandfather, Art Fletcher. Art was employed there for about thirty years as maintenance man and was well known and liked by everyone in the company. I took the interview in anticipation of my March graduation as another option in case I was not accepted, as I expected to be, in the Westinghouse Fellowship program.

Before I arrived back in New York, Art told the President and the Personnel Director with whom I had interviewed at Norden, about my changed situation and my availability for employment. By the time I got home there was already a letter in the mail offering me a job as an Assistant Engineer (or was it Engineering Assistant?) at a starting salary of five thousand dollars a year. It was a godsend and after appraising our personal situation, I readily accepted my first engineering position.

Gail's return home and the anticipation of a long recovery caused a major problem for the Wilcox household. They lived in a five room railroad type apartment and readily welcomed us to the household in our desperate hour of need. Blanche and Ranny gave up their room at the front of the house to accommodate Gail and me and the baby. The whole family seemed to take the disruption of the house by the newcomers with good grace; everyone was more concerned about Gail's recovery than their own comfort.

With each passing day, Gail seemed to get better and stronger and eventually was able to get out of bed and move around freely. The christening of the baby that we had delayed while we waited for Gail to recover was finally scheduled for a Sunday in December. We decided to name the baby Ranseler John after his grandfather and father. This christening and the small party we had with it was to be the last happy ceremony that Gail would participate in.

Before Christmas arrived, her condition had deteriorated again and she was forced to stay in bed. We took her back to the New York Hospital where we were told that her condition was terminal and there was nothing they could do for her except to try to make her comfortable and alleviate the pain. We were obliged to take her home.

We spent the next months at the Wilcox house with Gail eventually becoming completely bedridden. I worked during the week and came home at night and the weekends to care for Gail and Ranny. Eventually, with the help of the American Cancer Society, we were given the use of an adjustable hospital bed and the services of a visiting nurse who came to the house for an hour or two each weekday.

I set up a cot for myself between the hospital bed and the crib so that I could hear the demands from either side. Because I was a heavy sleeper and hard to rouse, I gave Gail a cane with which to poke me, if I wasn't responding to her or the baby's cries. (One night I was so hard to wake up even with the prodding of the cane, that Gail swung the cane into my crotch so that I was awakened with a loud yell and sore testicles.)

I had to go to the New York Hospital for instructions on how to take care of the patient. It became my duty to administer the morphine shots in the evening and on the weekends when the visiting nurse was not on duty, to rub down the back to try to prevent the inevitable bed sores, change the bed linen, (which was quite a delicate task with a patient in eternal pain), provide the bedpan, and toward the end when Gail became too weak to perform most functions, to feed her.

(In the midst of all this anguish, some humor shone through. While I was at the hospital waiting to see the nurse who would instruct me in my nursing duties, I overheard the nurse talking to another patient, a woman of about forty. The nurse told the woman that on her next visit the doctor wanted her to bring her stool. The woman was a bit perplexed and wondered why the doctor wanted her to bring a chair (stool). The nurse told her that she meant a specimen of her feces (or poo-poo as she told the woman).

The poor lady blanched and said, "How am I going to bring that." The nurse suggested a shoe box.

The woman said, "But I have to travel in the subway."

I was quietly laughing as I pictured this woman carrying a box of poop in the Subway and the faces on the people around her as the scent wafted past their noses. I also imagined a purse snatcher grabbing the box hoping to find something valuable in it and his dismay when he finally opened the box.)

Gail went rapidly downhill; the pain was getting greater and was unbearable. Her weight declined so that as the spring of 1957 progressed she turned into a mass of bones with little flesh. While talking to her, I kept up a spirited façade with encouragement that things were changing for the better. She played this charade along with me, but I believe she knew that there was no hope. When alone, I would cry for her pain; it was so intense and with no hope for relief that I was becoming an advocate for mercy killing. It got so bad for her that I increased the amount and the frequency of the morphine to ease her pain; I figured that she was not going to live to be addicted and the only thing that could be done is to lessen her agony.

After a courageous battle of nearly a year, Gail finally died as I sat by her side in the bedroom on the afternoon of June 24, 1957 as Ranny lay in the crib alongside innocently gurgling some incomprehensible baby talk and not aware that he had just lost his mother. She was only 23 years, four months, and twenty days old when she died. The funeral service took place at St. Joseph's Church and Gail was buried in the military cemetery at Pine Lawn in Suffolk County. Finally, she was beyond suffering.

THE EMERGING ENGINEER

In 1956 when I left school it was still a year before man first put a vehicle into orbit; in October 1957 Russia launched the Sputnik into orbit starting the world on an exploration of space that is still continuing. It would be four more years before the Soviets put a man into space (Yuri Gargarin in April 1961) and prompted the United States to dedicate itself to putting a man on the moon before the end of the decade.

Computers were still scientific laboratory curiosities, the vacuum tube was just being replaced with the transistor, and engineers were still relying on that most ancient of calculators, the slide rule. Computer aided design (CAD) was well in the future and we were still designing equipment by hand.

It was in this 'state of the art' world that I started work at the Norden-Ketay Corporation almost immediately upon my withdrawal from Tri State College and my return to New York when we first became aware of Gail's cancer. I was assigned to a program for the United States Navy to design and construct a "Stabilized Element for an Electronic Sextant" (SEES). This was a high accuracy, state of the art electro-mechanical structure that provided a spatially fixed base for a large navigational sextant that automatically tracked the sun or the moon and was built by the prime contractor, Collins Radio Corp. of Iowa.

Our program director was Albert F.W. Parr, a former Army Intelligence Officer who spent the end of the war as a translator interrogating German war prisoners. (The F.W. in his name, of course were initials for Frederick Wilhelm.) I worked under the Mechanical Engineering group leader, Andy McMillan, but answering directly to his two subordinates, Bob McIntyre, who was responsible for structural design and analysis, and Harvey Holman, who was the lead man for the mechanical and electro-mechanical subsystems.

Norden Laboratories, the division I was working for, was located in White Plains in Westchester County. There was a scarcity of parking near the plant so I joined Art Fletcher every morning in walking two miles to catch a bus from Astoria Boulevard to Manhattan to pick up a train at 125th Street to White Plains where the station was a stone's throw from the office.

On my first day on the job I was handed a stack of documentation and told to read up on the project that I would be working on. My perusal of this dry and difficult to comprehend material lasted about two hours when I was pulled off the reading to perform some trivial engineering task. That was the last of the reading; after that initial task, I was continuously deluged with new and more challenging tasks.

I worked closely with Bob McIntyre and under his tutelage soon became very familiar with practical applications of structural analysis. We also got very involved in Steel and Aluminum fabrication of the large structure we were building.

The high accuracy specifications for the SEES necessitated the temperature stabilization of the very large castings that were key elements in the program. There was no facility in the country that had the capabilities for the high and sub-zero temperatures we needed for the stabilization process and the job of designing and building this was given to me; (under a very small budget and a very tight delivery schedule.) This was to be the first engineering design task of any magnitude that I would be solely responsible for. Making use of all the tools at my disposal, including constant brain picking of the experienced engineers around me, I completed the job on schedule and with one hundred percent success.

I couldn't have had a better program to expose me to the practical application of a wide variety of engineering disciplines; besides the structural analysis and the design of the heat treating/deep freeze stabilization facility, I was putting to use many of the things I learned at Tri-State; heat transfer, statics and dynamics, thermodynamics, and metallurgy (however, in the study of metallurgy, I never did find out whether a 'platinum' blonde was a native metal or just a common 'ore). It was here too, that I became familiar with one of the elementary principles of engineering; "The angle of the dangle is directly proportional to the heat of the meat, provided that the mass of the ass remains constant).

It was not too long before I began to feel like a *real engineer*. I felt that the only thing I lacked that could hold me back from advancement was my Bachelor's Degree in Engineering; I was determined that I would return to school to complete my credits for this at the earliest opportunity.

When Gail died in June of 1957, I was devastated; it was hard for me to accept that she had died so young and that I was left alone with a son, Ranny, who had not yet seen his first birthday. It may seem a bit insensitive, but after living through these past months with Gail being constantly in pain and knowing that even the morphine in large quantities was not giving any relief, her passing was somewhat of a blessing to both her and the family because it finally gave her peace.

During that summer, I purchased my first new car, a 1957 Ford, at the end of the model year for about $1800 (about a tenth of what it costs today, 45 years later.) Other than the modest loan to purchase the used Hudson that I was currently driving, this was the largest loan that I had committed myself to but I felt I could cover it as I continued to work at Norden's and saved for my return to finish the last six months of my degree requirements. In the meantime, I wanted to stay with Ranny so that he would know who his father is and to get acquainted with him.

Blanche was most anxious to assume the entire burden of raising Ranny but I didn't feel this was appropriate. I did however take advantage of her willingness to help by staying at the Wilcox house after Gail's death to allow my mother-in-law to take care of Ranny when I went to work. I took care of him in the evening and on the weekends.

I was informed by the registrar at Tri-State that if I discontinued my matriculation from college for more than a year, I would subsequently lose my G.I. Bill entitlements. I signed up for the fall quarter and took some vacation time to return to Indiana to start attending classes again in September. Having locked in my entitlements for another year by attending the first day of classes, I immediately withdrew from school to return to New York and my 'secure' job at Norden's.

It wasn't too long after getting back to work that Norden started to lay off some employees during the 1957 economic slowdown that seemed to hit a large number of businesses and especially those in the defense industry. It was about October or early November after a series of weekly Friday layoff announcements that the company informed us that on the following Friday there would be another and final layoff. If further cuts had to be made, they said, the entire company would have to shut down. That Friday came and I was not on the roster of layoffs; I went home elated that weekend knowing that I was still employed and that I would be riding out this crisis until the company either solved their problems or shut the doors.

When Monday rolled around, however, my fortunes fell like the leaves that were then falling from the trees. Al Parr called me into his office and told me that another employee and I had been slated for the layoff on Friday but had been overlooked in the announcements; that day was to be my last day of work at Norden's. Before this time, I had planned on working another year, completing the current project at Norden's, and returning to school in September of 1958 after I had saved enough to make life a little easier than my first two years in Indiana had been. Now I resolved instead to return to school in the spring and to graduate by the summer of that year, if I could get a job in the interim.

With the sagging market jobs were scarce, particularly for Engineers. Even so, I was fortunate to get several job offers; most likely because of the low salary I had been collecting at Norden because I lacked my degree. I turned down a job at the Armour Elevator Company, which after Otis was the second largest elevator manufacturer at the time. I was offered the position of Chief Engineer (with no staff) even though I did not have an engineering degree and had no experience in the elevator industry. However, the salary offered was well below even the paltry salary I was being paid at Norden. (I was making about $125 a week at Norden; Otis' initial offer was $65; later increased to $98 after my declination of their first offer. They must have been desperate for a low paid lackey to offer such a job to a neophyte.)

I finally accepted a position with the Kollsman Instrument Company in Elmhurst which was much closer to home than Norden. The job would entail test and evaluation of a new star tracker that had already been designed and built. The job was not too challenging nor was it very interesting but I didn't really care about what I would be doing just as long as I was collecting an adequate paycheck until my return to school in March. (I had Ranny's expenses to take care of and I had been paying a regular stipend to Blanche for room and board; her child care services, fortunately, were gratis.)

I wasn't at Kollsman long enough to become a member of the Engineer's Union (which was mandatory) when the union called a strike. The company was making an offer of a three percent raise spread over two years and the union was holding out for more.

I continued to report to work because I wasn't a member of the union and was not entitled to the small stipend the union workers received for time spent on the picket line. The Striking workers on the picket line verbally abused me each day that I entered the plant to work and called me 'scab', but I continued to break the picket line convinced I was entitled to stay on the job as a non-union member. This situation lasted about two days before management reluctantly gave in to the union's demands for my removal from the job and I was informed that I would have to leave the premises

I was out of work again for about four weeks before the union settled the contract dispute. After being on strike for over a month the union in the end agreed to the original company offer of a three percent raise. It would take more than the full two year term of the contract for the raise to equal the amount of pay lost to the workers during the strike. I could never figure out why they went on strike if they could have made the same settlement months before without striking.

This was a significant loss of pay for me but it did not dampen my resolve to return to school in March for the spring term even though it would mean that I would be quite destitute for six months if I couldn't find part time employment in Angola; especially having to make the monthly payments on the car I had purchased this past summer.

While the workers at Kollsman were on strike, I did manage to pick up some odd jobs with a private contractor from St. Alban's, cleaning and waxing floors for commercial establishments.

RETURN TO INDIANA

I quit the job at Kollsman in March and drove to Angola to reregister in school during the worst snow storm of the winter. The snow was piled so high along the Pennsylvania Turnpike that I felt I was driving through a ten foot high tunnel of snow. Many drivers were stranded at the rest stops along the road; I heard on the radio that at one of the rest stops, Frankie Avalon, a popular singer of the day, was also held up and entertained the other travelers who were marooned with him.

I took a single room at the home of Ray Hemmert, one of the professors in the Mechanical Engineering Department, who was currently serving as the Acting Department Head while Professor John Humphries was on academic leave completing his Doctorate requirements.

Professor Hemmert was an ardent Catholic and the faculty advisor to the Newman Society, the campus Catholic organization. As such, Hemmert and I had many lively discussions on his porch and in his living room; primarily about the Catholic religion. He was constantly on me to attend the local church and to join the Newman Society. He could not understand my abandonment of the Church and at times became rather overbearing in trying to get me back. I was fortunate that I only had him for one class during these final days at school as he carried this fortitude into the classroom where I was taking "Steam Power Plant Engineering." With any other instructor I probably would have carried the course with a straight A, but Hemmert was so piqued at me that the best I could get out of him was a B; even though I thought the work I did was exceptional. (I moved out of the Hemmert house after that quarter and took up residence for the next three months in a room at a house being rented by another student and his wife.)

One of the other students residing at the Hemmert house was a Bolivian aristocrat, Arturo Pabon Balanza. (Pabon was the family, or father's name and Balanza was the Mother's maiden name which in the Bolivian tradition was appended after the last name.) Arturo was not a particularly good student but was dedicated to completing the degree requirements as ordered by his father in Bolivia. I tutored Arturo from time to time for a small stipend.

Most of the time, Arturo and I ran around in different social circles. One of his close friends, another student from Bolivia by the name of Gonzalo Patino, was a scion of the famous Patino family that dominated the Bolivian tin industry and controlled the country with their connections and wealth. This was during a period of radical change for Bolivia and the then President was in the process of nationalizing most of the mining industry. During the previous Christmas school recess, Arturo and Gonzalo could not return to the uneasiness in Bolivia and spent the time at the home of the Bolivian Ambassador in Washington, D.C.

My most memorable experience with Arturo was the Easter Sunday that we spent in Detroit, Michigan after a week's field trip sponsored by the school and on which we visited several manufacturing plants as part of our engineering curriculum. This trip included a visit to the Ford automobile plant at River Rouge and the Ford Museum in Dearborn. Arturo, who had his car taken away on orders from his father after Arturo was involved in a bad accident, enlisted me to drive him to Detroit for the field trip. After the business of the week we parted our ways on the weekend; Arturo visiting with friends in the exclusive Grosse Point section while I visited in-laws on the 'other side of the tracks'. I was to pick up Arturo on Easter Sunday afternoon for the return trip to Angola.

This was about my third weekend trip to Detroit and on most visits I had taken advantage of the invitation extended by Gail's cousin Peggy, to sleep over at her house in the northern end of the Motor City.

Peggy was one of two daughters who lived in Detroit under the watchful eye of their mother, Jenny, the older sister of my father-in-law, Ranny. Peggy and her six children lived in a house provided by the Social Services Department and her sister, Julie, lived in the downstairs apartment of a house a short distance away owned by her mother, Jenny. Julie was also on welfare along with her twelve children; the oldest of which had just turned eighteen when I was visiting that spring.

The spouses of the two sisters were ne'er-do-wells who were unemployed most of the time and on occasion would show up unannounced when they weren't bumming it on the road. A typical place for them to spend some of their idle time was Fort Lauderdale, Florida, where they would live off one of the widows or divorcees during the season that these lonely women would be plentiful in that city.

The last I heard of Julie's husband on my last visit to Detroit was a report that he was hitch hiking to Florida and had been picked up by a driver in Georgia who, unknown to this drifter, held up a gas station along the way, got back in the car and drove away. The driver and his passenger were picked up by the police before leaving the state. The driver, I understand, paid fifty dollars as a bribe to the jailor and was released, while the unwitting dupe got locked up for a year in a Georgia prison.

Julie had an advanced case of Multiple Sclerosis and was confined to a wheel chair and had limited use of her hands. She was a pretty lady in spite of her ailment and she and the children were doted on by Jenny. One weekend when I was visiting Detroit, Jenny came into Julie's apartment to check up on her and found her elder daughter trapped helplessly under her husband who had returned for one of his brief and unwelcome visits to the family. Unable to summon help because of a speaking problem Julie was struggling to breathe under the weight of this despicable man. He was completely naked and had passed out into a drunken stupor after having sexually forced himself upon the poor helpless woman.

Jenny, who was a woman of no modest proportions, picked up the unconscious bum, carried him to the front door, and threw him into the street while forcefully telling him to get his ass out of her sight and out of Detroit before she kills him; something I was convinced at the time that she would have done in an instant. She threw his rancid clothes at him and the last that was seen of him was his bare ass running down toward Ten Mile Road. (His subsequent stay in that Georgia prison received no sympathy from his deserted family in Detroit.)

I was always welcome at Peggy's home any time that I was in Detroit, primarily because I was family, but also because every time I stayed over I brought a case or two of Stroh's Beer, a local product, which cost less than three dollars for a case of twenty-four 12 ounce bottles. Weekends with this unpretentious group of Peggy and her friends was always a relaxed time and social amenities were never an issue.

The plumbing in her small house was a bit eccentric and there were times that a bath and a shave were not available. The toilet was usually out of order and could not be automatically flushed. With six children in the house and a continuous stream of visiting friends, the toilet was often gross beyond description. At these times I would haul in buckets of water from wherever I could get water; either outside at one of the working faucets or at a neighbor's house, to manually flush the foul-smelling bowl. The Easter weekend that I was in Detroit with Arturo Pabon was one of those 'easygoing' times.

After a Friday night and a Saturday of partying with Peggy and her friends, both at home and at one of the local bars, I drove to the bus terminal where I was to pick up Arturo at 3 P.M. for the return trip to Angola. I would have stayed with my hostess a bit later but Arturo had insisted on getting back so that he could study for a Monday morning exam.

When Arturo arrived at the rendezvous point, however, he told me that he had met a lovely young lady at a party on Saturday night and had been invited to join the family for Easter Dinner. When he explained that he had to meet me early on Sunday, they implored him to bring me along. I was reluctant to join Arturo because I was unshaven and, quite frankly, looked like a slovenly bum; hardly dressed to grace someone's home at dinner. Arturo's insistence and his revelation that his 'date' would be providing a companion for me for the afternoon, convinced me to drive him out to Grosse Point.

When we pulled up to our host's home, I was awestruck. I had just left a rundown hovel on the north end of the city and now here we were in front of a huge mansion just a block away from the banks of Lake St. Clair.

As we approached the front door, I became very hesitant about going on, but Arturo insisted that I not deprive him of this opportunity to see his young lady again. We were greeted at the door by the Butler, a new experience for me, and we were led into the front hall, a majestic room that was larger than the entirety of any of the apartments I had ever lived in. A grandiose staircase reminiscent of the mansion at Tara in the movie "Gone with the Wind" was at the end of the hall opposite the massive double door.

The Butler ushered us into a Living Room or Parlor through French doors on the left side of the hall; an immense room centered on a large fireplace that served as a focal point around a sitting area with three large sofas. The room was occupied by four or five gentlemen attired in suit and tie, and an equal number of elegantly dressed ladies. The two young ladies who were to be our companions for the day were elsewhere in the house and the Butler was sent to tell them of our arrival.

We were informed that because of the late hour; it was then about four in the afternoon; the present company had eaten dinner but the girls had waited for our arrival. While we waited for the girls we were introduced to the guests around the room. I felt quite out of place in these elegant surroundings with these nattily dressed people. I was unshaven, unkempt, and looked more suitably attired for a barroom brawl over in Hamtramck than for a social meeting with such distinguished company.

In spite of my dishabille, I was soon put at my ease by the warm and friendly greeting, which seemed sincere, and I fell into relaxed conversation with one of the men who stood by the mantel of the fireplace sipping what appeared to be a glass of port wine; no doubt of a superior vintage. It turned out that he was the father of one of the girls, Tina, who was to be my companion for the day and was a cousin of Arturo's young lady. Tina's father was the Manager of a large, local manufacturing company and a graduate Mechanical Engineer. We hit it off quite well as he asked me about school and my standing in the class and I queried him about his company. He was very impressed that I was the top student in the class and pursued with avid interest more information about me. I felt that I was in an interview for a job.

Just as this conversation was becoming more spirited, two lovely young ladies entered the room. They were both about twenty years of age, and I was soon to learn, seniors at Michigan State University at Lansing. They came into the room with such enthusiasm that the subdued atmosphere soon evolved into a burst of noisy conversation and laughter.

I was introduced to the cousins. Charlotte, Arturo's girl, greeted me with such fervor that I thought she was not going to release my hand, which she had taken into her two hands with a tight grip that belied their softness. She seemed to be very much at ease here in her own home.

Tina was equally warm and after some brief small talk amongst all of the guests in the room, Charlotte excused us from the parental company and led us into a palatial dining room on the other side of the center hall. The dining room had to be at least thirty feet long and in the center of the room was the largest table I had ever seen; set for dinner at one end for four people. It had obviously been reset for us while we awaited our hostesses in the living room. On one side of the room was a large French door that looked out upon a large terrace with a formal garden beyond; this was, indeed, Tara.

The four of us took seats at one end of the table, with Arturo seated alongside Charlotte and facing Tina and me. It seemed to me that there was enough room at that table for another two dozen diners.

The butler offered us a glass of red wine from a bottle that I knew had to be a quality vintage even though, at the time, I was not familiar with fine wines. We all accepted the wine that was poured for us and Charlotte offered a toast to our meeting. (I got so caught up in the part that I was playing in this scene from a movie that I completely forgot how grubby I looked and eagerly joined in the spirited discussion that ensued and that never seemed to find a lull.)

Two maids served a fine gourmet dinner of several courses; I was so involved in the conversation, asking and answering questions about ourselves, that I can't remember exactly what we were eating; I only knew that when we finished with dessert and coffee that I was very sated and ready for the ride down the shore road when Charlotte suggested an after dinner drive.

As we left the house Tina volunteered to take us in her car which I was to find out was a recently purchased large Buick that sold for about twice the price of my bare bones Ford. I insisted that I do the driving in my car with Arturo and Charlotte sitting close together in the back seat and Tina joining me in the front.

We drove about two blocks when Charlotte pointed out what was probably the largest mansion in Detroit; she said that it was the home of Edsel Ford whose name would later be found on one of Ford's biggest follies, the Edsel Automobile.

As darkness fell upon the city, we returned home to *Tara*, said our farewells to the other guests, and started the two to three hour trip back to Angola. We kissed the girls goodbye (a very chaste kiss, I wish to note) after exchanging addresses with promises to keep in touch. I left Detroit with a feeling that a door to a unique opportunity had been opened to me both professionally and personally, having hit it off so well with Tina, and more especially her father.

On the drive back to school, I was relating how overwhelmed I was by the wealth represented by the house we visited and Arturo said, "That was nothing; you should have seen Tina's house where we were last night; it was twice as big and twice as impressive." (Arturo, himself, came from a very wealthy Bolivian home. He lived on a ranch which he claimed was only a modest spread, but at one point indicated that it took a whole day on horseback to travel from one side of his father's ranch to the other.)

Tina and I wrote to each other no more than two short letters each after she returned to Michigan State. Her last letter included an invitation for Arturo and me to join her and her cousin at their sorority gala dinner and dance, a black tie affair. I couldn't afford the rental of a tux but Arturo offered to pick up the entire cost of that weekend so that I could drive him. The same sense of misplaced pride that prompted me to throw away Dewey Currier's cigarette butts had me decline his offer and I never got to see Tina again. I assumed this would close the door to any ideas I may have had about approaching her father for a position at his Detroit Company.

My father-in-law's sister Jenny was the chef and owner of a restaurant concession operating in one of the local bars in Detroit City. She served simple fare and had a good neighborhood business. She always implored me to come to the restaurant for a meal and to bring a friend if I were traveling with a fellow student.

On one of the Detroit visits, I was traveling with one of these students, Al Capone. His given name was Bernard but it was a natural for everyone to call him "Al." Al, like me, a native New Yorker had married one of the local Angola girls while in school and I often visited them at their modest apartment in Angola for conversation, a meal, or to help Al with his school work.

Al had one trait that did not endear him too well with many people. Just about every sentence of his conversation was punctuated with the vulgarism "fuck" in a variety of parts of speech; noun, verb, adjective, adverb, or interjection. One of the first things I did when suggesting to Al that we go to Jenny's for a free dinner was to insist that he curb his proclivity to 'F' his way through every statement. With Al's promise to watch his tongue, I took him to Jenny's for dinner.

She gave us an excellent steak dinner, something we as penniless students had not had for a long time. During dinner, Jenny stopped by for short periods to chat and Al was a model of proper speech, while I had my fingers crossed that he would not fall into one of his usual linguistic lapses.

After dinner, Jenny came by our table again and said, "How was the steak boys, enjoy it?" Al blurted out with enthusiasm and without hesitation, "That was the best fuckin' steak I ever had." I cringed but Jenny very graciously ignored it and moved on.

After graduation, Al would take a position with Grumman Aircraft, Corp. in the aircraft engines department. I didn't find this out until ten years later when I joined Grumman. He eventually moved to a Florida division and we lost touch after his transfer.

In the few times I was in Detroit during those last months of school before graduation I usually stayed at Peggy's house. I did spend a couple of nights at the home of Julie's oldest daughter, Julie and her husband, Chuck. There were always people coming and going and Peg's house was a hub of activity. Peggy and the kids had a lot of friends and the door was always open to everyone. Chuck and Julie's house, on the other hand, was a welcome harbor when I wanted a less frenetic environment.

One of Peggy's friends and a regular visitor at the house was a young lady by the name of Marlene. Marlene was very attractive and well proportioned and I came to believe that she came over more often when I was visiting the city. When we weren't gathered at Peggy's house we would congregate down at one of the local bars. If I arrived and no one was at home at Peg's, I knew exactly where to head; the local watering hole.

One Friday evening I had accepted an invitation from Chuck to spend the weekend at his house, so when I arrived in Detroit I immediately headed there. No one was home when I arrived but by prearrangement Chuck and Julie had left me the key to the house in the mailbox. After stowing my gear at the house, I drove over to Peg's house and finding no one there, I headed for the bar where I was sure I would meet up with many of my new found *cousins* and friends.

The bar was relatively quiet for a Friday night but I did run into Marlene there. She told me that Peg, Chuck, and many others went to a party on the northern outskirts of the city and that I could join them out there. My unfamiliarity with the area prompted Marlene to volunteer to show me the way.

She left her car at the bar and joined me in my Ford. (Marlene's car was an old used car that she had picked up for ten dollars and had by that time driven over forty thousand miles without servicing or even an oil change. However, it did provide transportation.)

As we drove to the party, I realized that we would be passing by Chuck's house along the way and suggested that we stop there for a drink before continuing. Marlene readily agreed. I had brought the now expected case of Stroh's Beer to the house earlier so upon our arrival I got each of us a drink. After a couple of beers things started to move in the direction that we had both anticipated when we decided to stop at the house. I moved close to Marlene, the conversation became more intimate and in a short time we were wrapped in a tight embrace.

It didn't take long for the both of us to silently assent to the next step. Feeling very macho, I picked Marlene up in my arms and without objection she permitted me to carry her into the master bedroom. Continuing this manly act, I tossed her onto the bed with her feet toward the headboard. As she hit the bed, I heard a sickening sounding thud. Marlene gave a short gasp and then was quiet.

When I threw her on the bed she had banged her head on the footboard and was knocked unconscious. At first, I got frightened because I thought I had killed her; she lay there so stiff and quiet. I attempted to revive her and it seemed that she wasn't breathing. My thoughts were racing in all directions;

How will I explain a body in the bed to Chuck and Julie?

Where should I bury the body?

As these crazy questions ran through my head, Marlene let out a sigh; enough for me to know that at least she was still alive. It took a few more minutes before she regained full consciousness and a bit longer for me to regain my composure. The ardor of a few minutes before though, had been extinguished. After she sat up, we returned to the living room, finished our beers and without too many words returned to the car to join our friends at the party with me feeling like a poor man's version of the most famous of klutzes, Inspector Clousseau.

All was not play; studying went on at full pace and I worked hard to maintain my standing at the top of the class. Part time jobs were scarce and so was money. I went days without having a decent meal while I waited for another job or the small monthly stipend from Uncle Sam. I learned to eat very cheap. A box of three packets of Lipton's Chicken Noodle Soup sold for thirty-nine cents, which I would purchase and ration to myself. Each packet made a quart of watered down soup. I waited until the hunger pangs were effecting my work and the hunger was too distracting before I would 'cook' up my pot of chicken soup to eat with whatever stale bread or crackers (or nothing) that I had on hand.

Graduation day came on August 29, 1958; dropping out of school for 18 months had stretched what would have been a 27 month matriculation into nearly four years. I sent invitations to the family in New York to attend and I had thought that my being the first amongst all the brothers and other relatives to complete a college curriculum and receive a Bachelor's degree would encourage someone in the family to make the trip to Indiana to join me for the ceremonies and help celebrate this auspicious occasion. I don't think any of them could afford the expense of the trip or the time from work.

In my last weeks at school, I was called by Al Parr at Norden asking me if I would like to return to work there on the SEES project that I had worked on for over a year and to take the equipment out to sea aboard a navy ship for sea trials and evaluation. I had enjoyed the challenge of the work at Norden as well as the people I worked for and with, so I readily accepted the position once I was satisfied that the salary was appropriate.

I attended the graduation ceremonies and received my sheepskin but I did not attend any of the other ceremonies associated with the graduation week including one recognizing me for being the top student in my class. As soon as I received my degree, I hopped into the car and headed back for New York where I would be starting back at Norden Labs the first Monday after my return. I missed my son, Ranny, who I hadn't seen in six months and hoped he would recognize me when I got home just before his second birthday on September 27.

1958-1970

1958-1970

RENEWAL

I returned to New York feeling that a new life was beginning for me; I had my Bachelor of Science Degree in Mechanical Engineering, a job waiting for me at Norden's in White Plains, and I would be renting an apartment as soon as I could find suitable quarters. I planned to take Ranny with me and relieve my Mother-in-law Blanche of the child care that she had provided since Gail's death. I hadn't considered how to take care of Ranny during the day but as in most things I figured I'd cross that bridge when I came to it. For now, I was single, young, and full of great visions for a successful future in Engineering and an even better future for my son.

I stayed at the Wilcox house on 45th Street for a short time as I started work at Norden's in White Plains on the first Monday after my return. I couldn't wait to get back into the swing of things on the job, most particularly to collect a regular paycheck. I was now a full fledged engineer with a Bachelor's Degree and no longer an engineering aide. At Norden I was assigned to the SEES (Stabilized Element for an Electronic Sextant) program as expected where I would be assuming responsibility for the successful completion of its acceptance tests aboard the U.S.S. Compass Island, a cargo ship that had been converted to a platform for evaluation of many military navigational, tracking, and other systems requiring validation at sea.

As I would be the only Norden person permanently assigned for regular duty on the Compass Island, my first task was to become familiar with the details of the many complex electronic and mechanical systems on the system as well as a knowledge of some of the systems from other contractors to which our device would be integrated. It was a formidable task for a 'greenhorn' like me, but I was always happiest when presented with this kind of a challenge.

Shortly before my return from Indiana, brother Bob had completed his tour of duty with the United States Army in Germany and had been discharged. He had taken up residence in Astoria in a rented room at the apartment of an elderly gentleman named Artie. When I went over to pick up Bob one evening to go out to one of the local pubs, I saw the terrible condition of the apartment he was living in so I suggested that the two of us rent a place together. I had just been looking at a reasonably priced garden apartment in Flushing with two bedrooms that I thought would meet our needs very well. It was a four room second floor apartment with a separate bedroom for each of us. When Bob took a look at the place he jumped at the chance to share the new accommodations with me.

Because I would be periodically going out to sea aboard the Compass Island for extended stretches of time over the next few months, Blanche eagerly volunteered to take care of Ranny until I could come up with some alternative arrangements; when I moved to Flushing, Ranny continued to live at the Wilcox's in Astoria.

Before moving in, Bob and I went to Schlossman's furniture store in Jamaica, famous for its low priced and widely advertised furniture sales (actually it was junk, but what did we know?). We purchased a living room set, a bedroom set for Bob and some miscellaneous pieces to complete our initial decorating attempt. I believe the total cost of all the pieces: bed, dresser, sofa, end and coffee tables, chairs, etc.; was no more than three hundred dollars (that was probably also the life expectancy of the furniture – in days).

I was fortunate to pick up a used but complete bedroom suite from a neighbor for forty dollars. (When Jean would eventually marry me and join me to live with this 'beautiful' furniture, she would refer to it as "early depression" style and was most anxious to replace it at the earliest opportunity.)

Bob and I moved into the apartment in early fall and invited many of our Astoria friends over for a housewarming party. The bathtub in our only bathroom served well as a beverage cooler when filled with blocks of ice and plenty of beer. We didn't have enough chairs for everyone, but no one seemed to mind having to sit on the floor (even though the wood floor was still a bit gritty from a recent sanding that had not been sealed and finished.)

We settled into a routine with both of us working; Bob driving and delivering for Consolidated Laundry in Brooklyn (where we got our sheets, pillowcases and towels – an unofficial fringe benefit) while I continued working for Norden in White Plains with periodic trips aboard the Compass Island of one to two weeks duration. (At about the time we moved into our apartment in Flushing Norden was moving the main plant from White Plains to Stamford, Connecticut which would add about another half hour to the commute to work; and this was before the opening of the Throg's Neck Bridge.)

On weekends I would pick up Ranny during the day and bring him back to Astoria in the evening when I would either go partying or bar hopping depending on the opportunities. Most weekday nights I would also stop by to see him as well.

A FATEFUL NIGHT

It was not too long after our move to Flushing in the fall of 1958 that I was invited to one of these weekend parties; a birthday party for Barbara Estivo one of the girls associated with the group that Bob hung around with, the "Six Corners Crowd", so named for the six corners formed at the intersection of 31st Avenue, 43rd Street, and 30th Road in Astoria. (They did spend most of their time however, congregating at the bar on 44th Street or on the street corner outside.) Most of the guys and gals associated with the Six Corners group were contemporaries of Bob and about five years my juniors. Most of my old gang were either married by this time or were still in the service. Through Bob, I had gravitated to this group of neighborhood characters, most of whom would have been good subjects for a Damon Runyon story.

I didn't realize it when I accepted Bob's invitation to join him at the "Let's Go Club" for Barbara's party that this would be a night that would profoundly change my life.

All of the usual 'suspects' from the Six Corners were there. Of course there was my brother "Herman the German" Bob (as he had been dubbed because our Grandpa Beiser's name was Herman and the boys felt it was ethnically humorous, particularly on an 'O'Leary'.) Bob was accompanied by his femme fatale of the moment, Marylou O'Connor, a recognized comedienne of the group who was always quick with an amusing retort no matter what was said.

There was Warren "Putsy" Finley, well liked by all, accompanied by his later to be wife, Dolores. In a few years, Warren would play a key role in my run for Governor of New York State in 1966 (more about that later). Warren and Dolores were later to be divorced and Warren would die at a relatively early age after a long bout with cancer. We saw him several times in the months before he died at a time when he was in pain and rapidly losing his battle, but he never lost his sense of humor or his pleasant manner.

(I always got a kick out of the nicknames of some of the guys in the Six Corners Gang; besides "Herman the German" and "Putsy", there were "Harry the Horse", "Icky Stick", "Monk", "Zombie", et.al.)

Annie Kelly and Matty Roland were also there that night. They were also destined to be married; several times. I don't know how many times they split and wound up getting remarried but Annie filled in the interim times with other gentlemen (and other kids). When she was ready to return again, Matty was always there anxious to oblige.

There were quite a few others from the Corners that went through the marriage and divorce cycle. Amongst them were Barbara Estivo, our current birthday girl, and Tommy Doran, brother to Tese who herself married and divorced Hank Sirokowsky; Pat Curtain and Tom O'Connor; Lee Yetter and Barbara Flood also joined this revolving door group.

Not all of those at the party wound up in a broken marriage. Bob's girl of the hour, Marylou would eventually marry Rich Smith. They are still together after more than forty years and are currently living happily in retirement at Port St. Lucie, Florida. Jean Yetter and Jimmy Cox, another surprisingly successful couple are presently living in Massapequa Park. (Jean was a cousin to my sister-in-law Marilyn.)

Patty Mellini, another party goer, was scheduled to marry George (can't remember his last name) and had all arrangements made for the wedding and reception. Jean and I had even accompanied them on the weekend before the big day when they purchased the furniture for their new house. During that week, George showed up at Patty's house to tell her he was calling off the wedding; he had second thoughts and said he wasn't ready to get married. Patty eventually married Eddie McKinley to live 'happily ever after' in Otego, New York with five or six children.

We still keep in touch with many of the people who attended "The Party". This group also included; Bill Rucker and Eileen Deegan Rucker; Annie's brother, Eddie Kelly; Jimmy Baxter; Tony Gillan; and Sharon Duffy.

There was, however, one very beautiful and shapely girl in attendance that stood out above all the others and caught my attention. Bob had briefly introduced me to Jean DePaolo about a month before when she flitted in and out of Coyle's Bar where Bob and I were fueling up for the night's activities. I didn't think about it much then nor in the interim but on the night of the Estivo party, I tried to learn more about her, especially after seeing her in that form fitting black dress. I asked her to dance to the music that was playing on the record player and we danced several slow Fox Trots together; that was the extent of my dancing talent, not having yet learned the Lindy, Cha-Cha, Meringue, or any of the other popular dances of the time.

I offered to drive Jean to her home; an apartment on 12th Street on the other side of Astoria where she lived with her parents, Joe, a sanitation man, and Rita, who was at that time working for Servomechanisms, a company that produced small electrical motors for the defense industry. Jean also had two younger brothers, Joe, 13 and Steve, 10, living in that small residence; an apartment house without central heating. Jean declined the invitation at first, particularly when she thought that I was getting a bit too aggressive when she was retrieving her coat from the coat room, but she eventually agreed to accept the ride. We did not have much time to talk at the party and at that late hour it was evident that there wouldn't be much additional conversation before we arrived at her home.

When we got to 12th Street I offered to walk her to her door but she again was reluctant. (I would later find out that she lived on the top floor of a four story walk up.) I knew even then that this was a special girl and I wanted to pursue our brief introduction further. I asked her for a date for the next weekend. She hesitated again, but with a little persistence on my part she eventually agreed to go out with me and we agreed that I would pick her up then.

When I got home to our apartment in Flushing that night, I told Bob about the date I had arranged with Jean for the following weekend and kept him awake for a long time extolling the virtues of this fantastic young woman. Bob listened politely even though it was obvious he just wanted to get to his room and get to sleep.

I told Bob that night that even though we had just met, I was going to marry Jean. He was convinced that it was the drink talking. He was probably right; why would an innocent eighteen year old girl consider starting up a serious relationship with a twenty-six year old widower with a two year old child and who was a 'man of the world' compared to this inexperienced girl who had just graduated from high school about five months before? However, I was so smitten that I was convinced that this relationship was pre-ordained to succeed.

I was eager for that week to end as I constantly thought about that first date. When the weekend finally rolled around, I went to pick up Jean at her home, walked up the four long flights of stairs to the top floor and nervously stood at the door waiting to be greeted. The only one there to welcome me at the door was Jean's mother; Jean was not at home.

While I was driving to 12th Street to pick up Jean, Bob was headed over to Coyle's Bar where the gang always kicked off the night's activities and was also the place where we would all gather at the end of the night; often to be followed by a final stop for coffee at the "Modern Age" diner after the last bar closed for the night. When Bob arrived at Coyle's he was surprised to see Jean there with some of her friends getting ready to go out for the evening.

He went up to Jean and said, "What the hell are you doing here? You're supposed to be on a date with my brother tonight. He's headed to your house now to pick you up."

Jean said, "Oh! Was he serious about a date? I didn't think he was."

Bob didn't tell her the full extent of my lovesick ravings of the week but he did strongly suggest that I had been looking forward to this evening and would be very disappointed if she didn't show up. Jean decided to honor her commitment for the evening's outing and called her mother at home from the public phone at Coyle's to tell her that a gentlemen caller would be arriving soon and that he should wait for her as she would be home shortly. What I had hoped would be the beginning of a fruitful association had started out on a low note.

For our first date we went to a cocktail lounge in Flushing, the Blue Note, where we talked for several hours before leaving well after midnight for home. Jean was a bit reserved and quite shy at this early stage of our relationship. I felt that I did most of the talking but I was determined to find out more about this mysteriously quiet young woman. I sensed that, in spite of her reserve, this was the start of a long friendship and returned home that night filled with eagerness for our next date and firmly determined to pursue her all the way to the altar.

Over the next weeks, I continued this relentless pursuit until I became her steady date every weekend. The fact that I was previously married and had a young son didn't seem to deter her from accepting my suit; perhaps it was because she and her father, Joe, came from a similar background; when Jean was three, her birth Mother, Marie Gennaro, and her father were crossing the street in Astoria one day when they were hit by a speeding vehicle, killing Marie and almost doing the same to Joe who wound up in the hospital where, if his mother had not intervened, would have had his leg amputated. At his mother's insistence the doctors did not remove the leg and Joe, while not incapacitated, spent the rest of his seventy years with a slight irregularity in his gait.

AT SEA ON THE OCEAN, AT SEA AT HOME

The next months were very busy. When I wasn't at sea aboard the Compass Island for the sea trials and acceptance tests, I was either dating Jean or taking Ranny on an outing, or more often spending time with both of them while Jean and Ranny became acquainted.

It may have been self-centered of me at the time, but my first concern in my current courting of Jean was not who would be a good mother for Ranny but rather who I felt would be the perfect wife for me. I assumed that whoever that was would be the right one for Ranny. As it turned out, I was absolutely right in this assessment.

My work aboard the Compass Island was sporadic but the days I was on duty there I was busy ten to sixteen hours a day; starting with the installation and alignment of the equipment on the ship and culminating in the completion of the acceptance tests at sea.

The Compass Island was equipped with large outboard mechanical fins on the hull that were controlled by a gyroscopic stabilizing system to coarsely neutralize the roll of the ship while at sea. As our equipment was used to provide a stable base that also neutralized the roll and pitch of the ship to provide a highly accurate 'artificial horizon' for the electronic sextant, it was necessary for the ship to go through a certain level of these motions to complete our evaluations under all conditions.

One day while out at sea, the seas were so calm that we could not accomplish the tests we had planned for that day. I asked the Captain of the ship to 'reverse the feedback' from the gyros in the roll stabilization system so that we could artificially roll the ship for our tests. We had the ship doing a constant roll cycle of about twenty degrees port and starboard and continued this for the entire day; about eight hours. I was so busy with the work that I was doing that I didn't realize what effect this constant roll was having on the crew; even the 'old salts'. When I went down to the Officer's mess for dinner, I was only one of about four diners who showed up; the rest of the crew was either sick in bed or throwing up off the fantail (the rear end of the ship.) I was directed by the Captain not to mess with the roll stabilizers in the future and to wait for a normal sea to conduct the tests.

All was not work during my time aboard the Compass Island; while there the ship made stops for a break in Bermuda and in the Virgin Islands at Saint Thomas. During our short stay in Bermuda I went to dinner with some of the other contractors before returning to the ship. When back aboard I was standing on one of the upper decks smoking while watching the returning crew members; it brought me back to my own navy days when we were coming back from liberty. As I stood peering down at the dock, I saw one of the returning sailors riding at top speed down the center of the dock on a rented motor bike. Without any attempt to hit the brake, he headed straight toward the end of the pier where, with the sailor locked to the seat, the bike flew off into the darkness into the water below. Some of the sailors on the deck watch fished the sailor out of the water; I don't know whether they ever retrieved the bike.

This was not to be the last of the evening's entertainment. As I continued to observe the returning crew, I noticed that a mesh cargo net was laid out on the pier to take aboard cargo; or so I thought as I stood there. As the midnight curfew for the crew approached, more of the sailors were returning, many in various states of inebriation. Some of them were so drunk that they lay down on the cargo net and passed out. There were about ten to twelve sailors sprawled in the cargo net when the net started to rise, lifting the besotted sailors off the pier and onto the main deck of the ship; they were completely oblivious to what was happening to them.

Meanwhile, back on the home front, I was relentlessly pursuing Jean with persistent tenacity. On New Year's Eve we had one of our most memorable evenings together. We attended a New Year's Party and Dance hosted by the Astoria Rambler's Social and Athletic Club and held at the Steinway Lodge, a waterside catering place in Astoria overlooking the East River. Both of us remember that as a special and romantic evening with beautiful, live music to which we danced into the late hours of the morning. I especially remember the two of us waltzing alone on the outside terrace, ignoring the winter cold and just enjoying the beauty of the night and caught up in the rapture of the moment.

We dined out fairly often while I was courting Jean and during one stretch we made a determined effort to try all of the available ethnic foods, from the more usual Italian, Chinese, and German to the less common Japanese, and others. Of course, the best part of each evening was the "conversation" that ended the night before getting Jean home; which was never on time if you were to ask her mother.

We loved to share the jazz scene together. We visited Birdland in Manhattan, the Village Vanguard in Greenwich Village where we swayed to the smooth bent trumpet of Dizzy Gillespie who resembled a blow fish when he blew that sweet horn, and we listened to Della Reese at the Safari Club at College Point. When we weren't watching and listening, we were dancing at one of the many local dance clubs. Jean taught me how to Cha-Cha, Meringue, and do a reasonable Lindy. Some of this dance instruction took place at the Astoria Ramblers Club house on Thirtieth Avenue and Thirty-first Street just steps away from the el (the elevated subway).

The club house was located on the second floor above a local 'Gin mill' and served us for club meetings, social nights, and the 'stag parties' that we euphemistically referred to as 'football movie nights'. These were the nights when some of the most gross 8 millimeter porn films were shown to the club members and any of the public that were prepared to pay a dollar or two for a night of 'entertainment'.

Jean got caught up in my anxiety to get married and at one point we agreed to forgo the formal ceremonies and to elope during one of my frequent trips aboard the Compass Island. We made plans to meet when the ship arrived in Norfolk, Virginia one weekend to get married there or in Maryland, which was nearby. Our elaborate plans went astray when Jean's parents became aware of our intrigue while I was at sea doing my duty and looking forward to our rendezvous in Norfolk. Shortly after leaving the Brooklyn Navy Yard on another of our voyages, I received a telegram from Jean on the ship telling me that she was reconsidering our plan and had a better alternative (but was not reconsidering our marriage plans.)

Jean's mother and father convinced her that she 'owed' it to them, as their only daughter, to have a proper, formal wedding. When I arrived home, I went to the DePaolo apartment where we (Jean and I, her Mother and Grandmother) discussed our plans to get married. After a thorough discussion, I agreed to go through with a wedding in Church to be followed with a reception. We set a tentative time for the fall, which was about six months away.

When we 'shopped' around for the right Church to get married in, we encountered a few obstacles. We wanted to get married on a Saturday afternoon rather than a Sunday for the convenience of the people who had to work on Monday and who we planned to invite to the wedding and reception. In those days, if you wanted to get married in the afternoon, most churches only permitted this on a Sunday - for a Saturday wedding Our Lady of Mount Carmel, Jean's parish church, required an early morning Nuptial Mass, as did St. Joseph's, which I considered my home church even though I was living in Flushing at the time.

We eventually made arrangements for a ceremony on Saturday afternoon at St. Patrick's Church at 39th Avenue and 29th Street in Long Island City, using the address of Jean's Aunt Helen and Uncle Anthony to establish Jean's residence in the parish. The date was set for September 12th and the reception was to be held at Ricardo's Restaurant on 21st Street in Astoria. Ricardo's had just expanded from a small neighborhood restaurant to a large catering facility.

We made plans for an attendance of one hundred guests at a cost of $8.50 per person. This price included: a cocktail hour and a dinner with an open bar for four hours, the wedding cake and the band, invitations to the wedding, the wedding photographer, a limousine, and the wedding night at the Commodore Hotel in New York City. With all of this there was not much left for us to do but send the invitations and get the wedding dress; and, of course, the wedding rings.

Officiating at our wedding was a newly ordained priest, Father Edward Richards. This was only the second wedding at which he presided; the first was his sister's nuptials. When we went through the compulsory pre-Cana conferences where Father Richards advised us in the obligations of the marital state into which we were about to enter, Father seemed to be a bit embarrassed and unsure of himself. I guess that he was a bit intimidated that with very little practical experience under his belt, he was trying to advise a man who had been married for nearly five years before and had a son that was approaching three years of age.

My brother Bob consented to be my Best Man and Anne Mulraney, a lifelong friend of Jean, would be her Maid-of-Honor.

In the following months, I successfully completed the acceptance tests for our equipment aboard the Compass Island and before the wedding date was re-assigned to work at Norden in the Stamford, Connecticut plant on the development of a 'spring-mass accelerometer', a precision component that had multiple uses in Navigation and Missile Guidance systems.

As the wedding day approached, Bob agreed to find other living quarters. He made arrangements with Warren Finley to share an apartment with him on 44th Street in Astoria. Poor Bob! It wouldn't be too long before Warren himself would marry Dolores and Bob would again be "kicked out" of his home. This is probably one of the key prompts for Bob to marry his first wife, Peggy Carpenter.

One Saturday night that summer of 1959, I was returning from a DePaolo family event with Jean sitting alongside me in the front seat of my Ford and her Father, Mother, and Grandmother sitting in the rear. As I was driving down Roosevelt Avenue in Corona beneath the elevated tracks, a fast moving tow truck came barreling through a red light as I approached that corner with the light in my favor. He collided into the front side of my vehicle and sent the car into a spin as I hit the brake to stop a good distance up the road.

I managed to stay composed and as soon as I determined that everyone was unhurt, I exchanged driver information with the tow truck operator who was denying any responsibility for the accident that he had just caused.

My car was still functioning so I drove my passengers to their apartment in Astoria; they were now living on 21st Street and 31st Avenue where they had recently moved. Once they had bid their farewells for the evening and I was alone in the car, I broke out into a cold sweat and with my hands trembling uncontrollably, I decided that I was in no condition to drive. I walked to the Wilcox place on 45th Street and slept on the sofa there until the next day.

On Monday, Jean and I went to my insurance agent, Sydney Schwartz, a retired policeman with an office in Flushing to report the accident and to make arrangements for the car's repair. Recently joining Sydney in his office was his son, also named Sydney, who had recently passed his bar requirements as an attorney and was starting off his practice with his father's indulgence.

When we finished with Sydney, Sr., he had his son speak to us about the accident. Junior suggested that we retain him as our counsel to represent us in a suit against the driver and the tow company. Our property damage was covered with our collision insurance with a small deductible and none of the passengers were injured, all suffering no more than a moment's fright; but Junior insisted that in many accident cases the real damage to the body may not be apparent until some time afterwards and that a suit should be brought on our behalf to cover ourselves in case of this eventuality.

Besides, he insisted, the other driver will no doubt sue us and we should beat him to the courts. Junior sent us to a doctor of his acquaintance to examine both Jean and me. Jean did have a chipped tooth that was unrelated to the accident but the doctor credited this to the collision.

When the doctor examined me and asked about how I felt, I told him that I had no injuries. He squeezed my left shoulder and asked, "Does this hurt?" I said, "No."

He squeezed harder and asked the same question. He repeated this several times until he squeezed hard enough for me to wince and say, "That hurts!"

He marked down in the record that I exhibited pain in the left shoulder at which time he sent me into an adjoining room where he subjected me to some thermal therapy; after which I was instructed to return the following week.

I returned to the doctor the following week and he had the nurse put me into the therapy machine. When the doctor came in after this session, he asked how the shoulder was, as he examined it with his fingers. I said, "That shoulder is fine, (the right shoulder) but I thought I had pain in the left shoulder." He just ignored me, put some jottings in the record, and I decided that this would be my last visit to this crackpot.

I mention this here only because, although over the next months and years we would have no further contact with the doctor, lawyer, or insurance company about this matter, this incident would have a profound effect a few years in the future.

Jean, by the way, had her tooth taken care of by her dentist on Steinway Street in Astoria. One day I accompanied her to the dentist on a Saturday morning and had Ranny in tow as we would be spending the day on an outing together. The waiting room at the dentist was filled with young women waiting to be tended to; this dentist evidently attracted a lot of young women.

As Ranny and I were waiting for Jean to come out of the examination room, Ranny said he had to go to the bathroom. There was one toilet right off the waiting room where I immediately took Ranny to take care of his needs. While there I availed myself of the opportunity to relieve myself, telling Ranny to stand aside and wait for Daddy. As I stood by the bowl, that little blond headed mischief maker looked up and said in a loud, stentorian voice, "Gee Daddy, you got a big wee-wee." I was sure his piercing voice was heard on the next block.

I walked into the waiting room with all eyes panned in my direction and I was positive that they all had a lascivious leer on their faces with all eyes burning their way into the front of my trousers. I quickly left the office to take Ranny for some 'fresh air'.

Our wedding took place as planned in St. Patrick's Church and the reception at Ricardo's was such a huge success that we kept the band on and continued the open bar for a time after the contracted end time. Jean and I stayed on for the entire wedding reception and afterwards, before moving on to the Commodore Hotel for the wedding night, stopped at the Brauhaus German Restaurant on 86th Street in Yorkville where we finally ate dinner accompanied by a bottle of Rhine wine.

Without dwelling on the privacy of the events of the rest of the wedding night, I would like to mention that early on Sunday morning as we were preparing to move on to the rest of the honeymoon schedule, there was a knock on our hotel door. I went to the door and asked through the closed partition, "Who's there?

The voice on the other side said, "I received a call that there's a broken pipe in the room and I'm here to fix it."

I told the unseen intruder outside the door, "There's no problem with any of the pipes in this room and we don't want to be disturbed."

We packed up and left the hotel in mid-afternoon hoping to have an early dinner at Mama Leone's, a famous Italian Restaurant in Mid-Town Manhattan. Unfortunately, Mama Leone's and most of the other restaurants that we attempted to eat at were closed on Sunday either all day or until the evening. We settled for our Wedding Breakfast/Lunch/Dinner at a Kosher Restaurant, Phil Glickstern's on the West Side. We agreed it was terrible but it was our honeymoon so who cared? (How many people have stuffed cabbage for their honeymoon breakfast?)

We had reservations to spend the week at the "Jack-o-Lantern" resort in the White Mountains of New Hampshire. Along the way, we would spend that Sunday night in a quaint old hostel in Holyoke, Massachusetts, "The Yankee Pedlar Inn", where we were assigned a room in the third floor 'attic'. The room was comfortable but was provided with two single beds which caused me a bit of chagrin until I decided to butt the two beds together. (In the morning, Jean, being modestly embarrassed about the rearrangement of the room, cajoled me to separate the beds again so that the chambermaid would not know about our overnight intrigue.)

The room feature that stands out most in my mind (not to mention the activity that the room encouraged) was that we had to walk through the closet to get to the bathroom. [We would return to this same room on one of our anniversaries about twenty five years later, while we were traveling from a Conservative Party picnic in Sullivan County to Boston. Although the inn expanded greatly, this old room in the original building was still in the same condition that it was in 1959. As on that first visit, the room was furnished with two single beds; this time however, having learned to appreciate Jean's reserve, I didn't put the beds together.]

On Monday we arrived at the Jack-o-Lantern to start our honeymoon week. The hotel fronted on the main highway with a series of motel type rooms lined up along each side of the main building which housed the office, restaurant, and recreation hall. We were assigned to one of the private and isolated cabins set off in the woods behind the main building. On top of that main building was a giant Jack-o-Lantern about ten feet in diameter, which could be seen for miles by drivers approaching from the south.

Our cabin was comfortable, clean, and nicely appointed; we knew immediately that we were going to enjoy our week in New Hampshire as long as the food was reasonably edible.

New Hampshire is a beautiful state and in mid-September the leaves were just starting to turn color; not yet in full bloom but still picturesque. In addition to more traditional honeymoon activities we did a lot of sightseeing that week: The Lost River Glacial Cavern, Franconia Notch State Park, The Flume, The Old Man of the Mountain (described by Hawthorne as "The Great Stone Face"), Six-Gun City, a poor rendition of a western pioneering town and, the highlight of our tourist activity, we made the treacherous drive to the top of New Hampshire's highest mountain, Mount Washington. This was quite a terrifying experience. There were no guard rails along the narrow road to the top and at several places the road narrowed down so much that only a single car could barely navigate the way. Fortunately we didn't run into another vehicle at these points coming down the mountain, nor coming up on our return down. Jean was especially frightened on those cuts of road where she was sitting on the outboard side of the road looking down the steep slope where she felt we were about to fall. It was cold and windy at the top of the mountain but the view of the New England states was spectacular and well worth the treacherous journey.

One 'exciting' evening was spent at a local drive in theater; not a common destination on most honeymoons. When we arrived at the theater, there was only one other car in the entire complex. Before long the crowds really swelled - to about six cars. Before the show commenced I went to the snack bar to get some goodies. When I got there, the girl working behind the counter was scurrying about excitedly. She said to me as I approached the counter in a voice that betrayed her distress, "I didn't expect such a large crowd tonight", (it probably was large by New Hampshire standards!)

All good things must come to an end and at the completion of our New Hampshire visit we had to return to the mundane world of work and parental responsibility. We arrived at our apartment in Flushing in the early evening and would spend one more night alone before picking up Ranny in the morning. Jean had resigned her job as an administrative assistant at the Republic Steel Corporation in Woodside and was eager to start her new life as the stay-at-home Mother of a young boy, Ranny, who was about to turn 3 years of age on September 27th, but she also approached the future with a great deal of apprehension; not knowing what was in store for her in this unaccustomed role.

A NEW FAMILY; AND GROWING

We were really starting out from scratch in our Flushing apartment. The only furniture we had was the cheap living room set of a three piece sectional and coffee table from Schlossman's, an ugly looking kitchen table with an enameled metal top and four chairs that were questionably stable, the pre-war bedroom set that was sturdy, functional, but outdated, and, for Ranny's room, we had a single bed that we purchased to match the small maple chiffonier that Jean brought from home.

Other household items were equally scant, with pots, pans, dishes and silverware that just about provided us with the necessities. The living room floor that I had sanded was still raw and unfinished and Jean insisted that I finish this before anything else was done; a chore I readily completed, being most anxious to please my new bride.

We had no television set and were given an old black and white set from Jean's Aunt Helen and Uncle Anthony. This large console set was outfitted with a metal jacketed seventeen inch tube and was so heavy it had to be carried by three people to get it up to our second floor apartment. The television set needed repair regularly and I was often obliged to remove all of the vacuum tubes to take to the local drug store to check out in the tester that was available there for free public use.

I was making about sixty five hundred dollars a year at the time and was carrying only one debt; a monthly payment of about $50 for the next twelve months to finish off three years of payments for our only vehicle, the 1957 Ford that I had purchased two years before. The rent for our garden apartment was $115 dollars a month. I had told Jean before we got married that we wouldn't have much of an income to start with but that I had 'great potential'. So we were starting out with no material wealth, but with things that were more important: a lot of love, a lot of dreams for the future, and a lot of chutzpah.

Jean was even more inexperienced than I was in the rearing of children but, necessity being the mother of invention and other things, she learned very quickly. The anxiety of her new found position was further exacerbated when almost immediately after the wedding day, she became pregnant.

Our youthful love for life and our confidence that the future would only get better helped to get us through these early years; and though there were times when things looked bleak, our sense of humor and love for our small family kept us working together.

Jean and Ranny formed an attachment almost immediately upon moving into our new home. Jean was a fastidious housekeeper and always accomplished her chores early in the morning. The apartment was small and sparsely furnished, which simplified the cleaning tasks quite a bit. This gave Jean time to spend with Ranny at the local park or walking to the shopping areas along Northern Boulevard or Francis Lewis Boulevard; not too far from home.

With little spare cash, life was pretty simple for a time and our entertainments were also simple. Restaurants, which would later fill a large part of our lives, were never contemplated as an affordable alternative; all of our meals were eaten at home. We learned to eat with the simplest (and cheapest) cuts of meat and we had not yet developed a palate, or the purse, for fine wines.

Until we got married, I had been in the habit of eating no breakfast and simply grabbing a container of coffee on my way into work. Jean insisted that a good breakfast was necessary and got me into a routine of having a healthy breakfast in the morning, which I would have continued to forego had she not gotten up in the morning to prepare it.

We had no medical insurance in those early days; most companies didn't provide this as a fringe benefit. Fortunately we never had any serious problems that required much more than an inexpensive doctor's visit. We did have the maternity expenses for the pending addition to the family but the doctor charged a reasonable fixed price which included all of the pre and post natal care as well as the actual delivery of the baby. For Ranny's regular pediatric care, Jean took him by bus to the State health clinic in Corona.

While there she would often visit her Aunt Helen and Uncle Anthony who were living in Corona not too far from the clinic. Jean's Grandmother, who we all called Nana, started to live with Aunt Helen around this time. Even though she was a Democrat Nana and I hit it off well from the beginning. While I knew that many of the other members of Jean's family had reservations about her marrying me because of her youth and my prior marriage, not to mention Ranny, Nana was supportive of our relationship from the beginning.

Nana was a grand lady with increasing health problems that she never let slow her down. She was widowed in her thirties after bearing ten children in quick succession. There were moves at the time to separate her from the children but she would not allow her family to be torn apart. Times were hard but, with determination, hard work, and lots of love, she held the family together and saw most of them reach maturity and get married. Rita, Jean's step-mother, was the second oldest of the offspring.

Nana, or Florie (the same name as my mother), was active in the Astoria Democrat party and was friendly and familiar with all of the big name politicians and office holders in Queens County. She worked in the campaigns of Jim Delaney, the local Congressman, Tom Mackell, the Queens County District Attorney, and other well recognized officials of the time. Although in later years she was prohibited by health problems to drink alcoholic beverages, she still liked to have a glass of scotch and water from time to time. On these special occasions, on her visits to our house, I would give her a tall glass of water and a thimbleful of Scotch to quench her thirst.

Interestingly, when Nana applied for her Social Security; a small pittance but an earned entitlement; she had difficulty proving her place of birth. Her mother was emigrating from Ireland while she was pregnant with Nana and the records of the time were unclear whether or not Nana was born on the ship, on Ellis Island, or sometime thereafter. The Administration gave her the benefit of the doubt in the end, assumed that she was born on American soil, and issued the approval for her small social security check. (This tale was told to me at the time by a source that I don't recall and has since come into question as to its validity. I choose to believe it because it is a good story.)

Many times over the years I knew her, Nana would often spend time with Jean and me and we would take her to some of our local parties and dances. She always felt that she could relax with us while she was out of earshot of her six concerned daughters, any one of whom would have cast a disapproving eye over Nana's night on the town. With all of her health problems and her occasional forays with us she still lived an active life until her death in 1988 at age 86.

Jean, Ranny, and I celebrated our first Christmas together in our garden apartment on 191st Street in Flushing. The first three and a half months together were relatively uneventful and it was a peaceful time of our lives; getting to know each other and settling in to our new life. Little did we know at the time that the following year 1960 would bring profound changes into all of our lives.

The first change in this first year of marriage was a blessing. In the early morning hours of June 8th, Jean woke me to tell me that she was about to have the baby. We didn't know at the time whether it was going to be a girl or a boy but we were soon to find out. I quickly dressed Ranny while Jean calmly got ready for the trip into the New York Hospital located on the East Side of Manhattan. We had previously arranged to have the baby delivered at that great institution. Jean was unruffled and Ranny thought we were in the midst of an exciting adventure, while I was so nervous that I didn't know if I could drive us safely to the hospital. Because Jean did not yet have her driver's license, as the only driver in the house I had to compose myself for the trip.

As we excitedly drove through the quiet night lighted by a large full moon, we heard Ranny utter in wonderment as he gazed out at the night sky from the back seat, "Hello, Moon!" This cracked us up and helped to relieve the tension that was building up as we drove west along the Grand Central Parkway, thankful that there was so little traffic at this time.

When we arrived at the hospital, Jean was checked in and after the doctor's brief examination; I was instructed to go home where I should wait for a call as it would be some time before the baby arrived. (More recent customs have the father at the expectant mother's bedside and often even participating in the delivery. Not having the stomach for it, I have always been thankful that this wasn't the practice in 1960.) I followed the directive and took Ranny back to Flushing and waited for the call that came in shortly after 11:19 A.M. informing me that Jean had given birth to a beautiful, healthy young girl who we were to name Patricia Ann, (the Ann for Jean's maid-of-honor and soon to be Patricia's godmother). Jean had wanted the name Patricia but when my brother Dan and his wife Agnes had a girl several months before and gave the newborn cousin that name, Jean was considering giving our newborn a different name but I convinced her if Patricia was the name she wanted, that's the name she should use. It's a good thing she did because that's what everyone calls her today. (Actually, Jean wanted to name our new daughter

"Dawn", but after recalling that Dawn was the name of one of the cocker spaniels I had in Indiana, she decided to go with 'Patricia'.)

Shortly after her entry into the world, Patti was baptized at our new local parish church, St. Andrew Avellino in Flushing. Ann Mulraney and Bob sponsored Patti as Godparents and we followed the Christening with a small party at our apartment. We then continued our modified life with a family of four and we had not yet celebrated our first anniversary.

The next major change in our lives in 1960 was my leaving Norden to join some former colleagues in a newly formed company in New Rochelle. This took place shortly after Patti was born.

Al Parr, the former Manager of the SEES program at Norden that I successfully saw through to completion aboard the U.S.S. Compass Island, formed a new subsidiary to Hydrapower Corporation, an established small Westchester company that wanted to expand their business from the manufacture of hydraulic components into the military electronics field. Al took Andy McMillan with him to the new company to provide the Mechanical Engineering expertise and another former SEES engineer, Herb Berman, to do the design of the electronic control systems. Harry Grossman, although not one of the technician on the SEES program, also came from Norden's to handle the assembly, testing, and other manufacturing tasks, and Jim Fay was brought from the outside to do the drafting.

The new company was to be called Powertronic Systems, Inc., a subsidiary of the Hydrapower Corporation.

Al, through his industry and Navy connections, obtained the first contract for the budding young company to Design, Develop, Build, and Deliver an "East-Seeking Gyrocompass" to be used in the U.S. Navy's Anti-Submarine Warfare program. One of the systems used to track enemy submarines underwater was a craft called a "fish" that was towed behind a destroyer and housed sensitive sonar gear, which for accuracy, had to be positioned a minimum distance behind the large mass of the mother ship. There was a requirement that was not being currently filled to measure the heading of this "fish" and to transmit this information back to the mother ship. There was very limited space and limited electrical power in the 'fish' to accommodate the required system. Al, with his extensive experience in the design and application of gyroscopes and gyroscopically driven systems, conceived the idea of building the Gyrocompass System or "Remote Heading Indicator" using a single gyroscope to establish both the stabilized platform for the device and the capability of determining accurate heading information. This was an entirely new concept and had never been done before and presented a formidable design problem for the new team.

A key part of Al's proposed system was what he called a "Schuler Tuned" accelerometer, another untried concept that would require development. At the time Al and the others went over to Powertronics from Norden's, I was continuing my work on the development and test of the spring-mass accelerometer. Because of this experience, Al gave me a call and asked me if I wanted to join them at the new company. At the time, I had a great respect for Al's technical and management talents and with Al's optimistic line of Bull-shit, I was convinced that this would be a rare, though risky, opportunity.

As I was considering Al's offer, it was announced that Norden, which had been recently absorbed by the United Aircraft Company, would be moving all of their facilities to Norwalk, Connecticut; a move that, although it would probably add to the security of the job, would add another half hour to an already long commute. This move convinced me that it was time to leave Norden and to roll the dice at Powertronics with Al Parr and the others. Jean was a bit nervous about the move but, as she has always proven to be, was fully supportive of my decision to leave the security of the present job for the uncertainty, but possibilities, of this new adventure. I received a modest raise in salary with the move to Powertronics, but the economics didn't play a major part in my decision to change jobs at the time; it was strictly the challenge of a new adventure.

When I signed up with the new company, the entire staff was housed in one room of the Hydrapower plant at Pine Court except for Harry Grossman, who was in a small workshop that abutted the 'main' office. The day that I came aboard, the fledgling company was making a move to new quarters around the corner from Hydrapower. The facility consisted of a corner retail store which was to be converted to our manufacturing and test area and an upstairs residential apartment that was used for our offices. The single bathroom and toilet facility that we all shared still had the old residential bathtub in it. The accommodations were far from luxurious but everyone was so filled with enthusiasm for the new company and the one program we would all be working on, that we weren't concerned about the present surroundings.

I would soon find out that we would be developing the new system as a sub-contractor to the Telephonics Corporation on Long Island, the prime contractors to the Navy. The contract was not one of the cost plus fixed fee government contracts that were common in the 1960's and we were to deliver the system for a fixed price of twenty-eight thousand dollars. Al Parr had evidently done a good job of convincing our Hydrapower backers that even though the costs would 'somewhat' exceed the contracted price; a small investment by them in our development costs would be paid back many fold when we got the expected production contract.

Shortly after I settled into the new position and the new office and had started my analysis of the accelerometer requirements, our lease on our Flushing apartment was expiring, so we used the opportunity to move to a new home.

In the short time that we had been married; less than a year; Jean and Ranny were both establishing local friendships in our garden apartment complex. Jean became very friendly with the couple next door, Dotty and Mike Meyericks and their family, while Ranny, as kids will do, was quick to make friends on the block. It would be difficult uprooting the family from these budding relationships but we needed more room with the recent addition of Patti to the household.

We rented a small attached house on 202nd Street in Bayside, not too far from our Flushing apartment. The house belonged to the family of a United States Navy man who was presently stationed outside the New York area. The house would be available for a limited time as Mr. Rehder, the owner, would be retiring from the navy in a year or two and his family who were with him at his current station planned to move back into the house at that time. Although we had this time constraint, the monthly rental was well within our budget and the house was in a reasonably good, 'ready to live in" condition, so we decided to rent the house without a long term lease and would worry about our future housing needs when the time came to move.

As we settled into our new house Jean was anxious to get rid of the antiquated "depression" furniture that we had started out with, but I was initially reluctant to take on the burden of the monthly payments until we were better able to afford it. Before that year was over I recalculated the practicality of buying new furniture and determined that we could get most of the pieces that Jean had selected at Gertz, a now defunct department store located in Flushing. We went one weekend to purchase the colonial style pieces for our living room, dining room, and bedroom. We did this before Christmas and we were promised delivery of the furniture before the holidays.

In anticipation of the delivery, expected before the end of the year, Jean sold off the Schlossman furniture that adorned our living room. In the interim, we used two beach chairs in the otherwise bare living room to watch the small portable television that sat atop a small bookcase. These were the only things we had in the room. (The bookcase came as a 'free' gift with the set of Colliers' Encyclopedias; our first major purchase while we lived in Flushing shortly after we got married. I recently threw out these Encyclopedias after forty-four years of use; they were a bit out of date and any time that I need any information today, I'm sure to find it on the internet.)

The furniture didn't arrive by Christmas time and we were soon to learn that it would not be delivered until March. I was thankful that Jean hadn't sold off our bedroom set or we would have been spending our nights in sleeping bags. The beach chairs served our needs because we had no alternative but they were old and frayed and not long for the world.

One night as I was sitting comfortably in the beach chair; a lounging type model; Jean arrived home from an errand and rang the bell expecting me to answer it. When I didn't answer the bell after a reasonable time, she used her key to open the door. When she came into our sparsely furnished living room, she doubled up with laughter; what she had found was me wedged into the chaise with my butt on the floor and my legs pointing up in the air. When Jean had rung the doorbell I moved to get up to answer it when the worn chair suddenly collapsed and I found myself in a position where I couldn't move.

After Jean regained control of herself, she did manage to assist me in getting extricated from the chair that had me confined.

(This episode reminds me of another night when another incident occurred that caused me great discomfort but provided more great entertainment for Jean.

On the small enclosed front porch on the front of the house, we had a 'high riser' that functioned as a sofa during the day and was convertible to a double bed at night by lifting a metal shaft of about one inch diameter, that extended the length of the bed and was pivoted at each end. The shaft, when properly pushed all the way down, locked in place and secured the bed.

One torrid summer night, our bedroom became unbearably hot. We did not have air conditioning so we decided to sleep on the high riser because the porch was much cooler than our bedroom. I opened the high riser by pulling on the shaft which opened the bed; however, I neglected to lock the bar in place. When I lay down on the bed, the moveable side of the bed collapsed and the shaft swung around and caught me on the throat and took the wind out of me.

I attempted to push up against the shaft, but this only increased the pressure on my throat. Jean heard the commotion and came into the room to find me gasping for breath and unable as yet to talk because of the impact of the bar on my throat. Jean did not panic. Instead she doubled up with laughter at my predicament and was so weak from the laughter that she couldn't help me. Every time she tried to help me, I would gasp and she would laugh more. She finally did get control of herself and I was finally saved from the strangulation that was sure to ensue.

Later on that same evening, after we had both recovered from the earlier incident, and we were both sound asleep, fire trucks, responding to an alarm, came down our street with their flashing lights filling the porch. These lights must have prompted me to start dreaming about a fire in the house, which dream woke me up in a panic. While I was still half asleep I jumped up on the bed and ran for the door, stubbed my toe on the same bar that had choked me earlier and tripped off the bed and into the wall. Needless to say, that Jean, who was a light sleeper, woke up in time to witness my sleep walking act and again had a merry time laughing at the show that I was involuntarily performing for her delight.)

In my engineering profession, I had learned early on that a new design should always be checked and double checked and, preferably, checked by someone else. This was the only way we could assure the success of the design. I should have carried this practice over into our home. When I calculated the financial impact of all of our furniture purchases, I had made a small error, and not one in our favor. When I discovered that our monthly payments were going to be substantially more than we had anticipated, I realized that the next few months would be financially lean ones. We were fortunate that we had not yet spoiled ourselves with gourmet cooking, fine wines, and high living.

We managed to make it through these days on a more stringent budget and accustomed ourselves to living within our means. The only time it really became a cause for concern was on New Year's Eve. All of the neighbors that we had become quite friendly with in a short time, had a practice of visiting each other's houses on New Year's Eve and each one was prepared for the holiday callers with food and drink. After making sure that the children had a memorable Christmas with a tree and many presents from Santa, we were so broke that we had nothing, not even a bottle of beer to offer the neighbors if and when they came to our house.

When New Year's Eve came around we reluctantly decided to turn off all the lights in the house so that no one would be encouraged to knock at our door. Jean and I spent the evening in bed watching television. The movie that night was about Charles Edison when he was a boy. After that awkward and embarrassing evening, I was determined that this would be the last New Year's Eve that we would be forced to 'hide out' in the bedroom.

We may not have had much money during our short stay in Bayside, but it was probably eighteen of the happiest months we've had. The kids were happy, healthy and always well fed and well clothed. We gave them plenty of attention and plenty of love. The neighbors were all wonderful people and we grew especially fond of Fraser and Gloria Stone and their family of 'Newfies" (Gloria and Fraser were from Newfoundland), and Pete and Jane Villano who shared the driveway between our homes.

We even had a curious fondness for our next door neighbor Mrs. Wine, an elderly widow who often displayed a bit of eccentricity. Behind her house was a rickety garage that had been built by her late husband. The doors were hanging askew off the hinges and the windows on the garage doors were adorned with lace curtains that the good Mrs. Wine regularly washed, pressed, and hung on the line to dry.

Mrs. Wine's husband was still with her in the house; his ashes were in a jar over the mantle in her living room which abutted our living room. The separating wall between our two houses was thin enough to permit us to hear much of what was going on in the other's house. Our portable television was also a bit eccentric and would often go blank with no apparent provocation. Tapping the top of the television proved to be an effective way to get the television working again. We soon discovered that we didn't have to get up out of the chair to rap the T.V. and could effect the same result by banging a foot on the floor.

Mrs. Wine did not take too kindly to the banging on the floor and would inevitably retaliate by banging on the wall to express her displeasure. After a while, it became a contest between us. When she became persistently annoying, I would bang back on the wall while yelling to her, "I'll knock your old man off the mantle if you don't stop that banging."

She would always find a way to even the score. One afternoon while I was sitting on the open back porch reading a book and Mrs.Wine was sprinkling her lawn by hand with the garden hose, I felt a splash of water, looked around and saw that she was watering in the direction away from me. It took a few more times of catching the spray before I glanced over fast enough to catch her deliberately spraying me with the hose. I didn't say anything to her and silently smiled at the old gal.

(Pete and Jane Villano were a few years older than us and had a couple of boys past high school age. We assumed that they were well beyond the child bearing years. However, about two years after we moved away from Bayside and had not seen the Villanos for a long while, Jean woke up one morning and told me she had a strange and unbelievable dream about Jane Villano having a baby. We both laughed at the absurdity.

Later that same day, Gloria Stone called Jean to say hello and informed her during the course of the conversation that Jane was, indeed, pregnant. This was not the only time that Jean has displayed this E.S.P. over the years.)

Those early years of marriage in Flushing and Bayside were times when we didn't have the resources for outside diversions so we often entertained ourselves at night by playing games such as Yahtzee, Milles Bourne, Checkers, Monopoly, and any number of card games from cribbage to rummy.

I continued to attend most of the Astoria Rambler weekly meetings in Astoria on Friday nights and, as long as my luck was holding out fairly well, I participated in the after meeting poker games. The winning streak I carried over from the Navy was still with me so I didn't have to dig into our limited household income; that is until I purchased a book advertised in the New York Times guaranteeing to improve one's poker winnings. After buying and reading the book, my luck rapidly declined and I haven't been able to win at the game since.

POWER-TRONIC SYSTEM, INC.

At Power-tronics the fortunes of the infant company began to go from bad to worse. The development of a unique accelerometer was a key part to packaging the system in the limited envelope that we had been assigned. My initial analysis of the physical requirements for the device indicated that Al's concept would not work. I evaluated the idea in several different ways but the numbers kept coming up negative. We could find no flaws in the analysis which meant we had to find another way to solve the stabilization problem.

Fortunately for us, Sperry had just developed some new, low cost gyroscopes in a size that could fit into our design envelope and budget; provided we could keep the power consumption down to an acceptable level. Al began to get a bit panicky but did not reflect this to the money people and continued to convince them that we would still be delivering the system under the original timetable and budget.

The monetary constraints left us little room to design what some of us thought would be the 'best' system; instead we started to skimp on analysis and costs with predictable results. These judgments were especially worrisome in the areas where we needed state of the art components to fulfill the system requirements.

Typical of the bad decisions that were made was the one by Al to use germanium transistors in the electronic controllers instead of the more expensive silicon transistors. I suggested to Al that we should do a thorough heat transfer analysis of the system to assure that the Germanium units which had a low upper temperature operating limit would not be overstressed. Al ordered me not to waste time on this and to concentrate instead on our more serious mechanical design problems.

I did as he said during the day but at night and on my own time I went through the thermal calculations several times and the results were irrefutable; if the ambient temperature reached 85 degrees Fahrenheit, the transistors would blow. We had added too many additional thermal loads onto the system into a too confined space as a result of our inability to avoid using the extra gyros. When I called this to Al's attention, he said that the system would never be subjected to that high a temperature (even though the specifications for the system called for a much higher temperature resistance.) He was the boss, so after making the objections we proceeded as ordered.

A couple of months later when the system was assembled and was undergoing tests in the laboratory, the air conditioning in the building went out on one of the hottest days of the season. The temperature in the lab was rising and I cautioned Al again about the sensitivity of the germanium transistors. Just as the room thermometer hit 85 degrees, the temperature inside the unit peaked and most of the germanium transistors blew. We were all dismayed that the system failed and would have to be reevaluated, redesigned, and rebuilt, but I was silently thinking "I told you so!" when my analysis had been verified right on the button.

This was only one of many bad decisions that were made in an attempt to build the system "on the cheap" so that Al could cover his butt with Milton and Harry who surely would have cut the funds off and terminated the whole company had they known the fiasco we were being led into.

One of the false economies that stand out in my mind was when we wanted to send the system out for a professionally painted finish. It has always been my opinion that, if a system doesn't look good, you've lost half the battle of getting it accepted by the customer.

In 1960, one could get an automobile painted at the Earl Scheib paint shop for $29.95. Al wanted us to mount the system on top of one of the older vehicles and to run it through Earl Scheib's shop. He didn't get his way on this one but we wound up hand painting the equipment.

Things may not have been quite so bad if we had more contracts coming into the house, but this was our only job; and it was one that was costing our investors. We had a Sales Manager who had the responsibility of making the contacts and soliciting new jobs and he was out on the road most of the time doing just that; or so we thought. He would return to the office about twice a month and at other times would be in contact by phone. It came to our attention, when we called one of the potential customers that our sales manager was supposed to have seen several times, that he had been there once for a short time, left some information and departed.

When we checked further into his activities of the past several months we found out that he was seeing very few of the prospective customers he was supposed to have visited. When he was out of town he would usually check into a hotel or motel and sit in his room drinking himself into a stupor. We got rid of the drunkard and searched around for a more reliable and sober sales representative.

Before the Remote Indicating Gyrocompass system was delivered, Al Parr; probably sensing the failure of the program that was his brainchild, negotiated a new position for himself with a company in the Bronx and took Andy McMillan and George Epstein (a personal friend of Al's who pretended to be a design engineer with credentials) with him. Andy had actually bailed out of Powertronics several months before and had taken a new position with another company; he gave this position up to join Al in the new venture in the Bronx.

The rest of the staff; Herb Berman, Harry Grossman, Jim Fay, and myself, along with one junior technician that we had recently hired; were left with the task of trying to get the system in at least good enough condition to be accepted so that we could collect the twenty-eight thousand that we were under contract for.

As for the System we delivered; it was eventually accepted and we received payment for it but the last I heard, about a year later, was that the system had been left on a solid surface, not even on a moving vehicle, and over long periods had measured errors of ±180 degrees, which essentially said the system was worthless.

Fortunately for those of us staying on with the foundering company, Herb Berman had a more simpatico relationship with Milton and Harry than Al did and this *kinship* encouraged Milton and Harry to continue their financial support and give us a chance to build up the business with the team that we had left. Herb took over the reins as the President, I was to be the Chief Mechanical Engineer with Jim Fay to do the design work on the board, and Harry would continue as the director of the Lab. In the next few weeks, we would take on Walter Young who was a top notch sales representative with contacts in government and business, and John Acuto, a Servo Design Engineer. With this small contingent and some new ideas, we were ready to go out and 'wow' the world with our engineering talents.

With a proactive Sales Manager and a small crew of competent engineers that were willing to take on the most difficult development jobs, we soon found our niche in the defense and space industry. The first contract we picked up was a small one but got a foothold for us in building precision, electronically controlled, gimbaled systems. The small two axis mount for an infrared sensor tracking system was an advance on the state of the art in precision, speed, and accuracy and we delivered it to the government in record breaking time. It took some innovative design approaches and a lot of chutzpah to bypass some of the more conventional techniques but in the end the customer was more than satisfied. In the coming months, this unorthodox approach to meeting nearly impossible delivery schedules or extraordinary design requirements would become our modus operandi and would result in our successfully winning some tough contracts.

These times were exhilarating ones for all of us; when we weren't busy on a proposal for a new job, we were actively working on the boards and in the lab to develop some "bread and butter" products, which hopefully would give us some modest production and a continuing market so that we wouldn't have to rely on the one of a kind developments we were most often bidding on.

One of these potential production items was a "magnetostrictive delay line", which Herb gave to me as a project as we were waiting for decisions on several outstanding proposals that we had submitted. Herb's plan was to develop a new magnetostrictive delay line (MDL) that would be a step up from the offerings currently on the market and could get us an entry into the slowly growing digital computer market. This was in the days before the development of the microchip and the computers of the day were large devices that were full of hardware. The delay line was one of the items used to store data as electro-mechanical impulses along a stationary coil of wire.

Herb wanted to develop this improved version of a delay line in thirty days with the total in-house cost of the parts not to exceed five dollars and ninety five cents. (Where he came up with this number I've never been able to figure out.)

Always one to enjoy a challenge, I accepted the job, but first I had to ask Herb, "What is magnetostrictive?" He wasn't quite sure himself but trusted that I would be able to find out.

(Magnetostriction is the characteristic of certain metallic alloys to constrict or expand when subjected to an electrical pulse across a wound coil of wire. The pulse then travels the length of the wire at the speed of sound through that material and has the inverse effect on a coil of wire at the other end of the wire; that is, the constriction of the material imparts an electrical impulse into a second coil at that end. The time for the impulse to travel the length of the wire from coil to coil determined the "time delay" of the MDL. A series of these pulses could be stored as binary bits for use as a memory device on one of the early electro-mechanical computers.)

I had a lot to learn and a lot to do in a short time. I had to bone up on Acoustics, Magnetostriction, Magnetostrictive materials such as Vanadium Permandur, and all of the other problems that arose as I got deeper into the study. I got all of the information I could from the Engineering Library in Manhattan and followed up on all the leads I could. I even went so far as to contact one of the top experts in the field who I discovered in my research had written a definitive treatise on magnetostriction about 35 years before in 1927 while he was employed by the National Bureau of Standards. He had retired but I tracked him down to his retirement home in Virginia and called him there to "pick his brain." He was delighted that someone had read his ancient articles which were still applicable today and he turned out to be a font of information for me; without his help I wouldn't have had much of a chance to complete this project in the narrow time frame we allotted to it.

Working day and night I managed to get a prototype unit developed, built, and tested, and verified that we met all of the stringent specifications we had imposed on ourselves. I even priced up all of the tooling necessary to go into production and met the per unit costs as Herb wanted. (Of course, to meet the stipulated $5.95 total parts costs, we would have had to make a production run of several hundred thousand to write off the tooling and material costs.)

We put Walt Young out on the road to peddle our new product and were well on our way to making a start in the market when the whole computer industry started to change with the new solid state developments. We never sold one MDL but I had a lot of fun beating the clock on a difficult job.

Life at Power-tronics was anything but dull; every day brought new challenges and we found most of our market on new developments that were always moving up another step in accuracy, speed, acceleration, compact size, or some other characteristic that most of the other companies avoided because of their high risk. If we didn't stick our necks out, however, we may never have landed a job based solely on the depth of our company resources. (In other words, we bull-shitted our way into most of our contracts with assurances of producing "wondrous" results, heretofore unattainable—and we usually delivered as promised.)

One example of how far we stuck our necks out was a proposal on a gyro stabilized two-axis tracking mount for accurately positioning some cameras and sensors of various kinds which were to be mounted aboard a K-135 tanker plane that had been converted especially for this program. The device was to be used to make measurements of an eclipse of the sun which was to occur about three months after the issuance of the contract. The aircraft was to be operated at a location above the Arctic Circle where it would fly along parallel with the movement of the eclipse to maximize the exposure time of the total eclipse. The equipment to be built had an extremely tight specification for accuracy, had to operate in an exposed environment at high altitudes, and had a delivery date from which there was no latitude; the solar phenomenon was not going to take any excuse for a missed delivery. There were not too many companies that wanted to bid on this job, but for Power-tronics these kinds of challenges were becoming routine.

With the tight delivery schedule we had no choice but to make many quick decisions; each "seat-of-the-pants" decision making the program a bit more risky. Fortunately we had an excellent man at the end of the process in putting the system together and assuring that it functioned the way we wanted it to. Harry Grossman was a graduate of the RCA Institute and was the best technician I've ever worked with. He didn't have an engineering degree but he could run technical circles around most of the engineers I've had to deal with over the years. I developed the habit on many of these jobs of relegating many of the completion tasks to Harry because we didn't have the luxury of enough time to do a detailed analysis of many of the design details. I had the draftsmen insert onto the layout drawings the initials 'LHDI' (let Harry do it). Harry by this time had merited my full confidence that the job would be done and it always was.

(Harry and I not only established a close professional association but wound up becoming the best of friends and confidants for many years; sharing many holidays and family events together. Harry and I worked together for 33 years and there has been a huge hole in my life since he died of colon cancer in 1993.)

By the way, we did deliver the Solar Eclipse tracker on time and it functioned beautifully, meeting or exceeding every expectation.

One of our proudest achievements was landing a job with the National Aeronautics and Space Administration (NASA) competing against thirty-five of the top companies in the country for a high accuracy tracking mount to be used at Huntsville, Alabama and which had to maintain stability and accuracy over extreme and rapidly changing temperatures and climatic conditions. I was told by the engineers at NASA that the primary reason we got the job was because of our offer to do a spectrographic analysis of the metal alloys in the structure as an assured way to offer the stability required; ours was the only proposal that had addressed this aspect of the job and it made our proposal stand out. Actually the claim of the benefits of a spectral analysis was a cock-and-bull story that I had conjured up but it had evidently caught the attention of the engineers evaluating our technical proposal. (We did do the spectral analysis but it didn't prove a thing about the equipment but it satisfied the customer.)

This job entailed the design of highly accurate and highly sensitive air-bearings and the only way to get the kind of results we needed was to hand adjust the system after assembly and test and to disassemble, rework, reassemble, and retest several times. This process was delaying the delivery for which we were already quite late to the point where the contracting officer at NASA sent us a telegram with an ultimatum; we would deliver the promised equipment by a specified date (about a month away) or the contract would be canceled and NASA threatened that we would never do work with the government again.

Harry and I took the warning very seriously and worked on the equipment seven days a week while we stayed at the factory, and only took enough time off to catch a nap from time to time. We made the new delivery date and Harry accompanied the equipment to Huntsville for testing where it was evaluated and accepted.

This was the story of our lives during those times; we worked late hours and most weekends and we were constantly rushing to get either a proposal out of the house or to complete the design and building of the equipment for which we had won a contract. During the earlier years while we were trying to get a start in "a" business, I saw little of the family, did not take a vacation, and was oblivious to the fact that Ranny and Patti were growing up rapidly around me as work was occupying most of my time; not to mention the three to four hour round trip commute every day from Long Island to New Rochelle.

In his rounds of the government agencies, Walt Young had made a contact at the Smithsonian Laboratories in Boston and had the Program Director give me a call to discuss his requirements and our capabilities to fulfill his needs. The Laboratory was engaged in a program to measure the continental drift around the world and required at least sixteen high accuracy and highly stable tracking devices. Each unit would be installed at a different point on the earth and all would be synchronized together to determine the small amount of drift between the continents over an extended period of time.

While the Program Engineers at the Smithsonian were attempting to get the necessary funding for the project, I spent a great deal of time on the phone and several trips to Boston working with them to resolve the many technical problems. In the end, this investment in time was about to pay off. The Smithsonian got the money for the project; several millions of dollars, and we were the lead contender to get the job. When we bid on the job we had a good handle on all of the technical problems and felt confident that we would win the competitive bidding contest. To make sure that we didn't leave any stone unturned, we agreed amongst ourselves to really tighten the belt on the pricing end of the initial contract for the development unit. We decided to forgo any profit and to make it up when we got the production job.

Everything went as planned; we submitted our proposal and waited to hear the results. Walt got a call from the contracts officer in Boston and a meeting was set up in New Rochelle to resolve some last minute changes and additions and (we didn't know it at the time), to sign the contract to go ahead.

Before this meeting had taken place, and unrelated to this job, we had moved from our converted retail store to a larger, more modern facility a short way up the road on Main Street.

When the entourage of engineers and administrators arrived at our plant, Walt and I greeted them and escorted them to our new conference room, while Herb remained in his office upstairs. We were directed by Herb to make no commitments to the Smithsonian representatives without first discussing any contract changes with him; even the smallest item should be left open for further evaluation by Herb before any agreements were made.

It turned out that the guests from the Smithsonian had only minor items to clarify and Walt and I felt comfortable that we would have no problems

464

putting this contract to bed before the day was over; but we followed Herb's direction and withheld any commitment until we spoke to him.

Typical of the magnitude of the "changes" that were discussed was the addition of a Power On indicator light on the main control console. This was a trivial item and one we would have included as a normal addition on any of our equipments but it was not specifically mentioned in our proposal, and again, we hesitated to make the decision on the spot. If it was up to me, I would have just agreed to the "one dollar" light, signed the contract, and started work on the project; but Herb had been quite explicit in what he wanted.

Before we broke for lunch and after we had discussed all of the changes needed, Walt and I excused ourselves and went upstairs to have our meeting with Herb. We reported to Herb that the meeting went extremely well and that the changes and additions that were requested were minimal in both cost and impact on the program and that we were ready to add a modest amount to the price, which we knew would be completely acceptable. Herb had other ideas.

He said that after all the time that the Smithsonian has invested to get to this point in the process with us; they would have to award us the contract even if we added on a substantial amount to the price. Walt and I disagreed and strongly stated our case to Herb but he was adamant. He wanted to; for instance; charge several thousand dollars just for the addition of the Power On indicator light. His desire to now show a profit drove him to want to put outlandish prices on all of the small additions. Walt and I both said that we could not, with a straight face, go back to the customer and justify these outrageous demands and suggested that if he insists on doing this and wanted to stiff a customer who could put us in the multi-million dollar business, he would have to present the case at the afternoon's meeting.

After a pleasant lunch with our soon-to-be customer, we sat down again to close the deal. Herb not only made his presentation with a straight face, but he also made an ass out of himself and, by association, Walt and me. When one of the engineers asked him how he justified such a high price for a simple light bulb and socket, he replied, "It is not only the cost of the parts; it's all of the design changes that have to be made, etc. etc."

The stunned group, were taken aback by the afternoon's turn of events. After a couple of hours listening to Herb's fantasies, they packed up their gear to leave and told us they would be in touch. Herb was still convinced after they left that they had no recourse but to grant us the contract.

After an anxious wait of about a week, Herb asked Walt to call up to inquire about the status of our proposal. Walt came back after contacting the Smithsonian buyer and told us that the contract was going to another company. Walt did not tell Herb but told me later that the buyer told him that they had come to New Rochelle with intentions of signing off on the contract the day that they visited but after Herb's presentation all of the Smithsonian people agreed to not go through with the award and to go with another bidder. The buyer said to Walt (about Herb), "To be quite honest with you, after listening to Herb we decided that we couldn't do business with that Jew Bastard." I didn't blame Walt for not telling this to Herb.

This was not the first time that Herb made a terrible decision and it would not be the last. He tried to squeeze too much out of limited resources. He would often refer to "Parkinson's Law", which stated that any job will expand to fill the time allotted to complete it. Herb took as a corollary, the inverse of this, that if you allot less time than required for a job, the worker will manage to get the job done in that time. Unfortunately, "Herb's Law" didn't work in the real world and we would often find ourselves trying to complete a job in less time than the job actually needed. This led to short-changing the minimum required analysis and consequent difficulties in meeting our objectives.

We had expanded our staff quite a bit; we had taken on a staff of draftsmen and designers, engineering help, and additional technicians in the lab. We were fortunate in having act as our support staff, the crew from our parent company, Hydrapower, which provided us accounting, purchasing, bookkeeping, and other back-office functions. Herb demanded that all of the workers put in overtime when necessary, without pay. John Acuto, Harry Grossman, and I tried to get Herb to pay the working staff for this overtime but Herb said that they were "management and professional" staff and should expect to put in long hours. We felt that we three could be expected to put in the extra time without compensation because we had a stake in the future of the company, but that the others were simply hired as workers and should be compensated.

I insisted that even if we don't pay the men for the work, we should keep accurate records of the time on the job so that we would have a record for monitoring the progress and for use in future bids. This mistreatment of the staff almost proved to be the undoing of the company.

The Federal Department of Labor sent in an agent as part of a routine inspection of our labor policies. After interviewing all of the workers, the agent asked for and received from us all of the time records for the entire staff. The Labor Department concluded that, just as we had unsuccessfully insisted against Herb's objections, all of the working staff should have been paid for their overtime over the course of the last couple of years and that the company would have to pay all of the back pay due to the workers or face other charges and fines. We were left with no alternative except to comply with the order.

Milton Cohen would have closed us down at that point, but he bit the bullet on the payment because we were on the verge of getting some of the largest contracts we had up to that point.

We should have realized in those earlier days that Herb's erratic judgments were only a harbinger of things to come.

A BIG MOVE

I was so busy at the office in New Rochelle that before I knew it many months had passed in our rented house and we were notified by the Rehders that they would be returning to Bayside in the spring of 1962 and we would have to vacate as originally agreed; we did manage to get nearly two years at the house but we would be sorry to leave. This was going to be difficult for all of us. Ranny was very friendly with Donald Stone and some of the other neighborhood boys and Jean and I had come to know and be fond of all of our neighbors. We would often party together at one of the houses; quite often at the Villano house next door.

Typical of the parties that we had was a barbecue that we had in the Villano's back yard during the warm summer. I would often be called upon to sing or lead the rest in songs. That summer night they probably wished they hadn't got me started. I sang continuously, entertaining the whole neighborhood, until the sun was coming up and we finally disbanded.

I was even growing fond of Mrs. Wine, the old curmudgeon next door. After this night of singing and after I had retired to my bed as the sun was rising, Mrs. Wine started to dump heavy items down the stairs in her house. The clangor could be heard through the thin separating wall to our house and every time she dropped another item I was jolted out of my elusive sleep. This was her intent, I suppose, after my having kept her awake all night with my serenading.

Fraser Stone and I would sometimes get together and knock off a bottle of Scotch together and talk. After a few drinks we would often conspire to leave New York to open up a hunting lodge in Newfoundland. Fraser was a great carpenter and a native "Newfie" so he not only knew the area well but was in a position to take the lead in building whatever accommodations we needed in the deep woods.

Homesteading was still being carried on in Newfoundland and had not been terminated when they elected to join the Canadian Federation in 1948, not too many years prior. Fraser convinced me that we could pick up two large tracts near the mountains to homestead, which we would then join together for our mountain hunting and fishing retreat in a remote area where moose, trout, and salmon were plentiful. In the sober light of day these wonderful plans never materialized but we had a great time planning and dreaming.

However, now that the Rehders were returning we had to find new quarters. We preferred to stay in the Bayside or Flushing area and went out apartment hunting in those communities. Everything we looked at was either out of our price range or, for those that we could afford, did not meet our minimum housing needs.

We looked at one apartment nearby that had a reasonable rental but found it was a "do-it-yourself" monstrosity. None of the rooms had a dimension that exceeded eight feet. The toilet was located underneath the staircase requiring one to bend forward while sitting so as to not hit the head on the underside of the staircase and it was impossible for a man to stand in front of the bowl to relieve himself.

In the Master Bedroom there was a shower curtain hanging on a bar mounted against and parallel to the wall. I asked the owner what the curtain was for. He told us that this was the closet; at which point he pulled the curtain back and revealed a recess in the wall no deeper than two or three inches. That was a closet?

With the poor selection of available apartments, we decided to look at some new homes. There was a new development going up in Smithtown on Long Island with Colonial Style homes selling for $17,000. We drove out one weekend to look at the model homes and were seriously considering purchasing one of the homes. When I realized the length of the commute from Smithtown to New Rochelle, we decided that we would pass on the Smithtown house.

There was an advertisement for a house in Westbury, also on Long Island, in the Sunday newspaper that seemed to be a real bargain at less than $13,000. After checking out the mileage from Westbury to the office and determining that it was just about at the limit of what I would care to travel, we called and made an appointment to see the advertised house.

When we arrived at the Westbury house that weekend in the company of a real estate agent, a woman who was presumably the present owner answered the door and immediately started to give the agent a tongue lashing.

"What the hell are you bringing these people here for? You know this is an inter-racial neighborhood and that's why I'm getting out."

The agent insisted that we see the house and the woman let us in.

This wasn't a house; it was a small box. There were four small rooms in a house that was no more than fifteen feet wide. Upon entering the house there was a small enclosed porch of about six feet in depth with a living room immediately behind that was about ten feet deep. On the far side of the living room were two doorways into a bedroom on the right and the kitchen on the left; each room was about half the width of the house. There was barely enough room in the bedroom for a small double bed.

It didn't take us long to decide that all we wanted from this house was to get out. At that point, the real estate agent said he had something more suitable not too far from this place and in a 'better' neighborhood. We then spent the rest of the day going from one house to another that were all in a price range just 'slightly' above the selling price of the Westbury house; and always a little bit further from the city line; an aspect that we didn't appreciate at the time because each successive home was just a short distance from the last.

We looked at some terrible resale homes and were about ready to call it quits for the day when the agent told us that he had a place in Plainview that was slightly higher in price but would probably meet all of our requirements. This was the first time that I had even heard about a community called Plainview but we were willing to look at this one last house on that day. The Plainview house was going for $17.990, which the agent assured us was a 'steal' at that price. We felt that we were willing to go for almost that much in Smithtown in Suffolk County and put up with the longer commute so why not purchase this house in 'close-in' Nassau. I didn't realize that Plainview was as far to the east in Nassau as one could go; it is located right on the Suffolk County border.

The house that we were shown was a ranch style without a basement and had in-the-floor hot water heating. The house was part of a multi-house development and was originally built as a single story ranch style with three small bedrooms, a living room, a kitchen, and an attached garage. When we looked at the house it had been altered by John Trask, the present owner, whose family presently occupied the house, with the garage converted to a small family room with a bar and a detached garage built to the rear and side of the house with a long driveway.

The original front entry to the house was directly into the living room. One of the bedrooms had been converted to a hallway with a staircase leading up to a dormer extension on the second floor which had two bedrooms and a toilet without a bath or shower. We were told that the piping was under the floor for the addition of the new plumbing and was ready for the installation. (We would later find out that this was not true.)

There was an enclosed unheated porch in the rear of the house and a patio of two foot square black and white concrete blocks set in a sand base in a checkerboard pattern.

The house seemed to meet all of our current needs and with four bedrooms even allowed for expanding the family.

Earlier in the day, during our initial discussions with the real estate man, we were told that under the G.I. Bill, we could purchase a house with no down payment. With this in mind and with the agent assuring us that my check would not be cashed but only held until we closed on the house and would be returned if I could not get a mortgage, I put down a binder of five hundred dollars on the house even though there were insufficient funds in the bank to cover it.

With the decision made to purchase the house, the agent took us immediately to a firm that started the paperwork to clear a mortgage for us. I would provide them with all the necessary back up information by mail. Pending approval of our loan application, we were on our way to becoming home owners. The contract signing was set for the next week and the insurance agent set us up with an attorney from Plainview to represent us. The closing would come soon after the mortgage approval.

It wasn't until a few days after the contract was signed and we were waiting for the closing that I became aware of something I hadn't been informed of before; closing costs. I was told that these costs included: 'points' for the bank to cover the lower interest rate that I would get as a qualified veteran (at that time the mortgage interest was 4½ percent), filing fees, mortgage tax, the bank's attorney's fees as well as my own attorney's costs, and other fees that would add up to about $1500; not a large number today but in 1962 to a young struggling couple it was a formidable amount. I had no idea of where or how we would get the money to cover these closing costs but we were not about to lose heart.

When Jean asked me where we would get the money, I reassured her that, "The Good Lord will provide." I trusted that with his help we could work something out.

As the closing date approached and we had still not figured a way out of our financial problem, we were beginning to get a bit concerned. Then, with less than two weeks remaining before the closing, we received an unexpected telephone call from Sydney Schwartz, Jr. our attorney who was representing us in a suit against the truck driver who had collided with us in 1959 (pg.436). I had completely forgotten about that episode and gave up a long time ago that any settlement would be made. Now, out of the blue, Sydney called to say that the insurance company for the other driver had made an offer to settle; the amount was less than $5000. Upon inquiry about the cut for Sydney and the Doctor, we found out that we would have enough to cover the closing costs with a little left over to help with the moving costs; another item that did not figure into our calculations.

Yes! In the end the Good Lord did provide -- even for those of us who are always living on the edge and have shown little faith.

We were now home owners; the Trasks had moved from our Plainview house to their new home in Old Bethpage, and the Rehders would soon be in Bayside to take over the house we were presently occupying. Before we could move however, I had to get the house in order for our move and arrange to move our household goods within a couple of weeks. I was about to become a typical suburban homeowner and would soon be forced to learn all of the crafts needed to make the house livable; painting, wallpapering, carpentry, gardening, etc.

On the day of the move in April of 1962, the moving van pulled up to our house in Bayside with three workers, ready to start the move to Plainview.

We had everything ready to be loaded into the truck and the workmen started to take everything that we indicated out to the truck. Everything went smoothly until a saleswoman came to the door while we were in the middle of the disorder and confusion of directing the three workers and trying to keep Ranny and Patti from getting in the way. Ranny was five years old at the time and Patti was not yet two.

About a month before our move, we had taken advantage of an advertisement in the paper to have a 'free' professional picture of the children taken at Gertz, the Department Store in Flushing where we had purchased our furniture. Jean had taken Ranny and Patti in for the sitting for the photo and the saleswoman was now there on our moving day to show us the proofs of all of the pictures that had been taken at the photo session. She attempted at this inopportune time to encourage us to purchase additional pictures; assuming that just seeing such wonderful pictures would entice us to buy. Jean had told her at the beginning of her unwelcome visit to come to see us in Plainview as we were too busy moving; which she could readily see. The woman stubbornly insisted on showing Jean the pictures and invited herself into the house.

Jean, not being one to intentionally cause discomfort to anyone, even the most crass and pushy people, politely listened for a short time as the woman spread the photos across the dining room table which had yet to be loaded on the truck. When Jean realized the magnitude of the decision that would have to be made in selecting the pictures and, not wanting to make any hasty or costly decisions, told the woman to make an appointment to see us in Plainview in about a month, after we settled in. The woman persisted in pursuing the sale on the spot and was finally told to just send us the one free photo as promised and forget the rest of the pictures; and out the door she was led.

The moving men in the meantime had completed the loading of the furniture into the truck and were ready to hit the road. Before they left for

Plainview, I wanted to make one last check of the house to make sure they had taken everything as directed and I asked the movers to wait a few minutes while I assured that nothing was left off the truck. When I came down from my upstairs check, where I had discovered that they had an additional large piece of furniture to put on the truck, I learned that the movers had already started out for Plainview on the truck.

I jumped quickly into our car and headed for the Clearview Expressway and the Long Island Expressway hoping to intercept the moving van before it had gone too far. About two or three miles from the house I saw the moving truck on the LIE, raced alongside and honked the horn to signal them to stop. I told them what had happened and after they initially argued against going back to the house, my persistence finally forced them to relent.

When we returned to the now almost empty house in Bayside, the workers loaded up the forgotten piece into the van and our family loaded up into our car. We started to follow the truck along the LIE and, along the way, decided to pull ahead to arrive in Plainview before the movers to greet them at the house. The LIE was not too heavily traveled at that time of day and we expected the truck to be following close behind.

However, it was three hours after our arrival before the van finally pulled up in front of the house. The driver simply said they got caught in traffic on the expressway and got stalled in getting to the house; an assertion I found difficult to believe but I was not going to debate them until all of our furniture was off the truck and into the house.

When the unloading was completed the head mover handed me the bill for the balance of the moving. I was astounded to discover that he had included an uncontracted cost for three hours of additional time for the three men; I don't recall the exact sum but it was quite substantial for the nine man-hours. I told them I could not, and would not pay them for the time that they had wasted somewhere between Bayside and Plainview, a drive that would normally take no more than forty-five minutes.

They said they couldn't accept less than the total balance including the added overtime and that they had been directed by their boss to bill us for the time. They were not going to leave until I paid them. The three men sat down on the stairs leading to the second floor and said that they were going to sit there and would charge for any additional time until I paid the requested amount. By happy chance, we had the telephone installed before we arrived at the house and, getting the telephone number from the spokesman for the workers, I called the moving company office and asked for the head man.

After my explanation and complaint, the manager told me the same thing as the workers; that I would have to pay for the overtime and, if there were any complaints, I could take it up with the office after the payment and after the workers had left. Instead of arguing with the uncooperative voice on the other end of the line, knowing full well that I was not going to convince him over the telephone, I waited for him to hang up and then talked into the dead phone.

"So, you agree that I should just pay them what we had originally contracted for and we will settle this between us when I call the office in the morning. Okay, I'll pass the word on to them and I'll call you tomorrow." I said this loud enough for the workers to hear me. When I hung up I repeated what his boss supposedly said. He seemed a bit reluctant but didn't want to antagonize his boss by calling him back and asked me to pay him so he can leave.

When I went to write out a check, he told me that under the contract he could only accept cash or a certified check and he looked like he was ready to do his sit down again. As we arrived at the house earlier my sister, Helen, who lived in nearby Hicksville had come to greet us. At first I had thought that this was a terrible time to be visiting, as we were moving into the house. At this point she unexpectedly became a godsend. Helen volunteered to take my check and cash it under her cashing privileges at one of the local retail stores.

I wrote the check and Helen ran out to get the cash. When she returned shortly after, I paid the movers, got them out of the house, and started to get us settled in for the night, happy to be rid of the intruders.

In the days that followed, the moving company continued to badger us for the additional and unwarranted bill for the extra hours that they continued to say we owed them. I simply ignored them and eventually they gave up on trying to collect, implicitly acknowledging that they were in the wrong.

We adapted to our new home at 36 Sunrise Street very quickly. We had moved into a perfect neighborhood for our young family; the neighbors were very friendly and there were a huge number of young children on the block; Ranny and Patti fit right in with the other children and soon made many friends. It wasn't too long before we had all become an integral part of the circle of friends on our end of the block.

The neighbors were all fairly young and, the houses were only about twelve years old. Most of the residents were relative newcomers to the community and had young and growing families. Most of our families would establish close and life long friendships; not only the kids, but the parents as well.

We were fortunate to have selected a community that was already establishing itself as one of the best school districts on Long Island and was fast becoming one of the most desirable places for parents to buy into because of the outstanding educational system in place in the Plainview-Old Bethpage School District. Because of this, taxes were higher than most of the other school districts on Long Island and would increase each year at a higher pace than the average. (I heard it said by some of the home owners, who seemed content with the high taxes in the Plainview-Old Bethpage School District, that they welcomed the higher school tax levy because it helped to keep out "certain undesirable elements". I would later find out what these "code words" meant.)

Ranny started first grade at the Fern Place School in the fall of 1962 along with his new found friend, Ronny Rahilly, who lived next door to us. Ranny would later join the local Cub Scout Pack and would also become one of the star players in the Plainview Little League.

One day while I was working on the lawn in front of the house, I noticed Ranny, who was then just shy of six years of age, riding up the sidewalk toward the house on his tricycle. Standing between him and our house was one of the neighbor boys, who, when Ranny approached, stood in the way of the bike and with hands defiantly on hips, challenged Ranny to pass him at his peril. Ranny, not wanting a confrontation, instead, pedaled his tricycle into the street and rode around the challenger.

When Ranny arrived at the front of our house, I asked him what had happened. He told me that the kid up the block wouldn't let him pass. I told Ranny that the next time this 'bully' got in his way; he should just get off the bike, punch him in the nose and drive right on by.

It wasn't too long afterward on that same day and while I was still working in front of the house that I saw Ranny again approach this road block. This time, when the harasser again challenged him, Ranny got off the tricycle, walked up to his tormentor and without hesitation gave him a quick right to the center of the face. The bully was so stunned that he did not respond. Ranny got back on the tricycle and returned to the front of our house without a comment. I gave him a pat of approval on the head and he seemed quite pleased with himself.

The bully no longer tried to intimidate Ranny after this confrontation. Ranny learned an important lesson in life; to always stand up to bullies because they will usually back down when you don't shy away from the challenge. After this, Ranny not only was not bothered by this neighbor boy, but he and the boy, Wayne Whittall, became very good friends.

I became an assistant coach for Ranny's Little League baseball team during his first year of organized baseball. The following year, I would take over as manager of the Colormart team (Colormart was a local paint and wallpaper store that sponsored one of the teams) with Ranny as one of my players. At every game that we played, the parents, particularly the fathers, were constantly on my back about letting their boy play more of the game. The parents were a persistent nuisance but I chose to ignore them and I played the boys the way they were supposed to be played; every boy got a chance to play a fair share of the game no matter how badly he played. We were in the game to win, but more important for the boys, we were in it to have fun and develop a sense of sportsmanship. Most of the other managers seemed to be interested primarily in winning games and left many of the poor players sitting on the bench during the whole season even though the league rules called for 'all' boys to play in every game, if only for a short time.

By playing the team my way, all of the boys shared equally in the satisfaction when we finished the year winning the division championship and earning a chance to play in the Regional finals. In the finals, we capped our year by defeating the All-Stars from the opposing division by a score of 14-1 to sweep the regional title.

I was especially proud of Ranny and the team because we were offered the opportunity to play with all of the best players from our division because the division we were to play against had a three way tie which prompted them to select the best players in the entire division instead of holding a playoff to select a team. I opted to play with my team the same as we had played the season; without the 'ringers' and with every boy again playing his fair share of the game. The boys realized they were against very stiff competition but they accepted my decision. They played their hearts out and gave us a great victory against what should have been a much superior team.

We celebrated this victory in our backyard where we had a 24 foot diameter above ground pool where the boys could swim and where we served the team a sumptuous barbecue of hotdogs and hamburgers. The boys had a special treat when they dumped the fully clothed team manager into the pool in honor of our win. (Perhaps, it would have been more appropriate to dump some of the other parents into the drink after their boorish behavior during the season.)

After that very successful year I was looking forward to bigger and better things for the following year, but affairs got so busy at the office that it was the last time that I had a chance to serve as a volunteer in the Little League.

It wasn't too long after our move onto Sunrise Street before we fell into the mold of typical suburban home owners; mowing lawns, doing house repairs and remodeling, participating in the school activities like P.T.A., commuting forty-three miles each way to work, and spending weekend nights drinking canned beer and entertaining or being entertained.

The thing that captivated us most about the neighborhood was the people who lived there. To us, Sunrise Street became not just houses, but the people in those houses. They were a diverse bunch of blue and white collar workers, professionals, and civil servants and we all related very well and we were to enjoy many memorable years together; both pleasurable and sad.

The most popular entertainment for all of us in those early days was entertaining each other in each other's homes; most weekends found us at another gathering of the 'block' with any occasion used as an excuse to hold a party. In this way we came to know each other and to share in the mutual maturing of our families.

The 'Mayor' of Sunrise Street was Neil Sheehan, a New York City Police Detective who lived across the street. Neil, whose Christian name is 'Cornelius', was at the center of all neighborhood activities, whether it was organizing our annual block party, telling "Boo Radley" spook stories to the kids, or playing practical jokes on one of the neighbors. He was a good cop and a tough cop; but around the block when off duty he was always the first one in line to help a neighbor in need.

Neil was always a constant source of entertainment with his practical jokes. I especially recall the story of when he took Bob Eatz's patio furniture and nailed it on the roof of Bob's house. Bob, upon arriving home in his car, noticed this unexpected scene and said to his passenger as he turned the car onto Sunrise Street, "Well, look at that. Some asshole has put his furniture on the roof.... Say, wait a minute! That's my furniture... and my roof!"

There was another time at one of the annual Labor Day block parties when one of the neighbors (who will remain unnamed) had imbibed a bit too much booze and retired early in the day to his house where he passed out on the couch. At the instigation of our resident joker, some of the neighbors went into the house while our unidentified drunk was snoring away and painted the head of the sleeper's penis with a bright red nail polish.

Later that evening, while the festivities were still underway, a loud piercing scream filled the neighborhood. It wasn't long before everyone realized that the shriek emanated from the house of the recently decorated dupe. His wife ran to the house to investigate, returning a short time later; doubled up with laughter. The butt of the joke had awakened to go to the bathroom where he discovered that his recently painted staff had turned a deep crimson color. He thought that he had contracted some terrible venereal disorder and went into a state of shock. (Though unrelated to this event, he moved from the neighborhood shortly after this incident but left the block with another popular "Neil Story" to add to the legend.)

On the evening of November 9th, 1965, the entire Northeast Region of the United States, including New York City and Long Island, was hit with a massive blackout. The electrical grids had overloaded and it took several hours to return the region to normal power levels. The blackout became the subject of many television specials and several movies, one of which highlighted the increase in pregnancies that were attributable to that night's blackout. Without any radio or television and no lights by which to read, there weren't too many activities that one found practicable on that darkened night.

In the late afternoon of November 10th, while we were all still talking about and were still troubled by the loss of power on the previous day, all of the homeowners on the block received a telephone call that was ostensibly from LILCO, the local power company, informing us that they would be switching to new generators at exactly 6 P.M. that evening and that all of the residents were to turn off all of the lights in the house and anything else that used electricity; refrigerators, fans, etc. This, they said, was necessary to prevent another overload on the system and another blackout. With the previous night's calamity still fresh in mind, we did as we were requested and awaited the promised call from the power company to inform us when we could put the lights back on so that we could prepare our dinner.

I walked outside the front door to observe the darkened houses. I noticed Neil Sheehan standing in front of his house. As the lights went out in one house after another, Neil was blowing at each house as if he were blowing out candles. I went over to ask what he was doing and he burst into laughter. I realized almost immediately what had happened. Neil had made all of the calls and had everyone on the block turning off their lights while he played candle snuffer.

It was a great coup for Neil; everyone responded to the orders because of the recently experienced trauma, and this time Neil, again had a great laugh at the expense of everyone on Sunrise Street.

A NEW ADDITION

As we were becoming part of the life on Sunrise Street, an additional life would soon join us in our household. There were about fifty children residing in the fourteen houses at our end of the block, the houses that would usually participate in our annual block party in September, and that number would be increased by one on March 10, 1964 when a beautiful baby, our daughter Eileen, was born at the Central General Hospital in Plainview.

Patti may have been a bit concerned at first at being replaced as the baby of the family but she did not show any of the signs of resentment that I had shown when my sister Marilyn was born in 1935. Eileen was readily accepted by all of us and was a very welcome addition to a home full of caring and love. Of course, we had Eileen baptized at the earliest opportunity at Our Lady of Mercy Church with Jean's brother Joe and Gloria Sullivan, Jean's childhood friend standing as the godparents.

We moved Patti from her downstairs bedroom which was adjacent to our room to make room for the new baby.

(There were two bedrooms downstairs and two upstairs. One of the rooms upstairs had not been in use in the two years that we had lived in this house. This was the room that we assigned to Patti. It was situated at the end of a long, narrow, and (to a young four year old mind), dark and scary hall. Patti never said anything at the time and it would be years later that we would find out that she was continuously frightened when she went to bed in that *faraway dungeon* and would quite often run down the hall in the dark of night to Ranny's room to jump into bed with him to find some security and comfort.

This arrangement lasted for four years, when we rebuilt the second floor of the house to accommodate bedrooms for the entire family and converted the downstairs bedrooms to a large family room or den.)

In the next years as we watched our brood grow into a healthy and happy family. Jean and I were pleased to see the children grow up not only physically healthy but also emotionally well adjusted. We were delighted to witness each of them as they went through all the stages of growing up, from the first steps of walking and the first spoken words, to the celebration of birthdays and holidays, the start of school and the successful completion of school at graduations, as well as the making of the first Holy Communion and Confirmation at Our Lady of Mercy Church.

All three of the children were active in school, neighborhood, and group activities.

Ranny was a Scout, participated in Little League Baseball and the Police Boys Club Football as a defensive end and in these sports he received his share of winning trophies. He participated in some of the theater put on by the school, most notably, a lead role as Mr. Banks, in the stage production of "Mary Poppins". He played the clarinet in the school band, an instrument at which he became very proficient. He was especially proud, as were we, when he was singled out by the band director to play the alto saxophone in one of the special concerts because of his talent on the reed instruments.

He was also self teaching himself on the piano that Jean's Aunt Florie and Uncle Henry gave us. It was an upright player piano with the player mechanism removed. We painted it with a soft red antique finish, had the piano tuned, and it has performed ever since as an instrument of musical and aesthetic beauty – not bad for the price!

Jean became co-leader with Betty Romaine of Patti's Brownie troop and, subsequently, her Girl Scout troop. Patti's award winning athletics included playing on the first place girl's basketball team and on the synchronized swimming team. In her earlier years she had a brief flirtation with ballet but did not maintain an interest in the ballet.

Patti sang in the chorus in school, but we were most surprised by her performance in the musical "Oklahoma". She never told us the part that she was playing and we assumed that because of her participation in the chorus that she would be playing in one of the group roles. We were bowled over when we went to the performance and found that not only did she have a major role as Ado Annie, but that she was magnificent in the role; well poised and displaying a lot of talent. I taped this performance from the orchestra seat with a portable cassette tape recorder; I still have that tape today.

Patti took piano lessons from a Mrs. Maripodi who gave musical instruction at her home around the corner from us.

Eileen had a brief flirtation with the scouts but because Jean was the leader of Patti's troop and Eileen was obliged to attend most of those activities, Eileen had already had her share of scouting.

Eileen also participated in the school theatrics and had at least two memorable featured roles; one in elementary school as Gretel in "Hansel and Gretel", and later on, as Grandma Tzeitel in a production of "Fiddler on the Roof."

Eileen's instrument was the guitar and her attempt at athletics was as a member of the twirling team where she was presented with the largest trophy that any of our kids ever received. Patti was probably a bit perplexed at the size of this trophy compared to the ones that she had previously received for first place in basketball, swimming, and other activities. Eileen received her gargantuan trophy for "perfect attendance."

These were, indeed, happy days for us. We didn't have much in the way of material things but I did have a steady job and we were all in excellent health. Since joining the new venture at Power-tronics in 1960, I hadn't taken a vacation in four years and our family outings consisted of day trips to Jones Beach or Sunken Meadow Park in the summer or, perhaps, a day at Lollipop Farm, a now defunct animal farm in Syosset. With my taking on the position as Chief Mechanical Engineer at the office, my workload increased immensely. (The paycheck did not move up at a corresponding rate.)

It was 1964 before I felt that I needed some time off and we decided that we could afford a trip to the Catskill Mountains where we spent a week at a family resort just outside the town of East Durham called, "The Shapanack" My brother Dan and his family had been going there each year and we were convinced that this was the kind of inexpensive, fun place for a young family.

We left Eileen, who had just turned one, with Jean's mother and father for a week and the four of us shared one room at the Shapanack. The room had no private bath facility and we had to share a bathroom in the hall with three or four other families. There was no air conditioning and no window in the room but as we spent most of the day outdoors or at the resort sponsored activities this did not prove to be too much of a hardship.

The total cost for the entire family for the one week stay, which included three full meals a day for each of us plus entertainment, was only 105 dollars. The activities included swimming in an Olympic sized pool, softball games, hayrides, horseback riding on sway backed nags, and an event each evening in the recreation hall; a country singer such as Joe Omehundro, dancing, or games.

We returned to The Shapanack the following year, this time bringing Eileen with us. As we were now veterans of the resort, we were housed in a two bedroom suite with a private bath; but still no air conditioning. The tariff had increased to 155 dollars for the entire family.

In 1967 we returned for the last time, spending this week with Chris and Marion Eckhoff and their three children. Many of my brothers and their families continued to vacation at the Shapanack for many more years after this, but now, sadly, the family owned and run resort has closed its doors.

Our house soon became a gathering place for much of the family on holidays and special occasions. While the children were still young and eagerly anticipating Santa's annual visit on Christmas, we would do what most parents did, stay up into the wee hours of the morning, setting up the toys and gifts under the tree, while imbibing, of course, in some *Christmas Spirits*.

Invariably, Jean's mother and father, being anxious to see the grandchildren opening their gifts on Christmas morning, would arrive shortly after sunrise with brothers Joe and Steve in tow, to start our day. We didn't have much sleep but youth and the spirit of the occasion kept us alert for the entire day. Mom and Dad would stay for a sumptuous holiday dinner and usually, because of a problem driving in the dark, they would leave before sundown after spending the day at the house. Some years we would be joined by other members of Jean's family; Nana (her grandmother), or some of the many aunts and uncles and their children.

Typically, about the time that Mom and Dad left, our other invited guests from my side of the family would start to arrive, having finished their exchange of gifts and family dinner earlier in the day. There would normally be my sister Helen with her husband Leroy and their only daughter Carol; my brother Dan with his wife Agnes and their children, Diane, Patti, Danny, Maureen, and Billy; brother Fran with Marilyn and their kids, Kathy, Gary, Gerard, and Marilyn; and brother Bob. After Bob married Peggy Carpenter she also joined us for the holiday festivities. Quite often my father and his bride, Mary would join us sometime during the day.

Invariably, after a day of heavy celebrating with much food, much spirits, and much chatter passing our lips, the partying would go on into the morning hours, sometimes so long that we watched the sun rise on the next day while the children slept on beds, sofas, or on the floor somewhere in the house. By the time everyone had left we were always too exhausted to do the cleanup until we had a few hours sleep.

These were wonderful days when all of us were filled with youthful plans and exuberance for the future and our conversations were lively and covered a full range of topics, from national and international events, to our own busy activities, and the future of our youngsters. There was never a lull in the action and very often we would wind up in group games that had us all laughing hysterically.

Just as our parents did before us, we made New Year's Eve a night for the parents while the children slept. Most often we would party at the house of a neighbor, friend or family. On occasion, we would celebrate the New Year at a church sponsored party in the basement of the school or a reasonably priced affair at the American Legion Hall or Knights of Columbus.

By the time we moved to Plainview, the old tradition from our childhood of dressing up on Thanksgiving and knocking on doors begging, "Anything for Thanksgiving?" had been abandoned. Halloween had become the costume and "trick or treat" day for the new generation.

Easter was still the day for new outfits and welcoming the spring. The Easter Bunny still brought the surprise baskets to the young ones and Jean still continued to eat all of the ears off the chocolate bunnies; placing the rest of the mutilated bunny carcass into the basket.

Most of the year was spent working long hours at Powertronics in New Rochelle with its long commute, with the weekends devoted to home maintenance, inside and out.

These weekends would also entail a great deal of family entertaining. There were very few weekends that went by without getting a surprise visit from some member of the family and their brood. It was fun, but most often would force us to postpone some necessary expenditure for household improvements so that we could provide refreshments for the guests. Jean had at various times taken part time employment to help supplement the family income. She worked as a saleslady in the local bakery on the weekends, did baby sitting, and was an early telemarketer. (She worked for a time making phone calls from the house to inform people that they had won free dance lessons at the Arthur Murray Dance Studio. She quit this job after one of the lucky winners told her that he couldn't accept because he had no legs.) She also worked at various times in sales at the old Abraham and Straus Department Store in Huntington, Georgetown Manor on Route 110 in Melville and on Jericho Turnpike at the North Shore Design, a purveyor of upscale furniture, accessories, and design service. While doing all of this, she did manage to complete the curriculum at the Wilsey Institute of Interior Design.

I particularly remember her job at the Bakery because there was many a Sunday while she was at work that we would be visited by some of these surprise guests. If it was a money short week, I very often called Jean at the bakery before she came home; Sunday being her payday; to ask her to pick up a case of beer or something else for the guests. It was difficult getting ahead financially at that time but neither of us ever wanted to make any guest feel unwelcome in our house. In the end, we survived quite well.

**TWO COCKER SPANIEL
PUPS, INDIANA, 1954**

**OUR CABIN ON LAKE JAMES,
INDIANA, 1954**

**(l. to r.) DAD, HELEN, MARY
DAN & MARY WEDDING 1952**

**JACK ON CAMPUS AT TRI-STATE
1956**

**JACK WITH ANDY McMILLAN
AT NORDENS 1956**

**JACK AND RANNY
1956**

**JACK
FLUSHING, 1959**

**JEAN AND RANNY AT
PENNER LAKE PARK, NEW JERSEY
1959**

MR. AND MRS. JOHN J. O'LEARY
SEPTEMBER 12, 1959

JEAN, 1959

PATTI AND RANNY, 1861

**PATTI, EILEEN, RANNY
CHRISTMAS 1964**

**PATTI THE BALLERINA
1965**

EASTER, 1966

CHRISTMAS, 1966

FAMILY TREK TO SUBURBIA

We were not the first family members to move out onto Long Island. The slow exodus from the city began in the mid 1950's when Helen and Lee purchased a Cape Cod house in Hicksville in Nassau County.

Daddy and Mary followed a few years later with the sale of their house in Astoria. They bought a split level house in what was then part of Levittown. This section of Levittown became nationally known when it was featured in a best seller of the times, "The Status Seekers". Most of the previously constructed homes in Levittown were inexpensive homes built without basements after World War II to provide an opportunity for returning servicemen to afford a home of their own. These homes proved to be very popular and started a mass movement of families from the city to suburbia over the next twenty years.

The development of houses that Dad and Mary bought into was significantly more upscale than the preponderance of homes surrounding them. Most of the new homeowners did not want to be associated with the 'common folk' in Levittown and petitioned the United States Post Office for a mailing address and zip code in Wantagh. It took some time, but the

Post Office finally came through and designated this limited area as part of North Wantagh with the same mailing zip code as Wantagh. They were still part of the Levittown (Island Trees) School District but they were content that they would no longer have to be associated with the riff-raff by virtue of their address.

Fran and Marilyn were the next to make the journey east when they purchased a Cape Cod house in Massapequa Park as a joint ownership with Marilyn's parents, Bill and Gert Ryan. Our move from Bayside followed some time after that and it wasn't too long before Danny and Agnes decided to leave their apartment in Astoria to buy a house in East Meadow into which they moved their family along with Agnes' widowed mother, Ellen Gibney (who all of us affectionately called 'Grandma' Gibney'.)

Bob was living at the time in Ridgewood with his first wife, Peggy. After their childless marriage ended in an amiable divorce, it was some time before Bob married Tina and they moved to Central Islip in Suffolk County. The area of Islip Town that they lived in would incorporate as the Village of Islandia after they moved from their first home, a condominium, to a single family house nearby where they would raise their three girls, my goddaughter Doreen, Brenda, and Erin; and where Tina would pass away in 1993 after a long bout with cancer.

Marilyn and Donald and their seven children would spend a few short years in Hempstead before Donald and Marilyn went their separate ways and Marilyn moved back to Queens. She returned to residency in Nassau County after all of the children had grown and left home, and eventually took up permanent residence in Florida.

On Jean's side of the family, her mother and father made their first move to Long Island well after most of the O'Leary's had established residence in the suburbs. Their first house was a small place in Farmingville which they soon exchanged for a lovely little house in Bay Park in Nassau County; a house close to the water. After Jean's father died, her mother, Rita, spent a couple of years sharing an apartment near the water in Bay Ridge, Brooklyn with her sister, Vera. When Vera died, Rita came back to Nassau County to take an apartment in the Town of Hempstead Senior Housing in Wantagh, where she lived until she passed away in 2004.

Jean's brother, Joe, who was a supervisor for the Metropolitan Transit Authority in New York City, moved to a house in Westbury with his first wife, Nancy; continuing to live there with his second wife, Sue and two of her children, Andrea and Billy. When Sue died, Joe remarried for the third time, sold the house and moved to another house in Westbury.

Jeans youngest brother, Steve, a retired New York City Police Captain, is the only immediate family member (other than some nephews and nieces) that still lives in New York City. He and his wife, Anna, a well known fashion designer, share a cooperative apartment on 57th Street near Sutton Place, not too far from the Queens Borough Bridge.

This migration of the family took place over the last fifty years. Although most of the next two generations have established their homes and jobs on Long Island, some of them are starting to move to other areas of the state and the country to make their lives.

SEWING THE POLITICAL SEEDS

I was not into any political activity at all (other than as an armchair political philosopher) before moving out to Long Island in 1962. The closest I came to any intent to actively participate in the political arena was when I was a boy of less than ten years of age and told Mother that someday I would be President of the United States; after all, isn't it true, as we believed then, that anyone can become President of the United States? Other than that childhood foray into fantasy, my only connection with anything political was that I registered to vote and enrolled as a Democrat in Queens in 1959; never giving any thought to why I chose that party other than that Daddy was a Democrat and a union man and I thought that it was appropriate to follow the lead of the patriarch of the family.

The first Presidential election that I voted in was in 1960 when I voted for Richard Nixon, a Republican. Although I didn't give it much thought at the time, I believe my inclinations were away from the Roosevelt New Deal, and his successors, and to a government more directed toward the individual's right to care for himself. This tendency toward conservative thinking was influenced by my spare time reading prior to that time.

In the little time I had for other things, between establishing myself as an Engineer in a struggling young company and doing the domestic thing with home and family, I did as much serious reading as I could - not too many fiction novels and primarily books on economics, philosophy, and government. The writings of Russell Kirk, particularly "The Conservative Mind", introduced me to traditional conservatism and an appreciation for the "permanent" things. Bill Buckley, with his "God and Man at Yale", opened my mind to the shortcomings of the liberalism that dominated our national politics and universities.

My economic literary diet consisted of large servings of Henry Hazlitt, Frederick Hayek, and Ludwig von Mises – later desserts would be served up by Milton Friedman. I did not ignore opposing theories and Kenneth Galbraith's, "The New Industrial State" proved interesting while not convincing.

M. Stanton Evans, Frank Meyer, and other of the contemporary conservative writers were also on the menu; and, of course, one of the most influential books of the time, "The Conscience of a Conservative", by Barry Goldwater, who would be the Republican Candidate for President in 1964.

By the time we moved to Plainview the roots of activism were being further sown through intra-family discussions about the state of the state, the nation, and the world; conversations that were usually facilitated and enhanced by a few beers shared during those long nights that found us on many occasions greeting the rising sun in the morning. These discussions intensified after 1962 when I became a homeowner and more sensitive to the growing tax burden in suburbia.

It was at that time that my brother Bob, a regular weekend visitor at our new home, had become very active with the about to be established Conservative Party of New York State, which was being formed by a group of conservatives led by J. Daniel Mahoney and his brother-in-law Kieran

O'Doherty in reaction to the Republican Party's radical turn to the left after the election of liberal Nelson Rockefeller as Governor in 1958.

Now, in 1962 with assistance from William Buckley, publisher of the leading conservative magazine National Review, and several other prominent conservatives, Mahoney and O'Doherty initiated the statewide effort to place a candidate on the ballot for Governor by getting sufficient signatures on designating petitions for that purpose; a formidable task at which they proved to be eminently successful, to the chagrin and active opposition of Governor Rockefeller and the Republican Party.

David Jacquith, a prominent business man from upstate New York agreed to run for Governor as the candidate of the fledgling party. If the party was successful in getting more than 50 thousand votes in the race for Governor in the November elections, the party would have a permanent place on the ballot and be an officially recognized party; at least for the next four years until the next election for governor.

[The early history of the founding and the rapid growth of the Conservative Party during the first five years from 1962 to 1967 can be found in the spellbinding book, "Actions Speak Louder" by founding father, J. Daniel Mahoney, Arlington House, New Rochelle, New York, 1968.]

Brother Bob had married in September of the previous year to Peggy Carpenter. At the time, Bob was driving a truck for the Consolidated Laundry Company. Peggy was the sister of John Carpenter, Bob's foreman at Consolidated.

Foregoing a formal wedding and reception, Bob and Peggy eloped and married, and then returned to New York to start their new life in an apartment in Ridgewood in Queens County. This community would prove to be one of the hotbeds of conservative discontent and a prime source of the early support of the new conservative party. Bob was one of the early proselytes and became active with and an official of the newly formed Alexander Hamilton Conservative

Club in Ridgewood. (This is the club that would later help to elect the first Conservative State Assemblywoman, Rosemary Gunning Moffett not too long after the party had won its permanent place on the ballot.)

Bob tried to interest me in joining the conservatives but I had a full plate at the time. I had recently taken over the new position as Chief Mechanical Engineer at Powertronics and with our move to a new house in Plainview; I did not have the time or the inclination to get involved with the conservatives although I sympathized with their seemingly quixotic goals.

In addition, I had been recently introduced to the local Plainview Republican club by Frank Rausch, our next door neighbor who was a block captain for the local County Committeemen and who was himself to be a Republican Committeeman in the not too distant future. I joined the club and resolved to find some time to participate actively with these local Republicans. In the fall of 1962, our first year in Plainview, I volunteered my services to the club's finance committee. Our first fund raising event was a Halloween costume party at the American Legion Hall on Southern Parkway. I immediately felt at home with most of the members and before that election season was over I had agreed to be a block captain for Gus Maggio and Al Schupp who were the County Committeemen for our election district.

(Unlike Mahoney, O'Doherty, and their followers, I still had not yet found the disillusionment with Nelson Rockefeller or the State Republican Party and had even participated in a campaign rally for the Governor held at the old Long Island Arena in Commack in October. I was introduced to Rockefeller at the rally and this would be my last personal contact with him until a dozen years later when he was Vice President under then President Gerald Ford.)

The first four years after we moved into our new home were to be extraordinary ones politically. In March of 1962 there was a huge rally at Madison Square Garden sponsored by one of the more active conservative groups, the Young Americans for Freedom. The rally featured Barry Goldwater as the main speaker and the Garden was filled with enthusiastic conservatives to hear this Arizona Senator who was being touted as a potential candidate for President in 1964. The size of the crowd in a liberal state portended well for the new conservative party that was being started in New York.

In November of 1963, President John Kennedy was assassinated during a motorcade in Dallas, Texas; a terrible tragedy for the nation; but equally bad for the country was the accession of Lyndon Johnson to the presidency and the introduction of the vast spending programs of the "Great Society" including Medicare, the largest spending program ever introduced by the federal government.

Another major event in 1963 was the march on Washington by a crowd of about 300,000 demanding equal rights for black citizens. It was at this march that Martin Luther King delivered his famous, "I have a dream..." speech. By the end of 1963, the number of American troops in Vietnam had increased to 15,000 (by the end of 1964 this would increase further to over 100,000 troops after the Congress passed the Tonkin Gulf resolution authorizing Presidential action in Vietnam. By the end of 1966 there were nearly 400,000 American troops engaged.)

An activist Supreme Court was busy in those years declaring prayer in school as being unconstitutional, backing the one-man, one-vote obligation on the states in apportioning their legislatures, while the Congress was passing the 1964 Civil Rights Act and other ground breaking legislation.

The nation and the world were in a radical transition in those years. I felt that the Democrat Party under Lyndon Johnson was on the wrong path and I was looking forward to the 1964 Presidential election and a Republican candidacy by Barry Goldwater, who was leading the national conservative charge. At the time I felt that I could best serve this cause by remaining as a member of the Republican Party.

Goldwater did get the nomination for President in 1964 but was abandoned by the Rockefeller Republicans in New York and in the end lost the election in a national Johnson landslide. One of the highlights of the Goldwater campaign was an historic speech by Ronald Reagan on behalf of the Goldwater candidacy, which speech helped Reagan to become a principal national spokesman for the conservative cause.

I was greatly disappointed in 1964 by the lack of support of the local Republicans for their presidential candidate and it was the start of a disillusionment that would end with my inevitable break from the party.

With Johnson's election as President to a full four year term and the return of a Democrat Congress, and the expansion of the Great Society, as Johnson's radical changes to government were infamously called, the country was moving rapidly toward a more socialistic, welfare state. I was deeply disturbed by this further leftward drift of the nation but was so involved in trying to get our company, Powertronics, off the ground that I had little time to join in the growing conservative movement that was developing across the land.

Bob, and his bride, Peggy, continued to join us on most weekends and Bob's zeal for the successful new Conservative Party was starting to persuade me that the new party had much to offer as an alternative to the existing power structure. The race for Mayor in New York City in 1965 where the Conservative Party was represented by William F. Buckley, Jr. gained nationwide attention for the young party when Buckley garnered over 341,000 votes, outpolling the Liberal Party with over 13 percent of the total vote cast. The Conservative Party enrollment was growing and the party would continue to be a major player in State and local politics in New York for the next forty years.

I had not yet made the move to change my enrollment when Bob made a suggestion that was bound to shake up the hierarchy in the Conservative Party for the next few weeks.

MEANWHILE, BACK AT THE OFFICE

As I was going through my political metamorphosis, Powertronics was going through a very trying period. Over the preceding three or four years we had managed to win some very interesting contracts; none of them led to the hoped for production orders and an improved bottom line, but engineering wise, we were accomplishing some pretty spectacular technical achievements.

In 1966 we were winding up what was our major program up to that time. We had designed, developed, built, and were now delivering a high performance flight simulation table that was to be a key part in the nation's mission to land a man on the moon before the end of the decade; a goal set out so eloquently by President John F. Kennedy before he was assassinated in Dallas in 1963. We designed the FAT (Flight Attitude Table) under contract to Grumman Aerospace, Corporation of Bethpage, Long Island who were the prime contractors to build the Lunar Module which was destined to land on the moon in 1969.

At about this time, our parent company, The Hydrapower Corporation, was taken over by the Teledyne Corporation, a company whose primary raison d'être was the acquisition of smaller companies such as ours and with an insatiable appetite they were rapidly becoming a major conglomerate. Although Powertronics was not the Teledyne target, as a subsidiary to Hydrapower we were included as a part of the deal.

The consensus of our Powertronic staff was that this new circumstance put us in a very tenuous position. We had expanded staff with the increasing workload over the past couple of years, particularly the Grumman simulator contract, but at the time of the Teledyne takeover we seemed to be headed into a business slowdown. We knew that we would have to show an improved performance for the new masters and logically presumed that if we didn't, we would be closing the doors. There were several proposals out for new business but the new management would be sure to want *real* contracts in house. We didn't know what kind of assurances they would require to prove ourselves to them and we were, therefore, very apprehensive about the future

(This new arrangement had at least one side benefit for Herb Berman and me. As the key management personnel in our small company, the two of us, along with Milton Cohen, Harry Schwartz, and Jim Giampapa from Hydrapower, had been granted stock options in the Hydrapower Corporation before the takeover by Teledyne. As part of the deal with Teledyne our stock options were converted to options in the Teledyne Corporation, a big board stock that was rapidly growing, with periodic stock splits. Under the stock plan, we could exercise 30 percent of the options in July of 1966, 30 percent in 1967 and the remainder in July of 1968.)

Because of the insecurity that all of us felt under this new regime, some of the employees were looking for other employment, while others were exploring a second job as a hedge against the future. Harry Grossman, for instance, got involved with a California company called "Holiday Magic", a distributor of a line of cosmetics that was marketed at home parties. Opportunities were available at many different levels and the rewards were purportedly proportional to the level of entry and the amount of money invested.

The base level was as a salesperson, doing the direct selling at home parties. This required no investment, except in time for training, and realized the smallest commissions.

The next level up was as an organizer or manager of a group of salespeople, which required a small investment of about one hundred dollars. The supposed potential of this position was only limited by one's ability to recruit new sales personnel.

Level three was as a Master Distributor which required an investment of 2500 dollars for cosmetic stock at a substantial discount resulting in a high commission on sales for the Master Distributor. Organizers answered to the Master Distributor and had to purchase stock through the MD.

At the top of the hierarchy was the General Distributor who not only received the largest wholesale discount but was also entitled to a stipend of 5000 dollars from those Master Distributors aspiring to buy out and move up to their own general distributorship.

Harry bought in as a Master Distributor and encouraged me to attend one of the high pressure recruiting seminars in the evening in Manhattan. After listening to the rosy picture that was painted for us by the high pressure salesmen, and with a feeling that I had not much to lose, I joined up as an organizer and started to recruit salespeople to work in my group. Jean was my most diligent volunteer and immediately started to present cosmetic demonstrations in the homes of friends and neighbors..

After a month or two of purchasing necessary stock, which included even the forms for ordering the stock, and with a respectable coterie of workers, I finished the first months activity netting as a profit a grand total of eighty cents (and this only by including Jean's sales into the calculation.) This new endeavor was obviously not going to work for me. In fact, the only ones that made money on this scheme were the schemers at the top, who made their money by selling *distributorships,_*

Harry would also eventually retire from the cosmetic business, particularly after discovering that many of the people using the cosmetics were getting severe allergic reactions and rashes.

With the shadow of an uncertain future hanging over my head and particularly with some of the unwise management decisions being made by Herb Berman for Powertronics, I was primed for a new adventure when in August of 1966 Bob made an extraordinary proposal that I was easily persuaded to consider.

STARTING AT THE TOP

The summer of 1966 was an unusually hot one. Bob and Peggy visited us quite a bit that season to escape the heat of the city. Our political discussions became more spirited: the animation of the debate being directly proportional to the amount of beer consumed. Bob was continuously waxing ecstatic about the Conservative Party and as the party's fortunes improved dramatically in the four years since it established itself as a recognized party in the state; he had become one of the most active members in Queens County. He gave us regular updates on the party activities in the state and was greatly concerned that summer about the upcoming party convention which was to be held in Saratoga Springs in September to nominate a candidate for Governor of New York State in that year's election.

It was mid-August when Bob told me that the party leaders, Dan Mahoney and Kieran O'Doherty, had still not been able to find a suitable candidate for governor and that the convention was to be held on September 7th. (This was the last year that statewide candidates were selected by party delegates elected for that purpose at a primary election that was held in June. Since

1966, statewide candidate designations have been made by a meeting of the State Committee or by designating petitions. Bob was an elected delegate to this convention.)

During one of our weekend exchanges in August, Bob said that what the party needs to run for Governor is some *new blood*; someone who has not run for office before but who could bring to the race some executive experience in the private sector, someone fresh and young, who could appeal to the overburdened taxpayers of the state who had lost confidence in the professional politicians and would eagerly support a man *of the people*. It didn't take him much longer to suggest that I would make a great candidate for the Conservatives for Governor in the 1966 election, and as they had no one ready to go with only about three or four weeks left before the convention, he could probably get a majority of the delegates support my candidacy. I, of course, told him that he was a dreamer and that I had no desire to take on that burden.

After prolonged discussion; and a few more beers, I began to see some merit in Bob's proposal. I asked Bob if he could get me an interview with Dan Mahoney and the State Committee to discuss the possibility of such a candidacy. Before the night was over Bob had agreed to write a letter to Mahoney and offer my services to the party. Bob wrote a strong letter on my behalf, which elicited no response from Mahoney but in a follow-up telephone call by Bob to Marty Burgess, the Executive Director of the State Party, a meeting was arranged between Burgess and me for early that week at the party headquarters in New York City.

The Conservative Party Headquarters office was located at 141 East 44th Street in Manhattan. I arrived on time for my appointment with Burgess. The office was a single small room accommodating two desks along adjacent walls; one for Executive Director and the other for a secretary. The desks and what may have been a couple of small tables were piled high with papers and campaign paraphernalia and it appeared that very little, if anything was filed in any orderly fashion.

Marty was the only one occupying the office at the time so we would have a private conversation to discuss the possibility of my candidacy. He moved a stack of papers from a chair alongside his desk and asked me to sit. From the outset, Marty was adamantly against my candidacy and didn't hesitate to let me know. It was evident that he was speaking on behalf of Dan Mahoney in discouraging my attempt to run.

We discussed money for the campaign (of which, I had none) and the fact that as an unknown with no experience there would not be any support for such a candidacy. He made a special point of noting that I was not an enrolled Conservative and that they would prefer not to run a Republican.

I suggested to Marty that, if I could show a broad base of support amongst the general electorate that he seriously consider my candidacy as being viable. As I sat there, the thought came to my mind how I could accomplish this. I told Burgess that within two weeks I would have his desk piled high with letters of support as an indication of the seriousness of my candidacy. He politely said that I could try to accomplish this but that he doubted if it would avail anywhere near the support I would need in a Statewide race.

I left the office, having formulated a plan in my mind of how to get a letter writing campaign underway.

I called Bob that evening and laid out my scheme. We would start a telephone chain calling campaign asking everyone we know to write a letter to the Conservative headquarters in support of my candidacy, and each of these callers in turn would call as many of their friends and relatives in New York as possible, and to do this immediately as time was very short. The convention was not even a month away.

I was stunned by the positive response that we received when we started this phone chain. Everyone that we called enthusiastically supported my attempts to wrest the nomination, and with few exceptions made many calls to their friends and relatives. The campaign was underway and letters started to pour into State Headquarters which must have had them quite perplexed. Everyone I know pitched in with enthusiastic passion; friends, family members, neighbors, co-workers, and friends of these friends. My brother Danny stationed himself outside St. Raphael's Church in East Meadow on Sundays to get the parishioners to sign on to the campaign. He was surprisingly successful and had a good part of the parish signed up before we finished this effort.

As we closed in on the day of the convention there was still no serious opposition and Mahoney and O'Doherty were still trying to put together a statewide ticket; but they would not even speak to me. Bob and I decided that, if we could elicit so much support in such a short time and without even discussing the issues I would be running on, that perhaps there really was a silent majority out there waiting to pull the lever for a fresh face for Governor. We discussed carrying the fight upstate to the convention floor and decided that if we can get some initial support from some of his local party comrades, we would go all the way to Saratoga Springs.

Bob set up a meeting between me and Serphin Maltese, his local Ridgewood leader, and another meeting with Ted Dabrowski, the Queens County Conservative Chairman. Maltese was friendly and non-committal, but also not disparaging of my effort. Dabrowski, on the other hand was strongly supportive and, I believe in his own mischievous way, he thought that an outside challenge to the leadership would be a fitting way to protest what was developing as a regime that was becoming too autocratic and not open to reasonable suggestions by top leaders such as he himself. Dabrowski was not supporting my candidacy as much as he was trying to send a message to Mahoney and O'Doherty about the way they were attempting to leave other leaders and workers out of the decision making process.

Through Bob's efforts, I started to receive some significant support from Conservatives who were delegates to the convention and decided to pull out all of the stops to get the nomination for governor.

Warren "Putsy" Finley and Ernie Schoof, good friends of Bob's, who worked in a New York City advertising firm, volunteered to create campaign posters and flyers for the convention. We had the flyers printed up in large quantities and would use these at the convention and in a mailing prior to the convention to solicit both physical support and financial contributions.

I reserved a suite of rooms at the convention hotel in Saratoga Springs for Bob and me, and we decided to arrive before most of the delegates so that we could be there to greet them as they arrived. Through Jane and Ellen Dostal, Sunrise Street neighbors, I had arranged to have a large number of the neighborhood high school girls attend the convention and was arranging for a bus to transport them to the convention hall. We were preparing to provide them with uniforms and 'O'Leary for Governor' sashes and signs, but this whole effort fell through when they realized that the Convention was mid-week in September and this was also the first week of school.

This mid-week scheduling of the convention also discouraged some of our many supporters from attending as they didn't want to lose a day's work. In the end, our campaign entourage consisted of Bob and me, and a lot of campaign signs – and a lot of balls.

At the office, when I went to Herb Berman's office to tell him that I would be taking two or three days off to attend the nominating convention upstate, he seemed to be a bit upset. He was aware of my effort to get the Conservative Party nomination and had even sent a letter of support on my behalf; although he would not participate in the telephone campaign effort. He pleaded with me, that if I did not receive the nomination at the convention not to accept a spot on the ticket as the candidate for Lieutenant Governor. I assured him that I had no intentions to and that I planned to go all the way.

Bob and I arrived at the Holiday Inn in Saratoga Springs about noon on September 6th. We were assigned a suite of two large rooms on the second floor overlooking the courtyard which was the first thing that was seen upon entering the front entrance to the hotel. We could not have been better situated. The two large windows in the suite were prime locations for our large "O'Leary for Governor" signs, which would be the first thing to greet the delegates as they arrived later that day and the following morning. This was quite an unexpected bonus, especially for the low rate that we were paying for the entire suite, 37 dollars a day for the two of us.

The convention did not start until the next day and our plan was to entertain and talk to as many delegates as we could accommodate in our suite and to visit the many county delegations that were sponsoring their own hospitality suites. Most of the delegates would be arriving before evening and some would only be making a one day trip for the convention and would not be there on the eve of the convention.

The first thing we did after stowing our gear and hanging the signs in the window was to purchase our hospitality supplies: booze, beer, soda and mixes, and snacks. After preparing the room for guests, Bob went to the lobby to invite some of the early arrivals to join us in the suite for cocktails and conversation. On one of his first contacts, Bob found out that Mahoney had settled upon a candidate that he would be recommending to the delegates the next day; Paul Adams, the President of Roberts Wesleyan College, a small college of about 600 students in Rochester. Dean Adams was a Republican who had been recommended by the Monroe County Chairman, Leo Kesselring.

Now that the leaders had decided on a candidate our task was to take our case directly to the delegates at the caucuses that would be going on that entire evening. During our rounds of the delegations we discovered that a third candidate had entered the race, Donald Serrell of Garden City, another Nassau candidate but the only enrolled Conservative of the three contenders.

As I presented my credential to each group that we spoke to, I started to pick up much delegate support from across the state. I believe much of the support was forthcoming because of a discontent amongst the delegates for the same reason as Ted Dabrowski; they felt that they had been left out of the decision making process and did not want to just rubber stamp the Mahoney dictated candidate.

The first major support came from the Onondaga County delegation and before I left their suite they pledged the support of the entire County delegation for tomorrow's first vote. With each delegation we spoke to, I was beginning to believe that, if we had enough time to meet the majority of the delegates before the convening of the convention, we had a good shot at getting the nod.

I met Dean Adams briefly during the evening and from our brief conversation I concluded that he was a personable man of character and intelligence and could well represent the party if nominated. However, at this point I had started to amass a respectable amount of support from many individuals and after a visit with the Queens County delegation had the support of Ted Dabrowski and his group.

As we made the rounds, it soon became apparent that Dean Adams was far from having a majority vote lined up even though he was the selection of the Mahoney crowd. The other candidate, Donald Serrell, was picking up a lot of support from some of the more zealous Conservative because he was the only one of the three who had enrolled in the Party.

I became aware during the course of the night that Serrell had turned off many of the delegates because he was too 'extreme'. He was reportedly a member of the John Birch Society which had been attempting to take over local party organizations across the state much to the chagrin of Mahoney and the more moderate majority of the party.

Our estimate of the support for the three candidates at the end of a long evening that ended for us at about 3 A.M. before we returned to the suite, was that Adams was ahead in delegates but was short of the necessary majority. Serrell and I were about even at this point and he may have even had a slight advantage with his Conservative enrollment. At one point during the evening, Joe Hayes, a confidant of Serrell and also a Garden City Conservative, approached me sometime after midnight as we chanced on each other in the hall between caucuses. While Serrell entered the room, Hayes collared me to ask me how things are going; he was obviously nervous about his own candidates showing and did not disguise this too well.

When I told Hayes my assessment at this point and indicated that while I think his candidate has picked up some support, he will never get a majority tomorrow. We both realized that if Adams were to be stopped, Serrell and I would have to join forces and one of us would have to step aside. I indicated to Hayes that I was in this to the end, win or lose. Hayes then proposed that I throw my support to Mason Hampton for Lieutenant Governor and he, Hayes, would get most of the Serrell contingent to back me for Governor. At this point I simply requested that Hayes bring Hampton around after the vote and declined his offer of support.

(I believe at this point, I was beginning to question whether or not I should be in the race at all. Although I was rapidly picking up on the issues and garnering a great deal of support, I was really wet behind the ears and had gotten caught up in the enthusiasm of the contest without evaluating all of the ramifications in time and money. I had a wonderful time running and met many wonderful, serious, and like minded people from across the state. Before we went to sleep that night, Bob and I sat in the room and I expressed some of my misgivings about the race.

After we left everyone for the night and returned alone to our room, Bob and I could hear many of the delegates debating the merits of the three candidates in the hall, in loud voices. We eavesdropped through the closed door.

Dean Adams seemed to have some support and was liked by most of the people who met him. However, his Republican enrollment was a problem for some and, though it had nothing to do with qualifications, there seemed to be agreement that with his mustache that someone offered "makes him look like Hitler", his appearance would militate against him.

On the other hand, there was general agreement amongst these 'hallway' delegates, that Serrel was a 'kook' and would prove to be an embarrassment for the party.

The assessment of me that came through the closed door was, inexperienced and a Republican; but probably a good candidate for the future.

All in all, I went to sleep that night knowing that I had done my best; had taken a Cinderella candidacy and made it appear viable, and tomorrow would be going into the convention with a respectable amount of support; perhaps enough to deadlock the convention on the first vote.

After breakfast early the next morning, I received a call from Ted Dabrowski. He wanted me to come to his suite to speak to the Queens County delegation before the convention was called to order by the chairman. Because Ted had turned into one of my biggest sources of support and guidance, I went right over to the room where I found the entire delegation from Queens in caucus, including many of that morning's arrivals.

Ted said that he had laid out his evaluation of the likely convention vote on the first ballot based on his discussions with most of the delegations. As we had also concluded, Paul Adams had the most votes going in but was well short of a majority. Serrell and I were even with neither of us likely to win on the first ballot. The problem as Dabrowski saw it was that if we have a deadlock on the first ballot with no majority winner, many of the Adams supporters and O'Leary supporters would be switching their votes to Serrell, because he was the only enrolled Conservative of the three, and that there was the possibility of Serrell's walking off with the nod for governor; a result that none of the Queens delegation wanted to see.

Ted proposed that I drop from the race before the first ballot and throw my delegate support to Paul Adams who everyone would feel comfortable with as the candidate. After all the effort I had put in, I was reluctant to just drop out without an opportunity to present myself.

515

Ted then proposed that I release my pledged delegates and that I would be put in nomination as the "Favorite Son" candidate for Queens County and that a nominal vote would be cast on the first ballot if not needed to assure Adams' first ballot majority. My votes would come from the Assembly district delegations led by Serphin Maltese and Rosemary Gunning, two of the party's upcoming stars.

After having met most of the delegates and starting to get a finer appreciation of the Conservative Party and its people, I did not want to be in the position of a 'spoiler' that would only lead to many good people being erroneously led into an election with a Serrell at the head of the ticket. I thanked Ted and the Queens delegation for their support and agreed to join in their plan. Gene Agoglia, a Ridgewood Conservative was selected to make the favorite son nominating speech. (I had prepared a nominating speech for Bob to deliver but Bob was happy to make the seconding nomination and let Agoglia do the nomination speech.)

The convention was called to order and after the preliminary business was conducted, a party platform was unanimously adopted with little debate. As was customary, because I was a candidate about to be nominated for the position of Governor of the State of New York, I stepped out of the main auditorium to listen to the nominating speeches from outside the hall. When the nominating speeches were completed, I assumed that the only order of business left was the casting of the votes so I decided to take a stroll around the grounds outside to get some fresh air and to return after the votes were cast.

I was in the courtyard when Bob caught up with me. He seemed to be in a very agitated state. He testily asked me, "Where the hell have you been"? "They're looking for you inside."

I said that I was just getting some air. Bob told me that someone made a motion to have each of the three nominees address the convention. I was not prepared for this. I am not much of a public speaker and even when well prepared would not ever be considered a William Jennings Bryan.

I asked, "When will I have to make this speech?" hoping that at best I would be the last one to speak.

Bob said, "Right now, they're introducing you now." He said this as we walked toward the door of the auditorium and I heard them announcing my name.

At first I didn't know what to do or what to say; I was very ill prepared and public speaking, again, was not my forte.

I remembered that I had written Bob's nominating speech which he didn't use. I asked if he had it. He had it in his pocket and I asked him to give it to me quickly, which he did. I figured that the words that I used in the nominating speech could be quickly turned around while I was reading it from the podium and be adjusted on the fly to have something comprehensible and meaningful to say.

As we entered the room to polite applause at the conclusion of the introduction, I was directed to the front of the room to a raised platform and speaker's lectern. I stepped up on the platform and noticed that the rear of the room was covered with movie and television cameras and bright floodlights. I had never been before this large an audience nor in front of so many cameras which seemed to me to be an infinite number of evil eyes.

My throat was parched and my knees wouldn't stay still. The sweat dripping down my face, I feared would be in my eyes so that I wouldn't be able to see the handwritten speech that I had to rely on.

Somehow, I managed to get the words flowing from my mouth. I mentally edited the written speech as I read slowly. The speech had all the platitudes about the great things that I would do for the state but I had to adapt the words on the spot to reflect "I will..." instead of "He will..." which would have been Bob's delivered version.

It seemed to me to be hours, but I'm sure the entire speech was no more than about ten minutes. When finished, I quickly left the stand as with a flick of the hand I acknowledged the polite applause from the delegates. Someone was kind enough to say to me as I walked to the rear, though with not too much conviction, that it was a good speech. I was just glad that it was over and for the first time was truly happy that the day was going to end the way it was planned with the Queens delegation that morning; without me as the nominee.

After the vote was taken, with Serph Maltese and Rosemary Gunning voting for me along with the delegates from their Assembly Districts, Paul Adams was declared the nominee after the first ballot with 238 votes. Donald Serrell got 68 votes, and I had my token vote of 12 votes. I had earlier spoken to the delegates that had pledged their support to me and had released them with the encouragement to vote for Adams, which most of them did.

The rest of this race is history. Governor Nelson Rockefeller was reelected by a large majority against the Democrat Frank O'Connor. Paul Adams made an outstanding race and got over 500,000 votes, beating out the Liberal Party Candidate, Franklin Roosevelt, Jr. and wresting the third row on the ballot from the Liberal Party. After only four years, the Conservative Party was the number three political party in the state and a force to be reckoned with in the future.

As for me, after returning home and back to work and the family, I enrolled immediately in the Conservative Party. After meeting with so many like minded conservatives, I felt that I had at last found a political home. I got as active as possible in the campaign on behalf of Paul Adams and joined the Hicksville Conservative Club which was just being organized by Leroy Sluder. (In three more years I would take over as Chairman of that club and one of the first things that I did was change the name to the Mid-Island Conservative Club to reflect the general geographic area within the clubs jurisdiction; including the communities of Hicksville, Plainview, Bethpage, Old Bethpage and Jericho and, later on the entire Town of Oyster Bay.)

(Oh! One of the first things I did after the Saratoga Springs convention was to enroll in a Public Speaking course at the Bethpage High School adult evening program.)

A RETURN TO REALITY

Now that my unsuccessful attempt to get the Conservative Party nomination for Governor was behind me, it was time to put all of my energies and expertise into making Powertronic Systems a profitable venture. We had a remarkable staff that was working together as a well oiled machine. We had a history of some very important advances in the state of the art in many of our delivered systems and there were many opportunities available for future contracts. We had the support of Teledyne and Hydrapower, who were anxious to see us succeed; but we didn't know how long they would be willing to carry us until we showed a decent profit.

The only impediment that we had in realizing our potential growth was our own management at Powertronics. By fiat, we wasted an enormous amount of resources on some of what I call *Herb's Follies*. One of these was Herb's insistence on breaking into the 'Flight Attitude Table' business; an area of the industry that had a very limited market and which already had at least two companies that were well established and had pretty well locked up that restricted market.

One of the federal government agencies had issued a request for proposal (RFP) for a Flight Attitude Table, which was advertised in the Business Commerce Daily that we regularly consulted for the latest business opportunities. We requested the RFP and upon reading the specifications it was obvious that the contract was geared precisely to one of the advertised catalog items that had already been developed by another company. Herb insisted that we devote all of our resources to getting this contract even if we have to forego any profit on the job so that we can get a foot in the door of that business.

This was a nearly impossible task, but after voicing our united objections and being overruled, we did our best to come up with a proposal that would meet the customer's requirements and would undercut the price that we knew the preferred vendor was charging for the equipment. Whereas the competition had already put his development costs behind him, we would be starting out from scratch. Herb felt, erroneously in my mind, that our experience with the Flight Table for Grumman gave us an edge on this job.

In the end, with fingers crossed, we submitted a proposal that did cut the price below the competition. This put the customer in a bit of a bind as they had already selected who they would be issuing the contract to, so they decided to recall the RFP and ask for a resubmittal with much tighter requirements. We became aware that the competition had already developed the next generation equipment and was prepared to deliver to the new specifications in the short delivery schedule requested. After finally realizing that this job was already pre-slated for one specific company, Herb finally agreed to throw in the towel. In the meantime, we had lost most of the time we needed to impress our new masters and had also turned down other proposals in which we had a good chance to be successful.

In the meantime, we did spend some time on a proposal for a portable and lightweight weather radar system for the United States Army. The initial contract would be for the development prototype and, as a piece of universal field equipment, would be going into production after the successful demonstration of the prototype. The first year's production would be for 100 systems for about 3 million dollars with future orders of 5 to 10 million dollars a year.

Because of the lightweight, weather-ability, and other unique problems, there were many difficult technical questions to be resolved, particularly in the Mechanical Design area; the electronic control problems being fairly straightforward. I came up with solutions to all of the problems and this was the key to our success in getting the contract.

This was a job that we could accomplish and make a slight profit on and the production potential was enormous for our small company. After receiving the contract, Herb wanted to improve the profit margin, but we had estimated the job so closely that his interference threatened the success of the job. In spite of Herb's meddling, we put together a system that was readily accepted by the Army.

It was about this time, that Teledyne must have reviewed the performance of the company and decided to terminate our activities. We closed the doors at the end of May in 1967 with Teledyne paying off the employees with a modest termination pay of a few weeks pay. Herb and I were kept on as consultants on a retainer for three months to be available if there were any problems with the Weather Radar System we had just delivered. (This system, by the way, went into production by another company using our design for the expected 3 million dollar initial buy.)

I immediately started the search for a new position in the business. Several of Powertronics' competitors made substantial offers but I turned them down; I believed that each of them were more interested in picking my brain about Powertronics prior business than in fully using my engineering expertise.

I finally accepted a reasonable offer from Grumman Aerospace Corporation located in Bethpage, a short drive from my home in Plainview. I would be starting work in the Simulation Section of the Systems Engineering Department. George Mayer, who would be my boss in this new job, hired me to do all of the Mechanical Design work on a new Simulation Laboratory that he had proposed that would be built by Grumman for a gross expenditure of 50 million dollars and would be *the* leading facility of its type in the air and space industry. I was hired based on my experience with Grumman in the successful delivery of the FAT table. Grumman was familiar with my work and were most anxious to merge me into their operation.

(George Mayer's dream for this new, state of the art facility never came to fruition when the company decided not to spend that huge sum to build. While George left the company shortly after this rejection, I stayed and spent the next 26 years in the simulation end of the business at Grumman, working on every major program from the A6 Intruder and LEM, to the F-14 Tomcat Fighter, and many others along the way. Over twenty years after George Mayer left the company, Grumman would invest the Fifty Million dollars in an updated simulation facility and I would finally get to do the job I was hired for in 1967.)

After closing Powertronics in May I was out of work for six weeks before accepting and starting in the position; my longest period of unemployment while not attending school in over fifty years. I was further fortunate in accepting a position that did not require the hours of commuting that I had become accustomed to in all of my past engineering positions; I was now just minutes from home to the office. I now was home for dinner every night and most weekends and got to share more time with the kids who were now 11, 7, and 3. I also had more time to get involved in political activities, which would soon occupy much of my time. A different life was ahead of me and the family.

GRUMMAN AEROSPACE CORPORATION

After seven years of living on the edge at Powertronics, my initial introduction to Grumman seemed like the start of a long overdue vacation. George Mayer continued his unsuccessful quest to convince the company to build his proposed multi-million dollar simulation facility, while Harry Grossman and I were not given any meaningful assignments pending a management go ahead on designing the equipment we were hired to build. (Harry, another refugee from Powertronics, accepted a position at Grumman and started two weeks before me.)

Neither Harry nor I were accustomed to sitting around doing nothing but checking the stock market returns each day so we convinced Mayer that we should start the design of a large motion simulator that was part of the anticipated new facility. Harry assumed responsibility for the electronic design, while I tackled the Mechanical and Systems design. Harry and I had established a close working relationship at our previous job and, with this close rapport, we soon completed a cutting edge design for this state of the art motion device. It wouldn't be too long after the completion of this design that Mayer would learn that his proposal for the simulation facility had been rejected by the management because of its high cost and we would never get to test the viability of our design.

(As there was no pressure on getting this job completed, a luxury we were not used to, Harry and I took time during the day to discuss improvements we wanted to make to our homes. Harry had moved to Long Island shortly after we had started to live in Plainview; he bought a house near to us in Old Bethpage.

The result of this home improvement planning was that in early 1968, Jean and I undertook the first major renovation of our house in Plainview with the removal of the poorly constructed dormer from the house, which we replaced with a new second story addition. We gutted the two downstairs bedrooms and constructed a new den or family room and the entire family now moved to the new bedrooms on the second floor.)

At this time, I was assigned to work on the Orbiting Astronomical Observatory, or OAO, which Grumman was designing for the National Aeronautic and Space Administration (NASA). In the short time that I worked on the OAO before its launch into orbit in December 1968, I assisted in the design and development of the mechanisms used to deploy the satellites solar power panels and played the key role in the design of heat pipes to assure the temperature stability of the vehicle while in orbit.

It wasn't long before I went to work on the design of a simulation program to test out a new automatic carrier landing system (ACLS) for the A6A Intruder, an all weather fighter aircraft and a work horse of the Grumman inventory that had been flying for several years and would continue to serve even into the next century. I soon developed a reputation for the quick and successful completion of some of the most complex programs, and usually within an impossible budget. (As one of my colleagues, Jack McCullagh, so sagely observed, we were continuously being asked to; in his words; "make cake out of dog shit.")

Just prior to putting the finishing touches on the A6 simulator project in the spring 1970, I had to go to the Plainview Hospital to have my gall bladder removed; this would take me out of action for about six weeks. As all the major problems in setting up the simulation were already solved, there was no difficulty in turning the project over to another engineer for its successful completion.

(I had been suffering intermittently from these gall bladder pains for much of the previous two years. The old family retainer, Doctor Jacob Rand, had been treating me for a duodenal ulcer and for two years I had been instructed to avoid spicy foods, including tomato sauces on pasta, alcohol, and other possible ulcer irritants. As the pains were usually of short duration and did not occur daily, I assumed that I was progressing toward a cure.

When the pains became too intense and were occurring almost daily, I decided to seek a second opinion from a local internist. After a series of tests, gall stones were declared to be the cause of my distress and were removed at the Central General Hospital in Plainview on March 25, 1970. I remember the day well because it coincided with the 20th anniversary of Mother's death.)

THE CONSERVATIVE PARTY

When I returned from the Conservative Party convention in Saratoga Springs in September of 1966, I took the first steps in what would become a long ideological journey. The youthful party was only four years old but had already made a permanent impact on the politics of the state. The Buckley mayoralty race in New York City in 1965 and the wresting of the third line on the ballot from the Liberal Party in 1966 set the stage for even greater electoral successes for the fledgling party.

I became a dedicated adherent of the conservative cause and committed myself to work with the responsible leaders within the party to help further the party goals.

It was very difficult in those early days, however, to determine who the real, responsible leaders of the party were. Once the party took over the coveted Row C on the election machine, its newly acquired status made the party a target for every radical group or individual that saw an opportunity to assume a position of power or influence within the party to further their own personal agendas. The John Birch Society, a rabid anti-communist organization, was typical of those who attempted to take over the party, particularly at the local club level. The takeover attempts by these forces that were inimical to the goals of the party would occupy a great deal of the party's energy in its first decade. This distraction however did not stop the party from moving forward; the party was filling a void in New York's political arena and continued to attract more dedicated adherents.

My first focus of attention, of course, was to my new position at Grumman and the furtherance of my engineering career, but with my concern for the acceleration of the welfare state under Jack Kennedy, which was further exacerbated by the "Great Society" programs of the Johnson years, I determined to make my modest contribution to the conservative cause by working with the leadership of the party at the state and county level and, especially through working with the recently established local Conservative club in my home town.

Events were moving rapidly within the party after the auspicious vote for Governor realized by Paul Adams. In Nassau County, at the beginning of 1967, the Republican Party, under the leadership of Chairman Ed Speno who had previously prohibited his candidates from seeking or accepting Conservative Party endorsement, started to change its tune when they recognized the growing voting power of the Conservatives. In an attempt to ameliorate the anticipated effects of the vote on Row C in 1967, in the early part of that year Speno offered to support Mason Hampton, an enrolled Conservative attorney from Malverne, for the position of Nassau County Clerk. The price asked for this endorsement, however, was too much for the Conservative Executive Committee under the leadership of Chairman Jim Marrin,

Marrin speaking for the committee, after consultation with State Chairman Dan Mahoney, said that the Conservatives could not go along with a deal where there would be no fundamental change in the tax and spend proclivities of the two major parties and no future Conservative Party input into the policies of the County government just for an endorsement for a purely administrative post, the County Clerk. The Conservative Party decided to field its own candidate for Nassau County Executive; A Werner Pleus, a Plandome Attorney and a Harvard Graduate, against the Democrat incumbent, Eugene Nickerson, and the Republican challenger, Sol Wachtler, Supervisor of the Town of North Hempstead. It also ran a full slate of Conservative candidates for the other countywide races.

Speno was incensed that the Conservatives wouldn't go along with his proposed deal and prohibited his candidates from accepting the endorsement of the Conservatives. This Republican embargo of third party support effected only the Conservative Party and did not extend to the long established Liberal Party. Most of the Republicans in the Town of Oyster Bay accepted the endorsement of the Liberal Party while shunning the Conservatives. This included Ralph Marino, the Republican candidate for Supervisor, and the remainder of the Republican town ticket. The only exceptions were two renegade Republicans who went against the party dictates and accepted the endorsement of the Conservatives; Carl Grunewald who was running for the Oyster Bay Town Council and William Buckman, who was seeking a seat as a Trustee of the Jones Fund. The Conservative vote would prove to be the deciding vote in these two races in November.

The Pleus campaign was run on a shoe string, but running hard on the issues of taxpayer relief and a cut in government spending, he garnered over 57,000 votes in Nassau County, far exceeding any expectations from the political pundits. The Democrat, Gene Nickerson, won reelection by a slim margin and it was the Conservative vote that was instrumental in denying the election to Sol Wachtler. The Conservative vote also provided the margin of victory not only for Grunewald and Buckman but also helped to put two Democrats on the bench, David Gibbons to the County Court and Henry Kalinowski who was elected to the 4th District Court.

The party was now in a position to start seriously influencing the course of government; at least in many of the counties of the state, including Nassau, but the state government and the Republicans were still under the domination of Governor Nelson Rockefeller and his liberal wing of the Republican Party. At that time Rockefeller had his sights set on becoming President of the United States and was determined not to be foiled by the new thriving party that he, in a way, helped to found. (Many of us have sardonically referred to Rockefeller and Senator Jacob Javits as the 'founding fathers' of the Conservative Party – there wouldn't have been a party without them.)

If the party could now pull together as a cohesive unit, the future looked very bright. However, with success came a factionalizing into many disparate groups, each trying to dominate the party. 1968 would bring more successes but would also witness the start of party discord from many individuals who, heady with the accomplishments of the past five years, would now attempt to dictate the party's future. I continued to support Jim Marrin, the elected leader in Nassau, and worked with him in his attempt to maintain party discipline and unity during the troubled times ahead.

With the universal recognition of the party's rapidly growing strength in the State, it was probably inevitable that there would be many people who would take that new found esteem and attempt to use it for their own purposes; but for the nonce, Marrin was in control and had the support of most of the key leaders.

In late 1967, after the Republican failure to recapture the County Executive's seat, Chairman Ed Speno, decided to resign as Chairman and was succeeded by Joseph Margiotta of Uniondale in January, 1968. Margiotta would prove to be a very pragmatic politician and being unconstrained by the strong anti-Conservative stance that Speno had taken; opened the lines of communication to the Conservative Party and early in 1968 made a deal with Jim Marrin to give Republican support to Conservative Mason Hampton for a seat in the United States Congress in exchange for supporting the candidacy of William Cahn, the Nassau County District Attorney.

This accommodation between the parties infuriated Noel Crowley, a Syosset attorney and a Vice-Chairman of the Nassau Conservative Committee. Crowley united the Conservative dissidents against Marrin and his followers and challenged the endorsement of District Attorney Cahn by running himself in a primary election against Cahn. Crowley was encouraged by the close, 8 to 7, vote by the Executive Committee in favor of the Cahn endorsement; a vote in which Crowley had abstained..

The County Executive Committee responded by removing Crowley as Chairman of the Oyster Bay Conservatives, a post to which he was appointed by Chairman Marrin. The committee would have also stripped Crowley of his Vice-Chairmanship but the nineteen member Executive Committee couldn't legally remove an officer that had been elected by the entire County Committee.

Shortly after the Executive Committee vote on Cahn, a meeting of representatives of all of the Conservative clubs in the County was called by Ralph Scinta, Chairman of the Wantagh Club. The meeting, to discuss the developing situation in the county concerning District Attorney Cahn, was to be held in a local restaurant but when news of the meeting leaked out and members of the press showed up at the meeting place, it was moved to a more private locale, Scinta's appliance store on Merrick Road in Seaford. I attended this meeting to represent the Hicksville Conservative Club.

Noel Crowley did his best to stir up the 45 Conservatives in attendance against the decision of the County party to endorse District Attorney Cahn in exchange for the Hampton congressional endorsement. Jim Marrin, who also attended the meeting, remained silent during the entire three hour session as many in the group sat on washers, dryers, and stoves.

I was not convinced by Crowley's arguments and along with many of the others felt that it was well worth an endorsement for District Attorney to have an opportunity to elect for the first time an enrolled Conservative with the stature of Mason Hampton to the United States Congress. Hampton had run an excellent race as the Conservative candidate for State Attorney General in 1966 and had gained much respect for himself and the party and would prove to be an exceptional candidate for Congress.

I observed that most of Crowley's support came from those members who had their own agenda and seemed to want to use this occasion to challenge the leadership for purposes other than the overall good of the party.

Crowley also wore another hat in the party hierarchy; he was the elected Assembly District Leader from my Assembly District. When the Crowley inspired malcontents announced their plans to run a primary against Cahn and to further announce that they would be running against Marrin's reelection as Chairman at the July County Committee meeting, Marrin asked me to run a primary against Crowley for the party position of Assembly District Leader in the June primary. I was still a relative newcomer to the party and Crowley had been active with the party since its inception and was well known and respected in the district, but I accepted the challenge and agreed to take him on.

In April Marrin stunned everyone when he announced that he would not be seeking reelection as Chairman, citing business reasons. Two of Marrin's supporters, Austin 'Pete' Verity and Fred Morlock were mentioned as possibilities to fill Marrin's seat. The Crowley crowd immediately challenged for the leadership by offering Walter Stevens, John Shulman or James Patterson as the dissident candidate for the Chairmanship. This was the first year in which the Nassau Conservatives had a significant split in the leadership, but it would not be the last.

The sides having been chosen, it turned out to be a very bitter and acrimonious primary election for both the public offices and the party positions. I lost the election for Assembly District leader to Crowley by a vote of 95 to 93; disappointing, but not too bad a showing for a relative newcomer against one of the party's most prominent leaders. When the smoke of the primary cleared, both sides were claiming victory but it was apparent that there was no clear cut winner. The committeemen that were elected at the primary election were almost evenly split between the factions. The upcoming county committee organizing meeting in July promised to be a real battle for the Chairmanship.

The meeting of the committee was held in a large room at the New Hyde Park Inn on Jericho Turnpike. The governing by-laws of the County Committee at that time permitted the use of proxy voting so all of the members did not have to personally attend. In the short time between the election of the committeemen and the meeting, both sides actively solicited proxies from the non-attending members. In many cases there were duplicate or forged proxies and this would prove to be an undoing of the proceedings.

The meeting was held in the evening and could not be called to order until all the challenges to the proxies; and there were many; had been resolved to the satisfaction of both sides. Both the Marrin group and the Crowley dissidents were challenging every opposing proxy. This process lasted until well past midnight. Some of the attendees who had patiently waited for hours had to leave and gave a proxy to the leader of their faction. This further aggravated the proxy delay.

The bar at the Inn had been open during the evening and many of the participants were fueling up their aggressions at the bar while waiting for the meeting to officially get underway. When Chairman Marrin finally called the meeting to order, it was becoming clear that his side had a slim advantage in the vote. The dissidents were determined to delay the proceedings hoping to cut down the vote by outlasting the other side. The meeting turned into a shouting match, which intensified with each parliamentary delaying tactic by Crowley and his minions. There were by this time of the early morning many drunks who were getting beyond control.

After the debacle of the proxy battle, Marrin decided to amend the by-laws to eliminate proxy voting at all future meetings; allowing voting privileges only to the committee members in attendance. This further aggravated the arguments, with one side saying that this change would go into effect for the election of the officers and the other insisting upon the use of the proxy votes for the entire meeting. It was the Crowley group that wanted to eliminate the proxy votes for the elections at this meeting hoping that Marrin would lose enough live bodies in the early morning hours, confident that his followers would stay the course.

As it turned out, the hour grew so late that the management of the Inn insisted that we leave. Without having finished the first order of business which was the adoption of the by-laws, Marrin recessed the meeting to a time and place to be established.

As we left the meeting hall as the sun was coming up that morning, the parking lot turned into a boxing arena. With the heat of the verbal battle inside and the liquid courage that many were now feeling, there were several physical confrontations in the parking lot. There was further mischief discovered when Doctor Vince Joy, one of Marrin's supporters, found that his car tires had been slashed.

The bitterness of that night was to taint the party for years to come.

Marrin continued to perform the functions of Chairman and did not reconvene the meeting for several months. In the interim, the Crowley faction held a rump session of the County Committee to elect Maxwell Phillips of Lynbrook as party chairman. The Phillips designation was not recognized by the Marrin faction or by the County Board of Elections, but it did move Marrin to facilitate the convening of the full committee.

Because of the threats and fights at the original meeting in July, Marrin asked me if I knew someone who would act as the sergeant-at-arms to maintain order at the next meeting. I suggested one of our local club members, a sanitation worker in the Town of Oyster Bay, Dan Donovan, who was a Republican at the time and had a reputation for brawling in many of the local bars. At Marrin's request I asked Donovan to assume this responsibility. He did this gladly and recruited a half dozen of his fellow garbage men to provide the security at the meeting hall. The presence of this cadre of tough looking bruisers went a long way in maintaining order that night.

During the time between meetings, the original candidate for Chairman supported by Marrin dropped out of the running and Marrin prevailed upon John Sheehan, who was the first Chairman of the party until 1964, to seek the chairmanship and run for the remainder of the two year term.

The reconvened meeting held on March 13, 1969, while not completely harmonious, was less contentious than the melee in New Hyde Park and after a long evening a new Chairman was elected on the third ballot and the meeting was adjourned at 1:30 a.m.

There were three candidates in contention for the chairmanship; Sheehan, Maxwell Phillips, and Joseph Lamberta, an attorney from Massapequa. The first ballot had no majority vote winner when the secret ballots were cast, with Sheehan at 158 votes, Phillips at 149 and Lamberta at 127. Sheehan was still leading after the second ballot with 151 votes to 122 for Phillips, while Lamberta had dropped to 79 votes.

Before the final ballot, a deal was struck between Sheehan and Lamberta wherein Lamberta threw his remaining votes to Sheehan and was elected to the second leadership position, Executive Vice-Chairman. Sheehan then was elected County Chairman by a vote of 172 to 106 when the total vote cast dropped from 434 to 278 when a large number of delegates left the five hour marathon meeting.

There were three other vice-chairmanships voted on that night. After being elected Chairman of the local Conservative Club, one of the first things that I did was to agitate the leadership (Jim Marrin) for recognition for the loyalty and support of our local club during the past year of controversy. My request to make our former club Chairman, Michael Tisdell, a Vice-chairman was granted and Mike was elected along with Michael Camardi of North Hempstead, and James Harvey of Wantagh.

(It was speculated at the time that the chief provocateur of the dissidents, Noel Crowley, was motivated less by a sense of outrage about the endorsement of Bill Cahn, than his being pissed off that Mason Hampton, rather than he, had been given the Republican nod for Congress.)

In the general election in November of 1968, Richard Nixon was elected for his first term as President of the United States. The Conservative Party had wanted to support him on the Conservative line but Nelson Rockefeller, controlling the makeup of the slate of Electors for President in New York, would not allow them to share the Conservative line. Rather than run an opposing slate and diminish Nixon's chances in New York the Conservatives decided, by a narrow vote of the State Committeemen, not to run any electors that year.

James Buckley, a Republican running on the Conservative line for United States Senator against the incumbent, Jacob Javits, received more than one million votes on Row C. His 1968 run would set the stage for a future run with more success.

I was a candidate for public office for the first time on the voting machine, running for the State Senate against the incumbent Republican, Henry Curran. My workload at Grumman prevented me from doing any active campaigning, I spent no money and made no campaign appearances and yet, still pulled in a respectable vote; another visible sign of the growing appeal of the Conservative Party.

Unfortunately, Mason Hampton lost the Congressional seat in a close race against the liberal Democrat, Allard Lowenstein. Lowenstein was an anti-Vietnam war activist and an early supporter of the Presidential candidacy of

Minnesota Senator Eugene McCarthy, whose candidacy in the early Democrat Primary elections was instrumental in driving President Lyndon Johnson out of the race that year. I often think that had our party been united in 1968 instead of engaging in internal fratricide, Mason Hampton would have prevailed in that election.

This was also the year that history was made when two enrolled Conservatives, Charles Jerabek of Suffolk County and Rosemary Gunning Moffett of Queens were elected with Republican support to the New York State Assembly; the first time Conservatives were elected to the state legislature.

In January of 1969 I was elected Chairman of the Hicksville Conservative Club, succeeding Mike Tisdell of Hicksville. One of the first things we did under this new administration was to change the name of the club to the Mid-Island Conservative Club to encompass a larger geographic area, including, in addition to Hicksville: Plainview, Old Bethpage, Bethpage, and Jericho. (Later on, as some of the other clubs in the town became inactive, the club would encompass the entire Town of Oyster Bay.)

Nassau Conservatives greeted the New Year, 1969, with great confidence in the future. The vote, not only in Nassau but across the state, had gained new respect and recognition for the Conservative Party. The new Republican leadership in Nassau County was ready to 'break bread' with the Conservatives and, if the Conservatives could manage to overcome the internal feuding that had plagued us in 1968, the future was bright for us.

Pete Verity was asked by John Sheehan to take over the role of leader in the Town of Oyster Bay and he, in turn, asked me to work with him and the other Club Chairmen who were not in the Crowley camp. In this role, I was part of a small group of Oyster Bay Conservative leaders participating in a meeting called by the town Republican leader, Angelo Roncallo, to discuss the possibilities of our working together in the 1969 Town elections, which were the main focus of that year's election. In Oyster Bay, there were five positions open: Town Supervisor, which was then occupied by a Democrat, Michael Petito; three Town Council seats and the Town Clerk, all filled by Republicans. I felt this was a great opportunity to get our first elected Conservative in the Town of Oyster Bay, and the meeting with the Republican leaders would be a catalyst to bringing this about.

The meeting was held one evening in the early spring, surprisingly, at the home of the incumbent Supervisor, Democrat Mike Petito. Attending this meeting was the head of our Conservative delegation, Pete Verity, and most of the key leaders including me. On the Republican side was Angelo Roncallo and a small cadre of non-descript executive leaders who said and did nothing at the meeting except to nod approval at every utterance from Chairman Roncallo. The inclusion of Mike Petito was surprising but would soon be explained.

Roncallo took immediate control of the proceedings. He was a very imposing man. He weighed in at well over 300 pounds and from his centrally located seat in Petito's living room, dominated the initial courtesies and greetings.

Our leader, Verity, seemed to acquiesce in Roncallo's prime role in the meeting while the rest of the Conservative leaders and I waited for our cues from Verity. We would soon learn from Roncallo the reason for the meeting place and the inclusion of a Democrat.

I was stunned when Roncallo made his proposal. He had evidently had previous discussions with Petito and had come to terms with him.

Roncallo had come to this meeting convinced that the town's Conservatives had a great affection for Mike Petito and favored his reelection as Town Supervisor. Roncallo proposed that, if the Conservatives endorsed the three Republicans running for the Town Council, the Republicans would be willing to support Petito for Supervisor; this combination of endorsements would ensure the election for Petito and the Republicans.

Verity and the other Conservatives in attendance were ecstatic at the offer. Yes, they did like Petito, but I had always thought that we liked Petito, not so much because of his Conservative credentials (of which, he had none), but rather because he was a perfect foil against the absolute Republican control of the town.

As the conversation progressed favorably in the direction of consummating this unacceptable arrangement, and our Conservatives were coming closer to agreement, I felt that I had to speak out. While Verity frowned on me, I offered my observations of the deal. I wanted to know, "What's in this deal for the Conservatives? You're asking us to endorse three Republicans for the Town Council and in return you offer us the Republican endorsement of a Democrat."

Verity scowled but could find no words to give the obvious answer. There was no gain in this for the Conservatives and, if we had continued to nod our dumb approval for this arrangement, it could have only weakened the party in the eyes of the two major parties and our new found influence would have been used for no good conservative purpose.

Taking my cue, the other Conservatives, having been awakened from their inexperienced reverie, started one by one, to speak out against the deal. I spoke no more and was content that my few words sparked the move away from this imprudent agreement. Before the meeting was over, common sense prevailed, and there were no deals made that night.

(Before the year was over, the Republicans made an independent deal with Mike Petito to give up his race for reelection as Supervisor and gave him their endorsement for a seat on the Family Court, which along with the Democrat endorsement, assured his election to that post and gave the Republicans a chance to recapture the Supervisor's spot. Mike went on to win the Family Court election but was killed less than three month's after taking office, when he was shot by an unknown assailant while vacationing in Puerto Rico. He was shot on March 24th, the day I was being prepared in the hospital for my gall bladder surgery the following day.)

Before all of the endorsements were in for the 1969 town races, Pete Verity had scored a bit of a coup when he maneuvered the Republicans into backing Phil Healey of Massapequa for one of the Town Board seats. Phil was a Republican but did not have the backing of his local leader at the time because he was not one of the 'clubhouse cronies' who normally would be expected to get the nod. The Conservatives admired Phil's independent spirit and felt that this was as close as we were going to get to a conservative in office until the proud Republicans could be taken down a peg or two; their continuing dominance of the County had led them to regular success at the polls, which fostered an arrogant disregard of anything or anyone, non-Republican.

We did support the Republican candidate for Town Supervisor in the Town of Oyster Bay, John Burke, who would eventually wind up winning in the general election with the needed support of the Conservative Party.

Another successful candidate who won because of the Conservative Party vote was Town Council candidate, Lewis Yevoli, the first Democrat in living memory to sit on the board. Another Democrat, Louis Orfan of Bethpage, also received our endorsement for the Town Council but was beaten by Republican M. Halsted Christ of Muttontown.

The unsuccessful Republican in the town board race was Frank Hynes, a former Receiver of Taxes and the Republican leader of Farmingdale. Although we would later develop a cordial political relationship, I was extremely happy at the time to see Hynes go down in defeat. When sober, Frank was an especially congenial man, but unfortunately he had what we called "The Irish Curse"; he imbibed too often and too much in the 'sauce' and when the spirits hit him, he became belligerent and nasty.

His actions at our local Conservative club fund raiser at the Hicksville Knights of Columbus Hall were typical of his liquor driven hostility. Although he didn't get our endorsement and was running against our candidates who would be introduced during the evening's program, Hynes paid for admission and attended our dinner dance. As the Chairman of the Club and the emcee for the evening, I treated our uninvited guest with courtesy but did not feel that as an opponent of our candidate that he merited an introduction.

Frank cornered me in the entrance hall as I passed through during the evening and with a foul, liquored breath, pushed his nose into my face, and berated me for not having endorsed him and backing the two Democrats. I told him that his current behavior was more than enough to justify our decision. At this point, Frank called me a few uncomplimentary names and told me he was going to, "…beat the shit out of you." To which I politely told him, "You lay a hand on me and I'll kick your ass down those stairs."

At this point, Dan Donovan, who had been watching this interchange, stepped between us and mediated a standoff between us. Frank, who had previously heard me sing at another affair, said, "Well, at least you can sing. I'll give fifty dollars to your club, if you will go inside and sing me an Irish Song." I was to find out his motives for this unusual request in the next few seconds.

Not being one to turn down a chance for an easy fifty dollars, I quickly told him, "Okay, if you put up the fifty bucks, I'll sing you a bit of 'Danny Boy', if that will suit you."

He agreed and added, "…but only if you announce that this is being sung at the request of Councilman Frank Hynes." And with that he pulled out a fifty dollar bill to give to me.

I took the fifty and agreed to announce that this was a request by Councilman Hynes and that he was paying for the privilege of hearing me sing… but I said, "I will also tell them that this money will be used in the campaign to kick your ass in the November election." He chuckled at this, and assumed that I wouldn't be so impolite as to carry out the threat.

I went inside to the microphone, asked the band to back me up on a chorus of "Danny Boy", held up the fifty dollar bill and announced to the gathering that Councilman Hynes just donated fifty dollars to the club to hear me sing an Irish tune, that I accepted the donation and would use his money to help kick his ass in the election. At this point Frank was fuming and I thought that he would run across (or rather stagger across) the floor to punch me out. I finished the song, gave the treasurer the unsolicited donation, and there was no further trouble from Councilman Hynes for the rest of the evening.

When the results came in on Election night and I found out that Hynes had lost by only a whisker to Lew Yevoli, I chuckled to think that the fifty dollars that he gave us that night of the dinner-dance may have been instrumental in causing his defeat.

1970

"It was the best of times, it was the worst of times, it was the age of wisdom, it was the age of foolishness, it was the epoch of belief, it was the epoch of incredulity, it was the season of Light, it was the season of Darkness, it was the spring of hope, it was the winter of despair, we had everything before us, we had nothing before us, we were all going direct to Heaven, we were all going direct the other way..."

These words opening the classic, "A Tale of Two Cities", could have been written to describe the year 1970 as it affected our lives at 36 Sunrise Street, as well as those years at the end of the eighteenth century during the time of the bloody French Revolution as depicted by Charles Dickens.

1970 had started on a high note. The family was in good health and the children were doing well in school and in their extracurricular activities and we were all looking forward to the future with great hopes and greater ambitions.

Ranny was coming off a successful year of football; playing defensive end in the Police Athletic League. He was in love with the game and was looking forward to the summer when training for the new season would begin. He was playing the clarinet in the band and was now very proficient; the horrendous squeaking of the early days that drove us wild while he was practicing had been replaced with smooth melodies that now entranced. His musical talents didn't end with the clarinet as he self taught the piano; taking his cues from Patti, who was taking private lessons with Mrs. Maripodi, who had a studio at her home around the corner on Blanche Street. Ranny was maturing nicely in his adolescence and his voice had started to develop a deep resonance, relieved at times by a sudden uninvited rise in pitch.

While Patti was involved with music with her participation in the school chorus and piano lessons, Girl Scouts and synchronized swimming, she was developing into a beautiful and disciplined young lady. She needed no prompting to do her school homework and insisted on completing every assignment even when we encouraged her to ease up when it came time for bed. Her seriousness was balanced by a keen sense of humor and a sharp wit.

Eileen had started kindergarten and was a constant source of energy that kept us all amused. When she arrived home from school or any activity, the house would suddenly come alive with her loud announcement that she had arrived.

Jean, however, was the real spark plug of the family and the navigator that kept us all on the right path. I'll never figure out how she could handle so well all of the things that she undertook. She was working two part time jobs. One position was as a salesperson at the Abraham and Straus Department Store in Huntington where she was a "floater" where she had to know all of the departments and filled in where necessary. The other was as an interior designer and salesperson at the World of Décor, also in Huntington.

It was also about this time that she decided to go to the Wilsey Institute of Interior Design in Hempstead where she got her formal education in that field. With all of this, she still had a house to manage and a family to raise, which in itself was a full time job that she performed well. Student, salesperson, designer, mother, wife, home manager with all of its duties – I don't know how she did it and still have time to entertain family and friends; and we did a lot of that.

With the start of the New Year, I was assigned the task of developing a simulation program for the A6A Intruder. It was the kind of job that I had become used to and I thrived on the challenge of an inadequate budget, impossible delivery time, and state of the art design requirements. The program was nearly complete when I was hospitalized in March and, because I had everything in order at the time, the job was easily finished in my absence.

On the political front, I had just been re-elected in January to serve a second one year term as Chairman of the Mid-Island Conservative Club. The Conservative Party was coming off another great year at the polls and all Conservatives were looking forward to the 1970 political season with great confidence. In Nassau County, Noel Crowley and his allies were still lurking in the shadows ready to challenge the leadership again, but this time we were all prepared for any fight. Crowley was still the Assembly District leader but in the two years since I had lost the leadership to him by two votes, I had been building up my own local constituency and was ready to challenge him in 1970 at the primary election.

(We never did get to have the face off on Primary Day. When the designating petitions were filed in the spring for Assembly District Leader, we both challenged the other's petitions in Supreme Court. Mason Hampton filed the brief on my behalf and when Crowley first read it on the scheduled court date; he threw it on the law clerk's desk and stormed out of the courtroom. Shortly afterwards, he withdrew his challenge to my petitions and gave up the fight for leader because he had no valid legal response to Mason's well researched rebuttal. Thus, I became the new Assembly District

Leader without a primary fight and for the remainder of the year would wear two leadership hats; A.D. Leader and Club Chairman.)

The year was still young when we had the first negative event of the many that would cloud our lives that year.

As club chairman, one of my first actions was to appoint a program committee to assure that there would be an interesting speaker or some other happening to encourage more participation in our monthly meetings. Up until now, the attendance at club meetings was about fifteen to twenty members with an occasional surge in attendance to twenty five. For our February 1970 meeting, I had arranged to have a debate featuring our new Oyster Bay Councilmen, Democrat Lew Yevoli, and Republican, Phil Healey in a discussion with William Morris, the Housing Program Director of the N.A.A.C.P., and Neil Gold of the Suburban Action Institute.

The N.A.A.C.P (National Association for the Advancement of Colored People) and the Suburban Action Institute were threatening legal action against the Town of Oyster Bay for what they claimed were discriminatory zoning practices which were preventing the poor and minorities from buying homes in the Town of Oyster Bay. The two groups told the town that they would bring suit in federal court if the Town did not downzone at least twenty percent of the open land for low-income housing, claiming that the current zoning was unconstitutional.

The normally complacent town residents, from Bayville on the north shore to Massapequa in the south, were alarmed at what they considered to be a major threat to their neighborhoods. They expressed their fear that the downgrading of the town's zoning would threaten the suburban quality of life that they had become used to and open up the town for the development of urban ghettos. What they really feared, but no one said it openly, was that the town would open itself to large black communities.

I felt that our club could serve a major community service by holding an open public forum to discuss the merits and impact of the proposed down-zoning. I was looking forward to moderating this event which I anticipated would draw a large crowd. (The turnout at this event, held at the Hicksville Knights of Columbus Hall, was well over two hundred, interested and worried, citizens; the largest attendance at any Conservative club meeting in the county and a record that still holds forty years later.)

When the night of the meeting arrived on February 19th, a more pressing matter came up that I had to take care of and I missed the meeting. When I came home from work, I found out that Ranny had not returned home from school that day and we were concerned about his absence. In inquiring amongst his friends, we found out that Ranny, at the ripe old age of 13, had decided to leave home and find his adventures in the world. We rode around to the places that he usually hung out and called or visited some of his many friends.

We could not fathom why he would leave home. He was doing well in his studies and in his other activities, he was well liked by his friends, and he was at an age where the girls were getting attracted to him. After running out of options and places to look for him, we notified the police of Ranny's absence. The police did not seem overly concerned at this point and told us that they don't start any action on these reports until twenty four hours after the disappearance. It seems most of these types of departures are usually resolved within a day.

With our concern, I couldn't attend the meeting and did all I could to try to locate Ranny. Well before midnight, as predicted by the cops, he finally returned home. He was hungry, tired, and cold from the bitter winter's night. We were so glad to see him home safe and sound that there was no retribution. The only concern that remained was why he wanted to leave home; an answer to which we never got an answer. Perhaps it was just a need for adventure.

Ranny said that he was sorry for having made us worry and realized even more how great he has it at home; no worries about where he's going to sleep and eat or keep warm on the cold winter days. The aftermath of his brief adventure proved in the end to be very salutary. While he was doing well in school and we were having no discipline problems with him, he became even more settled in his daily routine.

(Dennis Kennelly, our club vice chairman, took over the moderating duties at the meeting for me. The meeting reportedly went very well and we stirred up more interest in our club and gained some recruits.)

The following month, I was hospitalized for removal of the gall bladder and didn't return to work for 5 or 6 weeks while I recuperated. While I was sitting at home occupying space, the Apollo 13 was making its journey from earth with the intent of putting the next two American astronauts on the moon. There was a problem with the command module and the planned landing was aborted for the three astronauts on board: James Lovell, John Seigert and Fred Haise (Fred Haise would eventually be hired by Grumman as a Vice-President in charge of Space Programs). The LEM was used as a "life boat" to propel the astronauts back from the moon. The Grumman Simulation Department played a key roll in this rescue effort and although I would have only played a miniscule part in the effort, I was disappointed that I was not available for this historic event, which was made into a major motion picture nearly 30 years later with Tom Hanks in a starring role.

While I was convalescing, my supervisor Nick Szuchy was proposing to the F-14 management the setting up of a parallel simulation effort to the contracted simulation that was being pursued by Carmine Castellano and an engineering staff of about 35. The management people were not satisfied with the progress being made by the project's simulation group and Nick convinced them that we could accomplish a significant part of the task with no impact on their budget; he told them that all of the equipment we would need was already available within the company.

When I returned to work, this task was given to me and I immediately made an appointment with Castellano to review with him the progress of his group and to use any of the work that they had already accomplished. I was surprised to find out that, even with 3 dozen engineers on the job for several months, there was nothing that they had done that was of any use to me. I had to put the whole package together myself.

Gathering information from all of the relevant design groups on the F-14 program, I was able to complete the design of the simulated cockpit to be used on a 3 degree of freedom motion simulator that could be tied in with our Analog computing department. One of the most important and difficult tasks (for me) was the development of a mathematical model of the aircraft dynamics. Even though the Castellano group was supposed to be working on the math model, they had nothing that was of use and I had to educate myself in that field. (I would discover years later when I came across the math model report from the Castellano group, that the model they published was exactly the one I had generated for our "off the books" simulator. Interestingly, even though they even went so far as to use the hand drawn sketches that I had used in my paperwork, there was no acknowledgement of my contribution although there were many other people mentioned in the report. It's a good thing that I get my satisfaction from a job well done and not from meaningless recognition.)

With the unofficial help of several of the shops, the design and implementation was completed in about two months and I had the project pilots in to fly and evaluate the simulator. I was to find out that pilots are not too fond of simulators as they were most anxious to get into the seat of the real aircraft. Their initial response to my simulator was therefore very negative and we did very few studies with the system at that time.

(The attitude of the pilot's would change later on in the year when the F-14 crashed during its second flight on December 30th. Bill Miller, the F-14 test pilot, who was flying that day and had ejected safely from the plane when a problem occurred in the control system, was most anxious to find out the reason why the aircraft failed. The only thing that they had that could accomplish the necessary investigation was my simulator that they had frowned upon earlier in the year. I was at home for the Christmas holiday when I received a call from my boss, Jack O'Brien, at three o'clock in the morning, immediately after the crash, directing me to come in and reactivate the simulator. After using the simulator to successfully identify the problems in the aircraft control system, the pilots finally gained a respect for my design.)

And still the Castellano group had not produced a simulator; in fact, that group never did deliver on the contracted requirements. A key part of this official simulator that they were purportedly designing was a visual display that was to be designed and built by a subcontractor who had, before delivering the equipment they were supposed to be developing, filed for bankruptcy, closed their business and left Castellano and his group up the creek without a paddle. I would eventually be asked to step in to complete the design and construction of that aborted visual display after our management finally closed down the fruitless Castellano effort. I finished this job successfully, using only the funds remaining from the original subcontract.

In the spring of 1970 the New York State legislature passed a bill that reversed the state's restrictions against abortions except in cases where the mother's health was endangered. The vote in the Assembly was very close – actually it was a tie vote until one of the Assemblymen changed his vote, where he had previously voted to maintain the abortion limitations, and cast the deciding vote to open the state to the unrestricted killing of unborn babies. This vote would hold great portent for many of the legislators supporting the change; including Senator Ralph Marino, Assemblymen Vincent Balletta and John Kingston, and the Assembly Speaker and one day gubernatorial aspirant, Perry Duryea. (Other than branding the supporters of this legislation as "pro-abortionists", the change in the New York law would become irrelevant after the Roe v. Wade decision of the United States Supreme Court in 1973, which Court "found" a constitutional right for a woman to have an abortion.)

It was about this time that Nassau Conservative Chairman, John Sheehan, asked me to run for State Senator in my district against Ralph Marino. I felt that I had a full plate and was reluctant to run. I was still recovering from major surgery, I was Chairman of the local Conservative Club and was about to take on Noel Crowley in a primary election for Assembly District Leader, and at Grumman, I had just been assigned the challenging task of designing the F-14 engineering simulator.

Two years before, I had permitted my name to be on the ballot against Senator Henry Curran knowing that I could not run any kind of a campaign. If I agreed to run again, it would only be to run an effective campaign and not to be just a name on the ballot. After much soul searching, I decided that I would find the time to campaign, while still accomplishing the other things that I had to do. I told Chairman Sheehan that he could count on me to carry the Conservative banner in the local Senate election.

(Two of the factors driving my decision were; one, the entry of James Buckley into the race for United States Senator in New York. Buckley had run a great race in 1968 for the same position, and was now challenging the major party candidates on Row C; and, a second factor was having Dean Paul Adams heading up our Conservative ticket as our candidate for Governor for the second time. We were hoping for at least a repeat of his historic showing in 1966 and I was confident that a strong campaign by local Conservatives would help to focus attention on the statewide races.)

As it turned out, I did not have to run a primary against Noel Crowley when he dropped out of the race following our brief confrontation in Supreme Court. This left me with time to work with Pete Verity of Massapequa who I was supporting for Chairman at our County Committee meeting. Verity won this election handily, in spite of the now diminishing opposition from the Noel Crowley faction of the party. Immediately after his election, Verity asked me to take over the post as Town Chairman in Oyster Bay; which I accepted. Jim Morrow would be leading Hempstead Town and Bob Valli, the Town of North Hempstead

One of the first significant decisions by the new 19 member Executive Committee of the party was to endorse a candidate for Councilman in the Town of Oyster Bay when a vacancy occurred because of the resignation of one of the incumbent councilmen that year. Although this position would not usually be up for election in an even numbered year, because of the timing of the vacancy, it would be on the ballot in 1970.

The Republican Party, which was dominant in Oyster Bay for years, appointed Warren Doolittle, a Hicksville attorney, to fill the vacancy until the November election. This was to be Verity's first opportunity to personally deal with Joe Margiotta, the Republican County Chairman.

After the meeting of the two chairmen, Verity came back to the executive committee with a report. He told us that he attempted to get an endorsement for a Conservative to fill the vacant position in Oyster Bay and that Margiotta said that he had already made the commitment to back Doolittle. Verity informed us that on further insistence, Margiotta agreed that the next vacancy on the Town Council would go to a Conservative. At first we assumed that as a quid pro quo for this deal, the Conservatives would back Doolittle in the 1970 election. Verity said that no commitments were made other than Margiotta's agreement to put a Conservative on the town board.

With that, Verity recommended that we back the Democrat, Louis Orfan, who we had supported the previous year but who had lost the election. Most Conservative leaders in the town thought very highly of Orfan, a personable and conservative choice, and went along with Chairman Verity's recommendation. Orfan did not get the support of his own Democrat Party that year. To enhance his chances in the general election, he filed papers for an independent line under the party name of "Bull Moose Party"; in homage to

Oyster Bay's most famous resident, President Theodore Roosevelt. Doolittle, as expected, won handily in November.

On May 4, 1970, there was a student protest at many college campuses across the nation, objecting to the bombing of Cambodia as ordered by President Richard Nixon in his attempt to bring the Vietnam War to an end. At Kent State University in Ohio, where the students joined in this protest, Governor James Rhodes called out the National Guard to help to control the demonstration which was punctuated by rock throwing, windows being broken, and an attempt to burn down the ROTC building. At one point the National Guardsmen opened fire on the demonstrators, with thirteen students being shot, killing four. Amongst the four students killed was Jeffrey Miller, a graduate of our local Plainview-Old Bethpage School District.

This incident at Kent State fueled the fires of the anti-war factions across the country and accelerated the pace of the demonstrations. Nowhere was this more in evidence than in the Plainview High Schools, where the students, many of whom knew Jeffrey Miller, were being whipped into a frenzy of demonstrations and threatened to upset the academic climate in the district. Many of the school district teachers and administrators were sympathetic to the anti-war movement and it appeared that no one was taking any positive action to quell the discontent.

(Kent State could have used a college president such as Samuel Hayakawa, a noted semantics expert who while acting-President of San Francisco State College, stood up to the protesting students and brought order to the school. His success in stemming any further riots during his tenure as President gained for him the title of "Samurai Scholar", and eventually led to his successful run for United States Senator from California in 1976, an election he won by over 250,000 votes.)

With no one seeming to address the growing discord in the school district, I suggested to Dennis Kennelly, who had become a close confidant of mine in the Conservative Party and who was an elected member of the local School board, that we try to rally the support of community leaders to help to bring some stability and order to our local schools. We enlisted John Burke, the Republican Supervisor of the Town of Oyster Bay, Martin Ginsberg, our local State Assemblyman, and Lewis Yevoli, a Democrat-Conservative Town Councilman.

A meeting was set up for May 17 to be held at the law office of Assemblyman Ginsberg. A mailing was sent out under the name of our new group, Citizens United for Reason in Education (CURE) with the sponsorship of Burke, Ginsberg, Yevoli, Dennis and me, inviting most of the local government, school, and civic leaders.

Dennis and I had wanted to limit the invitations to only those people who we thought could support a reasoned approach to the current problem. The other three insisted upon inviting many people who we knew were not interested in quieting the local demonstrations but were rather sympathetic to the anti-war activities and would attempt to use our group to further their own radical causes. As the three elected officials lent credibility to our effort and we needed their participation to get this effort off the ground, Dennis and I acceded to their demands and expanded the invitation list to include these dissenters.

The meeting was held to a standing room crowd at Ginsberg's office, and by agreement the Assemblyman presided over the meeting. After my initial introduction of the purposes for the establishment of this group, to bring order to our disordered schools in the wake of the Kent State shootings, the meeting soon turned into a forum for the very people that Dennis and I attempted to exclude. They dominated the discussion and were attempting to alter the modest goals we had set out to attain in support of the protesting students and the anti-war objectives. It became apparent that this disparate group of characters could never come to an agreement on any reasonable program and the meeting soon broke up.

Burke, Ginsberg, and Yevoli continued in their insistence on including the people who were trying to use the organization for their own purposes, which led me to dissociate with them and ultimately led to CURE never getting off the ground.

It would take some time, but stability finally returned to the school district. I still feel certain that with the right alliance of leaders without the discordance of some of the mavericks, order could have established more quickly.

By mid-summer I had finished the design of the F-14 Interim Simulator (as I called it), had been assigned directly to the F-14 project, and had laid the groundwork for an active Senate campaign that I would pursue in earnest beginning on Labor Day weekend. I planned a campaign fundraiser for late October and in the interim would use my own funds to bankroll a modest printing of campaign literature and bumper strips.

With all of the time spent on politics and work at Grumman, we didn't plan any kind of family vacation for 1970. (After a terrible vacation in 1969, we didn't feel it was such a big loss at the time. In the summer of 1969 we rented a house on Cape Cod, Massachusetts where we had planned a week in the sun. The weather was terrible all week and local activities were non-existent. The few hours that we managed to get on the beach were punctuated with the constant attack of sand flies which effected all of us except for Eileen, who at 5 years of age, was completely oblivious to the ravenous appetites of the local sand flies. We all became so disgusted with Cape Cod that we packed up early and went home before our rental expired.)

I was selected for my new assignment on the F-14 project at Grumman because of my extensive experience in the design and building of inertial guidance and navigation systems. Because of this, I was asked to write up test plans for the magnetic compass to be used in the cockpit of the F-14. When I informed my new masters that I had absolutely no experience or knowledge of the workings of the magnetic compass, they readily agreed to assign me to another task in preparation for the first flight of the plane; they asked me to develop test plans for the aircraft's weapons control system. Of course, not having any experience in this area, I was a perfect selection for the job.

Two things facilitated my entry into the world of aircraft weapons systems. First, was my assignment to Porfirio 'John" Viamonte, a young Cuban, who was an expert in this field and an excellent tutor. I learned a lot from him very quickly. Second, was that the system on the first F-14 was not a full blown version of the weapons system to be integrated into the aircraft. The Partial Armament Control System (PACS) was a much simplified version which enabled me to understand the equipment enough to complete the job without getting bogged down in the complexities of the system integrated into the production aircraft.

I woke up in my bed at home early on an August morning. My heart was aching and pounding as if it were trying to explode in my chest. I was in a cold sweat and both my arms were numb. Trying to catch my breath, I poked Jean to wake her up and told her that I believed I was having a heart attack; all of the classic symptoms were there. I was afraid to move even if I felt I could. Jean called Dr. Rand, our family physician, and told him what was happening. Dr. Rand told Jean to get me to the hospital immediately, that I was probably having a serious heart attack.

Jean drove me to the emergency room at the Plainview Central General Hospital where I was checked in and put into the Intensive Care Unit. The staff at the hospital started to run tests, particularly blood tests, several times a day. I was moved to a room in the main section of the hospital the next day and was kept on my back in bed for the entire time. Almost immediately upon my signing in at the hospital the symptoms eased up and I felt normal and healthy again, but the doctor insisted that I stay in bed until the tests were completed.

After two days of being inert in the bed, I was going to get up in spite of the doctor's orders when a patient across the hall from my room was checking out. He had a similar experience to mine and was cleared to go home. As he was waiting for someone to pick him up he stepped out of his room and from my bed I could see him in the hall. He suddenly collapsed and the nursing staff came rushing down the hall, were injecting him in the chest with large needles and were using the fibrillator on him to get his heart going. He died. After witnessing this incident, I spent the next two days obediently following the doctor's orders.

The results of the tests were indecisive and I've never had the same problem since that day. A few years after this, Pat Reilly, one of my co-workers at Grumman was relating his experience in a similar situation. He underwent surgery at the Mayo Clinic to install a metal brace on his spine and about four months later had the same 'pseudo' heart attack that I had had. The explanation he was given by his doctor at the time was that a blood clot must have been lodged in his circulatory system from the time of his operation and the clot eventually worked its way into his heart valves causing the stress he experienced. I think the same thing may have happened to me; the doctors never did give me a satisfactory explanation.

In September I was heavily into the campaign during my off hours. I was interviewed on several radio programs and by the local weekly newspapers. Ralph Marino, the Republican incumbent, and Jack Maisel, the Democrat challenger participated in most of the debates with me but I only saw my Liberal Party opponent, Lois Portnoy, once during the campaign. (She was the highlight of one of our debates at one of the local schools. She was an attractive and well proportioned young lady and when she arrived on the stage dressed in a mini-skirt, most of the men in the audience lost interest in the debate and seemed distracted throughout the evening.)

In most of the debates I brought up Marino's vote in favor of repealing the abortion restrictions in New York. He got so upset about my hitting him on this issue that he whined to me one night, "Why do you keep bringing up that abortion vote?" I simply told him, "Because you voted for it."

Patti and Eileen were a bit young to appreciate my running for public office but they enjoyed all of the hoopla that went along with it. The campaigning at super markets, the motorcades, the debates, and they could feel that something exciting was going on. Ranny, on the other hand, wanted to play an active role in the campaign. There was only one "O'Leary for State Senate" campaign button issued in the entire campaign and it was one that was hand made by Ranny. He was constantly urging his friends and classmates to get their parents to vote for me on the Conservative line. I appreciated all of the support the family gave to me during those days.

…then came that dark day in October.

On Saturday, October 17th, I was working at my desk in Grumman's Plant 15, putting the finishing touches on the acceptance test procedures for the weapons control system to be used prior to the anticipated first flight of the F-14 Tomcat, which was scheduled to occur before the end of the year. The entire staff of engineers that was working on the procedures was on an overtime schedule to facilitate the completion of the job so that Grumman could qualify for the multi-million dollar bonus, if they successfully completed the first flight on schedule. (Many engineers, such as me, were not being paid overtime for the extra hours and were given a daily stipend of two dollars for meals.)

When I answered the telephone that fateful afternoon, I was expecting only business calls on my line; I was surprised to hear Jean on the other end. She was frantically distraught as she cried into the phone, "Come home right away, Ranny hanged himself." I must have turned ashen white as I felt the blood rush from my head and my stomach turn. I said that I was on my way and hung up the phone before I realized that I had walked to work that morning and did not have my car with me; to walk home would take about twenty-five minutes. I asked Andy Schneider, one of my associates who was sitting nearby, to give me a lift home. Without hesitation, he agreed.

As we drove, I must have been ranting to Andy unintelligibly as my mind could not grasp what had happened and I didn't know what I would find when I arrived at the house. It took less than five minutes to drive the short distance to the house but it seemed to me like an eternity.

When I arrived at the house, the emergency ambulance from the Fire Department had already arrived in answer to Jean's first call, and one or two police cars were parked in front of the house. When I went in the front hall, there were emergency workers hovering over Ranny who was lying motionless on the floor of the entry hall; his naked body covered with a blanket. The medics must have been attempting to revive him from whatever state he was in and someone stopped me as I entered. One of the workers explained to me that they had done everything they could but were too late and there was nothing more they could do; Ranny was dead.

I must have screamed with the agony of what they were telling me. I fell to the floor and took Ranny in my arms as if hoping just by holding him and hugging him, I could force life back into his body, which was already turning cold. I was too weak to resist when someone pulled me off and escorted me into the living room where Jean was waiting, unbelieving what had just happened; by this time I was blinded with tears. Jean was equally grief-stricken and at this point both of us were inconsolable.

The rest of the day was like floating in an unrealistic dream for Jean and me. Patti and Eileen were still over on Sylvia Lane playing with the Kennelly kids at their house. We, or someone, called to let Pat Kennelly know what had happened and the children stayed away for the night with some friends; I don't remember who - but we were to lose track of much of what happened that week.

We must have made some calls to the family and it wasn't too long before the house was filled with family supporters; my brothers Dan and Fran, I remember, and my sister Helen, and Mom and Dad from Jean's family. Neil Sheehan, ever the helpful neighbor and a New York City Policeman, was an invaluable comfort and strength for us in those initial hours.

We held a wake at Wagner's Funeral Home in Hicksville when Ranny was returned to us; because of the way he died, he had to be taken to the Nassau County Medical Examiner.

Those days are mostly a blur in both of our minds. Even with the huge crowds of family, neighbors, friends, and well wishers, it was impossible to rid ourselves of our shared grief and pain. It was especially difficult for us not knowing why Ranny's life ended in such a terrible way. From all indications he was happy with his life and looking forward to the future with enthusiasm; he was seriously talking about going to the Air Force Academy in Colorado to be become a pilot when he finished high school. (Actually, because of a vision problem requiring him to wear glasses, he would probably not have qualified as a fighter pilot, but he still could have been accepted into the Academy with his grades and other talents.)

Dennis and Pat Kennelly were especially solicitous toward us during this time; Dennis took off from work and he and Pat spent the entire time with us throughout the wake.

I only remember a few of the people who attended the wake even though there was a constant flow of supporters. Senator Ralph Marino, my opponent in the election that year, stands out in my mind along with his Republican Town Leader, Angelo Roncallo for having attended the wake to express their condolences. I appreciated that they put aside the partisan politics to pay their respects to an innocent young man. Ranny had just turned 14 on September 27th.

It is very hard for me, even forty years later, to remember that terrible time in our lives without feeling a sorrow for a loss so profound that I will carry the memory of Ranny in my heart to my own grave.

Shortly after the funeral, I was called by a Nassau County Police Detective, who had been assigned to this case, asking me to come down to Police Headquarters in Mineola. I was informed then of the conclusions of the police investigation which, while not easing the pain in my heart, at least gave a reason for this horrific tragedy.

The detective told me that Ranny did not commit suicide, which was the prevalent interpretation of what had occurred. Ranny, being a maturing adolescent and inclined to explore the many facets of growing up, had been experimenting with increasing the intensity of the feelings of masturbating by adding the extra stimulus on the body that could be attained with pressure on the neck by applying a rope or a belt around the neck. The detective said that he had spoken to some of Ranny's friends at school and that this, indeed, was one of the things that was a subject of popular discussion amongst some of his classmates. From the state of Ranny's body at the time he died, I was told that he had evidently been experimenting with this pressure enhancement that he learned from his classmates at school and that he had slipped while applying the pressure of his belt. With no one around to help him, he was helpless in his dilemma and was unintentionally strangled; a terrifying accident

Knowing this helped to give some closure to this tragedy that had no other explanation.

I found it difficult going back to work, but knew that somehow we had to get on with our lives; we still had two young girls, Patti at 10 years, and Eileen at 6, who had a full life ahead of them. Jean wanted to move to get away from the memories of the house and I wanted to stay so that I wouldn't lose the memories. In the end, inertia won out and we stayed.

One of the most grueling times during this whole nightmare was my having to tell Patti and Eileen that Ranny had died when the girls came home the day after, on October 18th. They were both devastated by the loss and missed their older brother deeply.

John J. O'Leary

The day I returned to work, Gene Graziano, my supervisor on the project, greeted me with an admonition that I should be ready to get back to work and not to expect any sympathy from the company. I'm sure his intentions were to help me through my grief but he came across as so harsh and unthinking that I said nothing to him and simply walked out of the office and went home for a couple of days until I cooled off.

I don't want to dwell on this, the most terrible experience of my life. Then, as now, I had to get on with the rest of my life. Jean and I found comfort in each other, and the fact that we had the girls to keep us on track made a big difference in putting this dark corner of our lives behind us. We managed to slowly get past our grief, but to this day the memories, both good and bad, endure.

Although life had taken a terrible turn, I managed to keep the commitments I had made, particularly in finishing the last month of my campaign for the State Senate, and on the job at Grumman.

At the end of October, we went through with a campaign fund raiser at the Andiron's at Morton Village in Plainview. The contribution to attend was ten dollars, for which the supporters were given unlimited cocktails and a lavish buffet. Many of the neighbors and friends attended and the proceeds were enough to cover the costs of the campaign.

My heart and my mind were really not focused on the campaign, but I did attend the remainder of the debates and made my appearance on some of the local radio interview shows. On Election Day, I received a record breaking vote for a minor party candidate in that Senate Race; getting nearly 17 percent of the vote while riding the coattails of our winning candidate for the United States Senate, James Buckley, who won with about 35 percent of the vote. His opponents, Democrat Richard Ottinger and Republican Charles Goodell, split the remaining votes. That was the first, and the last,

562

time that a Conservative candidate running only on the Conservative line has won a statewide election in New York.

Paul Adams, our candidate for Governor, pulled in a substantial vote to keep the Conservative Party on the coveted third line of the election ballot for the next four years.

(I would later learn to my astonishment that two of my votes in the election came from enrolled members of the Liberal Party, arch foes of the Conservatives. One of these votes was the secretary to Lou Orfan, our candidate for Oyster Bay Town Council, and the other was the fiancé of Lois Portnoy, my Liberal Party opponent. During the campaign debates I had taken some radical stands on some issues that were not really germane to the senate race but did gain some attention to my candidacy. Typical of these stands was calling for the severing of diplomatic relations with Turkey because of their failure to stem the drug trafficking out of their country to the United States.

Both of my surprise voters had attended a debate in which I took some of these extreme stands and voted for me because of them.)

Shortly after Election Day, a full court press was turned on to get the F-14 up for the first flight. The assembly of the first model at our Calverton plant in Suffolk County was put on a 24 hour schedule and was running concurrently with the testing of the completed subsystems. The plane was rolled into a hangar dedicated solely to the F-14 and every engineer and technician that had a part to play in meeting the deadline was put on 24 hour standby; to be called out to Calverton at any time, day or night. On one day, I was summoned three times to the Calverton test pad to perform the tests on the weapons system that I was responsible for. Each time, by the time I arrived at the plant after a one hour drive, I was informed that some other higher priority job was being done and that I should return home and wait for the next call.

On one of those trips, I was in the hangar waiting for a chance to get onto the aircraft to start the tests when the sides of the fuselage started to "bleed" huge amounts of "red blood". One of the hydraulic control lines had sprung a leak and the high pressure hydraulic fluid was spilling out through the sides. Everyone was ordered off the aircraft while the lines were repaired; a major setback.

The "bonus" deadline was fast approaching and everything was being done to expedite the completion of the assembly and test of the aircraft. Shortcuts were being taken that I thought might be a bit risky. I had been to some of the laboratories and assembly areas where the "black boxes" for the subsystems were undergoing bench tests; the tests that were performed prior to installation into the system to check the "black box" for the specified performance. A directive was given to speed up this process by just checking that the system was functioning without doing any detailed testing of all of the performance parameters.

Later, while I was in and out of the Calverton assembly area, I found out that the process here was being speeded up by shortcutting the performance tests and going through a fast functional test as the equipment had already been "bench tested" back at the lab. I tried to call this dichotomy to the attention of the crew chief in the hangar but my warning reached the deaf ears of one whose only goal was to get the aircraft flying by a fixed date; a date fast approaching.

Shortly before that crucial deadline, I was called into the office of Renso Caporali, the leading engineer on the project. (Caporali was a damned good engineer and would one day rise to head up the entire Grumman Corporation and would be Chairman of the Board when Grumman was taken over by the Northrop Corporation)

Caporali told me that they were doing everything they could to expedite the first flight and there was too much testing, in too much detail, being done. He said that I had a reputation for getting impossible things done on an unrealistic schedule and that is what they wanted from me now. It was Friday morning. He wanted me to take charge of, not only the weapons control system, but all of the subsystems that were being tested in the aircraft, to take all of the long winded test plans that were developed and condense them down to the barest minimum necessary to get the plane off the ground and into the sky. He wanted this done by 10 a.m. the following Thursday, December 17th, less than a week away. He wanted it completely checked over by each of the responsible engineers on each subsystem, typed in final form, and on his desk at the appointed time. I, of course, knowing no better, said, "It will be done."

Without losing a minute, I got the names of all of the responsible engineers and set up emergency meetings with each individual to explain the goal and throw the responsibility onto them to do a quick turnaround in shrinking the size of their test procedures. Every one of them balked at first; probably driven by their pride in authorship of documents they had spent many months writing. But with the authority that was given to me, I laid out for each one exactly what was expected, and when, and told them that there was no alternative but to get the job done.

I rode herd on every one of them for the following days; reviewing, condensing, re-reviewing, and rewriting, until we were all satisfied that we had developed the minimal safe procedure to permit a confident take-off for the aircraft on the goal date, December 21st.

A staff of about five secretaries was put at my disposal so that we could work through Wednesday night to get the finalized document in order, typed and copied. I was in Caporali's office at exactly 10 a.m. on Thursday morning; I believe, much to his surprise. This was to be the last and most minimal testing that could be done without jeopardizing the safety of the aircraft and the test pilot – or so I thought at the time.

By the time the weekend had rolled around, it was decided that even this new procedure was too long and a more abbreviated test was to be run only on those systems necessary to get the plane off the ground, to fly around the airfield once or twice, and to land. A further condensation of the test plans onto a dozen three by five index cards was ordered and produced.

I was in the control tower on the day of the first flight, having had to deliver some papers to the tower. I was present to hear much of the chatter between Chief Test Pilot, Bob Smythe, who had the honor of taking the F-14 on its maiden flight, and the control tower. At one point while doing his taxiing run I heard Smythe over the loudspeaker saying, "I'm experiencing a strange anomaly here. When I hit the brake pedals, the wing sweep is changing." The F-14 was fitted with wings with a variably controlled wing sweep to optimize the flight characteristics at different speeds. On this first flight, the wings would be fixed in the fully extended position for the low speed take-off and landing. There would be no high speeds on this flight. The orders were to just get it off the ground and back safely and we've locked up the bonus.

Someone said, "Get the chief." I assumed they were getting someone who was responsible for the systems in question.

When the chief got to the tower, he was informed about the 'anomaly'. His only reply was, "That's not supposed to happen." Someone told Smythe, now taxiing on the runway what the chief had said, and Smythe said, "Okay, I'll try to stay off the brakes."

Before long it was decided that the engines were running, the flight control system was usable, and the plane could, with fingers crossed, safely be taken up. Smythe taxied one last time to the end of the runway, turned around and, without any hesitation, gunned the engines and was in the air. He took the plane in a high pitch up and was off into the blue. He leveled out at a fairly low altitude and flew a small circuit around the airfield while commenting on how well the aircraft seemed to be handling. He was directed to land after the second go around, which was carried out without incident. There was a bedlam of celebration in the entire complex as the word rapidly spread that the job had been accomplished.

I went home and started to get ready for the rapidly approaching Christmas holiday. While we were still hurting from Ranny's death, we wanted the kids to have a normal and happy holiday. I was taking the entire holiday week off and wouldn't be returning until after the New Year – or, again, so I thought.

On December 30th, as I was enjoying the vacation at home, the work on the F-14 continued. Bill Miller was the F-14 project test pilot and would be doing most of the flying to evaluate the aircraft over the next months. Bob Smythe, being the Chief Test Pilot, took the prerogative of the boss and made the first flight to collect not only the glory but the bonus normally given to the pilot of the first flight.

Miller had been taking the F-14 up for longer and longer flights after some of the questionable items were cleaned up in the hanger after the maiden flight. On December 30th, he had the plane up over the south shore when the control system failed and he had to eject while the plane crashed into the ocean. I heard this bad news on the radio, but felt there was nothing that I could contribute to the company at this time. Miller was okay but the aircraft was gone.

At 3 a.m. the next morning, I received a call from my then section head, Jack O'Brien, telling me to come to work immediately to get my F-14 simulator up and running because there was no second aircraft on the line and no other simulator to help in investigating the cause of the crash. I got up, got the necessary support staff in to help set up the simulator, and in the following few days, working with the pilot and engineers, we found out the probable cause of the failure.

(Jack O'Brien was a hard drinking Irishman. He liked to start off the day with three or four, Canadian Club Manhattans. This was often obvious on his arrival at the office in the morning.

Jack was also a lover of things Irish and would often entertain us with a tale or two about his kinsmen. Therefore, I wasn't too surprised one Saturday morning when Jack called me up at about 7 a.m. in the morning while I was still abed. Jean woke me to say, "You're boss is on the phone." She handed me the phone while I was still in bed and not quite awake.

Jack spoke to me in a voice that itself spoke with a whiff of the old Manhattans and said, "I want you to listen to this beautiful music," at which point I heard the strains of the bagpipes playing "The Wearing of the Green." I listened politely until he returned to the line and then with great difficulty managed to end the conversation.

This happened several months before the crash of the first F-14.

When Jean woke me that morning at 3 a.m. to tell me that my boss was on the phone, the first thing I said was, "I don't want to be listening to the 'Wearing of the Green' at 3 o'clock in the morning." When Jean said, "I believe he's sober, and this is serious." I took the phone.)

1971-1972

<u>MOVING ON</u>

We were happy to see 1970 come to a close. Jean and I were still harboring an intense grief and were finding it difficult to wake up every morning without thinking first of Ranny's not being around to cheer up our lives. Photographs of both of us that were taken at this time reveal the extent of our melancholy; the vacant gaze in our eyes with the dark rings beneath, the pale complexion, and the look of bewilderment were constant reminders of the past year's tragedy. It would be some time before we really came to grips with our loss and were able to relegate the memory to a corner of the mind that would permit us to get on with a normal life.

With the beginning of the New Year, I turned over the Chairmanship of the Mid-Island Conservative Club to Dennis Kennelly. Dennis proved to be a very able successor. While he was the First Vice Chairman of the club during my tenure as Chairman, he worked diligently on increasing the Club membership and at every meeting would bring in new members, many of whom he would personally pick up to drive to the meetings. I felt comfortable knowing that the club would be in good hands and would continue growing under his stewardship.

Giving up the chairmanship of the club after serving two terms gave me the opportunity to concentrate on my duties as the new Assembly District Leader and with Mike Tisdell serving alongside me as a Vice Chairman of the county Executive Committee, the two of us were in a position to offer a strong voice on that committee.

The Executive Committee was still broken down into factions. Chairman Pete Verity, who our club supported, had a majority of the committee in his corner; but there were still some of the Crowley supporters serving as voting members. Jim Morrow, who Pete had appointed to lead the Hempstead Conservatives, also had his own agenda. He had run for Assemblyman in his district in 1970 and, as many of us did that year, had received a remarkably good vote on the Conservative line. This race fired his ambition and he had his hat set to get a major party endorsement for a congressional seat in 1972. (I would find out in later years that Morrow was attempting to circumvent the Chairman and the committee and was talking privately to Joe Margiotta, the Republican leader.)

1970 would turn out to be the zenith of Conservative Party fortunes in the first two decades of its existence. The party line vote in Nassau County was a record breaking fourteen percent as demonstrated by the vote on Row 'C' for the judicial candidates; an extraordinary showing for a fledgling minor party. Nassau's vote on the line also contributed significantly to James Buckley's victory in his race for the United States Senate. Many Republicans voted that year for Buckley, which indicated to us that there was still a latent conservative vote within that party.

With this new found electoral strength, the Conservative Party was poised to start influencing the major parties, particularly, the Republicans, to implement some of the conservative reforms in our state and local governments. And while the state party started to make some moderate progress in opening up a dialog with segments of the Republican Party, it still could not penetrate the stranglehold that liberal Governor Nelson Rockefeller had on the state.

Nassau County Conservatives were also ready to share in the recent successes. This opportunity would soon slip through our fingers when Chairman Pete Verity met with Joe Margiotta to collect on the commitments ostensibly made by the Republican leader.

The first opportunity to collect on this promise for Conservative recognition came early in the year when a vacancy for the Town Council occurred in Oyster Bay.

Verity reported to the Executive Committee on his meeting with Margiotta to discuss that race and other things. Verity told the committee that he had wasted no time in demanding that Margiotta deliver on his promise to give the Republican endorsement for the Oyster Bay council to an enrolled Conservative. At this point, according to Verity, Margiotta denied having made such a promise and Verity, in his usual blunt and direct manner, called Margiotta a liar.

The majority of the committee supported Verity in taking this tough stance, even though the immediate impact was a breakdown in the negotiations between the two leaders. The committee felt confident that the Republicans would have to reopen the talks if they wanted the Conservative vote.

What happened next stunned the Conservative leadership in the county.

Margiotta would have liked the added insurance of the Conservative vote for his candidates even if he felt that the Republican line alone was sufficient in this Republican stronghold to carry most of the important elections. It was not the additional votes on his line that he was primarily motivated by, but rather, the possibility of Conservatives backing some Democrats, which in the past couple of years had led to the unexpected election of Lewis Yevoli to the Oyster Bay Town Board and a small number of Democrats to the bench;

a rare occurrence in Nassau County without dual Republican-Democrat cross endorsements.

Verity underestimated the reaction from Margiotta when he called him a "liar". Although Margiotta would have welcomed a palatable deal with the Conservatives, he did not want to leave the impression that "the tail was wagging the dog" and yet he didn't want to drive the Conservatives into the arms of the Democrats. But he was so pissed off at Verity for his insult in being called a 'liar' that he sat down with Marvin Christenfeld, the Democrat Chairman, and thrashed out an agreement whereby all Republican and Democrat candidates in future elections would be precluded from accepting the endorsement of any minor party.

This arrangement suited Margiotta because he felt that as long as the minor parties, including the then viable Liberal Party, were not backing Democrats, the Republicans would be assured of continued domination of the local governments into the foreseeable future. Christenfeld was content to continue the agreement of the two parties on the cross endorsement of their judges which assured the Democrats an occasional position on the bench.

This agreement would prove to be devastating to the Conservative Party in Nassau. The party's ability to influence the course of government did not reside in the party's ability to elect its own candidates on Row 'C' alone; the Buckley election being highly unusual. The party's 'legal tender' in the election process was the ability to effect the elections in marginal races by withholding the endorsement or endorsing one of the major party candidates; and perhaps somewhere along the line, arrange for a reciprocal endorsement of a Conservative candidate.

Yet, the Executive Committee continued to support Chairman Verity and was prepared to deal with these new circumstances. Our strategy was two fold; first, to convince some Republican or Democrat candidates to buck their party and to accept a spot on the Conservative line and, where we couldn't back an acceptable candidate, to run our own candidate and to leave no line blank.

Lew Yevoli and Louis Orfan, enrolled Democrats opted to accept the Conservative endorsement against the wishes of their party leaders, for the offices of Supervisor and Councilman in Oyster Bay. Francis J. Donovan, a Republican running for reelection to the District Court in Oyster Bay also decided to take the Conservative endorsement. He maintained that as a Judge he was prohibited from accepting or declining a partisan endorsement and therefore was obliged to run on our line if we filed the designating petitions for him.

Margiotta was incensed that Donovan would go against his party's dictates and decided to run a primary against him. As the time for filing the regular party petitions had passed and Margiotta could not sponsor a candidate through the normal primary route, petitions had to be filed for someone to run as a write-in candidate by submitting what is called an "Opportunity to Ballot" petition. As the name of the candidate to be running against Donovan would not be displayed on the voting machine, the candidate was selected primarily because of the brevity of the name so that the party voters would not have to tax their minds when they were requested to write in the choice of the party bosses.

Selected to run against Donovan was Carmello Tese, whose four letter surname gave him the prime qualification to run. Margiotta obviously felt that a longer named candidate would not be remembered at the polls.

The Democrats also tried to oust Donovan from their line but were unsuccessful in getting sufficient signatures on petitions in the short period allotted. The Republicans were successful in beating Donovan in their primary, so the ballot wound up with Republican Donovan on the Democrat and Conservative line and Tese on the Republican line. Tese went on to win the general election.

(Donovan would eventually change his enrollment to Democrat and run against his old Republican friends as a Supervisor Candidate in the Town of Oyster Bay in a later election.)

Yevoli and Orfan did not get the support of the Democrats and ran a quiet race on Row "C", losing the general election in November.

(A couple of years after this when I started a dialog with Joe Margiotta after I had become party Chairman, I heard another version of the 'cross endorsement ban' story.

Margiotta said that he never made a promise to back a Conservative for the next available seat on the town council and even if he had, an endorsement for his candidate that year would have been an absolute necessity to clinch the deal. He also complained about not knowing who the real spokesman for the party was; Jim Morrow was making independent overtures to Margiotta, Crowley was still working his deals on the side, and Verity appeared to the Republican leader to have a title but no control over the committee.

In retrospect, knowing both Verity and Margiotta, although I went along with Pete while he was the leader, I am inclined to believe the Margiotta version as being closer to the truth. I don't believe that a pragmatic and tough minded leader like Margiotta would have agreed to give a Conservative a major party endorsement in return for our backing of a Democrat.)

THE OTHER JOB

While politics, government, and the Conservative Party were becoming an increasingly significant part of my life, the family and my profession as an engineer at Grumman continued to dominate most of my time and energies.

Over the next several years I would continue to be called upon to undertake tasks that called upon many engineering disciplines for original, state of the art equipment designs. In addition to the mechanical and system design, most of the projects required a thorough knowledge of electronics, optics, thermodynamics, structural analysis, metallurgy, aircraft design and other disciplines. I was delighted that all of the things that I had learned in school and through my previous years experience were called upon to make every day a challenge for me. I wasn't getting rich from my efforts, but I was earning a respectable income while having a helluva lot of fun.

Just before the close of the year in 1971, I participated in Grumman's effort to win the contract for NASA's space shuttle. In six weeks, the small simulation team that we assembled put together a simulation of our proposed vehicle to permit evaluation of the landing characteristics of our proposed shuttle vehicle from reentry from orbit to landing at Edwards Air Force Base in California.

Jimmy Hunter, one of the early pioneers in the use of digital computers in simulator design, did most of the mathematical modeling using the work that he had done for the Lunar Module simulator. Orlando Vescio, a topflight mechanical designer, handled the cockpit and instrumentation design. It was my task to design the motion simulator to accommodate the cockpit and to design and construct the visual display which would be used to emulate the runway at Edwards.

This seemingly impossible assignment was completed in the short time allotted and although, in the end, Grumman was not successful in its bid (North American-Rockwell won the contract) those of us who worked on this project were extremely pleased with our successful contribution. In ensuing years, I would be called upon many times to meet similar tough design goals and usually in record time.

One of the proudest accomplishments was the successful completion of a simulator for the Forward Swept Wing (FSW) aircraft which would eventually culminate in the manufacture and successful flight of what would be designated by the Air Force as the X-29 experimental aircraft.

As I mentioned earlier in this narrative, the test pilots were always very critical of simulators in general, and engineering design simulators, in particular. It was a very difficult task to design a simulator that could convince a pilot that the machine he was flying on the ground was the equivalent of real flight. Of course, we used every artifice at our disposal to achieve a sense of realism, but we were always falling short of the perfection that most of the pilots expected.

The X-29 with its forward swept wing design was a highly unstable vehicle but its configuration provided excellent maneuverability. The stresses on the wings with this arrangement could not be accommodated with the materials and processes available prior to the time of this program and the then recent developments in miniaturized computer design. With the use of our simulator many of the revolutionary concepts involved in the design of the X-29 could be safely tested in the laboratory before committing the pilot to make that first flight test in an inherently unstable aircraft.

Chuck Sewell, the project pilot, flew the simulator for months and the design of the first aircraft was developed along with the aid of the simulator test flights. Our proudest moment as simulator designers occurred on the day of the first flight of the X-29 when, after a series of planned maneuvers, Chuck announced to the control tower that, "This aircraft flies exactly like the simulator."..., a rare compliment from a pilot. We knew our mission had been accomplished.

I've lost track of the chronology of the many programs I participated in during the decades of the 70's and 80's but for most of that time, every day was like a new adventure. I loved designing new systems and was constantly challenged in new and different ways; often in areas of engineering in which I started out with little or no knowledge... and always with success.

I always felt that engineering was more than a technical and scientific skill. To me, engineering was a creative art in which the exercise of intuitive facilities often dictated the result, rather than just strictly scientific logic and mathematical calculation. And for me, the results often had an aesthetic beauty that filled a corner of my otherwise bland engineering soul with the same feeling as Renoir's "Luncheon of the Boating Party" appealed to my more traditional artistic appreciation.

The diversity of programs that I played a key part in included a unique concept for a Vertical Takeoff and Landing Aircraft (VTOL). Grumman's aircraft design group was focused on an aircraft whose fuselage was hinged at the center and could be vertically launched and retrieved from a platform on a navy destroyer at sea. We dubbed this unusual configuration, "The

Nutcracker". After the aircraft was launched, the fuselage would swivel to the customary shape while transitioning from vertical takeoff to traditional forward flight.

I set up a simulation program on the same equipment that I used for my previous jobs on the A6A and the F-14 prior to its first flight. For nearly a year this simulator provided the major sales tool while Grumman tried to peddle this concept to any interested government agency.

The Navy sent top representatives from many different Federal agencies, including Admiral Connolly from the Office of the Chief of Naval Operations (CNO), Jack Crowder and Admiral Lee from the Naval Air Command (NAVAIR), and Admiral E. Adamson, the Commander of the Atlantic Surface Fleet. From the Air Force, we received hands on visits from General Gaddis and Colonel Johnson. Interest was even stirred up at the White House and President Ford sent his staff representative, Gus Weiss, to evaluate our "Nutcracker" concept.

The success of the simulator and the attention it was receiving from the Defense Department prompted separate visits from our own Chairman of the Grumman Board, George Skurla and Grumman President, Joe Gavin.

(Shortly after I resigned from Grumman in 1993 to assume the elected office of Receiver of Taxes in the Town of Oyster Bay, I had occasion to run into George Skurla while I was campaigning outside the Shoprite Supermarket in Plainview. He was leaving the store with his basket full of groceries and stopped to talk to me; although he didn't recognize me from our "Nutcracker" encounter. He was retired from Grumman and was now a private citizen.

We had an interesting chat about our respective careers at Grumman and he spent nearly an hour talking to me. Some months later, he stopped in to pay me a visit at the Receiver's office to introduce me to his wife who accompanied him that day, and again spent a significant time talking about "the old days". Too bad we didn't establish this kind of rapport while he was still Chairman of the Board and I was a working engineer.)

While continuing to pursue my engineering assignments, I took advantage of some of Grumman's in-house, after-hours training programs, including a stint at Management Training and an introduction to computer programming (FORTRAN). From the latter experience, I decided that I had no interest in getting involved in this aspect of computer technology; it bored me.

After the award of the shuttle contract to North American, Grumman received a piece of the action from North American, a part of which included the provision of Engineers on-site in California. My good friend, Harry Grossman, was one of the engineers assigned to this job which would take him out of New York for two years and would break the continuity in our side-by-side working relationship that we established much earlier at Powertronics.

When Harry returned to New York, he was selected to work on a ship's simulator at the Maritime Academy at Kings Point where he would in a short time assume the position of managing engineer. This simulator, the Computer Aided Operational Research Facility (CAORF) was perhaps the first major simulator that employed computer generated visual displays as a prime element of the system.

The CAORF, while ground-breaking for the times, was archaic when compared to today's technological marvels. The heart of the CAORF system was a computer generated image system which was displayed on a 30 foot radius cylindrical, wrap-around picture screen using multiple colored television projectors. The Sperry Company designed and built this part of the system. At the center of the screen was a facsimile of the control room on the bridge of a typical cargo vessel.

The simulator was intended for use by harbor pilots and ship's officers to train for maneuvering ships into different ports of the world. Included in the computer data bases were models of New York Harbor and Valdez, Alaska, the terminus for the recently opened oil lines from the oil fields at Prudhoe Bay on Alaska's North Slope.

(Valdez was to become the scene of the largest oil spill in North American history on March 24, 1989, when the Exxon Valdez oil tanker ran aground at Bligh Reef, spilling over 10 million gallons of crude oil into Prince William Sound. Exxon brought in over 10,000 workers for the massive cleanup that was dictated by the EPA and other government agencies. The city of Valdez with a population of only 3500 people at the time grew enormously overnight, which proved to be a major logistical problem.

It cost Exxon an average of $1,000 each day for every worker; a staggering sum when multiplied by the number of people on the payroll for the cleanup.

The difficult task of cleanup was slow and the major cleanup work has long since been completed, but even today long term damages are still being evaluated on the fish and wildlife that were affected.)

By today's standards, the CAORF simulator design was very primitive, but served a useful function in spite of its limitations. The computers of the day could not attain the speed of today's personal computers and were very limited in memory capacity. Some characteristics of the real world had to be sacrificed because of these constraints. For instance, the texture of the water was omitted and there were no audible sounds on the control bridge. These deficiencies made it impossible to determine from the simulated environment what the ambient conditions were, such as, sea state, wind velocities, etc.

Some of the limitations of the simulator led at times to some bizarre occurrences. Because of the limited memory, the system would only display on the screen the more important elements. To accomplish this, the computer would prioritize these features and delete or insert them as necessary as the ship made its simulated run through a bay or channel. This led to such phenomena as buildings or other structures popping in and out of the picture. It was really strange to be standing on the bridge, finding a navigational landmark, and then having it suddenly disappear; only to suddenly reappear seconds later.

My close relationship with Harry and his familiarization with my personal abilities was instrumental in getting me involved in the CAORF to provide some of the necessary design enhancements to the system including the design of a pelorus for the ship's simulator and the design of supplemental means to add texture to the visual display and to add realistic sounds normally heard on the bridge of the ship during varying environmental and weather conditions. This last task necessitated on-board studies on several merchant vessels taking me as far south as Savannah, Georgia.

(On one of these ship visits, I was to pick up a cargo ship, the Sea Land Market, a large container ship, coming into New York harbor and which was scheduled to make a transit into the Narrows, through the Kill Van Kull, and to dock at a pier in Elizabethport, New Jersey. I would be making recordings of the environment on the bridge during the transit. An associate, Jack McCullagh, accompanied me on this late night journey.

We were taken by small boat to the Ambrose Lightship in the harbor where we waited with the harbor pilot who was to meet the ship for the planned passage. After about a two hour wait, we were alerted at about two in the morning to join the pilot on deck to board the Pilot Boat which would transfer us to the Sea Land Market which was even then steaming into the bay.

The Pilot Boat was a small motor launch manned by one man and barely accommodating our small party. The harbor was rough as we heaved and rolled into the darkness on that moonless night. I couldn't see a thing in the murky gloom after we sailed some distance from the lightship until we finally arrived alongside one of the largest container ships in the merchant fleet; the Sea Land Market.

We pulled alongside the ship in the pitch black as the bow wake of the ship added to the constant heaving of our little craft. We were like a cork bobbing in the merciless fury of a stormy sea. The Sea Land Market sat motionless as we hove to. Through the darkness a single beam of light appeared from the main deck of the ship to illuminate a Jacob's ladder which was dropped from the main deck, about 40 feet above our unstable little vessel.

Without hesitation, the pilot grabbed the ladder, jumped on, and quickly climbed onto the ship. Jack and I were told to follow the pilot. We both hesitated. I'm sure Jack was thinking what I was; only a crazy man would jump off our wildly bobbing boat in the pitch dark with only a narrow beam of light to see, and to grab onto a treacherously unsteady piece of rope. I imagined both of us floating in the bay.

After much cajoling by our boatswain, we bit the bullet and made the attempt. I tried to time my move to mount the ladder at the peak of one of the swells. I was successful in the attempt, but at the end of my slow, unsteady climb up the ladder, the palms of my hands were sweating in the cold night and were engraved with the impression of the rope ladder from my vice-like grip.

Arriving on the main deck of this huge vessel was like stepping onto terra firma after leaving our wildly oscillating "cork". After this harrowing experience in the dark of night, the rest of the assignment was a 'piece of cake'. We set up our operation on the bridge with movie cameras and audio recorders to monitor the environment as experienced on the bridge.

As it turned out, the ship was so new and the bridge was so well insulated from the external sounds that we went home with no usable data. We had to schedule some additional trips out on the open sea on other cargo ships before we recorded any useful information to suit our purpose.)

LIFE GOES ON

At the end of that terrible year, 1970, Jean and I were trying to set a pattern of normality in the house, in spite of the devastating loss of our only son in October. We had to do this to provide some stability for Patti and Eileen, now 10 and 6 years of age and not fully comprehending the events of the year. While it was difficult to deal with, we, too, had to come to grips with the death and get on with life.

During the holiday season we did not deviate from our established customs of decorating the house and a Christmas tree, and inviting family and friends to the house to celebrate the occasion. On one of these evenings we had the Eckhoff family and the Salt family over to the house. Looking back at the pictures that were taken at that time, Jean and I looked like "death warmed over"; our grief was still written in our pale countenances.

(George and Pat Salt were immigrants from England, who we and the Eckhoffs had befriended and shared holidays and family outings with. George worked at Grumman as a structural analyst on our commercial aircraft, especially the Grumman G-2, a small jet airliner used by many of the corporations. They had three boys, and the Eckhoff's were the godparents of one of the boys.

Chris and I sponsored George for his American citizenship when he decided to become a naturalized citizen. We had all grown very fond of each other and on our several Christmases together, exchanged gifts.

At some point George accepted a position in Seattle, Washington, with the Boeing Aircraft Company and although we would miss the family, we wished the family well in their new venture, expecting to hear from them shortly after they arrived in Washington.

Weeks went by and we and the Eckhoffs never heard from George or Pat. We grew more concerned with each passing day. We didn't know whether they had arrived safely in Seattle and speculated that they could have been the victims of foul play while driving out to the west coast and no one would be the wiser. After all, having quit Grumman, no one at that company had a reason to be concerned and, if George did not report to Boeing for work there was no reason for them to inquire about his whereabouts. Additionally, with no family in the United States, the Salts could disappear and no one would know...or care.

It was about this time that Dennis Kennelly was transferred to Seattle by his employer at ABC. When he and Pat returned to New York for a visit, we told Dennis of our concerns about the Salts and Dennis, never the bashful type, picked up our phone, called Seattle and tracked down the missing family. It had been months since we last saw the Salts and they sounded very embarrassed when we expressed our concern for them. They had arrived safely in Seattle as planned and evidently chose to cut out of their lives, the godparents of their son and the sponsoring Americans for George's citizenship.

PRINCESS

Somewhere in this narrative I must make mention of the last member of the family to join the household; our dog, Princess.

When we lived in Bayside before moving to Plainview in 1962, we had adopted a young mixed breed pup that we called "Fluffy". This was the name that Ranny had given to his favorite stuffed animal.

Fluffy was as black as pitch and we were soon to find out that his toilet habits were as black as he was. Perhaps with more experience we could have trained Fluffy better but it seemed that whatever we did, Fluffy was never trained from his bad habits of excessive barking and excessive bowel movements. Wherever we let him roam in the house or outside, he would leave a trail of dog poop in quantities that greatly belied both his size and the amount of food we gave him.

After a time of patient attempts at housebreaking the pup we finally realized that we could not deal with this dog so we turned him over to the Bide-a-Wee home in Wantagh with the hopes that someone more adept at training would adopt him and give him a home where both he and his new master would be happy.

This experience made us hesitant to bring another dog into the house; a resolve we maintained for several years after our failure with Fluffy... that is, until about 1967 when Ranny, who was then about 11 years old, pleaded with us to get a dog for him. He pledged to take care of the dog, to feed him and train him, and most importantly, he said that he would clean up the dog doo whenever necessary. With Ranny's fervent promises we adopted a medium sized female dog; a mix of Collie and Dalmatian. Ranny selected the name for the new member of the family; Princess. One of the first things that we did was to take Princess to the veterinarian for a physical checkup and to be spayed; we did not look forward to dealing with a litter of pups in the future and we understood that spaying of the dog would make it easier to train and gave the dog's a more domestic disposition.

We all quickly grew very fond of the new addition, and with Ranny keeping to his word to care for the pup; we did not endure the difficulty that we had with our last canine house guest.

However, it soon became apparent that Princess was a hair-shedding breed and the carpets were loaded with dog hairs. We trained the dog to stay in either the kitchen or dining room, neither of which was carpeted, but the shedding continued and with Jean's allergic susceptibility to this household pollution, we were forced to find a solution to the problem.

During the first year, we allowed Princess the freedom of the entire backyard and side yard that were entirely enclosed with a chain link fence and Ranny dutifully cleaned up the droppings in the back yard where Princess soon found her domain. There were many snowfalls that first winter with Princess, and the grounds remained snow covered for weeks at a time before completely defrosting.

It was after one of these periods of constant snow that we noticed after the thaw that the back yard was covered from end to end with dog doo; Ranny had not cleaned up any of the droppings in weeks and we were not aware that it was piling up under the snow. This condition was dramatically called to our attention on the first warm day after the melting of the snow, when the entire neighborhood also participated in enjoying the newly introduced fragrance. Together with Ranny, we remedied the immediate situation and to prevent further contamination of the backyard, we constructed an addition to the fence to set aside a dog run for Princess, limiting her to a 40 x 9 foot dog run area on the side of the house, with free access to our covered and partially enclosed back porch.

This solved one problem but I soon noticed that the accumulation of dog doo was reaching a critical magnitude. We had provided a garbage pail to Ranny to deposit the droppings and had lined the pail with a plastic bag to be put out regularly for the garbage collection. It came to my attention one day; probably caused by the aroma; that the garbage pail was about one third full; evidently not having been put out for collection for a long time. I confronted Ranny and asked him why he had not put the pail out for collection in such a long time. His response was that the bag was not filled yet.

(Can you imagine the consternation of the garbage men if they found at the curb, a thirty gallon plastic bag of dog doo, especially if when they tried to lift it, it broke open over their feet, as it surely would have given the heavy load in the bag?)

Ranny eventually established a reasonable routine with his dog and Princess melded into the household routine; except for her shedding problem. Eventually, we restricted Princess to the rear porch and the dog run; except for the times when she was taken on a leash to be walked through the neighborhood. Although the back porch was not heated we permitted Princess to live the entire time in the restricted area. We were told by the dog experts that dog's should be either a house dog, with limited exposure to the extreme elements for long periods of time or, if the dog was to spend the major part of the time in the outdoors, should not be permitted into the house. It was our understanding that a dog exposed to the elements for long periods would develop a thick, protective coat of hair. This was borne out by our experience with Princess who adapted very well to her living conditions.

We would periodically permit her into the house for periods of time but still restricted her to the kitchen and living room. During storms where there was thunder and lightning Princess would become so frightened that we had to take her into the house to calm down her tremors.

After Ranny died, Princess became the responsibility of the entire family. In her later years we permitted Princess to spend more time indoors as she started to fall into bad health. Her final days came in 1979 when she suffered from arthritis and other ailments that made it painful for her to be petted or touched. She started to step into her food and when she began defecating in her food and water bowls, I was selected to take her to the vet for evaluation. The vet offered no hope for Princess and suggested that she be put to sleep, which I agreed to on the spot while trying to control the heartache that I was feeling. When I told the family on my return home; it may have been my imagination; but I felt as if they looked at me as that cruel man who killed their beloved dog.

NEW BEGINNINGS

By the time 1972 rolled around the Conservative Party in Nassau was already showing signs of deterioration. The party had been losing some of its most active people since the escalation of challenges to the leadership in the previous four or five years by the likes of Noel Crowley and his cronies. Every time candidate endorsements by the party were contested in the primary elections and the party leaders were successful in beating back the challenge, the disgruntled losers; instead of backing the choice of the Conservative voters; packed up their bag of grievances and ceased working on behalf of the party. Every year we were witnessing less active people to do the necessary political work.

With the introduction of the ban on cross endorsements by third parties agreed upon by the Republican and Democrat Parties, the Conservative Party was dealt a blow to its growing stature, and those Conservatives who were sponsoring their own agenda deserted the party when they recognized that, without the ability to endorse and thereby influence the policies of the major party candidates, the Conservative Party had lost its most effective weapon in reforming government in the county and state.

When the time came for selecting candidates, Conservatives in Nassau had no choice but to run Conservative candidates only on the Conservative line, or to run no candidate in selected races against 'friendly' Republicans or Democrats. The executive committee managed to put together a slate of candidates for the November 1972 elections and decided to run no candidate against Congressman Norman Lent and Assemblyman Philip Healey; two of the officeholders that we felt would carry on our conservative work even without our endorsement.

In an otherwise bleak political year, the only bright spot was the fact that, for the first time in several years, we did not face the prospect of a party primary and its consequent fallout...actually another indication of the sad state Nassau Conservatives had fallen into.

1972 marked the year when the two-year term of Chairman Pete Verity expired. Although many of us still supported Pete and would have been happy to have him run for another term, Pete announced just before his term expired that he would not be running for reelection. Jim Morrow from Levittown, a 33 year old Social Studies teacher at Baldwin High School, expressed his interest in taking over the helm. Morrow was the Executive Vice Chairman and someone who had run for office on the Conservative line with distinction and was a candidate for the Assembly again in 1972. Most of the committee were not enthusiastic about a Morrow chairmanship because of his past failure in proving himself as a leader when assigned the task of organizing the Town of Hempstead by Chairman Verity; a job that Bob Valli and I had effectively done in our towns of North Hempstead and Oyster Bay.

Verity was very opposed to Morrow as a successor and, about one week before the scheduled County Committee reorganizing meeting, he asked me to run for the position. Before that time, I had not considered myself a contender for the job and really had no aspirations for a position that was all work with no pay, and no appreciation. Pete pleaded with me to take on the task with the argument that Morrow did not have the organizational skills to run the party and he, Pete, was afraid that the party would accelerate in its decline under Morrow's stewardship. Morrow had been a good candidate for the party and no one questioned his ability as a candidate or his Conservative credentials but Verity was adamant in his opposition to Morrow assuming the post of Chairman.

I was convinced to run when I decided that the party needed someone in charge who would at least concentrate on our need to organize what little resources we had remaining and agreed that Morrow would live up to Verity's expectations of failure as a Chairman. I reluctantly accepted Pete's challenge and planned, if elected, to serve one two-year term as all of the previous Chairmen had done. I promised myself to do the best I could to hold a disintegrating party together during the next two years.

The decision to run having been made, the first order of business in the contest for the chairmanship was to get a majority of the County Committee to support my candidacy. One week before the meeting was to be held, there were two other candidates vying with me for the post.

Thomas Brenker, a research specialist from Massapequa had joined Morrow and me in the race. Chairman Verity was more strongly opposed to Brenker than he was to Morrow and let this be known through the local newspapers. The previous year Brenker had been thrown out as a member of the Massapequa Conservative Club but had been reinstated on a technicality. I don't remember the particular malfeasance in that incident, but whatever it was, it prompted Verity, who was one of the founders and self appointed guardians of the Massapequa Club, to devote extra effort on my behalf to assure Brenker's defeat.

I believe that a prime reason for Brenker's entry into the race was to put an additional obstacle into my path; assuming quite correctly that in addition to Verity, I had the support of most of the Executive Committee members. Brenker was carrying a grudge against me since the previous election in 1971 when I was Chairman of the Oyster Bay Campaign effort and Brenker was shepherding the campaign of Conservative Mario Colleluori for Town Clerk of the Town.

Brenker, Colleluori, and John Scarpa met with me at my home for a meeting to discuss ways that the town campaign committee could assist in the Town Clerk race. Their main proposal was to focus our main efforts on behalf of Mario with the intent of winning that race on only the Conservative line... evidently the astonishing win of Jim Buckley for the United States Senate in 1970 filled many a head with visions of glory... or more likely, visions of sugar plums.

Their chief strategy to reap the highest vote was to dramatically introduce Colleluori to the world. They proposed that the town campaign, which had a meager treasury, finance the exclusive rental of a Long Island Railroad train, to be taken from Montauk to Pennsylvania Station, making whistle stops at all of the stations along the way, ala President Harry Truman in 1948.

While I wanted to burst out laughing in their faces at this preposterous plan, I treated it seriously and simply told them that we didn't have the funds for their venture. Brenker got pissed off at my refusal and I am sure carried this malice into the race for County Chairman in 1972. What I did offer and we did accomplish successfully was an old fashioned motorcade with all of our candidates participating. Escorted by the Nassau County Police, we took a convoy of about 30 vehicles from the north to south borders of the town, making stops at every major shopping center to permit the candidates to greet the voters.

The organizing meeting had been set by Verity to be held at Levittown Hall on Saturday, July 8th, my fortieth birthday. When I told Jean that I was running for Chairman, she was very supportive as she has always been in all of my "adventures". However, when I told her the meeting was to be held on my birthday, she was strongly adamant in her insistence that I not attend the meeting. I told her that I had to attend, if I expected to have a chance of winning the election to be held that night. The meeting could not be postponed or the venue changed as all the notices had been mailed to the committeemen and the statutory requirement was for the meeting to be held on or before July 10th. Jean finally relented to my obstinacy but had to reveal to me that she had planned a surprise birthday party for me on the 8th. Although this put a crimp in her plans and she agreed to reschedule the party for the following week, she was very gracious about it and, as a comfort to herself, said that, at least now I would be able to help her to order the alcoholic refreshments for the party.

On July 8th when the committee met for the reorganization, the meeting could not be called to order because of the lack of a quorum; 200 members in attendance were required for the quorum and at 9:30 P.M., an hour and a half after the scheduled start time, there were only 196 members signed in and Verity was about to postpone the meeting. Miraculously before Verity acted four additional members arrived and signed in; even later there would be some additional members arriving.

After the preliminary roll call and other formalities, the first order of business proposed by Tom Collins of Freeport was a change in the by-laws to make the quorum 100 instead of 200 members; a proposal that was adopted after a lengthy discussion.

When it came time for the nomination of candidates for the Chairmanship the announced three were placed on the ballot to be joined by a late entry into the race, Edmond Farrell, an ardent anti-abortion advocate who believed that this should be the single most important issue for the Conservatives to pursue.

The candidates were asked to make brief speeches to address their plans for the new administration. I called attention to my six years of service to the party, the support of the prior chairman and a majority of the Executive Committee, and called for discipline within the party and a rebuilding of the ailing organization. (Later on Grete Gebauer, a native of Germany and one of my supporters, approached me to tell me what a fine speech I made, especially "...vere you called for za discipline.")

When the votes were counted the final tally was: O'Leary 113, Morrow 91, Brenker 8, and Farrell 5 for a first ballot win. In putting together the remainder of the slate of officers prior to the vote for Chairman; all deals having been made for the support of the larger delegations; there was no opposition to my recommended slate which included; Bob Valli for Executive Vice-Chairman; three Vice-Chairmen, John Donovan of Freeport, Cliff Riccio of Wantagh, and Dennis Kennelly of Plainview (I insisted that Dennis be put on the ticket), Kay Belton of Wantagh for Secretary, and Alan Smith of Wantagh as Treasurer. The appearance of so many Wantagh people on the slate was indicative of the relative strengths of the organized Conservative clubs.

I made a brief acceptance speech to thank all of the supporters as I watched most of the losers leave the hall. I could sense even then that the next couple of years would be even more difficult with less and less workers to join in the rebuilding of the party. I was quietly confident that with time, patience, and hard work, I could make the party whole again.

Before leaving Levittown Hall in the early morning hours of July 9th, I searched out Pete Verity to attempt to arrange a meeting with him for the following day to get the party files from him and to discuss with him the transition to the new administration. Verity told me that there were no files to be had and that I was now the chairman and would have to figure things out on my own with no help from him. So my biggest pre-election supporter turned his back on helping me in getting adjusted to the new responsibilities.

...and so I entered a new and challenging adventure!

<u>END PART I</u>

INDEX

S

Salt, George, 585, 586

Salt, Pat, 585, 586

Scarpa, John, 594

Schenkel, Warren, 374, 375

Schmeling, Max, 18

Schneider, Andy, 559

Schoof, Ernie, 511

Schupp, Al, 500

Schwab, Gramdma, 74, 84

Schwab, John 'Pop', 74, 84

Schwartz, Harry, 504

Schwartz, Ruth, 200

Schwartz, Sydney, 436

Schwartz, Sydney, Jr., 473

Scinta, Ralph, 531

Serrell, Donald, 512-516, 518

Sewell, Chuck, 579

Sharkey, Jack, 18, 150

Shearer, Margie, 115

Sheehan, Jean, 141

Sheehan, John, 535, 537, 551, 560

Sheehan, Neil, 480, 482

Sheehan, Vinny, 93

Shulman, John, 532

Shultz, "Dutch", 202

Sirokowsky, Hank, 425

Sister Isabel, 107, 109, 110

Sister Mary Clement, 27, 281

Sister Mary Honorata, 27

Sister Mary Magdalene, 111, 112, 116, 118

Sister Mida, 95

Sister Philomene, 82

Sister Rose Magdalene, 115

Skurla, George, 580

Sluder, Leroy, 518

Smith, Alan, 596

Smith, James (boxer), 163, 164

Smith, Richard, 425

Smith, Sarah, 3

Smythe, Bob, 566, 567

Sokol, "Dutch", 22

Spellman, Francis Cardinal, 331

Speno, Ed, 528-530

Steiner, Buzz, 320

Steiner, Doctor, 95

Sterman, George, 318, 320

Stevens, Walter, 532

Stone, Donald, 468

Stone, Fraser, 452, 469

Stone, Gloria, 452, 453

Sullivan, Gloria, 483

Szuchy, Nick, 548

T

Tese, Carmelo, 575

Thatcher, Turner, 169

Thomson, Kay, 115, 139

Tina, 411-413, 440, 495

Y